DREAMS OF A
GREAT
SMALL NATION

DREAMS OF A GREAT SMALL NATION

*The Mutinous Army that
Threatened a Revolution,
Destroyed an Empire,
Founded a Republic,
and Remade the Map of Europe*

KEVIN J. MCNAMARA

PUBLICAFFAIRS
New York

Book Design by Timm Bryson
Map Design by Mike Morgenfeld

The Library of Congress control number is 2016930908
ISBN 978-1-61039-484-0 (HC)
ISBN 978-1-61039-485-7 (EB)   943.703
First Edition
10 9 8 7 6 5 4 3 2 1

TO KATRINA

Whose love, patience, and understanding make all things possible

CONTENTS

CHAPTER SEVEN

THE AMBIVALENT INTERVENTION 221

CHAPTER EIGHT

THE MOMENT OF TRUTH 255

CHAPTER NINE

THE VIEW FROM SIBERIA 289

CONCLUSION 317

LIST OF MAPS

Life is warfare, and the sojourn of the stranger in a strange land.
MARCUS AURELIUS
Meditations II[1]

ACKNOWLEDGMENTS

I WISH TO acknowledge the assistance and support of Max Boot, Richard Immerman, John Lehman, and Richard Pipes, all of whom encouraged and assisted me in this project. A big thanks to Neal Orkin, who brought to my attention the five-volume work *Cestami odboje: Jak žily a kudy táhly čs. legie* (The Road to Resistance: How the Czech Legion Lived and Fought) that was published in Prague in the 1920s. Thanks also to Alan H. Luxenberg, president of the Foreign Policy Research Institute, for his enthusiasm, as well as to the generosity of the Earhart and Tawani Foundations, all of which was absolutely decisive in making this project possible.

I owe a special debt to the late Russell F. Weigley, the scholar and teacher who introduced me to the subject of military history. Ivo Reznicek, the nephew of a legionnaire, agreed to render the stories of the legionnaires into English, settling accounts for the scolding he received as a boy in communist Czecho-Slovakia, where he was reprimanded by his teacher for speaking in class of his uncle's exploits in the Czecho-Slovak Legion. The staffs at the Immigration History Research Center Archives at the University of Minnesota, the special collections library of the Historical Society of Pennsylvania, the National Czech and Slovak Museum & Library, and the Vancouver Public Library were helpful. Many thanks also to Anne Applebaum, Mary Andrejka, Andrew Bultas, Edward Chlanda, Robert Faltin, Stella Gabuzda, Arlene Gardiner, Elinor Gay,

George E. Glos, George Hanc, John Hanc, Penny Heger, Tomas Jakl, Frank Kaderabek, Mary Kaderabek, Sarah Kaderabek, Radomir Luza, Jerry Machalek, Paul Makousky, Joan McGuire Mohr, Lukas Pavlicek, Daniel Pipes, Helen Rappaport, Miloslav Rechcigl Jr., Sandra Scott, Jim Stroner, Ivan Vilimek, and Milos Zika. An especially large debt is owed to my wife, Katrina, and my daughters, Hilary, Whitney, and Julia, for their patience and understanding during this long trek, which consumed many more years than the legion's epic journey.

FOREWORD

WORLD WAR I and the Russian Revolution remain the two most significant events of the twentieth century and the little-known story told in these pages had significant impacts on both of them. We know that the war originated in Sarajevo, now the capital of independent Bosnia-Herzegovina, but the conflict also had much greater consequences in Eastern Europe and Russia than it did in the West. While the Western Front's near-limitless casualties were personally horrific and socially traumatic, the combatant nations survived. Indeed, these battles are often quizzically recalled for their waste of human life in an otherwise inconsequential exercise of power.

The war in the east was far more consequential, casting adrift multinational empires, ancient dynasties, and entire societies amidst the collapse of four regimes—Austro-Hungarian, German, Ottoman, and Russian—that governed much of the earth. Governments were deposed, new nations created, old ones destroyed, dictatorships and democracies founded, the map of Europe redrawn, and the twentieth century forever altered. And while peace finally dawned in the west on November 11, 1918, war-borne conflicts continued to roil Russia, Eastern and Central Europe, the Balkans, the Caucasus, and especially the Middle East. Conflicts continue today in all these places.

War's crippling consequences ushered in the Russian Revolution, giving birth to a regime that would lead to a decades-long global cold

war that divided Europe, east from west. When communist rule collapsed in 1991, more than half a dozen European states were liberated
from Moscow's grip, and the Soviet Union imploded into another fifteen
smaller national units. German anger at losing the Great War prepared
the ground for World War II and the Holocaust. The collapse of the
Ottoman Empire left behind many states throughout the Balkans, the
Caucasus, and the Middle East that still struggle to establish stable governments and mutual peace. Austria-Hungary's collapse gave birth to
Czecho-Slovakia, Poland, and Yugoslavia, which served as trip wires and
hostages for hot and cold wars. Azerbaijan, Czecho-Slovakia, Georgia,
Moldova, Ukraine, and Yugoslavia have splintered into smaller units,
and conflicts continue to simmer today in places like Bosnia, Crimea,
Georgia, Kosovo, Moldova, Nagorno-Karabakh, and Ukraine.

ALMOST ONE HUNDRED years later, the epic tale of the Czecho-Slovak
Legion recounted in these pages remains little known in part because
it became lost between the lines of the multiple histories of a tumultu-
ous time. The story remained obscured because it played out in Eastern
Europe, Russia, and Siberia, lands that even today lay just beyond the
borders of Western curiosity. In the West, World War I recalls mostly the
Western Front; the Eastern Front is much less known, characterized by
Winston Churchill as the "unknown war."[2]

After 1938, the story behind the founding of Czecho-Slovakia was
overtly suppressed after Nazi Germany occupied the small nation, where
anti-German sentiment had for centuries walked hand in hand with
Czech nationalism. It was suppressed again after 1948, when Czecho-
Slovakia became a Soviet satellite. Prague's new Russian occupiers buried
the memory of the armed founders of Czecho-Slovakia, who had auda-
ciously fought and—albeit briefly—defeated the Red Army, threatening
the very survival of the Russian Revolution. It was not until 1991, when
the communist regimes of Russia and Eastern Europe collapsed, that
original source material surfaced.

Yet another reason this story remains little known is that the views of the men at the center of it were largely ignored. The firsthand accounts of the Czech and Slovak legionnaires that have surfaced shed light on their personal motivations, assumptions, opinions, fears, and ambitions. These accounts reveal new aspects of the story, different from those previously ascribed to the participants by historians who—much like the Habsburgs—treated them as mere objects. For too long, the legionnaires themselves were less important than what politicians, generals, diplomats, historians, and journalists wished to make of them.

This is the first English-language book to make extensive use of collections of eyewitness testimony in a history of this episode. In my research, I arranged to have more than one hundred long-neglected personal accounts by the legionnaires translated into English for the first time from a five-volume work, *Cestami odboje: Jak žily a kudy táhly čs. legie* (The Road to Resistance: How the Czech Legion Lived and Fought), published in Prague between 1926 and 1929. I also drew from dozens of memoirs, diaries, and letters of individuals who personally encountered the legionnaires. Many of these texts were translated from Czech, German, or Russian. Most of them are very obscure and a handful have never been published.

This is the history of a time "when everyone had gone crazy in his own way, and when everyone's life had existed in its own right, and not as an illustration for a thesis in support of the rightness of a superior policy," to quote Boris Pasternak.[3] This is not "Whig history," which Herbert Butterfield famously criticizes as the historian's tendency to draw a direct causation from a messy, less desirable past to an ordered and more perfect present, strongly implying a sense of linear progress or beneficent evolution in human affairs. "We may believe in some doctrine of evolution or some idea of progress," Butterfield writes, "and we may use this in our interpretation of the history of centuries; but what our history contributes is not evolution but rather the realization of how crooked and perverse the ways of progress are, with what willfulness and waste it twists and turns, and takes anything but the straight track to its goal, and how often it seems to go astray, and to be deflected by any conjecture, to return to us—if it does return—by a back-door."[4]

About dates: Before February 1918, Russia followed the Julian (Old Style) calendar that in the twentieth century was thirteen days behind the Gregorian (New Style) calendar used in the West. That January, the Bolshevik government decreed that Russia would convert to the Gregorian calendar at the end of the month. As a result, January 31, 1918, was followed the next day by February 14. Where noted, Old Style dates are given for most events inside Russia prior to January 31, 1918; they do not correspond to the dates for simultaneous events outside of Russia. They are identified as "OS." Gregorian dates are identified as "NS."

A common name for the Czechs and Slovaks: The Slovaks were subsumed into the new state that was established with the Czechs in 1918 amidst broken promises for their own autonomy, and the new state became known as "Czechoslovakia," which had the unfortunate effect of making one entire people seem secondary or subservient to another, a problem the Slovaks corrected when they seceded from "Czechoslovakia" to establish the Slovak Republic in 1993. As a result, I refer to the Czechs and Slovaks who fought side by side to create a new state as "Czecho-Slovaks" and the state they created as "Czecho-Slovakia." This punctuation was used by early advocates of the new country, including Tomáš G. Masaryk and Woodrow Wilson.[5]

Place-names: I have rendered the names of cities and towns as they existed at the time of the events in question, but have placed their current names and host countries in parentheses after the first reference, as in Königgrätz (Hradec Králové, Czech Republic), Pozsony (Bratislava, Slovakia), Austerlitz (Slavkov u Brna, Czech Republic), and Lemberg (Lviv, Ukraine). If the name of the city or town has not changed, but the country has, I note the current country. In order to help readers more easily follow the action of the Russian Civil War, however, I use only the current, familiar names of Siberian cities, some of which were changed after 1918.

Cyrillic transliteration: The system used in this book is that of the American Geological Institute Translation Center (recommended by the US Department of the Interior, Board of Geographical Names, Washington, DC), but names that are familiar in the West are rendered in familiar Anglicized fashion. So, Nikolai, except for Tsar Nicholas, and Lake Baikal instead of Baykal.

LOSING A GREAT WAR

EARLY IN 1918, it would not have surprised the leaders of France, Great Britain, and the United States to finally lose the Great War to Germany and Austria-Hungary. More than three years after the assassination of Austrian archduke Franz Ferdinand in Sarajevo, and the deaths of tens of millions of civilians and soldiers, Allied Russia collapsed in the east, Germany's armies swiveled toward the west, the soldiers of the Central Powers were coming in numbers never before seen, and the Allies braced for defeat. This growing conflagration on the Western Front, however, overshadowed equally dramatic and consequential exploits on the Eastern Front, which became lost between the lines of the histories of a tumultuous time, when the final horrors of the war melted into the growing chaos of the Russian Revolution. While the collapse of the tsarist regime in Saint Petersburg and the subsequent offensives by Germany are widely known, they have tended to eclipse a parallel saga of historic scale, the epic misadventures of an unlikely army of émigrés, deserters, and traitors, most of them former POWs, a rough beast slouching toward Siberia.[1] The improbable exploits of these reluctant warriors will link the two most significant consequences of the Great War: the triumph of Soviet rule in Russia and the collapse of Europe's Habsburg monarchy and its Austro-Hungarian Empire.

WHILE THE WAR dragged on, in one sense it was a great success: determined to achieve a balance of power on the Continent, as well as ever more killing power for its armies, Europe had achieved an equilibrium of slaughter. None of the alliances, sophisticated war plans, or new technologies—tanks, planes, trains, telegraphs, machine guns, or chemical weapons—had yet led to an overall armistice, let alone victory. On all fronts, armies fought to a bloody stalemate even when, more often in the east, sweeping offensives smashed through trench lines and took entire armies prisoner.

Having defeated Serbia (1915), Romania (1916), and Russia (1917), Germany and Austria-Hungary now turned to the west and attacked with unprecedented power and fury. Among Allied leaders, tension grew, tempers flared, history paused, and the Allies prepared for the worst. "The possibility is admitted in government circles," the US ambassador in London wrote to warn Washington, "of a disastrous end of the war."[2] The diary of "Colonel" Edward M. House, President Woodrow Wilson's most trusted adviser, noted on March 30 that "there seems to be a general inclination to be 'rattled.' All the dispatches we are receiving from the other side indicate it, and the most demoralizing feature of the situation, as the President and I see it, is the poise which seems to be failing the French and British governments at this time."[3]

Twenty-one days into Germany's onslaught, on April 11, 1918, British field marshal Douglas Haig—outwardly calm and stubbornly determined to continue the fight—took pen to paper. While anger, despair, and cynicism were as rife in the trenches as they were in the halls of government ministries, Haig addressed his message, "To all ranks of the British forces in France." In handwriting as neat as his uniform, his sentences as clipped as his mustache, the field marshal beseeched his men to endure:

> Words fail me to express the admiration which I feel for the splendid resistance offered by all ranks of our Army under the most trying circumstances. . . . Many amongst us are now tired. To those I would say that victory belongs to those who hold out the longest. . . . There is no other course open to us but to fight it out! Every position must be held

to the last man; there must be no retirement. With our backs to the wall, and believing in the justice of our cause, each one of us must fight on to the end. The safety of our homes and the freedom of mankind alike depend on the conduct of each one of us at this critical moment.[4]

By June 1, the Germans were ten miles closer to Paris than they were in April. The next day the Supreme War Council met outside of Paris, where the distraught commander of all Allied forces, French marshal Ferdinand Foch, in the midst of endless arguments, wailed, "The battle, the battle, nothing else counts!" Three days later, Sir Maurice Hankey, a former Royal Marine and secretary to the British war cabinet, wrote in his diary, "I do not like the outlook. The Germans are fighting better than the Allies, and I cannot exclude the possibility of disaster."[5]

SUCH WAS THE state of mind of the Allied leaders through the middle of 1918, following the collapse of Tsarist Russia and the subsequent German offensives, events that would prompt urgent and persistent demands by the Allies for the resurrection of an Eastern Front in Russia, demands that would drive their decision-making until the end of the war.

Russia Collapses

RUSSIA HAD STRUGGLED to hold off the combined armies of Germany and Austria-Hungary along the Eastern Front since 1914. Three years later, Saint Petersburg's population had swollen with masses of peasant-soldiers and war-industry workers, leading to severe and persistent food and fuel shortages, which idled factories, chilled homes, and emptied stores. The pain of families losing more than 4.3 million men to death, wounds, disease, or POW camps was exacerbated by cold and hunger. Popular anger was stoked by persistent rumors of German influence over the tsar's court.[6] Tsarina Alexandra was German-born and she engineered the appointment in 1916 of another inept prime minister, this one with a German surname, Boris V. Stürmer. Salacious rumors spread surrounding Alexandra's chief adviser, the mysterious, disreputable monk, Grigory Rasputin. In the streets, revolutionaries blamed a regime that was failing on both the battlefield and at home. Growing demonstrations led to scattered violence against the police, the normally heavy-handed Cossacks hesitated, yet Tsar Nicholas II insisted on a military crackdown on the protestors. Thus began the February Revolution of 1917 that toppled the 304-year-old Romanov dynasty.

With the fall of the imperial regime, and Russia's professional army dead and buried, military discipline evaporated and the Imperial Army began to buckle and collapse. Russian officers were ill-trained and feared the embittered peasant-soldiers, who were as likely to shoot their officers as enemy troops. A series of hapless provisional governments yielded only chaos and frustration. Ragged soldiers, many of them deserters, straggled home and angrily joined the ad hoc revolutionary councils, or soviets. The chief Petrograd Soviet of Workers' and Soldiers' Deputies in Saint Petersburg ignored the Provisional Government, whose ministers were cowed by the radical Petrograd Soviet, and began issuing orders.

On November 7, 1917 (NS), a secretive, ruthless band of socialists known as the Bolsheviks, led by Vladimir Lenin and backed by Germany, orchestrated an overnight coup, and the new Soviet regime immediately sought an armistice with the Central Powers. Opposition armies began to organize in the Russian hinterland and rival parties to the Bolsheviks emerged in Saint Petersburg. Unable to win a majority in elections to the new Constituent Assembly that was promised by the Provisional Government, the Bolsheviks shut down the parliament in January 1918 and proclaimed a new Russian Socialist Federal Soviet Republic. In March 1918 the Bolsheviks renamed their faction the Russian Communist Party and fled advancing German armies by moving the capital to Moscow. Reluctantly, they ratified the Treaty of Brest-Litovsk with Germany on March 3 (NS), which formally ended Russian combat in World War I.

Two things followed the signing at Brest-Litovsk—Moscow opened its POW camps and began shipping home more than 2.3 million German and Austro-Hungarian POWs, most of whom expected to be thrown back into combat on the Western Front. More ominously, the enormous armies Berlin and Vienna deployed in the east were turned and hurled against the Western Front.

Germany Attacks

ON MARCH 21, 1918, with the Russians safely out of the war, the first of five German offensives was launched to drive a wedge between the British and French armies, seize the English Channel ports behind the British, occupy Paris, and take France's surrender. The Spring Offensive opened before dawn with a firestorm of six thousand artillery pieces erupting along a fifty-mile British front, where the lines quickly began to break.[7] About 3.2 million shells exploded the first day, a third of them chemical weapons. A witness to the artillery fire, Winston Churchill, called it "the greatest onslaught in the history of the world."[8] After hours of explosions, flames, and choking gases, no fewer than thirty divisions of well-supplied Germans advanced rapidly through the smoke, across the muddy moonscape of the Somme. They overran British defenses, capturing ninety thousand prisoners.

Parisians fled the city and the French government made contingency plans to follow. On March 23, Kaiser Wilhelm II, the king of Prussia and emperor of Germany, declared triumphantly: "The battle won, the English utterly defeated." The same day, British ambassador Lord Reading was quickly ushered into the White House to see President Wilson, bearing an urgent telegram from Britain's prime minister, David Lloyd-George. It read: "You should appeal to the President to drop all questions of interpretation of past agreements and send over infantry as fast as possible without transport or other encumbrances. This situation is undoubtedly critical and if America delays now she may be too late." At the end of their hushed meeting, Wilson said, "Mr. Ambassador, I'll do my damnedest!"[9] The United States was entirely unprepared to become a world power. It became indispensable before it would become reliable. Meanwhile, the German offensives continued into the summer and as late as mid-July, victory by the Central Powers still looked possible.

America Awakens

"GOOD LORD! YOU'RE not going to send soldiers over there, are you?" No other comment so clearly reveals how unprepared the United States was to enter the Great War than this astonished remark US senator Thomas S. Martin, the Senate majority leader and chairman of the Senate Finance Committee, had made the previous year, in April 1917. One of the last surviving Confederate veterans of the Civil War serving in the Senate, Martin, then sixty-nine, a stout man with a full head of white hair, was listening as a military officer testified about a $3 billion request from the White House to create a much larger US Army. Itemizing the many expenses to be covered by this enormous appropriation (equal to more than $50 billion today), Major Palmer S. Pierce listed training camps, rifles, artillery, and airplanes, then added, "And we may have to have an army in France." Senator Martin's flabbergasted response is even more revealing when one realizes that it was uttered on April 6, 1917, the same day that the US Congress—including Martin—voted to declare war.[10]

In the immediate wake of the declaration of war, it was widely assumed that America's contribution would be limited to loans and war supplies for the Allies. General John J. Pershing and his superiors subsequently agreed that US forces would be assembled, trained, and supplied for their first offensive—in 1919. If Washington had stuck with its original strategy, the war would have been lost. It is not widely appreciated that US involvement in World War I became solely focused on holding off the 1918 German offensives instead. An effort unprecedented in history was undertaken to recruit, train, and ship sufficient numbers of troops to France before the Allies were defeated. The total number of Americans in uniform swelled to almost 4.8 million, 2 million of whom were shipped to Europe and almost 1.4 million of whom saw active combat.[11]

They barely arrived in time. As late as July 15, with another offensive under way, Berlin's leaders anticipated a big victory, German chancellor Georg von Hertling recalled. "That was on the 15th," he wrote. "On the 18th even the most optimistic among us knew that all was lost. The history of the world was played out in three days."[12] The German advances gradually slowed and the Allies, with US help, began to turn the tide of the war by August 1918.

The Austro-Hungarian Trans-Siberian Czecho-Slovaks

FOLLOWING RUSSIA'S WITHDRAWAL from the war in March 1918, Moscow began shipping home more than 2.3 million German and Austro-Hungarian POWs aboard trains from camps across all of Soviet Russia. More than 200,000 of the men in Austro-Hungarian uniforms hailed from the more obscure corners of the Habsburg realm, and they were known to their rulers—but almost no one else—as Bohemians, Czechs, Moravians, or Slovaks. They and their leader, a philosophy professor named Tomáš G. Masaryk, wanted a nation of their own. And they were willing to fight for it. From his London exile, Masaryk had traveled to Russia under an assumed name early in 1917 to persuade the men to fight for France on the Western Front, in return for which the Allies would consider creating a new nation, Czecho-Slovakia. Between 50,000 and 65,000 of these Czechs and Slovaks would throw in their lot with Masaryk.

On May 14, 1918, in Chelyabinsk—a Russian frontier settlement on the steeper, more fractured, eastern slopes of the Ural Mountains, the gateway to Siberia—about eighty Hungarians, hardened survivors of war and imprisonment, former POWs being returned to the Austro-Hungarian Army, sat waiting in the last three cars of a westbound train otherwise full of refugees.

Their steam-powered locomotive was replenished with wood and water. The bored, brooding veterans awaited the sudden jerking motion that would bring the creaking wood-and-steel train back to life and resume its languid journey west through the Ural Mountains, in the direction of Austria-Hungary. They had survived the Eastern Front, hellish conditions in Russia's POW camps, and several Siberian winters. And now many of the men—still loyal to the Habsburg dynasty—understood that they would be thrown back into combat. If no longer imprisoned, they may have felt doomed.

Across the platform stood a train facing east crowded with men who had also worn Austro-Hungarian uniforms, but these strangers appeared to be in better spirits. They were Czechs and Slovaks—part of the more than fifty thousand in Russia who had become followers of Masaryk— washing down stale black bread and blood sausages with kettles of strong tea. Strangers in a strange land, they had reason to be hopeful that they might win a nation for their people. Unlikely as it seemed, this was their moment.

The cars that carried the Czechs and Slovaks had been moved off the main track onto a siding, due to what Russian authorities claimed was a shortage of locomotives. These men, a handful of whom had deserted to the Russians and fought in a special unit of the tsarist army, won the new Soviet regime's permission to organize their own trains and depart Russia via Siberia, keeping a small number of weapons for self-defense.

Their eastbound trains were destined for Vladivostok, a distant port on Russia's Pacific coast more than thirty-one hundred miles away. In Vladivostok, the men hoped to board Allied ships that would circumnavigate the globe and deposit them in the trenches of the Western Front alongside their former enemies, the French. In return for fighting with the Allies, it was hoped, they would win freedom for their peoples. At least that was the plan.

If Russia decided to turn them over to Austro-Hungarian authorities, many of them would face certain imprisonment and possible execution. Several hundred of these men had innocently emigrated to Russia long before the Great War in search of jobs or land and had enlisted in the tsar's armies in 1914 as a prudent obligation. A few thousand more had served in the Austro-Hungarian army on the Eastern Front, but deserted to the Russians. For these men in particular, firing squads awaited them back home and the Austrian authorities were unlikely to exercise great care in deciding which among them was guilty. Those spared execution and deemed able to fight would be returned to the Austro-Hungarian army, perhaps to die facedown in the mud or snow for the privilege of preserving a German-speaking empire that held them firmly in second-class status.

Most of the Czechs and Slovaks traveling to Vladivostok, however, were newly released captives of the Russians. This motley legion had assembled because one elderly professor from Prague thought it was a good idea.

The Professor

IN THE LAST years of the war, from hotel rooms and apartments across Europe, North America, and Russia, Masaryk and a handful of associates had established a virtual government-in-exile. They energetically publicized the cause of Czecho-Slovak independence and lobbied the Allies for support because the world knew nothing of Czechs or Slovaks. "I was afraid that a short war would fail to liberate us, even if Austria were defeated," Masaryk recalled. "We weren't ready, and the warring powers were all but ignorant of us. So I gave a great deal of thought to how long it would last. Much as I feared a short war, I reproached myself for being so cruel as to wish it long."[13]

Masaryk had traveled to Russia with a forged passport in May 1917, dodging bullets and cannon fire across Russia, to negotiate with the Provisional Government. While there, he encountered Albert Thomas, the French minister of armaments and munitions on a diplomatic mission and had made a fateful offer, that the Czech and Slovak POWs be shipped to Europe to support France's badly mauled army.[14]

French lines were at that moment struggling to save Paris without, as yet, significant assistance from US troops. Thomas agreed to Masaryk's offer. The Bolsheviks also concurred, happy to rid themselves of the nationalist Czechs and Slovaks. Masaryk put out a call for volunteers to enlist in a Czecho-Slovak Legion bound for France. Tens of thousands responded.

Initially planning to remain in Russia a few weeks, Masaryk spent the next year there recruiting, educating, and organizing Czech and Slovak POWs across Russia. He then prepared to sail across the Pacific to the United States. Masaryk desperately needed to raise money, publicize the plight of his people, and seek the support of the United States.

"The army was harmonious and its spirit good," Masaryk later recalled. "True, I expected that it would meet with many a difficulty on its long journey, though I was convinced that, by avoiding interference in Russian affairs, it would end by reaching its transports safely."[15]

While the upheavals of war and revolution slowed his journey toward Vladivostok, Masaryk's trip was uneventful, as dozens of trains holding his 40,000–50,000 volunteers fell in behind him, rolling slowly across southern Russia and Siberia. Amidst the chaos of revolutionary Russia, however, his accord with Moscow began to unravel.

Incident at Chelyabinsk

SOME LOCAL BOLSHEVIKS resented the legionnaires for leaving Russia and using up scarce supplies of weapons and locomotives. At each station along the Trans-Siberian Railway, the Bolsheviks demanded that the Czecho-Slovaks surrender more of their meager supply of arms in exchange for access to locomotives. These requests irritated the Czechs and Slovaks, who saw many Russian locomotives pulling the westbound trains returning POWs, their former comrades, who were still loyal to Germany and Austria-Hungary. The legionnaires suspected that Germany and Austria-Hungary were in league with the Bolsheviks.

By late April 1918 the legion's first trains had reached Vladivostok, but all the seventy to eighty trains carrying the Czechs and Slovaks at different points along the Trans-Siberian had completely halted following a series of contradictory orders from Moscow. Sitting on railroad sidings like the one in Chelyabinsk, watching the westbound trains roll past, the legionnaires were stretched across almost five thousand miles and not moving. Angry and frustrated at the delay, the legionnaires called for a conference at Chelyabinsk.

While they were under strict orders to avoid involvement in Russia's domestic conflicts, delegates from across the legion urgently shared their fears that the Bolsheviks would prevent them from boarding Allied ships. But morale at Chelyabinsk remained high. Almost every day, the former shopkeepers, dentists, farmers, professors, factory hands, and bank clerks drilled and did calisthenics. The lowliest enlisted men and the highest-ranking officers all addressed one another as "brother."

PERHAPS FROM THE sheer boredom of sitting around a train station in the middle of nowhere, the Czecho-Slovak units and the Hungarians slowly sought each other out. They had lived under the same Austrian regime, worn the same uniforms, and survived captivity in Russian POW camps together. So, they greeted one another and compared stories. The men joked and teased one another. After years of isolation, they were eager to learn about lost comrades, the progress of the war, or news from home.

Unlike the Czechs and Slovaks, however, who were somewhat more experienced in foraging food and supplies along the Trans-Siberian, the Hungarians remained formally in the custody of an impoverished Russia in disarray. "Nobody was taking care of them," said Cyril Toman, one of the Czechs.[16] "So they were starving and kept going to our boys, begging bread from them. We would give them bread, tobacco, sugar, and sometimes even leftovers from our kitchen."

They were "extremely grateful" for the food, according to another Czech, Sergeant Gustav Becvar.[17] "Many friendships had sprung up, and when at last an engine arrived for the refugee train, a group of legionnaires gathered to say good-bye to their departing friends."

"Suddenly, a locomotive arrived," recalled Toman. Shifting easily into that tone of droll cynicism for which Bohemians are well known, Toman added, "It was hooked up to the cars, and the Hungarians, thinking that they were leaving, rewarded us handsomely."

As the train carrying the Hungarians began to ease away from the station at midmorning on the fourteenth, a loud Hungarian curse was heard, and a hunk of iron flew from one of the windows of the moving train, striking and seriously wounding a Czech on the platform whose last name was Ducháček. Collapsing, his body rolled under the wheels of the Hungarians' train as it lurched forward.

The Czechs erupted in pursuit of the slow-moving train, their footsteps crunched wildly across the gravel railbeds. They leapt onto the running boards of the steam engine and forced it to stop. They surrounded the cars, bearing rifles, and demanded that the Hungarians produce the person who threw the iron. Fistfights and scuffles broke out everywhere. Becvar noted that "only the strenuous efforts" of Czech officers saved several Hungarians from being lynched on the spot.

"The prisoners were laughing at us, though," said Toman. "They were shouting, 'Fuck you! God-damned Czechs!' Our brothers lost patience, ran into the cars and threw all of the prisoners out. They brought them back to the location of the incident. Again they demanded that either the culprit admit his deed or the others turn him in. The prisoners kept laughing and making comments. That made our boys angry. They started to smack the prisoners' faces and poke them with their rifles. It was only then that one of the prisoners pointed out the culprit."

This time, the officers could not restrain their men.

"The brothers, irritated to the extreme, threw themselves at him and beat him to death," according to Toman. Using the term "Austrian," as most people did in habitual reference to any soldier wearing an Austro-Hungarian uniform, Becvar said, "When, after a few minutes, calm was restored, the Austrian's limp body lay still upon the ground."

ONE

UNDER ENEMY EYES

This empire is doomed. The instant the Emperor shuts his eyes, we'll crumble into a hundred pieces. The Balkans will be more powerful than we. All the nations will set up their own filthy little states, and even the Jews are going to proclaim a king in Palestine. Vienna already stinks of the sweat of the democrats; I can't stand being on the Ringstrasse anymore. The workers wave red flags and don't care to work. The mayor of Vienna is a pious janitor. The pastors are already going with the people; their sermons are in Czech. The Burgtheater is playing Jewish smut, and every week a Hungarian toilet manufacturer becomes a baron.

JOSEPH ROTH, *The Radetzky March*[1]

There has never been a revolution without espionage and conspiracy.

EDUARD BENEŠ, *My War Memoirs*[2]

"I Have a Message"

A WEEK BEFORE Christmas 1914, a sixty-four-year-old professor packed a bag inside his comfortable home on a gently curving cobblestone street perched on Letna Hill above the brooding, thousand-year-old hulk of Prague Castle. Tormented by a guilty conscience, the old man felt a desperate need to do something—*anything*—for the young men on distant battlefields, some of whom were dying for treasonous acts that he encouraged.

World War One's Eastern Front, 1917

"On leaving Prague our Czech soldiers had given vent to their anti-Austrian feelings, and we heard that, in the army, there was insubordination among them," recalled Tomáš G. Masaryk. "Soon came reports of military severity and even of executions. Our men were being punished for what I, a member of parliament, had advocated. Could I—ought I—do less than the simple soldier-citizen whose anti-Austrian and Slavonic feelings I had encouraged?"[3]

Accompanied by his youngest child, Olga, then twenty-three, Masaryk walked out into the shadows of Prague's fabled castle and through the narrow lanes that wriggled between rows of small buildings clinging to the steep slope that falls away from the walls of the medieval fortress that still commands Prague's skyline. So, too, did Czech nationalists cling to the memories of the castle's Saint Vitus Cathedral and Royal Palace, where in 1618 the Defenestration of Prague sparked the Thirty Years' War.

By 1914 a small German-speaking class of merchants and officials presided uneasily over a growing population of Czech workers. Tomáš and Olga Masaryk wound their way toward the Franz Josef I Railway Station through the city's gauntlet of ghostly statues, of persons real and imagined, hanging from arches, lurking in corners, framing windows. They guarded churches, walkways, and bridges; sat atop pedestals, horses, and cornices in poses of prayer and combat, standing watch and bearing witness as Masaryk departed his adopted city, unaware that his own image would one day take its place among the statues. Above them, the "one hundred spires" that pierced Prague's skyline, pointy shoots from the rich soil of the city's Romanesque, Gothic, Renaissance, Baroque, and Neoclassical architecture, were airbrushed in black soot, but something more ominous darkened Prague's streets, Masaryk knew; police suspicions of his people were growing and the authorities were arresting all of those they suspected.

Vienna clamped down hard on its subjects at the start of the war, creating a War Surveillance Office that effectively imposed martial law. While all combatant nations limited some civil liberties, according to a study of the "militarization" of Austria-Hungary, "In no other country had rulers gone so far, in advance, in this effort, as in Austria."[4] "With the layer of traditional politics peeled away," observes historian Maureen Healy, "the state intervened, through wartime decree, in the everyday lives of Viennese residents in unprecedented ways."[5] Three Czech political parties—including Masaryk's—were dissolved. Newspapers were closed, widespread censorship was imposed, and citizens' personal mail was regularly opened. Czech leaders, some of them members of the parliament, or Reichsrat, were imprisoned and sentenced to death. Civilian juries were suspended and military tribunals imprisoned hundreds, if not thousands, many of them under sentence of death. While at least some persons were executed for activities deemed treasonous, estimates of their number vary widely.[6] No doubt fear was palpable among Czech activists. Vienna's fabled "crawling army of informers" flooded police stations and government offices with anonymous reports of "suspicious" activity. Even Prague's small circle of Czech leaders could no longer trust one another. One of the political parties, the Young Czechs, led by Karel Kramář, was accused of accepting Habsburg subsidies for its newspaper, which it had to reluctantly admit. The Young Czechs struck back in March 1914 by exposing the source of this accusation, a rival Czech leader, Karel Šviha, as a paid police informant.[7] Indeed, Vienna cultivated widespread spying among its subjects, especially among Slavic activists, particularly if they traveled abroad.

Masaryk could not be too careful; he kept his plans to himself. Yet—as he had done twice before since the war began—he now bade goodbye to his American wife, Charlotte, and his three older children, Alice, Herbert, and Jan. Olga could provide domestic help for an aging academic living out of a suitcase, yet her presence also made him look more like a doting father than a subversive. Indeed, their cover story was that Olga was ill and they were seeking medical help in Rome.

"I thought at the time that I should be back in Prague in a few weeks," he said.[8] Instead, he did not see Prague, his home, or his family for four long years. He never again saw his oldest son, Herbert. Alice was arrested and thrown into prison, and Charlotte, already suffering from worsening heart disease, suffered increasing bouts of depression as a result of the hardships the family experienced; the combination eventually put her in a sanatorium. But there was no turning back.

Masaryk was already collaborating with the enemy.

At that time, Allied leaders knew virtually nothing about Austria-Hungary's many peoples; even academic specialists on the subject were very rare. London relied on a handful of civilian journalists and scholars who voluntarily advised their government, which is why Masaryk first contacted the British government through H. Wickham Steed, foreign editor of the *Times*. The two had met years before in Vienna, where Steed was a correspondent and Masaryk was a member of the Austro-Hungarian Reichsrat.[9]

Tall, spare, elegant, with a pointed mustache and Vandyke beard, Steed was an educated man, tireless traveler, and engaging conversationalist. He gave the impression, a contemporary said, of being more the seasoned diplomat than a workaday newspaper reporter. His initial impression of Masaryk was that he was "too unassuming to be able to hold his own amid the intrigues and chicane of the Austrian Parliament." In 1913 Steed, disgusted with the oppressive Habsburg regime, departed Vienna for the foreign desk of the *Times* in London. That same year, he published *The Hapsburg Monarchy*, which was translated into several languages and quickly banned by the Austrian government on the grounds that it insulted Emperor Franz Joseph I.[10]

"One afternoon, towards the middle of September, when I was about to leave my house, I found a strange-looking man standing on the threshold," Steed later recalled. "Thick-set, of medium height, unshaven, grimy in appearance and in dress, with features of the semi-Tartar type that is not uncommon in Bohemia, he seemed an unprepossessing fellow."[11]

The disheveled Emanuel Viktor Voska entered the foyer of Steed's home and began, "I'm Voska, the head of the Bohemian Alliance in America. I am an American citizen. I left Prague with 30 American citizens five days ago. In an hour I must catch my train to Liverpool with them. Before I left, the Professor said to me: 'In London, see Mr. Steed.

Tell him the Russians shoot at our boys when they want to surrender. Our boys wave handkerchiefs but the Russians shoot all the same. Tell Mr. Steed to find means of stopping it. Our boys want to go over to the Russians.'"

Flabbergasted, Steed replied, "How on earth am I to stop it? Did Masaryk say nothing else?"

Voska shrugged, "No, that was all. He just said, 'Tell Mr. Steed to stop it.'"

This exchange revealed that at least some Czechs, and perhaps other Slavs, in Habsburg uniform were trying to defect to the Russians in the first weeks of combat. It revealed that Masaryk was able to get word from men on the Eastern Front, which meant that his intelligence was very good. And it provided an early indication that, from the birth of the Czech and Slovak liberation movement, the actions of Czech and Slovak soldiers in Russia held the key to the struggle for independence.

Of course, the exchange also confirmed that Masaryk was a traitor. Habsburg subjects were being imprisoned and executed for much less egregious acts of treason than making covert arrangements for the wholesale defection of Austro-Hungarian troops. The Army High Command (AOK) had ordered the death penalty without trial for desertion, encouraging desertion, or any actions that led others to neglect or reject their military duty.

Masaryk's intelligence was accurate. Years later, after the war, a young Czech soldier, back home in Prague, confessed that early in September 1914 he and his comrades tried to surrender to the Russians, with deadly results. "On September 8, 1914," J. Javurek said, "we put up a white flag above our heads, but the Russian army either did not trust us or did not understand us, and so our whole home defense unit suffered terrible losses."[12]

"Another Absent-Minded Professor"

As BOTH A Czech and Slovak, Masaryk bridged an ethnic gap that appears much more significant since the Czech and Slovak Republics went their separate ways in 1993. Observers who understand how the Czechs and Slovaks emerged from feudal Europe under entirely segregated Austrian and Hungarian tyrannies can appreciate how improbable it was that the first president of their new republic in 1918 encompassed both ethnicities in his immediate family.

Masaryk also possessed a handful of the most crucial relationships anyone in his situation could hope for. While hardly a social butterfly, his acquaintance with leading British correspondents was just one example of the array of contacts he developed in precisely those Allied countries—France, Great Britain, Russia, and the United States—where they proved most useful. Russia and America, for example, also had the largest Czech and Slovak populations outside of Austria-Hungary. He also befriended public officials, wealthy industrialists, and influential writers abroad. He cultivated ties to Croats, Serbs, Slovenes, Montenegrins, and Macedonians—South Slavs or Yugoslavs—with whom he forged a unified front of oppressed Habsburg minorities.

THE DISTINGUISHED BEARING of the bespectacled, goateed, always-proper Masaryk—one of his closest associates later said he appeared just like "another absent-minded professor"—belied his humble origins. He was born on March 7, 1850, among what he would later call the "Moravian Slovak" peasants of rural Moravia, in a small village, Hodonín, which sat beside the Morava River, a languid curling border between Austria and Hungary. The Slovaks, an obscure people, farmed the agricultural northwest corner of Hungary, just across the Morava.

Masaryk's father, Josef, a Slovak from across the border in Hungary, was an illiterate yet hardworking manager of farmhands on estates owned by Emperor Franz Joseph I. Josef had started as a groom in the stables and was later promoted to coachman, then overseer. "I grew up amid such straitened circumstances," Tomáš recalled later, "that I took it as a matter of course that I was going to be a serf just like my father and the others."[13] His father's status was such that he had to ask his superiors for permission to send young Tomáš to school.[14] The key to Tomáš's

education, however, was the loving attention of his Czech-Moravian
mother, Teresie (Theresa), who, like many Habsburg subjects, possessed
an uncertain ethnic identity.

Teresie Kropáček, a butcher's daughter, was Czech, born in Moravia.
But her son thought of her as German, since she received some education
in German. To her husband and others, she spoke Slovak. Although she
worked as a domestic servant and cook, she could read. She taught young
Tomáš to read in German, his first language.

Tomáš was always devouring books. His haphazard education was improved at the age of eleven, when his parents enrolled him in a two-year
program at a school. He returned home after graduation wanting to become a teacher.

Tomáš was raised a Catholic, he played organ at church, and he later
bragged of converting a locksmith's wife to Catholicism. A Slovak priest
inculcated in Tomáš his first taste of nationalism, and Tomáš's sense that
his Slovak father was "ruthlessly downtrodden" led him to begin to hate
"our masters."

At fifteen, Tomáš entered a German secondary school in Brünn (Brno),
Moravia, where he did well and made the first of many key relationships,
this one with Brünn's chief of police, Anton Le Monnier. The chief hired
Tomáš to tutor his son, Franz, and took Tomáš under his wing, granting
him access to his library of German classics and other works. The young
Masaryk consumed the police chief's works in Latin, Greek, Czech,
French, Russian, Polish, Arabic, and English, some of which he could
translate. In 1869 Masaryk accompanied Le Monnier to Vienna, where
the Brünn official was named that city's chief of police.

In Vienna, Masaryk enrolled in the prestigious Academic grammar
school, where fellow Austrian students included future government
ministers. He socialized mostly with the handful of Czechs there, and
it was in Vienna that he became fully aware of the antagonism between
Czechs and Germans. Perhaps not coincidentally, he struggled with his
Habsburg Catholic faith. At age twenty, he renounced Catholicism and,
two years later, in 1872, enrolled at the University of Vienna.

The following year Tomáš's older brother, Martin, then serving with an artillery regiment, died of pneumonia. Masaryk was devastated. "From then onwards," he would recall, "I put my entire trust in philosophy, in which I sought and also found consolation." A month later, his benefactor and friend, Le Monnier, also died, leaving Tomáš isolated in Vienna and without financial support. Yet he was soon hired as a tutor by another wealthy family and again devoted himself to the study of philosophy. Unsurprisingly, the future philosopher-president favored Plato, well known for his advocacy of the rule of philosopher-kings. In March 1876 Masaryk was awarded his doctorate. In April his first published article appeared in the *Moravská Orlice* (Moravian Eagle), addressed to the Czechs in the Reichsrat. "In political science, the foremost principal is to act," he wrote.

Still a tutor in search of more gainful employment, he traveled to the University of Leipzig in Germany in the summer of 1877, where, he later said, "I had a momentous experience which fundamentally affected my whole life and intellectual growth—I met Charlotte Garrigue."

An American who was only a few months younger than Tomáš, Charlotte was the daughter of French-Danish immigrants to America, a wealthy family from Brooklyn, and she carried herself with "a noble, aristocratic bearing."[15] Charlotte was visiting a friend in Leipzig, and she and Tomáš were immediately drawn to one another. They quickly began a courtship that involved reading, learning each other's languages, fireside chats, and long walks. By August the couple was engaged. "Charlie" returned to New York and Tomáš returned to Vienna in search of a teaching post. In February 1878 Tomáš received a telegram from Charlotte's father saying she had been seriously injured in a fall from a carriage. The young Masaryk took a seventeen-day passage across the Atlantic to Brooklyn, where he was relieved to find Charlotte recovering. Without waiting, they married in New York City on March 15, 1878. Masaryk turned a theoretical preference for the West into a tangible American presence in his life.

"Masaryk's marriage was a union between two people who were deeply attached to each other, and who also shared a wide range of intellectual

and artistic interests," says Masaryk's biographer, Paul Selver. "In order
to symbolize the close harmony which thus resulted, Masaryk adopted
his wife's maiden name, and was known henceforward as Thomas Garrigue Masaryk." This was a highly unusual thing to do in 1878, a clear
demonstration of the couple's progressive views. Charlotte was Masaryk's
"closest collaborator."

On their return to Europe, the couple visited Prague before settling
in Vienna. Masaryk was appointed a lecturer at the University of Vienna
and made a strong impression on his students. One described him thus:

> A lean, slender man with a gaunt, longish face and short beard. Re-
> served in manner, and entirely without affectations. He wore pince-
> nez, and his eyes, though they already showed some signs of the strain
> due to close study, gazed clearly, steadily and penetratingly from a
> countenance which seemed, so to speak, veiled with cares. . . . His
> lectures were free from any appeal to the emotions. But his delivery
> was kindled with a sort of devout intensity.

At home, the couple spoke English and German to each other, with
a smattering of Czech. Their first child, Alice, was born in 1879, and
a son, Herbert, followed in 1880. Later that year, wanting his children
to be brought up with a religious influence but unwilling to make that
influence a Catholic one, Masaryk was quietly received into the Evan-
gelical Reformed Church. This was congenial to Charlotte, who had
been raised in the States as a Unitarian. While Masaryk remained a devout Christian until his death, he expressed strong anti-Catholic views,
in part due to the continued loyalty to the Habsburg regime of Czech
Catholic factions.

In 1882 a surprising turn led Masaryk to Prague, a city to which he
was a complete stranger until his thirty-second year. Responding to the
growing agitation of the Czechs for autonomy in language and education—indeed, serious street battles had broken out the year before between Czech and German students in Prague—the Reichsrat and the

emperor split Charles University in Prague into Czech and German sections. Masaryk straightaway applied for a position on the Czech philosophy faculty; his appointment was approved the same year. Astutely, Tomáš and Charlotte began speaking to one another in Czech, both at home and in public.

In the nominating papers submitted to none other than Franz Joseph I—the always scribbling, micromanaging emperor, taking the time to evaluate the credentials of a novice faculty appointee—the minister of education, Freiherr von Eyberfeld, assured his sovereign: "Masaryk, to judge by his disposition, will form a moderating element among the Czech professors."

The minister was sorely mistaken.

Professor Masaryk spent years speaking and lobbying on behalf of the minority Czechs and Slovaks during his years in the Reichsrat from 1891–1893 and again from 1907–1914. His learned speeches lent him the air of a visionary idealist, despite the fact that he possessed a pragmatic and logical cast of mind. A solitary and somewhat shy person, Masaryk by his own admission preferred reading to public speaking or meeting people. Yet he was principled, stubborn, and personally courageous. He waged a lonely campaign against the anti-Semitic canard of blood-ritual murders in defense of a Jewish drifter charged in the brutal murder of a young Czech woman. While his research and testimony were perhaps decisive in lifting the defendant's death sentence, Masaryk became for years a hated and isolated figure.

As a politician, he was the sole elected representative of a Czech fringe party. But that modest perch was lost to him in March 1914, when the government of Emperor Franz Joseph I adjourned the Reichsrat, which had become hopelessly deadlocked by insistent and disruptive demands by its Slavic members for greater autonomy. The aging emperor now ruled by dictatorial decree. Masaryk's years as an advocate on behalf of the Czechs, Slovaks, and other Slavs made only limited progress in democratizing Austria-Hungary. As a teacher and scholar, moreover, his most productive years were behind him.

Meeting the Enemy

"WHEN [EMANUEL VOSKA] had gone," H. Wickham Steed "sat down to think out ways and means of doing what Masaryk wanted." Steed recalled from his years in Eastern Europe crowds singing *Hej Slovane* (Hey, Slavs), an anthem for Slavic peoples. Steed got a message to Masaryk, "If the Czech troops who might want to surrender to the Russians were to sing Hei Slovane at midnight in their trenches, the Russians might be warned to take the singing as a signal."

Steed immediately visited Count Alexander von Benckendorff, the Russian ambassador to London, asking him to forward this message to the Russian foreign minister, Sergey D. Sazonov. Steed repeated the instructions to be given to the Czechs and other Slavic troops, adding, "It would mean that Czechs were coming over into the Russian lines and must not be fired upon."

Voska had a second meeting in London—and almost everything else would ride on the outcome. Voska recalled his urgent departing instructions from Masaryk, "I must see Lord Kitchener personally and get his frank, confidential opinion on the probable length of the war. If he believed it would be settled in a few months, I was to do nothing."

With Steed's assistance, Voska wrangled an appointment with this greatest living British hero. Field Marshal Horatio Herbert Kitchener led the forces that reconquered the Sudan for Great Britain in 1898—with a young Winston Churchill serving under him in the Twenty-First Lancers—and later won renown and titles as the victor of the Boer War, commander in chief of India, and the virtual ruler of Egypt. Appointed secretary of state for war in 1914 and based in London, Kitchener immediately made a prediction that struck fear into the hearts of every European. Except, that is, Masaryk's.

The Germans were marching on Paris, Voska recalled, but Kitchener "talked quite impersonally, as though all this were someone else's trouble." Kitchener predicted that "it will be a long war. Three years at least, maybe four." The soldiers would *not* be home by Christmas. "The French underestimated the power of the German armies," he continued. "We'll lose Paris, probably. But we'll hold a line further south until we can bring our resources to bear. We'll win in the end, though. And if your people stand by, I'll do all I can to help you when we make peace."[16]

This was the first assurance that Masaryk's longer-term strategy might actually work. "For it was obvious," *Times* correspondent R. W. Seton-Watson recalled, "that not less than three years would be required to prepare the world for a program of complete independence, whereas if the war should only last half that time a strong case might be put forward in favor of a much more modest program of national autonomy inside the frame-work of the Habsburg Monarchy."[17] "For me," Masaryk said, "this question was very weighty, since the character of the work I meant to do abroad depended largely upon the duration of the war."[18] A Czech courier in London was found to take this news to Masaryk, while Voska sailed for New York, launching espionage and propaganda campaigns that top officials and historians will later credit for bringing the United States into the war.

SIMULTANEOUSLY, MASARYK BEGAN making arrangements to meet with key persons in the Allied countries in order to explain who the Czechs and Slovaks were, why they were unhappy as Habsburg subjects, and what they hoped to achieve if the Great War lasted long enough to weaken Austria-Hungary. While meetings of the Reichsrat had been adjourned since March 1914—the legislature did not meet again until May 1917—Masaryk retained formal immunity as a member of parliament, which he used in September to accompany his American sister-in-law to the Dutch port of Rotterdam, where she boarded a steamer for the United States.[19]

Once in neutral Holland, he seized his chance.

Urgently and insistently, he wrote to Steed on September 14. Failing to get an immediate response, he wrote on September 17 to Seton-Watson. Masaryk and Seton-Watson had met years earlier and by the summer of 1914 they were thinking of founding a new journal concerned with

European nationalism.[20] Writing from the Hotel Weimar in Rotterdam, Masaryk said,

> I came here to communicate with Mr. Steed: I asked him to come here or to send you or somebody who could grasp the full meaning of what I would have to say now. . . . I would like to hear what is going on, not only on the battlefields, but in the heads of those who will shape the future, perhaps the future map of Europe, at least of Austria. I wish that we Bohemians could say what we feel and what we hope. . . . [T]elegraph me here whether you have got my letter and whether I can expect somebody from England here—*now*.

The letter reached Seton-Watson only after Masaryk was forced to return to Prague on September 23.

This failure must have been frustrating.

"For three weeks there was silence," Seton-Watson recalled, "and then came a message through *The Times* correspondent at The Hague to Mr. Steed begging him to come over to Rotterdam, or to send a substitute." It was Masaryk again; Steed sent Seton-Watson to see him and—by what Seton-Watson later characterized as a "fortunate accident"—the British journalist was able to enter Holland in mid-October without having to show his passport. As a result, Masaryk's first meeting with an (unofficial) Allied representative was initially undetected by Austria's spies in Holland.

"We spent two days together, keeping mainly to our rooms for the day, and walking for miles along the quays after it was dark," said Seton-Watson, then thirty-five. "I took detailed notes of our conversation and immediately on my return to England drew up a memorandum embodying Masaryk's ideas, not only as to the internal situation in Bohemia and in Austria-Hungary as a whole, but as to the settlement which ought to follow the war, and the policy which the Allies should pursue." "An independent Bohemia" was the most Masaryk and his comrades dared hoped for. Russia's support would be crucial. Seton-Watson's memorandum noted that a kingdom would be more popular than a republic or democracy, suggesting a Danish or Belgian prince on the throne.[21] Complete independence, he said "is absolutely inconceivable unless and until Germany is crushed."

Turning Allied attention to their main objective—defeating Prussian Germany—Masaryk added, "A decisive blow can be dealt at Prussia in one of two ways—either directly or through Austria. To weaken or crush Austria-Hungary is the effectual way of weakening Germany." This was a point to which Masaryk would return again and again—independence for Austria-Hungary's peoples would destroy the Habsburg regime—and its destruction would finish Germany. He urged the restoration of "historical Bohemia-Moravia-Silesia," with the addition of the Slovak districts of Hungary, an audacious move, given his limited contact with Slovakia.

He also passed along very useful intelligence regarding the role of Romania in the war, which, he told Seton-Watson, was "obtained from secret informants inside the War Ministry in Vienna." His own nationalist agenda aside, he thought, *that* should get the Allies' attention.

Masaryk was not named in Seton-Watson's memo. He was identified only as the "informant," but his name was shared by messengers who conveyed the secret memo to the chief diplomats of the three major Allied nations, British foreign secretary Sir Edward Grey, French foreign minister Théophile Delcassé, and Russian foreign minister Sazonov.

More than useful contacts, journalists like Seton-Watson and Steed became advocates for Masaryk's cause and grew to admire how he rallied the Allies to his side. "Seton was converted by Masaryk to the cause of Bohemian independence," according to Seton-Watson's children. This is doubly important, since Seton-Watson "was the main unofficial specialist on Austrian Balkan affairs" for Grey and his staff.[22]

"Few understood at that time the importance of Masaryk's work or his unique ascendancy over the Slav peoples of Austria-Hungary," Steed later said. "Most British public men thought it a hare-brained business to take serious account of him or to suppose that an isolated Slovak professor at

Prague, who must be suspect to the Austrian government, could render valid service to the Allied cause. Even the strength of the Czecho-Slovak national movement was not understood."

A Holy Roman Mess

THAT MASARYK REMAINED a largely obscure person even after many years of service in the Austro-Hungarian Reichsrat—and that few officials in Paris, London, or Washington were even aware of the existence of peoples variously described as Czechs, Bohemians, Moravians, or Slovaks—was due to the fact that he, and they, were subjects of an interior European empire, Austria-Hungary, whose ancient roots and evolving complexity made it a difficult place to grasp.[23]

By 1914 Austria-Hungary resembled a fairy-tale kingdom, with its aging, crisply uniformed monarch, regal castles, dashing aristocrats, large estates, illiterate peasants, rolling hills, dark forests, wolves, gypsies, and legends of Count Dracula. Yet it was being swallowed up in an alien urban landscape of cities, factories, railroads, electric lights, battleships, early automobiles, and the second metro line in all of Europe.[24] It was becoming a place where bustling middle-class crowds no longer looked to the monarch and his fellow aristocrats for sustenance, guidance, or protection. The ruling aristocracy had come to seem majestically and powerfully irrelevant.

Still, Vienna had an impeccable pedigree. Unlike the modern, yet provincial, nation-states sprouting up all around it, Austria-Hungary emerged from the Middle Ages as the standard-bearer of Europe's older, more cosmopolitan, political tradition—Christian monarchial rule over disparate lands and peoples. By 1914 it occupied present-day Austria, Hungary, Czech and Slovak Republics, Croatia, Slovenia, Bosnia-Herzegovina, northern Italy, southern Poland, and western sections of Ukraine and Romania. Its 52 million people were squeezed into an area the size of Texas, yet it entered the war as a great power, second largest in land and third most populated in Europe.

Peoples & Nations, Central & Eastern Europe, 1914

Once the embodiment, if now the corpse, of the Holy Roman Empire, Austria-Hungary harked back to the fabled realm of Charlemagne. Each of these regimes shared a yearning to resuscitate ancient Rome's original empire of law, peace, and order, "the fairest part of the earth," said Edward Gibbon, "and the most civilized portion of mankind."[25]

The only common bond among Austria-Hungary's dozen or so nationalities was the Habsburg dynasty, which collected lands and peoples the way less powerful families might collect works of art. Croats, Czechs (Bohemians and Moravians), Germans, Italians, Poles, Romanians, Slovenes, and Ukrainians (Ruthenians) ended up inside the Austrian half of Austria-Hungary, while Croats, Germans, Hungarians (Magyars), Romanians, Serbs, Slovaks, Slovenes, and Ukrainians (Ruthenians) lived in the Kingdom of Hungary. "In all the Habsburg lands," noted one history, "Vienna was unique in one important respect. Here was at least partially achieved that supranational, cosmopolitan consciousness which was the dynasty's only hope for survival."[26] However, Europe's other peoples were merging into more homogeneous nations, while Vienna ruled a polyglot rabble. Viennese culture was exquisite, but the Habsburg empire was ungovernable.

AUSTRIA-HUNGARY, MASARYK HAD quipped on May 26, 1913, in the course of his last speech to the Reichsrat in Vienna, was like a good man who had somehow swallowed an umbrella—and spent the rest of his life fearing that it might open.[27] While Masaryk's metaphor is memorable, the realm is little remembered today in part because it did not fit the modern definitions of statehood. It represented neither a nation nor a people but a dynastic empire. And like most great empires—from the Roman to the Soviet—it slowly decayed from within until an unanticipated crisis caused the elaborate, aging edifice, hollowed out at its core, to collapse.

The Habsburgs inherited the historic mission of the Holy Roman Empire in 1273, when one of their own, Rudolf I, was elected emperor.[28] At first sporadically, and by the 1400s more permanently, the Habsburgs and the Holy Roman Empire were bound together, inspired always to restore a lost age—a Europe without nations, its many peoples united under one God and one emperor. The Habsburgs represented a faith more than a people and defined their realm more by traditions than by territory. The family laid claim to most of central Europe most of the time, but the seat of government moved with the emperor. Vienna was less a national capital than the principal address of the ruling family.[29] Austria's constitutions were revised whenever necessary—in 1848, 1860, and 1867—because the monarchy believed it was accountable to a higher law.

The 1867 constitution formalized what was essentially an alliance of the German rulers of Austria with Hungary's Magyar rulers, a partnership that oppressed all other ethnic groups. Austria-Hungary was further divided between its Latin Catholics and Orthodox Slavs. Like the neglected children of a bad marriage, it was the Slavs who were becoming most disruptive. Over time the principal achievement of the Habsburgs was their defense of Christendom against Islamic conquest. After Constantinople fell to Muslim armies in 1453, the advancing Ottoman Turks seized the Balkans in 1521, then laid siege to Vienna in 1529, the high-water mark of Islam's threat to Europe, until more recently. Unable to penetrate Vienna's fortress walls, Turkish armies returned to the city's gates in 1683, but Austria launched counterattacks over many decades that expelled the Turks from Hungary and the Balkans, confirming Austria's status as an essential European power. Yet this advance also planted the seeds of its final calamity. As Habsburg armies swept the Ottomans eastward, they occupied Bosnia-Herzegovina in 1878. The formal annexation of this province in 1908 sparked an angry reaction from its brooding Serbs.

Napoleon presented a more formidable challenge. After he defeated Habsburg armies, twice occupied Vienna, and crowned himself emperor, the Habsburgs in 1806 formally relinquished claim to lead the Holy Roman Empire, renaming their realm the Austrian Empire. And when the restive Kingdom of Hungary demanded equal billing in 1867, Vienna declared itself Austria-Hungary. No matter—its true realm was Christendom, ablaze in all its twilight glory.

As the fetters of feudal custom and Catholic piety slowly gave way, Vienna traded these institutions of genuine authority for more secular instruments of raw power—a large bureaucracy and a standing army. Indeed, concludes Habsburg military historian Gunther E. Rothenberg, "The army was one of the most important, if not the most important, single institution in the multinational empire of the Habsburgs."[30] If the army came apart internally, the unraveling of the empire could not be too far behind. As the belief took hold among its peoples that they were not merely Christians, serfs, or subjects—but Croats, Czechs, Germans, Hungarians (Magyars), Italians, Poles, Romanians, Ukrainians (Ruthenians), Serbs, Slovaks, and Slovenes—Vienna settled for obedience over loyalty and used cruder means to obtain it. Yet people's ethnic, cultural, and family loyalties crossed borders into neighboring nations, which would intervene in Vienna's affairs on behalf of their ethnic brethren, most fatefully in 1914, when Serbia and Russia went to war to defend Serbians in the Habsburg province of Bosnia-Herzegovina.

Attempting to blunt its subjects' demands, Vienna by the late 1800s allowed a parliament—the Reichsrat—to emerge alongside local assemblies, called diets, in the provinces. Yet this growing and increasingly raucous political arena—"Eight nations, 17 countries, 20 parliamentary groups, 27 parties," was the tally of one official—showcased Austria-Hungary's divisions.[31] In response to demands for greater democracy—and news of a revolution in Russia in 1905 that gave birth to a new Russian parliament, the State Duma—the emperor gave all males age twenty-four or older the right to vote in 1907. The next election destroyed the German majority in the lower house of the Reichsrat for the first time, electing 233 Germans and 283 non-Germans. Among the non-Germans were 103 Czechs representing seven political factions.

Still, the majority of high government posts remained in the grip of German-speaking officials. Paragraph 14 of the Austro-Hungarian constitution allowed the emperor to rule by decree when parliament was adjourned, a heavy burden to place on the shoulders of one individual, especially one so old. Vienna's 52 million subjects were largely subject to the rule of one man—a dictator in the guise of a constitutional monarch.

Indeed, 640 years after the first Rudolf was crowned Holy Roman Emperor, the empire's subjects probably took Habsburg rule for granted when, on December 2, 1913, on the eve of what they would call the Great War, Emperor Franz Joseph I celebrated the sixty-fifth year of his reign, a near European record.

The aristocratic families stood behind the throne. "As long as power was centered in Vienna and at the court, aristocracy mattered," notes historian Rita Krueger.[32] Yet the aristocratic class was reared in a non-national, multilingual, cosmopolitan milieu. They called themselves Austrians, but this term was merely shorthand for "Habsburg subjects." They were estate owners, soldiers, sportsmen, and statesmen, all of them measured by their pedigree. While the aristocrats who once dominated the officer corps gradually made room for professional soldiers of lower birth, the nobility retained its control of Habsburg foreign relations until 1918.

Vienna's German elite guarded its position jealously, while the Prussians were creating a united Germany farther north. Austria had been expelled from the German Confederation by Otto von Bismarck, who united the confederation's other Germans into a single nation in 1871. Even the Habsburgs gave way to nationalist fever. The Habsburgs began to impose German language and culture as aggressively as they deployed German soldiers and bureaucrats. By 1914 Germans represented only 24 percent of the population of Austria-Hungary but comprised 76 percent of the staffs of the central government ministries.[33] German-speaking bureaucrats insisted that all Habsburg subjects speak and write German. This demand bred resistance.

Vienna's Unloved Stepchildren

To THINK OF Czechs and Slovaks as a single people is a misperception, of course, one that would be rigorously promoted by Czech nationalists at the founding of Czecho-Slovakia in 1918—when Czech leaders rushed the Slovaks to the alter for an unequal marriage—and corrected by Slovak nationalists in 1993, when they broke from Prague and established their own Slovak Republic. There had never before been a Slovak kingdom or state. The Slovaks occupied a poor, rural corner of Hungary and remained largely invisible. While the Czechs and Slovaks shared a similar language and were long united in their opposition to Austria-Hungary, they had evolved entirely separately—one oppressed by Austria, the other by Hungary.

While the Slovaks had survived under Magyar rule since the tenth century, the more fortunate lands of Bohemia and Moravia next door were joined together in 1212 in the Kingdom of Bohemia, which enjoyed long periods of independence and—with its monarch entitled to elect the Holy Roman Emperor—genuine power. Local nobility at times cultivated Bohemia's intellectual life and cultural resources.[34] German clergy and tradesmen also began to appear as influential immigrants in the towns, and Czechs and Germans began to fight constantly.

Under Bohemian king Ottokar (Otakar) II, the Czechs suffered their first defeat at Habsburg hands. Count Rudolf I of Habsburg, who emerged from obscurity in present-day Switzerland, was anointed Holy Roman Emperor in 1273 in part to counter the growing power of Ottokar, who coveted the imperial crown. The feuding rulers came to blows and in 1278 the Bohemian king was killed at the Battle of Dürnkrut. It was this battle that first confirmed the Habsburgs' possession of Austria, after Vienna surrendered to Rudolf's siege. Bohemian nationalism reemerged in Protestant garb after John Hus, the rector of Prague's Charles University and an early critic of the established medieval Catholic Church, was condemned as a heretic and burned at the stake in 1415. Having pioneered a critique of the church later echoed by Martin Luther, Hus and his martyrdom spawned years of rebellion among the Czechs, who became largely Protestant.[35]

BOHEMIA'S STATUS AS an independent kingdom of the Holy Roman Empire—indeed, Prague served at one point as the capital of the empire—drew to a close, however, with the unexpected death of a single man in 1526. That was the year in which Louis II was killed in battle as Christendom fought the Muslim armies sweeping toward Austria to lay the first siege of Vienna. By marriage, the Habsburg dynasty inherited his kingdoms of Bohemia and Hungary. "Before the merger with Austria in 1526," historian Arthur J. May makes clear, "Bohemia and Hungary were kingdoms with brilliant pasts, national heroes, unique traditions and customs, and distinctive dominant tongues."[36] Yet the Czechs, Slovaks, and Hungarians would remain under Habsburg rule for almost four hundred years, and their essentially German Habsburg rulers would increasingly struggle to pacify their Slavic and Hungarian subjects.

The Catholic Habsburgs tried to repress the Hussite Protestant movement among the Czechs. After Bohemian Protestants were permitted to practice their faith in 1609, this simmering conflict—more religious than ethnic—erupted again in 1618 with the infamous Defenestration of Prague. When the Catholic archbishop of Prague ordered a new Protestant church destroyed, more than one hundred Protestant nobles and knights marched on Prague Castle, seized two royal officials and their secretary, and threw them from a window. While at least one was badly injured, all three survived. Some credited a heap of trash for breaking their fall, while devout Catholics saw the hand of divine intervention. Regardless, the rebels voted to depose their Habsburg ruler, Ferdinand II. "News of the 'defenestration of Prague' struck most European courts like a bolt from the blue," historian Geoffrey Parker recounts.[37] Europe's Catholic rulers rushed to rescue the Habsburgs. Thus began the Thirty Years' War, a bloody Protestant-Catholic conflict that spread from Bohemia to devastate most of Europe.

The Bohemians, however, were themselves quickly defeated in 1620 at the Battle of White Mountain, near Prague. At least twenty-six leaders of the rebellion, many of them Protestant noblemen, were executed in Prague's Old Town Square. Bohemian estates in Protestant hands were seized and awarded to loyal Catholics, many of them German, depriving the Czechs of a native, non-German aristocracy. Within a few years, thirty-six thousand families emigrated, rather than renounce their Protestant faith, and about five hundred of the land's 936 estates changed hands from rebel to loyalist aristocrats. From this point forward, the noble landowners virtually all spoke German while Czech was spoken almost solely among peasants and townspeople. In 1627 Vienna revoked the nominal independence of the Bohemian kingdom, reducing it to an administrative region. The steamroller of Germanization rolled on, Czech language and culture dwindled, and Czech Protestants were forcibly turned into Catholics. The shock troops of this Counter-Reformation, the Jesuits, boasted that one of their own converted 33,140 souls, while another bragged of burning 60,000 books.[38] "A German ascendancy as intolerant as that of the English settlers in Ireland was imposed upon the Czechs, and not seriously shaken till the nineteenth century," says historian H. A. L. Fisher.[39] "What remained as consequence until the end of the Habsburg Empire was the permanent alienation of the Czechs," concludes another historian, Robert A. Kann.[40]

Still, the national yearnings of Europe's peoples would not die. Indeed, the Thirty Years' War ended in 1648 with the Treaty of Westphalia, which recognized the right of Protestant states to exist independent of the pope and the Catholic Church, introducing the principle of national sovereignty into European law. By acknowledging the primacy of nation-states over the historic prerogatives of Christendom, the treaty undermined the pretensions of the Holy Roman Empire and began to erode the very legitimacy of the Habsburg dynasty. The same year that the Czech nation was so harshly subjugated—1620—the Pilgrims, another Protestant sect harassed by the established churches of Europe, landed at Plymouth Rock. Waves of Czechs and Slovaks would follow them to North America and, from across the Atlantic, generations later, exact their revenge.

Czech nationalism reawakened on occasion. Czechs, for instance, took to the streets in the European uprisings of 1848, as did the Slovaks, who went so far as to create a small army that fought their Hungarian masters that year. Czech and Slovak delegates to a Slavic Congress in Prague began to discuss the idea of a common state, though street disturbances on behalf of independence prompted the authorities to disperse the congress. Most of the time, peace prevailed in Prague. Yet Czechs and Germans lived peacefully mostly to the extent that they lived apart. Segregation was a way of life, with separate banks, swimming pools, soccer clubs, theaters, newspapers, playgrounds, and parks. Over time, German speakers felt increasingly threatened; by 1910, less than 10 percent of Prague's 225,000 residents spoke German.[41]

Lending weight to the national aspirations of Bohemia and Moravia was their growing status as "the center of Austrian industry," home to "three-fifths of all Austrian industrial establishments and production and nearly two-thirds of all persons employed in industry," according to Kann. Bohemia's rich mineral resources, along with its mining industry, were unparalleled in the empire.[42] In 1868 the Czechs founded their own large, independent bank, the Zivno, which began to fund Czech activist groups and facilitate the expansion of Czech industry.[43] As a result, the Czech lands were becoming ever more important to Vienna at the very time that the Czechs were becoming increasingly defiant of German-Habsburg rule.

In Hungary the rural Slovaks toiled in their fields and villages, invisible to Budapest, though by the late 1800s an occasional Slovak delegate would win election to the Hungarian Diet. Yet resistance—and anger—was rising in Slovakia's final years under Hungarian rule. Eleven Slovaks were sentenced for agitation against the state in 1906, thirty-three in 1907, and twenty in 1908. The perpetrators included parliamentary deputies, whose legal immunity was suspended for the sole purpose of punishing them. In 1907, moreover, Hungarian police fired into a crowd of protesting Slovak peasants, killing fifteen and wounding dozens more, an incident that came to be called the Massacre of Černová.[44]

AFTER THE HABSBURGS pacified their restive Hungarian partners by ceding them domestic sovereignty on their own territory in 1867 (creating Austria-Hungary), the Czechs returned to center stage as perhaps Vienna's most disruptive subjects. They did this from offstage, since the Czechs boycotted the Reichsrat for the next twelve years. Yet from the 1870s onward, Czech nationalists demanded that Czech be used as one—if not the only—official language in their own lands, a demand complicated by the large numbers of Germans in Bohemia and Moravia. While upwardly mobile Czechs would occasionally marry or otherwise assimilate into a German-speaking world, according to Elizabeth Wiskemann's pioneering study, "Most educated Germans, on the other hand, could never bring themselves to regard Czech as anything but a servants' language which they despised or, if they came from Vienna, they ridiculed. It is not an exaggeration that many of them considered it not fit to learn."[45] Language disputes, says Kann, emerged as "the permanent, unhealed wound of the national struggle."[46] Clashes over language laws would spark riots and the imposition of martial law in Prague and elsewhere.

Violent outbursts on this issue in the Reichsrat, Austria-Hungary's ineffective parliament, were notorious, drawing even Mark Twain to Vienna in 1897 to witness a legendary legislative brawl. "Yells from the Left, counter-yells from the Right, explosions of yells from all sides at once, and all the air sawed and pawed and clawed and cloven by a writhing confusion of arms and hands" went Twain's description of one thirty-three-hour Reichsrat session for *Harper's New Monthly Magazine*. Twain's timing of his trip to Vienna was fortuitous; this was indeed a historic moment.

The Habsburg-appointed premier, Count Casimir Badeni, had decreed that German officials must communicate in both spoken and written Czech to their Czech-speaking subjects. Many Czechs thought this was not enough, but most German officials flatly refused to learn Czech. The decree "unloosed the greatest storm in modern Austrian politics." Parliamentary fistfights prompted a summons for about sixty policemen or soldiers, who ejected a number of the Reichsrat's most unruly members. "It was an odious spectacle—odious and awful," said Twain, absent his usual humor.[47] German-speakers rioted on a scale not seen since the uprisings of 1848. Count Badeni was dismissed by Emperor Franz Joseph and his decree was withdrawn. This enraged the Czechs, in turn, leading to several days of "furious rioting" in Prague and other Czech towns; martial law was declared in Prague. With the Reichsrat paralyzed, the emperor invoked article 14 of the constitution, allowing him to rule by decree. "We have become," muttered the tight-lipped emperor, "the laughingstock of the whole world."[48] Thus ended the last serious attempt to bridge the Czech-German divide.

In Austria-Hungary's final years, there was much optimism in the air, despite ethnic and political divisions. Indeed, the advanced, modern, and experimental state of Viennese culture appeared to confirm the benevolence of a rising liberal faith in science, reason, and progress. Austria-Hungary was more prosperous than ever. "Materially, these were the most prosperous years that the Monarchy had ever known," historian C. A. Macartney said.[49] The most that Czechs were demanding—the most they could hope to gain—was a federal structure for the realm, one that would nurture and safeguard the rights of the Czechs, Slovaks, and other minorities. The Hungarians, after all, won such a status for themselves in 1867. These demands the Habsburgs resisted. Not without reason, Vienna feared that any further concessions would doom the empire.

When the Great War came, Vienna's fears came to pass.

An Unlikely Leader

IN PRAGUE, TOMÁŠ and Charlotte Masaryk had three more children— Jan in 1886, Hanička in 1890 (who died in infancy), and Olga in 1891. As a teacher, Masaryk cultivated a friendly approach to his students and encouraged them to ask questions, debate him, and join him for leisurely walks or chats in his home. That he treated his students this way astounded them and endeared many to him.[50] They included Serbs, Croats, and Slovaks, as well as Czechs, and he became a moral and intellectual example to young Slavs throughout Austria-Hungary. His Slovak students, especially, were inspired by him to create in 1896 a "Czecho-Slovak Society," and a periodical, *Hlas* (Voice), to work for the national unification of the Czechs and Slovaks.[51] Many of his students would become fellow activists in their respective nationalist movements. Yet Masaryk made his reputation in large part by puncturing his people's nationalist myths and attacking their occasional anti-Semitism. He refused to seek popularity for its own sake.

ONLY FOUR YEARS after arriving in Prague, he and another scholar, Jan Gebauer, published articles that exposed as forgeries two "historic" Bohemian manuscripts that had been embraced by the Czechs. Having surfaced in the early 1800s, one was "authenticated" by experts as dating to the early thirteenth century and the second to the ninth or tenth centuries. "Proof" of an ancient and enduring Czech culture, they became founding treasures of the National Museum in Prague. Yet reports began to surface that they may have been forged in the early nineteenth century by someone bent on creating a glorious Czech past. This led Masaryk and Gebauer to publish their articles in 1886 in the *Athenaeum*, a journal Masaryk had founded. It created a storm of virulent criticism.

A Czech newspaper called Masaryk a "loathsome traitor" and "a ghastly ulcer." Masaryk sued the newspaper after it refused to publish a letter of correction—and he lost the case. His subsequent appeal was also rejected. His publisher withdrew support, forcing Masaryk to finance the *Athenaeum* on his own. Instead of being promoted to full professor at the Charles University after three years, as stipulated at his appointment, he remained in a subordinate position for another fourteen years, without a significant increase in salary, a problem exacerbated by the arrival of more children. Even former students began to assume faculty positions above him. Both Czech political parties—Old Czechs and Young Czechs— repudiated Masaryk and his small band of followers. "The indignation against me," he later noted, "lasted a long time."

Yet the controversy gave birth to a tight-knit group of activists who would, years later, form a secret network of Masaryk's supporters. Subjected to endless snubs and insults, they avoided public places, used pseudonyms, and, according to one member, "tended to behave like members of a secret society," leading their critics to dub them Česká Maffie. Masaryk and the others adopted the epithet as their own and began in 1886 to publish another, more overtly political, periodical, *Cas* (Time).

Over time, Masaryk reconciled with the Young Czech Party. In 1891 he and Czech politician Karel Kramář, then aged thirty, won election to the Reichsrat in Vienna with thirty-four other members of the Young Czechs. Masaryk was forty-one when he returned to Vienna, this time a member of parliament, just as bitter legislative battles intensified between the minority Czechs and dominant Germans.

In parliament, Masaryk quickly established his credentials as a spokesman for the Bohemians and Moravians. Demanding educational autonomy for Czechs, better textbooks, and a second Czech university, his positions sounded treasonous to German ears. While speaking of a Czech "national movement" and demanding "state rights," "a full national life," and "self-determination" for Czechs, he envisioned a federated Austria-Hungary. This provoked a roar of disapproval from the Germans. "We shall *never* recognize Czech State rights," thundered a German deputy, "and with all of the means at our disposal we shall combat any attempt to bring about so preposterous a creation, which is directed against the national and economic existence of our people in Bohemia, Moravia, and Silesia."

Masaryk was soon elected to the Bohemian legislature and served in both the Reichsrat and the Diet. In 1893 he resigned from both following another falling out with the Young Czechs.

After a few quiet years, in 1899, the philosophy professor again became a target for intense public hatred. The dead body of a young seamstress, Anežka Hrůžova, nineteen, was found alongside a road in the woods outside the village of Polná in southeast Bohemia on March 29. Her throat had been slashed in such a way that no one doubted she had been murdered. Missing for nearly a week, her body appeared to have been moved after the murder, which perhaps explained why no traces of blood were found near the body. Yet this led the local villagers to another theory: young Anežka must have been killed by a Jew who took his victim's blood for ritual use. Among Polna's population of five thousand were about fifty Jewish families, which made finding a culprit relatively easy. Public opinion quickly fastened a guilty verdict onto Leopold Hilsner, then twenty-two, a drifter and handyman who was widely, and perhaps justly, held in very low regard.

Polná's local magistrate openly confessed that he issued the arrest warrant for Hilsner under public pressure. Hilsner's attorney was bullied by Polná's officials and followed by a hostile mob. While the actual evidence against Hilsner was flimsy, at best, the drifter was brought to trial, convicted, and sentenced to death—all within six months. His attorney filed an appeal. New witnesses materialized and defective memories suddenly improved. A wealth of new evidence accumulated, all of it for the prosecution. An anti-Semitic campaign was launched in the German press, blaming Jews for lung ailments, tight-fitting dresses, bad cookbooks, and foot-and-mouth disease in cattle.

A journalist who had previously been Masaryk's student wrote to him asking him to write an opinion piece in a Viennese newspaper. Masaryk wrote a long letter about anti-Semitism, urging a rejection of this "European disease" and all "anti-Semitic superstition." It prompted angry attacks. Stubbornly determined to defend himself, Masaryk in turn researched and wrote a thorough study of various ritual-murder allegations, which was published in several formats in both Czech and German. The second trial found Hilsner guilty of murder again, but Masaryk's actions were credited with the court's commuting of his death sentence to life imprisonment.[52]

As usual, Masaryk stood on principle and maintained a detached, scholarly approach. "Leopold Hilsner," he admitted, "is a notorious rascal who ought long ago to have been put into a reformatory." No matter—baser motives were ascribed to Masaryk. He was called "a hireling of the Jews and editor of a paper serving the cause of Jewry" by one published manifesto. Yet published attacks were the least of it—angry mobs descended on his home and lecture hall.

On Thursday morning, November 16, 1899, about twelve hundred people, encouraged by anti-Semitic newspapers, filled Masaryk's lecture hall and surrounding corridors. The professor, recovering from an illness, and his wife were escorted by a small group of still-loyal students through the boisterous, jostling crowd to the rostrum. As soon as Masaryk attempted to speak, the Czechs drowned him out with a roar of name calling and stamping of feet—ironically, the very same methods of protest being deployed at that time by the Czechs in the Reichsrat.

Masaryk took to the blackboard behind him: "I was not afraid to come here," he scrawled. "I therefore ask you to hear what I have to say." The mob roared its disapproval. Masaryk continued writing, denying accusations that, for instance, he was bribed to defend Hilsner. The crowd would not relent.

The university persuaded him to discontinue lecturing for a week. On November 27, the professor returned to the lecture hall, but yet another mob met him in the quadrangle and followed him into his classroom. The university made no attempt to restore order. Masaryk discontinued his lectures indefinitely.

As late as 1914 Masaryk was still able to read the occasional condemnation of his actions. Yet he would not back down. In 1913, when a Russian Jew was charged in Kiev with a "ritual murder," Masaryk was the principal speaker at a meeting of protest held in Prague.

IMPROBABLY, THE HILSNER affair did not end his political career.

Instead, Masaryk was persuaded by his supporters to establish a new political party. The Young Czech Party had supported the infamous Badeni legislation of 1897, a failed compromise that required German officials to use the Czech language. Riots in the Reichsrat prompted counter-riots in Prague, and Young Czech leader Kramář, as first vice president of the Reichsrat, expelled Germans from the chamber. The emperor dismissed ministers, disbanded the Reichsrat, and imposed martial law in Prague. The Young Czechs were weakened, Kramář's efforts on behalf of piecemeal reforms seemed futile, and Kramář and Masaryk found themselves drifting apart. "The fact is," Masaryk wrote to Kramář, "that you fear for Austria. I do not." Masaryk became the head of the Realist Party in

1900. In 1907, after the emperor awarded all males aged twenty-four or older the right to vote, and the German majority in the lower house was destroyed for the first time in history, Masaryk and a colleague formed a "bloc" of two Realist Party members.

Masaryk leapt into another cause célèbre. In 1908, to commemorate the sixtieth anniversary of Emperor Franz Joseph's accession to the thrones, the Austro-Hungarian foreign minister, Count Alois Lexa von Aehrenthal, annexed Bosnia and Herzegovina, provinces Vienna initially occupied in 1878, making a gift to his majesty of 1.8 million new subjects, mostly Serbs, Croats, or Bosnians. At the news, pro-Serbian disorder erupted in Prague, prompting the imposition of martial law.

Yet even before announcing his gift to the emperor, Lexa von Aehrenthal began a campaign of subterfuge and propaganda designed to bring Serb dissidents to heel. Sympathetic newspapers were fed stories of a pan-Serbian revolutionary movement headquartered in Belgrade. In July 1908 George Nastić, who later confessed to working for Vienna's secret police, published a fake memoir in which he claimed membership in a Serbian student revolutionary group, Slovenski Yug (the Slavic South), which fomented terrorism in Austria-Hungary on behalf of Belgrade. Reacting to its own propaganda, the police arrested fifty-three priests, schoolteachers, doctors, and public officials in 1908 and imprisoned them on charges of treason, subject to hanging.

During the Zăgreb treason trial, while 276 witnesses appeared for the prosecution—leading off with Nastić—only 20 of the 300 witnesses sought for the defense were allowed to testify. "No undue influence," said Masaryk's biographer, "was made to produce any illusion of impartiality."

Amidst the proceedings of the kangaroo court in Zăgreb (today the capital of Croatia), a leading Austrian historian and journalist, Dr. Heimrich Friedjung, published an essay in a Viennese newspaper that included accusations similar to those made by Nastić and the prosecutors.[53] Some of the men so accused filed a libel suit against Friedjung. After a handful of former Serb and Croat students of Masaryk's asked him to intervene, Masaryk demanded a formal parliamentary investigation into the alleged Serbian group, Slovenski Yug. His resolution was approved 167 to 132, and Masaryk followed that up with two trenchant speeches. In one, Masaryk said Nastić was flat-out "lying" and that the foreign ministry documents on which Friedjung relied were forgeries. Austrian newspapers called Masaryk a "vulgar parrot," and a judge in Zăgreb denounced him as a "scoundrel, a guttersnipe, a felon, an upstart, the scum of the earth."

The authorities pushed onward, sentencing thirty-one of the defendants to a total of 184 years of imprisonment, while acquitting twenty-two of the accused. An appeal led to orders for a new trial, but, reflecting the weakness of Vienna's case, the authorities declined. An appeals court later overturned the verdict. Yet the Friedjung libel trial proceeded, with Friedjung defending his article, which cited twenty-four documents supplied to him by the Austro-Hungarian Foreign Ministry. No originals of the documents could be produced. Finally, the forger stepped forward and confessed he had been hired by Austrian diplomats. Count Lexa von Aehrenthal offered to resign in June 1911, his reputation in tatters.[54] Meanwhile, in the Balkans, hatred and suspicion of Vienna intensified.

Importantly, both Steed and Seton-Watson covered these trials for the *Times*. The trials, Steed said, marked Masaryk "as the most public-spirited man in Austria-Hungary." Seton-Watson added,

> I remember very vividly his evidence at the trial. I as yet only knew him very slightly, and was still a little skeptical as to his political role, and as I listened in court, I felt as I was often to feel in successive crises of the Great War. There was in the man an austerity . . . a deliberate rejection of all of the arts of window-dressing. . . . The spell he cast was the result of closer acquaintance; it came from sheer force of character, from an insistence upon realities and fundamentals, stripped of all verbiage or ornament. There was the same uncompromising note in his private life: no alcohol, no tobacco, plain living, and high thinking.[55]

Hailed by supporters from Bohemia to the Balkans, Masaryk was also gaining recognition elsewhere in Europe. In 1910 he was feted on his six-tieth birthday with a book-length publication of his articles, in which Eu-rope's leading scholar of Bohemia, Ernest Denis of the Sorbonne, praised Masaryk.[56] Yet other Western European leaders were deeply skeptical—as was Steed initially—of the professor's political acumen. "Masaryk," re-ported the British ambassador to Vienna, Sir Fairfax Cartwright, in 1911, "is a fanatically honest man but absolutely devoid of political sense."[57]

It took Masaryk thirty-two years to reach Prague, and it took him another thirty-two years to reach the conclusion that Prague's peoples must finally be set free. Up until the war, however, Masaryk labored to avoid the outbreak of conflict. As late as December 1912, he was serving as a liaison for Serbian prime minister Nikola P. Pašić, who asked him to approach the new Habsburg foreign minister, Count Leopold von Berchtold, for a meeting in which Pašić could pay his respects and try to resolve the tensions between Vienna and Belgrade. Berchtold pointedly refused both the meeting and the offer of negotiations in a manner that was overtly rude to Masaryk as well as hostile to the Serbs. The Austrian antagonism toward Serbia gave Masaryk serious concern. "I feared," he said to a party meeting, "and I still fear, a European conflagration." And, he asked his fellow Czechs, "Are we prepared for whatever may befall?"

The Butler Was a Spy

WITH THE WAR under way, Masaryk traveled to Italy in December 1914, where he hoped to meet Allied representatives. He wrote twice to Professor Denis in Paris, who was sympathetic to the idea of remaking the map of Europe along ethnic and national lines. He had previously dispatched Voska to make contact with Steed in London, as well as to organize America's Czechs and Slovaks, recruit spies and couriers, and raise money.

In Prague Masaryk had begun holding secret meetings with a hand-ful of loyal Czechs he called his Maffie. The group included Edvard

Beneš, then thirty, a professor of sociology at Charles University who had known Masaryk as a teacher and mentor; Josef Scheiner, aged fifty-three, the national leader of the Sokol Organization, the Slavic network of nationalist-inspired gymnastic and cultural clubs; and Kramář, also fifty-three, the most prominent of all Czech politicians as the leader of the Young Czech Party.

Masaryk's thinking evolved dramatically from July to November 1914. Before Austria shelled Belgrade, the professor had pacifist leanings. By November he was wishing that the Great War would last several years and he had begun plotting his own insurgency. "My mind was made up, for good—Austria must be opposed in grim earnest, to the death. This the world-situation demanded. The only question was how to begin and what tactics to adopt," he said. "After careful consideration it was clear that we should have to leave the country and organize abroad our fight against Austria."[58]

While Masaryk spoke carefully, and shared his views sparingly, Vienna's spies, military courts, censors, and prisons were closing in on him. The Ministry of War assumed effective control of the civilian courts and of war industries, imposed censorship, and encouraged Habsburg subjects to spy on one another. Both a Czech member of the Reichsrat and a Czech editor were imprisoned in September. By late November one activist had been executed. Before Masaryk departed Prague, yet another was shot or hanged and before Christmas one more Czech journalist was executed. Overall, ten Reichsrat deputies—six of them Czech—were deprived of their offices and tried for treason.[59] "I was ready to escape to the Allies," he said, "the only question being how to manage my final departure. It took some time to make sure whether the police suspected me, for in Holland I had an impression that I was being watched. What I had already done was enough to bring me to the gallows, though, on the whole, little seemed to be known about it." Masaryk persuaded his fellow conspirators that, no matter what happened, they had to prepare themselves.

The small network of attorneys, journalists, and politicians who formed the core of the Maffie quickly extended its reach into other countries. From Julius Kovanda, a Czech butler in the home of the Austrian interior minister in Vienna, Masaryk received copies of confidential documents circulating among the ministers of Austria-Hungary—no doubt Kovanda was the source he mentioned obliquely to Seton-Watson and the one who provided him with information on the Slavic soldiers trying to defect to the Russians.

Masaryk employed basic espionage methods to avoid Austria's spies. In his trips to Holland, for example, he used coded messages and an alias, A. R. Mill.[60] With Masaryk abroad, a whole range of codes, forged documents, couriers, and secret methods of communication would be necessary. "We first of all agreed upon code-words for telegraphic communications," said Beneš. "We arranged whole sentences which were to mean that such and such a person was in prison, that *Cas* was suspended, that there was danger either of the betrayal or arrest of Masaryk, that further persecutions were being prepared, and so on, as the case might be."[61] Discreetly, Czechs throughout Austria-Hungary—and beyond—were recruited to serve as spies or couriers, mostly to acquire and transport information, or perhaps to watch a building or a person.

Ready to depart Prague, Masaryk told his comrades that what he most needed from them, especially those who served in the Reichsrat, was a promise not to disavow him or his work abroad, should it come to light. Masaryk received tacit support to serve as the spokesman for the Czech and Slovak resistance in part because most believed no one would listen to him; had they known the professor would become the world's leading figure for the movement, they might not have selected Masaryk—or anyone else. Yet Masaryk's leadership proved to be vital to the success of the Czech and Slovak independence movement.

Other leading Czech figures—including the most prominent, Kramář—were resting their hopes on a Russian invasion. They were encouraged by Russian leaflets promising the Czechs liberation and a report that the tsar had received a delegation of Czechs. In September the supreme commander of Russia's imperial army, Grand Duke Nikolai Nikolaevich, issued a declaration claiming that Russia aimed to fulfill "the national desires" of Vienna's subjects. Having visited Russia many times, engaged in long discussions with Tolstoy and Gorky, learned Russian, and read Russian literature, Masaryk was much less optimistic about Russia's role as a liberator. After all, Masaryk's well-regarded, two-volume study, *Russia and Europe*, which was published the previous year and was critical of the tsarist system, had been banned by the Russians.[62] Masaryk favored a democratic republic if independence came, yet he believed that another kingdom was the more likely outcome.

While Masaryk traveled, Beneš served as the principal liaison between Masaryk and the Maffie in Prague. Privately, Masaryk asked Beneš to be the conduit for documents from the Czech butler, Kovanda, in Vienna. In confidence, Masaryk also shared with Beneš his more detailed plans for a number of eventualities—what the Czechs should do in the event of a Russian invasion, if Russia was driven out of Bohemia, if Habsburg authority collapsed, or if Masaryk died. He provided Beneš with addresses for his contacts in France, Great Britain, the United States, and Russia. Someone drafted a map of "Slovakia" for Masaryk to use in arguing for its independence. "In short," Beneš said, "[Masaryk] had a complete political program for the future in which he had provided for all possible contingencies."[63]

MEANWHILE, IN THE United States, the former president of Princeton University, Woodrow Wilson, was very new to international politics. "It would be an irony of fate if my administration had to deal chiefly with foreign affairs," Wilson remarked shortly after his election, "for all my preparation has been in domestic matters."[64] As president he became known for his advocacy of the Federal Reserve Act, the first national child labor law, the Clayton (Antitrust) Act, the federal income tax, the first major tariff reduction since the Civil War, and the creation of the US Department of Labor. He was aghast at the war and determined to avoid it. Worse, behind the scenes, the president who "ordinarily gave scant attention to European affairs," said biographer Arthur S. Link, was increasingly concerned by an illness that was weakening his wife, Ellen.[65]

As war began to engulf Europe, Wilson appeared remote and distracted at a news conference on August 3, 1914. He gamely offered that the United States "stands ready . . . to help the rest of the world," perhaps as an intermediary.[66] Wilson was already preparing the first of ten neutrality proclamations, the first of which he issued on August 4, the same day he sent a personal message to each of the major combatant nations—drafted by hand at Ellen's bedside as she lay dying beside him—offering his "good offices" to broker a diplomatic solution. Every single nation rebuffed his offer, and Ellen died in her bed of kidney disease a few days later.

While Wilson was determined to avoid the European conflict, the president had a very clear-eyed view of how things might—or ought to—turn out, from the first months of the conflict. As far back as December 1914, in an off-the-record interview with the *New York Times*, Wilson said, "It seems to me that the government of Germany must be profoundly changed, and that Austria-Hungary will go to pieces altogether—ought to go to pieces for the welfare of Europe."[67] At a time when even highly educated Americans knew virtually nothing about the subjects of Austria-Hungary, Wilson had long since published *The State: Elements of Historical and Practical Politics*, which included the following: "No lapse of time, no defeat of hopes, seems sufficient to reconcile the Czechs of Bohemia to incorporation with Austria."[68] Still, conflicting priorities would cause Wilson to resist every step that would lead the United States to war and the Czechs and Slovaks to independence.

TWO

Inside Enemy Lands

It is lamentable, that to be a good patriot we must become the enemy of the rest of mankind.

Voltaire[1]

"Theirs Not to Reason Why"

On the distant battlefields of the Eastern Front, the actions of Czech and Slovak soldiers in the Austro-Hungarian army were more important to the cause of national independence than anything Tomáš G. Masaryk and his small network of conspirators could hope to accomplish on their own. In October 1914, for example, six companies of the Thirty-Sixth Regiment, whose soldiers were 95 percent Czech, surrendered to the Russians along the San River in Austrian Galicia. It remains unclear what drove these men, and a growing number of their comrades who followed them, into enemy arms. Was it a desire to escape harsh treatment by German officers and the searing horrors of war, or a desire to fight for the other side?

The testimonies of men who ended up in Russian captivity—or even Russian uniforms—confirm that their second-rate status at home and in the trenches created a predisposition to defect or surrender.

Bohemian Frank Prošek was one such person. A fellow Czech soldier recalled seeing him standing before a regimental court-martial, pleading for his life.[2] He had been caught a few days earlier by an Austrian patrol that assumed he was defecting to the Russian lines, rifle in hand. His likely sentence was a firing squad. The patrol and the military prosecutor had it all wrong, he countered:

> I'm an enthusiastic soldier, he told the prosecutor, but I am forced to labor under a serious and unjust disadvantage. As a Czech, I am subject to discrimination and ill treatment. Promotions go only to the Austrians. What chance did I have in this army; my race damns me in the eyes of my superiors. So I resolved to become a hero. I would surprise a Russian post, take it single-handedly, and bring back some prisoners. If I were successful, you would be forced to recognize my worth and promote me immediately. I might even get a medal!

"To the amazement of the regiment, the court accepted his plea," said the fellow Czech, Sergeant Gustav Becvar, "acquitting him of the charge of desertion." If that seemed too easy, it was. Becvar later learned from Prošek that the presiding military judge was, in civilian life, a Czech lawyer. His ruling was just one small example of how thousands of Czechs and Slovaks, entrusted with minor powers or insignificant positions in the military, the diplomatic corps, and other arms of the government, would take their revenge on the regime.

A few nights later, Prošek disappeared. Crawling into the deadly no-man's land that separated the Austro-Hungarian troops from the Russian enemy scattered among the rocks and trees ahead, Prošek actually survived. In fact, he eventually joined the hundreds, if not thousands, of Czechs and Slovaks wearing the uniform of the Russian imperial army.

The Česká Družina, a small unit of Czech soldiers in the Russian army initially composed of Czech emigres to Russia, played a unique and decisive role in turning unhappy Austro-Hungarian soldiers into a rebellious army. Czechs and Slovaks fighting for Austria-Hungary were welcomed into the Russian imperial army in ways few other soldiers could be. Indeed, they were explicitly encouraged to defect.

In March 1915, two days after an Austro-Hungarian attack on the Russians was repelled, food and other supplies were growing scarce. Most of the professional Austro-Hungarian officers had been killed and lesser men were put in charge. Amidst heavy snows, strong winds, and freezing temperatures, a unit of Czechs in the Ninety-Eighth Infantry Regiment held a line near Gorlice, a town on the Ropa River in Austrian Galicia. Their Austrian commander took advantage of the weather by having hungry Czechs tied to trees as punishment for eating meager portions of the reserve food supplies.[3]

"We all had had enough," recalled one of the Czech soldiers, Josef Křepela, "of that suffering, hunger, berating, and hitting that our commanders subjected us to, and a thought about an end to all of this torture was secretly growing inside us."

Each night fresh troops were dispatched to relieve the freezing, hungry men in the trenches, foxholes, barns, and shacks along the Austrian front above the Ropa River. Their commander, Lieutenant Reiman, spit out an ironic farewell to his Czech soldiers: "Auf Wiedersehen in Russland!" "And every morning," Křepela recalled, "when he learned about a guard who disappeared somewhere behind the Russian lines, protected by the barbed wire, he would waste no time writing a criminal report to the closest commanding headquarters." Once, when a good friend of Křepela's disappeared during a snowstorm, a laughing Reiman showed Křepela a copy of the criminal complaint he filed against the missing soldier, telling him, "The Russians must now have a whole regiment of you Czechs!"

As darkness fell one evening that March and another snowstorm gathered force, Křepela was ordered to take a replacement unit to the front. Under the watchful eye of their gun-wielding commander, Reiman, Křepela ordered thirteen young men huddling in snow-covered trenches into the storm. He led them through waist-deep snow toward a burned-out village on the Ropa River, which had been trapped between the lines of the opposing armies. When the men stopped to catch their breath behind a partially collapsed barn, Křepela decided to act.

"I looked into the faces of these boys, pale, with snowflakes on their freezing faces," he said. "How beat-up and absolutely non-soldierly they looked. It was evident they were not interested in any bravery, or a war medal, which they would gladly exchange for a piece of moldy bread now. Taking pity on them, I suddenly asked, 'Boys, would you like to go to Russia?' I will not forget the happy twinkle in the eyes of these poor wretches, who told me with one voice, 'Yes!'"

With desperate enthusiasm—but without any more of a plan—Křepela gingerly led the men single file toward Russian lines. Crossing a bridge over the Ropa after midnight, the men walked carefully past the dead and dying soldiers from both armies. Former enemies lay together mortally wounded in the same shattered homes, bleeding, delirious, softly crying for help. Discarded weapons were strewn about. In one house, two dead cows competed for space with the body of their dead owner. The stench drove Křepela and his men away. Taking refuge in another abandoned home, where a pale young girl, shell-shocked, wandered aimlessly from room to room, the men warmed black coffee and waited for the heavy snows to stop. By 3:30 a.m., they collapsed onto the empty beds and the floor, exhausted.

They awoke a few hours later to bearded Russian soldiers holding bayonets at their faces.

"Then," Křepela said, "happiness starts flowing through my body, and I shake hands with these good men, who are offering theirs. Moved, I speak the only Russian word I know—'*Zdravstvujte!*' (Hello!). We willingly gave them our rifles and all of our equipment, keeping only a beggars' bag holding nothing but bread crusts." Soon they were sitting on the floor with the Russians, forming a circle around a dim candle. "Are you all Czechs?" asked one of the smiling Russians. The Czechs nodded. Knowing what this meant, the Russian left.

A few minutes later, an officer wearing a Russian uniform entered the cabin. The officer lit a cigarette Křepela offered him, looked over the prisoners, and said in perfect Czech, "Hey guys, who among you is from Prague?" A confused silence hung in the air. "With open mouths, we look surprised. How did the Czech in the Russian uniform who is talking to us in such a friendly manner happen to show up here?" It turned out Reiman was right—a Czecho-Slovak regiment did exist in the Russian army, the Česká Družina.

The men gathered their meager belongings. After a three-hour march, the prisoners of war were put up for the night in the damaged remains of a school building. "We lay down on the cold floor not anticipating the crusade ahead of us," Křepela said.

Whether or not Czechs and Slovaks were defecting to the Russians or even surrendering too easily, according to historian Alon Rachamimov's analysis of the ethnic composition of Austro-Hungarian POWs inside Russia, "the national distribution of the POW population did not differ significantly from the relative share of each national group in the general population of Austria-Hungary."[4] If Czechs and Slovaks were more likely to surrender, their numbers relative to their fellow Hungarian or Polish POWs should have been larger. It is hazardous to assign singular reasons to discern whether Czechs and Slovaks surrendered too willingly, or defected, to the Russians amidst the chaos and bloodshed of large battles involving hundreds of thousands of men, machine gun fire, and explosions. Panic and flight were common, confusion was the rule, and raising one's arms in the air was no guarantee of safety. The very existence of the *družina* in Russia, moreover, was neither well known nor understood by many Czechs and Slovaks in the Austro-Hungarian army. "It sounded like a bed-time story for children to us," said Josef Divis, a Czech taken prisoner in April 1915, when he was introduced to the *družina*. "Many of us did not trust them. Some even laughed at them."[5]

THE MOST CONTROVERSIAL defection of Czech soldiers from the Austro-Hungarian army to the Russians occurred when 1,850 of the 2,000 men in the unruly Czech Twenty-Eighth Infantry Regiment disappeared into the Russian lines near the Dukla Pass, a gateway through the Carpathian

Mountains from Russia into Hungary (today, on the border between Poland and the Slovak Republic). The mass desertion followed informal contacts between Czech soldiers on both sides in early April 1915.[6]

In early March 1915 members of the *družina* on reconnaissance in the Carpathians had taken small numbers of men from the Twenty-Eighth as prisoners, Boris Wuchterle recalled, "who told us about the poor morale within the regiment." Nine members of the *družina* were assigned to venture through the mountains to make contact, first explaining to their mystified Russian comrades what they were doing and why. That night, in the darkness, the men found themselves behind the lines of the Twenty-Eighth, where they began capturing enemy soldiers. It took some time for the Habsburg Czechs to see that the men in Russian uniforms were also Czech. The *družina*'s soldiers told the Czechs they left behind—several wounded soldiers and their physician, who was also Czech—that the Russians would attack the night before Easter, but that the men of the Twenty-Eighth Austro-Hungarian Regiment should not fire their weapons or otherwise resist. The thirty-seven prisoners captured by the Russians gave up pertinent information about their unit. Another patrol from the Twenty-Eighth subsequently also surrendered to the *družina* when they were confronted and they also shared information on the positions of the Austro-Hungarian trenches and machine guns.

On April 3 (OS), Cossacks and Russians prepared to attack the Twenty-Eighth under cover of darkness. But members of the *družina* who stayed behind heard only silence. "It was only at twilight that a Russian 'hurrah' was heard, and the whole Twenty-Eighth Regiment went over to the Russians without a shot fired," said Wuchterle. Only the Austrian artillery fired at the enemy, wounding several Czechs.

Accounts such as this have been characterized as exaggerations by some who point to reports of at least some shooting, but even official Austrian reports concede that the gist of Wuchterle's eyewitness account is accurate. The debate about whether the men were indeed deserters "became the subject of one of the fiercest arguments inside the Austro-Hungarian army."[7] Reflecting official suspicion and anger, the entire Twenty-Eighth

Infantry Regiment was officially dissolved. Whatever the real motives of the men of the regiment, the *družina* was perceived to have lured Czechs into Russian arms. And this incident, says one historian, "was the first clear writing on the wall. The Austro-Hungarian authorities, civil and military alike, should have noticed that the war was unpopular with the Czechs, and that it was likely to become more so the longer it lasted."[8]

On Christmas Day 1915 amidst shooting between Austrian and Russian trenches, the members of the *družina* on the Russian side began singing "Stille Nacht," the German "Silent Night." The Austrians stopped shooting. When they were finished, one of the Czechs shouted a holiday greeting at the Austrians, to which an enemy soldier replied, "Wir danken" ("We thank you"). Members of the *družina* then began singing "Silent Night" in Czech, after which Czechs on both sides yelled greetings to one another.[9] In such modest ways, the *družina* worked its will.

THERE WERE MULTIPLE reasons Russia was taking so many Habsburg prisoners. One was the frequently shifting lines of combat along the Eastern Front, where violent, tumultuous offensives moved the lines of battle one hundred to two hundred miles in a few days.

The deprivations and horrors of a long war also fomented mutiny among ranks. The testimonies of many men reveal that the harshness of the fighting, shortages of food, inadequate winter clothing and shelter, and continued high casualties in failed offensives were highly discouraging. Better officers, more supplies, fresh reinforcements, and victories would have perhaps sharply reduced the numbers that defected to the Russian lines. Behind the façade of common uniforms, the army was long vulnerable to the same ethnic hostilities dividing Austria-Hungary. The army's Achilles' heel was that Czechs and Slovaks comprised a majority of the men in thirty-one infantry regiments, seventeen artillery units, twelve cavalry regiments, and eight rifle battalions.[10]

The mutual distrust between Habsburg officers and Slavic soldiers also naturally weakened the fighting spirit of the Slavs, which worsened after the multilingual officer corps was wiped out. The new officers installed were less cosmopolitan, knew fewer languages, and shared popular prej-udices against other ethnic groups. Czech or Slovak officers were likely to have their names and accents mimicked by their own Austrian or Hungarian troops. Such behavior gave Czechs and Slovaks a seemingly honorable reason to defect—fighting and killing fellow Slavic Serbs and Russians did not in any way serve their interests.

People Swoon, Prague Swears

CZECHS AND SLOVAKS went to war *almost* as willingly as any other group, at least at first, despite some modest protests and scattered arrests. Indeed, in the early weeks of the war in the summer of 1914, there was widespread enthusiasm for the Great War among the peoples of Europe, and it wasn't only the masses who cheered. Europe's keenest—and most unlikely—minds were also swept up in the fever for war. "Perhaps for the first time in thirty years," Sigmund Freud wrote to his brother, Abraham, late in July, "I feel myself an Austrian, and would like just once more to give this rather unpromising empire a chance." Freud hailed Austria's stern approach to Serbia as courageous and welcomed Germany's sup-port.[11] The Bohemian Austrian poet Rainer Maria Rilke, German novel-ist Thomas Mann, French scholar Emile Durkheim, and German scholar Max Weber also hailed the commencement of the war.

From the Czechs, there was much less enthusiasm.

"In Prague, there was not a trace of war-like enthusiasm," noted Rob-ert Seton-Watson.[12] One as-yet-unknown writer living quietly in Prague's Old Town neighborhood, Franz Kafka, then thirty-one, took note of the eruption of the war in his diary entry for August 2, 1914: "Germany has declared war on Russia. Went to swimming class in the afternoon."[13]

A German-speaking Jewish officer from Prague, Hans Kohn, noted that "the Czechs realized that a German victory might well strengthen German and Magyar control over the Slav peoples. In fact, the German chancellor, [Theobald von] Bethmann Hollweg, appealed to racial loy-alties in characterizing the struggle as an historic conflict between the

Germans and the Slavs. Thus there was no enthusiasm for the war in our regiment."[14]

One Czech recruit taking the oath as he was inducted into a home defense reserve unit, J. Javurek, recalled: "My love for the Austro-Hungarian Empire and Emperor Franz Joseph was the same as that of most of us Czechs. And when they were reading the oath to us, the Home Defense members of the Eleventh Infantry Regiment of the Home Defense in Jičín in August of 1914, I noticed sour faces on all of us, and when we were sworn in, I saw that instead of raised hands, many had their hands folded into fists." When they were marched to their trains under cover of night, Javurek said, "We scribbled on our train car, 'Export of Czech meat abroad,' and below that, 'Where is my home?'"[15]

Originally a popular melody penned in the early 1800s, "Where Is My Home?" was sung by Czechs with increasing frequency as the war dragged on. The song went:

> *Where is my home? Where is my home?*
> *Waters murmur across the meadows,*
> *Pinewoods rustle upon the hills,*
> *Bloom of spring shines in the orchard,*
> *Paradise on Earth to see!*
> *And that is the beautiful land,*
> *The Czech land, my home!*
> *The Czech land, my home!*

Historian A. J. P. Taylor says that in 1914 "only the Czechs were sullenly acquiescent."[16] Indeed, soldiers in the Second Battalion of the Prague-based Twenty-Eighth Infantry Regiment barely skirted insubordination as they were mobilized. Marching from their barracks, they threw away the Habsburg black-and-yellow flag and unfurled a red-and-white Bohemian standard. They sang *"Hej Slované"* (Hey, Slavs), the anthem popular among Slavic peoples. Scrawled on one of the battalion's wagons was the message, "Off to fight the Serbs, we don't know why!"[17]

In a report to Vienna on September 24, the governor of Bohemia wrote,

> Yesterday and the day before, troops were reporting for the frontline. The manner of their departure left a lot to be desired. The soldiers, though most of them older people, were accompanied by relatives and children; they were obviously drunk. The day before yesterday they were wearing badges in national colors on their forage-caps; some, though not very many, wore the Slav colors. Yesterday, their behavior was still worse . . . they carried three large white, red, and blue flags, and a red flag with the inscription: "We are marching against the Russians and we do not know why."

In addition, pro-Russian leaflets were turning up in Bohemia, Moravia, and Galicia.

Yet, historian Z. A. B. Zeman concludes, "Although there was a strain of pro-Russian feeling in the demonstration, it was neither the beginning of a revolution nor a unanimous expression of popular will against the Habsburg monarchy."[18]

No DOUBT ONE of the reasons the Czechs did not offer more resistance was the widespread assumption that the men would be home by Christmas. Millions would never see home again, of course, but the absence of a lengthy European-wide conflict during the hundred years prior to 1914 provided a—false—assurance that the war would be brief. Of the twenty-one wars fought in the nineteenth century, only one lasted more than a year. "The trend toward decisive campaigns and conclusive battles, followed immediately by peace talks, typified the modern wars of the nineteenth century in Europe," according to military analyst Béla K. Király.[19] Once assembled at a battlefield often some distance from a major town or city, opposing armies would commence narrow, if deadly, assaults. The side that began to suffer what it saw as unacceptable losses to its army would either flee the field, perhaps to fight another day, or capitulate and negotiate terms. Among combatants, casualties could be high, but professionals did most of the fighting, and civilians were less directly affected by large-scale, mandatory enlistments, or by the combat itself.

Of greater importance was the absence of any significant European conflict since the Franco-Prussian War—which lasted all of ten months— had ended in 1871. This was the longest period without war in European history. The last major conflict involving the Habsburgs was their defeat by Prussia at the Battle of Königgrätz (Hradec Králové, Czech Republic) in 1866, a conflict that some reference works call the Seven Weeks' War. Habsburg subjects up through the age of fifty—including the vast majority of men in uniform—had absolutely no recollection or previous experience with war. It was only natural that most soldiers shared the same expectation about the length of the war. "We were convinced that it would be a short war," said Kohn, the officer in the Czech unit, "probably over by Christmas, 1914."[20]

The Émigrés in Russia

WHILE THE LARGEST number of Czech and Slovak recruits for what became the Czecho-Slovak Legion would slowly emerge from POW camps across Russia, the army that would soon hold Russia's destiny in its hands got its start in the *družina*, the obscure unit of Czech and Slovak émigrés in the Russian imperial army.

Almost 900,000 emigrants arrived in Russia from Austria-Hungary between 1828 and 1915, among them tens of thousands of Czechs and Slovaks.[21] The largest number resided in the vicinity of Kiev (Ukraine), where there was a Czech High School, a Prague Hotel, and, by 1910, a weekly Czech-language newspaper, the *Čechoslovan*. In most combat nations, "enemy aliens" were subject to internment, deportation, and expropriation of their property. Unlike in most countries, however, where enemy aliens often lived on the margins of society, in Russia the Czechs and Slovaks were business owners, managers, landowners, professionals, engineers, foremen, and skilled workers. Yet, at the outbreak of the war, the Russian public began targeting any person whose ethnicity, religion, or former citizenship might link that person to Austria-Hungary or other enemy nations. By 1914 there were about 600,000 "enemy aliens" and 100,000 visitors from enemy nations in Russia. Of these, about 200,000 were Czech and 600 were Slovak, with 70,000 of them in farming communities in Ukraine. More than half had arrived in Russia since 1885 and many had never become naturalized Russian citizens.[22]

During the first week of hostilities, the Russian army sealed the borders to immigrants who might think of escaping the country. As early as July 25, 1914 (OS), the army ordered the deportation from areas under military rule of all "enemy-subject males of military service age," specifically, "all German and Austrian males age 18–45 who were deemed physically capable of carrying a weapon." This order was quickly extended to the entire Russian Empire and included women and children as well. As many as one-half of Russia's 600,000 "enemy" subjects were sent to camps or designated areas held under police surveillance. As early as September 1914, the government ordered the confiscation of all property belonging to anyone who was even *suspected* of belonging to a pan-German organization. Given the use of German by many non-German Habsburg subjects and the dearth of information regarding Vienna's non-German minorities, Czechs and Slovaks were easily targeted. "A sense quickly grew among officials that all enemy-alien property was fair game." Factories, farms, and stores could be confiscated, often at the behest of disgruntled Russian customers or competitors who turned their business disputes into acts of revenge by denouncing their "enemy alien" owners.[23]

Once it was clear that mere suspicion of enemy support or sympathy could cost an immigrant freedom or property, thousands of aliens applied for exemptions and persons of Slavic ethnicity received most of them. The first exemptions were granted to Czechs. Committees of Czechs and Slovaks sprang up in the major cities to petition the government. Delegations met with the minister of internal affairs, Nikolay A. Maklakov, and the foreign minister, Sergey D. Sazonov, solemnly pledging their allegiance to Russia.

The delegates also spoke to Sazonov about their desire to gain independence for their Czech and Slovak homeland and requested Russia's support. Sazonov expressed interest and requested a formal memorandum on the subject, which was shortly thereafter presented to Tsar Nicholas II, his ministers, and members of the State Duma, the Russian legislature. This was the first written proposal for liberation presented to an Allied government, preceding Masaryk's memo to the Allies by two months. The tsar received two delegations of Czechs and Slovaks, the first in Moscow on August 20, 1914 (OS), and the second in Saint Petersburg the following September 17 (OS). Initially, neither the tsar nor his ministers made specific promises—the tsar said only, "May God fulfill your desires." Sazonov indicated that realization of the Czechs' and Slovaks' goal of independence would depend on the Russian imperial army.[24] By November 21 (OS), however, the tsar announced Russian war aims that included an autonomous kingdom for the Czechs and Slovaks, but under the Habsburgs and within Austria-Hungary.[25] As a result, within weeks of the outbreak of war, the aspirations of the Czechs and Slovaks were on the Allied agenda.

Sazonov was not entirely surprised by Czechs' and Slovaks' expression of loyalty to Russia. Two Czech leaders, the radical Václav Klofáč—a sometime ally, sometime competitor to Masaryk in Czech politics—and Dr. Josef Scheiner, the leader of the Sokol Organization, had secretly traveled to Saint Petersburg in the first months of 1914 and promised Sazonov a revolutionary uprising in Bohemia in the event of war. While the two men may not have spoken for most Czechs and no uprising ever took place, this promise may have influenced Sazonov's fateful recommendation to the tsar in favor of war later that year.[26]

ONCE THE WAR broke out, the émigrés founded the Union of Czecho-Slovak Organizations in Russia, with an executive committee headquartered in Saint Petersburg; a military commission based in Kiev, which took the lead in organizing the *družina*; and a new weekly newspaper published in Saint Petersburg, the *Čechoslovak*.[27] From the very beginning, the organization's ultimate goal was independence for its people—the union adopted a resolution calling for an independent Czecho-Slovak state under a Slavic dynasty. Plans for an army were openly debated and, acknowledging the Slovak role, it was agreed that officers would give commands in both Czech and Slovak.

Czechs and Slovaks also began volunteering to form a military unit. Émigré leaders in Moscow, Saint Petersburg, and Kiev negotiated agreements with Russian military leaders to create the unit. The tsarist government gave its approval in August 1914 with stipulations that its commanders and at least a third of its lower officers be Russians, and that volunteers be—or become—Russian subjects. This would avoid charges that Russia was arming citizens of an enemy state, an act prohibited by the Hague Convention.[28]

On August 28 (OS), training in civilian clothes, the first émigré volunteers were given the standard Russian rifles with long, thin bayonets that rose above their heads. By early September about 750 men—all Czechs except for sixteen Slovaks—were formed into the three companies that made up the Česká Družina. Their insignia was a white-and-red ribbon affixed to their caps. The men were sworn in in Sophia Square in Kiev on September 28 (OS) at a grand ceremony that mixed elements of Czech and Slovak nationalism, Orthodox religious symbolism, and Russian imperial army protocol. It was the first time since 1848 that a military unit of Czech or Slovak volunteers stood armed and united to fight for their freedom. The unit left for the front on October 22 (OS) to serve with the Russian Third Army in Ukraine. They would become famous for being legionnaires, but the men referred to themselves as "brothers."

These brothers served in small units, performing reconnaissance and intelligence work on enemy locations, movements, and armed strength. They were valuable for their ability to read maps well, especially Austrian maps, and to interrogate enemy prisoners in German, Czech, or Slovak. They quickly distinguished themselves. Behind the lines, the émigrés raised funds for *družina* volunteers who were wounded or became sick, as well as for their families.

To let Czechs in Prague know about the *družina*, four men volunteered to don captured Austro-Hungarian uniforms, penetrate enemy lines, alert Czech leaders in Prague of their existence, and urge them to prepare for a Russian invasion. Two of the men were caught and shot.

Only one, Václav Vaněk, succeeded in reaching Prague. He later told colleagues that he asked the Russians to transport him to the front and fire at him as he fled back into the Austrian lines. He survived fire from the Austrian trenches, but was arrested. Habsburg authorities, however, could not disprove his contention that he simply escaped Russian captivity. Released, he met with Karel Kramář, the most prominent Czech politician in Prague, no doubt encouraging Kramář's pro-tsarist hopes. In order to confirm with his comrades that he accomplished his mission, the Bohemian reenlisted in the Austro-Hungarian imperial army, was again shipped to the front, where, again, he deserted to the Russians and rejoined the *družina*.[29]

THE EFFECTIVENESS OF the *družina* persuaded the Russian Supreme Command to allow the unit to absorb Czechs and Slovaks taken prisoner by the Russian Third Army—as long as the POWs volunteered. About 250 to 275 POWs had done so by February 1915. The entire *družina* numbered 1,433 by this time. Though small, units of the *družina* served with Russian forces in their offensive toward the Dukla Pass in early 1915, where they were credited by their Russian commanders with inducing the men of Prague's Twenty-Eighth Infantry Regiment to defect.

The slowness of Russian bureaucrats in approving applications for citizenship began to place members of the *družina* outside the protection of international law. While it is unclear how much thought each man gave to his legal status at first, the ex-POWs in the *družina* were, almost from the start, vulnerable to courts-martial and execution for treason, if apprehended by their former comrades. The Second Hague Convention of 1907 contained a provision "that prisoners of war liberated on parole and recaptured bearing arms against the government to whom they had pledged their honor, or against the allies of that government, forfeit their right to be treated as prisoners of war and can be brought before courts."[30] This status became one of many reasons the tsar's regime hesitated to enlarge the *družina* with POWs.

Even the Czech and Slovak émigrés who became Russian citizens must have felt at risk, knowing the rough justice Habsburg rulers meted out to their Slavic subjects. If they had been born in Austria-Hungary, it might have been difficult to prove their new Russian citizenship. Before too long, such thoughts congealed into a stark choice—either liberate their homeland or face possible execution in Vienna or Prague. Thus, the Česká Družina, notes Victor M. Fic, "gradually evolved from an army of Russian nationals into a revolutionary army of Austro-Hungarian subjects rebelling against the government to which they owed allegiance and giving armed aid to its enemy. This loss of international status, and thus of protection under international law, greatly enhanced the legal position of the Central Powers to shoot every volunteer captured on the front, as was often the case."[31] Indeed, cash rewards were offered by Austro-Hungarian field commanders for the capture of deserters and those suspected of disloyalty were routinely and freely executed in battle zones.

In June 1915 a larger *družina* became possible when it was opened to any Czech or Slovak of Russian citizenship who had been drafted to serve in the Russian imperial army. That door opened yet wider in August 1915, when Russia allowed all Czech and Slovak POWs captured anywhere in Russia (and not just by the Russian Third Army in Ukraine) to volunteer, and it waived the citizenship requirement. The union immediately dispatched representatives to POW camps to recruit soldiers, though the prisoners could also volunteer for civilian labor assignments. The weekly *Čechoslovak* newspaper, which reached many POW camps, also solicited volunteers. Yet by March 1916, historian Josef Kalvoda reports, only 343 POWs had joined the *družina* since its inception and the entire force stood at just twenty-three hundred men.[32] By the end of 1915 the unit's combat losses amounted to nineteen dead, twenty-three missing, and ninety-three wounded.[33]

FULLY 90 PERCENT of the soldiers captured by Russia were Habsburg troops. Of the 2,322,378 total prisoners taken by Russia in the Great War, 2,104,146 were Austro-Hungarian. Russia captured only 167,082 Germans—despite the fact that the number of Germans on the Eastern

Front equaled or surpassed the number of Habsburg troops from 1915 onward. These numbers have long fed suspicions regarding the loyalty of Vienna's Slavic soldiers and the quality of her military leaders. All the more remarkable is the fact that Austro-Hungarian POWs represented more than half the number of soldiers Vienna mobilized at the start of the war—3.8 million—and almost one-third of its total mobilization for the entire war—7.8 million.[34] Among them were 210,000 to 250,000 Czech and Slovak POWs—about 30,000 of them Slovaks.[35] From these few hundred thousand men the Czecho-Slovak Legion would emerge.

Instead of victory, Russia's offensives brought it more mouths to feed, men to clothe, and bodies to shelter—and burdened it with the care of millions of prisoners, when it could barely care for its own soldiers.

Once captured, Austro-Hungarian soldiers were made to march for days, sometimes weeks, before reaching a railroad station. The absence of harsh military discipline among starving, injured soldiers allowed ethnic animosity to surface. "The national antagonisms, artificially suppressed at the front with difficulty, broke out in full force here," recalled one Czech prisoner, Josef Kyncl, of his march through Galicia. "The Slavs, Hungarians, Germans, Bosnians, Romanians—everybody was cursing everybody else and people were fighting for the least significant things every day. . . . We would say that Hungarians like to fight, but we were not any better in those days of hatred and rough passions."[36]

Reaching a train station, the men were packed into modified boxcars called *teplushki*. Equipped to hold sixteen to twenty-eight Russian soldiers, each car would often be packed with as many as forty-five POWs. A row of unpadded wooden bunks lined each side, and the men slept two or three to a bunk, lying only on their sides, squeezed tightly together. An iron stove sat in the middle of the boxcar and a single latrine bucket sat near the unluckiest prisoner. The trains deposited the men at one of three sorting camps near Kiev, Moscow, or Saint Petersburg, where they were formally registered. The Czechs, Slovaks, Poles, Romanians, Serbs, Croats, Slovenes, and Ukrainians (Ruthenians) were separated from Austrian, Hungarian, and German prisoners, and shown preferential treatment. But the Russians were not able to provide the Slavs with better food, clothes, or medical care.

After minimal care for the seriously wounded, the men were herded into trains for a second journey, this one lasting weeks or months, to one of about three hundred POW camps, most of them in Siberia or Central Asia. The boxcars were locked from the outside, the men trapped inside for days without food or medical care. In bitter-cold winters, the stoves provided little heat and every window or gap in the boards was sealed with rags, mud, or straw. The men shivered in the darkness, choking on smoke and wretched odors. Days could pass before the Russians either fed the prisoners or distributed a handful of kopecks for them to buy their own food, wherever they could. The charity of peasants along the way kept many men alive and prisoners were sometimes able to slip away to beg among townsfolk.

There were not enough doctors, nurses, clean bandages, or medication for the wounded, which led to scores of infection-related deaths and to amputations performed without anesthesia. Yet, one Swedish nurse said, "In justice to the Russians it must be said that prisoners of war were not worse off in the Moscow hospitals than the Russian soldiers themselves, who suffered the same neglect due either to inadequate staffing or to brutal indifference."[37] Thousands died before reaching a POW camp, buried along the way if the ground was not frozen. Corpses were removed from the cars only when a train made a scheduled stop and the guards were changed. Occasionally, boxcars thought to hold scarce food for a town or city would be opened at the railroad station, only to discover dozens of dead prisoners, sometimes frozen. Some 140 bodies were found in a train that reached Penza in December 1914. Fifty-seven were found in Samara in February 1915. The men who survived such journeys emerged filthy, often emaciated, exhausted or dazed, diseased, and covered in lice.

PRISONER-OF-WAR CAMPS HELD between 2,000 and 35,000 men. Once abandoned factories, hotels, exhibition halls, prisons, stables, or warehouses, all of the camps were surrounded by stockade walls or twelve-foot-high barbed-wire fences with wooden watchtowers at intervals. Camp barracks varied in quality, with earthen huts dug into the ground a common form of shelter. Without adequate clothing or footwear, POWs endured average *high* winter temperatures of below-zero degrees Fahrenheit at most camps. Average lows dipped 15 to 50 degrees below zero.

Epidemics of typhus, dysentery, typhoid, and cholera swept through many camps. During the winter of 1914–15, disease took forty-five hundred lives at a POW camp near Novosibirsk and thirteen hundred at Krasnoyarsk.[38] During a typhus outbreak at Sretensk, the Russian personnel evacuated the camp and left the men to die. At Omsk, sixteen thousand POWs died the first year in wooden barracks largely unchanged from the four years Fyodor Dostoevsky spent there as a political prisoner in the 1850s, which inspired his first great novel, *House of the Dead*. Out of the 200,000 prisoners shipped to thirty camps across Central Asia, 45,000 never returned. Some prisoners recalled rats chewing on corpses of fellow POWs on barracks floors in the colder months, and stacks of frozen corpses piled outside when it was too cold to dig their graves. The diseased died slowly, the dead smelled terribly, and the "healthy" men swung back and forth between furious irritability and deathly apathy. Their stomachs ached with hunger, throats and lips were parched, wounds and infections festered and burned, fevers raged, and the men knew they were aging rapidly. Violent fights would periodically break the silences. Less often, one of the men would surrender to insanity. Final estimates for deaths among the Austro-Hungarian POWs range from 375,000 to 450,000. "Apart from the victims claimed by death in the early years," one observer recalled, "many of the prisoners were such mental and physical wrecks owing to the hardships they had suffered that no improvement in their material conditions could restore them to healthy manhood."[39]

Mercifully, 1916 brought significant improvements to the conditions in most POW camps. Larger epidemics subsided once the Russians began isolating the sick. Inoculations were administered, and hospital facilities improved. The building of latrines, bathhouses, and water supplies began to match demand. The prisoners started tilling vegetable gardens, sewing clothes, and making shoes or soap. The men even began to entertain one another with plays and musical performances, relying on the handful of actors or musicians among them. Teams came together, at least in the warmer weather, to play soccer, tennis, and horseshoes, and to engage in gymnastics.

The Russians observed the Hague Conventions regarding the treatment of imprisoned officers, giving them superior lodgings, a monthly stipend, and exemptions from work, which separated the officers from their men. In early 1915 the Russians had forbidden communication between officers and enlisted men. These two measures were of special value to those Czechs and Slovaks who were eager to join the Česká Družina or help with its recruitment, since their mostly Austrian and Hungarian officers could no longer discourage the enlistees, impede their efforts, or threaten them. On the other hand, all mail to and from POWs was still opened, read, and censored by the authorities in Vienna. An espionage unit in the censorship office kept tabs on all POWs suspected of disloyalty.

Many prisoners were allowed or encouraged to take jobs outside the camps. By the end of 1916, 497,000 prisoners were employed in farming, 35,000 in forestry, 294,000 in mines and factories, 169,000 building railways and canals, and 116,000 in other fields. Settled in some communities for years, several thousand POWs married Russian women. Yet prisoners were also beaten and flogged by their employers and many either died or became invalids as a result. It was in these workplaces that POWs came into contact with revolutionaries, and some would throw their lot in with the Bolsheviks.

In time, German and Austro-Hungarian relief funds began to reach the POWs. Yet while Vienna sent 85 million crowns worth of clothing, food, and medicine, supplies fell well short of the needs of the prisoners; Berlin's relief to its smaller POW population in Russia amounted to 4.4 times more per prisoner than Vienna's. The privations suffered by the imprisoned Habsburg soldiers embittered many. "For Austro-Hungarian captured soldiers," one analyst says, "it was clearly the Habsburg state that had abandoned them rather than the other way around."[40]

While Czech and Slovak soldiers had multiple reasons for defecting, the underlying issues of ethnic repression and political grievance became decisive only *after* these soldiers found themselves in Russian captivity, where they received, if little else, a lot more time to ponder their fate. Only then were they offered the opportunity to fight again. Thousands wanted to join the small Czech unit buried inside the Russian army, but this unit would not have amounted to much unless someone was prepared to organize these unlikely forces into a cohesive movement for national independence. Masaryk's efforts to gain Allied recognition for independence would be decisive in doing so.

Masaryk Slips Away

AT THE TICKET window for a connecting train at the Italian border in December 1914, as Masaryk and his daughter made their way to Rome, a clerk checked Masaryk's papers, paused, looked warily at him, and sadly admitted he had to telegraph the authorities for instructions. With growing alarm, Masaryk noticed his train starting to chug slowly away from the platform. Grabbing Olga's hand and his bag, he jumped onto the moving train, and the doors of history closed quietly behind him.[41] Thus went the first of many close calls for Masaryk during his exile.

All of the arrangements he could make, he had made; he even left a note for those who might arrest him. Resigned to the fact that his home might eventually be searched by the police, Masaryk drafted a letter explaining that his most important political documents were hidden, and that it would be a waste of time to ransack his house. It would do no good.

Traveling via Venice and Florence, Masaryk reached Rome on December 22, 1914. He met with Croatian, Serbian, and Slovenian subjects of Austria-Hungary who, like Masaryk, had escaped to Italy and were seeking independence, lobbying Allied diplomats to support a federal union of their South Slav provinces of Austria-Hungary with Serbia. Working closely with the Kingdom of Serbia, these exiles agreed to create a Yugoslav Committee to agitate on behalf of the proposed nation. Meeting at night in the darkened offices of Serbia's diplomats, Masaryk and the Yugolavs quickly agreed to coordinate their approaches to the Allies. Masaryk also contacted Russian diplomats, as well as the British ambassador, Sir James Rennell Rodd, who forwarded some of Masaryk's correspondence to London.

Another journalist sympathetic to the cause, Vsevolod Svatkovsky, summarized Masaryk's ambitious plan in a memorandum for Russian foreign minister Sazonov. This was the third diplomatic report Sazonov had received about the plans of the professor from Prague.[42]

Worried about the competing claims to Dalmatia by both Italy and the Yugoslavs—the Allies had secretly promised it to Italy—Masaryk nevertheless believed that Italy would remain neutral or, if anything, enter the war against Vienna and Berlin. He departed Rome on January 11, 1915, traveling by automobile toward Genoa, where he caught a train to Geneva. As he began making his plans to return to Prague, he received an open postcard from Vienna. It said only:

> The book which you want is out of print, and will not appear until after the war.

It was a coded message—the authorities were searching for Masaryk.

Masaryk discovered that Austria's ambassador to Rome had reported on his visits with almost every Allied enemy of Austria-Hungary—the Serbs, Russians, and British, among them. Vienna had issued an order to search for Masaryk. The order crossed the desk of the interior minister, Karl Baron Heinold, and found its way to his home, into the hands of his Czech butler, Julius Kovanda, who typed a copy for his intermediary, a popular poet working as a bank clerk, Josef S. Machar. Machar forwarded the postcard warning to Masaryk. A copy was also forwarded to Edvard Beneš, who sent both a courier and a coded telegram to Masaryk, warning him not to return. Crestfallen, Masaryk knew what this meant. Yet no one could be certain he received the messages.

This was too serious—Beneš decided to risk a border crossing. "I was alarmed at the thought that Professor Masaryk might cross the frontier and be arrested," Beneš said.[43] Listed among those to be drafted, Beneš was not allowed to leave the country and his passport was no longer valid. A friend who worked for the police provided him with the false papers that got him across the border. "In 1915," Paul Selver, Masaryk's biographer, writes, "a journey from Austria to Switzerland was quite a feat for a Czech of military age, and with a dubious political background, and the fact that Dr. Benes succeeded in reaching Masaryk at Zurich shows that he was not easily discouraged."[44]

Beneš met with Masaryk and Svatkovsky at Zürich's Hotel Victoria in February. The die was cast. They agreed that Masaryk, and anyone else who could join him, would organize Czech and Slovak émigrés to oppose the Habsburg regime in coordination with Czech and Slovak leaders inside Austria-Hungary. Masaryk would stay in Geneva. Beneš would return to Prague to serve as the principal liaison with Machar in Vienna and the Maffie in Prague. Masaryk told Beneš to cultivate a substitute in the event of his arrest, "because the connection with Prague must never be interrupted."[45] Both Masaryk and Svatkovsky would ask Kramář to join them in exile.

An enormous task lay ahead. "Austro-Hungarian affairs were imperfectly understood," Beneš said. "The Allies took but little interest in our cause, and if we desired to gain something for our nation during the war, we ourselves must get to work and draw attention to our claims."[46] The world was unaware of the Czechs and Slovaks. The French long mistook their gypsies for "Bohemians," converting a geographic error into a halo for the artists and drifters immortalized in Puccini's *La Bohème*. While the word "Bohemian" was generously applied to every free spirit in Europe, the real Bohemians remained a little-known people, lost in the dense, ethnic stew of Austria-Hungary. Goods exported from Austria-Hungary were typically labeled "Made in Germany" or "Made in Austria," rarely "Made in Bohemia," despite the fact that the Czech lands constituted the vital center of Habsburg industry. As late as 1914, one Western correspondent announced to his readers the "news" that "the ancient Czech (Bohemian) language still continues to be spoken in Prague!" Outsiders were confused by the various uses of the terms "Czech," "Bohemian," and "Moravian" in reference to the same people. One New York newspaper trying to shed light during the war on the identities of Habsburg subjects listed both Czechs *and* Bohemians.[47]

"It was strange," Masaryk recalled as he went immediately to work. "I was like a wound-up machine. I could think of nothing but our campaign against Austria; I saw nothing else, felt nothing else, I was hypnotized by it. The only thing I cared about was the war—what the day-to-day situation was, how things were going at the front—and whom to speak to next, how to reach people and arouse their interest. I would wrack my brains trying to outwit the border guards and get news to and from Prague. I forgot what it meant to sleep."[48] Alone with his thoughts at night, he wondered whether he, his associates, and their people were prepared. "Are we ripe for the struggle, are we mature for freedom, can we administer and preserve an independent state made up of the Bohemian lands, Slovakia, and considerable non-Czech and non-Slovak minorities?" Unanswerable questions aside, what was the short-term plan? "Our main task," he said, "would be to win goodwill for ourselves and our national cause, to establish relations with the politicians, statesmen, and governments of the Allies, to organize united action among our people in Allied countries and, above all, to create an army from among Czech prisoners of war."

"This was the crucial moment," said Selver, "when Masaryk accepted what might well prove to be life-long exile, in his devotion to a cause, the prospects of which, at that time, could scarcely be considered hopeful." Masaryk was sixty-five years old and faced a worldwide challenge in an age when horses still clogged city streets, telegraph and railroads linked only isolated pockets of the world, and dangerous steamship journeys were often measured in weeks. If he were not to die in obscurity, forever lost to his family and home, he would have to obtain a series of audiences with the leaders of the world's most powerful and distant nations, and then use languages he knew only secondhand to convince them, first, that his Czechs and Slovaks actually existed and, second, that the Allies must liberate them with a new map of Europe.

THREE

Masaryk's Exile

One man with a dream, at pleasure,
Shall go forth and conquer a crown;
And three with a new song's measure
Can trample a kingdom down.

Arthur William Edgar O'Shaughnessy, *Ode*[1]

Exile is the nursery of nationality

Lord Acton[2]

Couriers, Agents, and Allies Emerge

Tomáš G. Masaryk was heartened by reports from Russia that Czech and Slovak émigrés were received by the tsar and that the Česká Družina had been established.[3] Yet enormous political barriers—and the ruthless cruelties of war—awaited anyone who took up arms. While Czechs and Slovaks in the United States had organized themselves into the Bohemian National Alliance and the Slovak League of America, until April 1917 President Woodrow Wilson's vigilant neutrality prohibited any military recruiting or training on American soil. In France and Great Britain, however, Czech volunteer recruits for the Western Front suffered the same fate as so many regular French and British soldiers. Three hundred Czechs living in France—including thirty-seven Czechs from Great Britain whose offer to volunteer for the British army was declined—were inducted into the French Foreign Legion "for the duration of the war." Shipped off to the trenches on October 23, 1914, the Czech unit was quickly decimated. So many of its members were killed that the unit was disbanded.[4]

More successful were scores of obscure people—young and old, men and women, single and married—who began to step forward to volunteer as couriers or spies. Most were recruited by Emanuel Voska, the Czech-American businessman sent by Masaryk to the United States to raise money and recruit supporters and funnel information to British intelligence. A strongly built man from his years as a stonecutter, Voska possessed a round, powerful head; shrewd, yellowish-gray eyes; a determined jaw; and an air of authority. Having dabbled in socialist politics, he fled Austria-Hungary and crawled out of a ship's steerage quarters in New York in 1894, aged nineteen, speaking no English. Within fifteen years, he owned marble yards in New York and Kansas City, a quarry in Vermont, and part interest in a Czech-language newspaper. He married another Czech immigrant, fathered six children, and became president of the American Sokol, the network of nationalist-inspired gymnastic and cultural clubs of the Czechs.[5]

Voska's chief informant in New York was František Kopecký, a mail clerk at the Austro-Hungarian consulate who obtained government documents, blank passports, and information on Austrian military and intelligence operations. He worked under the code name Zeno. Voska called him his most valuable agent, though Voska also recruited the chauffeur to Germany's ambassador to the United States, Count Johann von Bernstorff; the personal maid to that ambassador's wife; and four additional Austrian consular officers in New York. More spies were recruited inside Vienna's and Berlin's consulates in Chicago, Cleveland, New Orleans, Saint Louis, and San Francisco, as well as among their diplomatic couriers.[6]

MOST IMPORTANT WERE the two younger men who joined Masaryk's organization, Dr. Edvard Beneš, a studious, tireless, young Bohemian with a cool and prickly demeanor, and Milan R. Štefánik, the handsome, passionate Slovak astronomer, explorer, meteorologist, aviator, diplomat, and French army officer, would also join Masaryk in exile.

Solitary, methodical, and always controlled, Beneš was the perfect aide.[7] While he was thirty-five years younger than his former professor, he carried himself with great confidence, which would serve him well when he began to negotiate, alone, with senior Allied leaders. And as a loner, he had developed few other relationships or loyalties. Critics saw arrogance beneath his confidence and a suspicious nature beneath his cool demeanor. Born on May 28, 1884, and christened Eduard, he later changed his name to Edvard, for unknown reasons. "Its only advantage," noted his biographers, "was that the new name would be easier to cut into stone." The tenth child of hardworking Bohemian Catholic farmers, Beneš became a freethinker at an early age and, later, a socialist. He first came to Masaryk's attention when Václav Beneš, his older brother and a supporter of Masaryk, asked the professor for help in getting Edvard French language instruction, a fateful choice. He began studying philosophy at Prague University in 1904 and then moved to Paris to study at the Sorbonne, where he came to know exiles from the Russian revolution of 1905. A semester in Berlin induced alarm at Germany's militarism, while two visits to England exposed him to a rather different kind of society. A member of the Social Democrats, he wrote articles for the party's newspaper and in 1908—the same year he became a pupil of Masaryk—authored a serious study of Austria-Hungary and the Czechs, arguing for a reformed, federalized empire. The following year, he married Hana Vlčková, a pretty blonde who became "his lifelong companion and the only friend he ever had," say his biographers. The marriage was a happy one, though childless. Money was not a problem, as Hana had some inherited wealth. Before the war, Beneš spent another year studying abroad in England and France from 1911 to 1912.

Sober, logical, analytical, reserved, prim and proper, Beneš was not so very different from Masaryk, though the older man could be warmer, as well as more combative. In September 1914 Beneš volunteered to work at Masaryk's party newspaper, *Cas* (Time). A few weeks later, as the war spread across Europe, the slight, balding young man, aged thirty, met Masaryk while walking toward the professor's apartment. Masaryk barely knew Beneš, who now confessed that he was sick of the continued infighting among Czech politicians and ashamed at the enthusiasm for the war in some Czech newspapers. Beneš poured his heart out to Masaryk. "He had reached the conclusion that we could not remain passive spectators of the war but must do something. He was restless and wanted to get to work," Masaryk recalled. "I said, 'Good. I am at it already.' On the way to the office I confided in him and we agreed at once." Masaryk trusted Beneš immediately, but Masaryk may also have appreciated that his grandiose plans were going to require some help. Regardless, Beneš proved to be invaluable to the independence movement. "Without Beneš," Masaryk said many times, "there would have been no republic."[8]

IF BENEŠ RESEMBLED a grim bookkeeper, the final leg of the triumvirate was more the dashing playboy. Milan Rastislav Štefánik was recruited into the movement by Beneš shortly after he moved to Paris in late 1915.

Like Masaryk and Beneš, Štefánik's origins were modest.[9] Born in Košariská in northwestern Slovakia, on July 21, 1880, Štefánik was the son of a Lutheran pastor and a mother whose two Slovak brothers were killed in the uprisings against Hungary in 1848. Young Štefánik was raised on Lutheran sermons delivered in Czech, unusual in Catholic Slovakia. By heritage, faith, and his Czech literacy, Štefánik was something of a rebel from the start. As child, however, his favorite pastime was to climb a nearby mountain to gaze at the stars through a paper telescope. Small, frail, and with a congenital heart defect, Štefánik more than made up for his physical shortcomings with relentless energy, wanderlust, and determination. He journeyed to Prague in 1898 to study astronomy at Charles University, where Masaryk was one of his professors. He also wrote articles for *Cas*. After earning a doctorate in 1904, he moved to Paris the same year for work. There he met Beneš, then a student, in 1905.[10]

As an astronomer and meteorologist, Štefánik traveled across Africa, Asia, Europe, and North America—including expeditions to Tahiti, Tunisia, and Turkistan—for the French government and its navy. In 1912 he became a French citizen and by 1914 he was made a knight of the Legion of Honor. As a result, he had strong, high-level connections among French politicians and journalists. In January 1915 he volunteered for the embryonic French air force. He took part in battles on the Western Front before he was transferred to Serbia, where he took on diplomatic assignments. He had tried to contact Masaryk soon after the professor went into exile, but without success. When the first formal demand for Czecho-Slovak independence was made public on November 14, 1915, Beneš suggested that it could be signed by Štefánik for the Slovaks, but Štefánik was still fighting in Serbia. He was seriously injured when his aircraft crashed in Albania on an Allied mission. Following a heroic journey on foot and by air and sea, suffering from internal bleeding, he reached Paris in December 1915, where he underwent an operation that saved his life, if not his health. In Paris, Beneš was reintroduced to Second Lieutenant Štefánik, now thirty-five, exactly a decade after their first meeting. A passionate, strong-willed, impetuous man who was not afraid to express his opinions, Štefánik was also more conservative than Masaryk or Beneš—he favored a monarch in Prague and feared democracy.

Yet Štefánik was about to open a very important door for the independence movement. He told Beneš that he had "powerful political connections in France" and shared his ideas on how to promote their cause.[11] The Slovak claimed that he had convinced officials to remove Czechs and Slovaks from France's lists of enemy aliens back in October 1914.[12] The independence movement now had among its leaders a prominent Slovak, without whom critics might have asked Masaryk and Beneš how they could purport to speak for the Slovaks. "The alliance of these three men was an ideal one," R. W. Seton-Watson recalled years later. "It was entirely untrammeled by conventions, but it rested on a sense of reality and very great tactical skill. They were always in the right place at the right moment."[13]

"Above All, We Needed Money"

"ABOVE ALL," RECALLED Beneš about the founding of the exile independence movement, "we needed money."[14] Masaryk concurred: "The truth was that we needed funds." Beneš, who was able to support himself throughout his exile, gave Masaryk four thousand crowns.[15] While small sums were raised in Prague, the exiles came to be supported by fund-raising among Czech Americans, an American millionaire who befriended Masaryk, and British intelligence.

The wealth of a growing class of professionals and business owners had fueled the Czech renaissance, in part through fund-raising campaigns, one of which built the Czech National Theater in Prague in a burst of national pride in 1881. While German theaters were gifts from German princes or government coffers, the Czech National Theater was built only after the Czechs raised most of the seven million crowns it cost. When it burned down scarcely a month after opening, the city and the emperor provided the funds to rebuild it. When plans to build a memorial to Bohemian preacher Jan Hus in Prague were launched in 1890, the Czechs raised ten thousand crowns in eight days. By April of that year, they had raised fifty thousand crowns. Before long, about three hundred people or companies had each donated a thousand crowns. Two hundred people attended the first official meeting of the Hus memorial group—and their speaker was none other than Masaryk.[16] In 1899 *Cas* appealed to readers for funds to expand the periodical from a weekly to a daily. The response was strong, raising the equivalent of ten thousand pounds sterling.[17]

Masaryk had these kinds of activities in mind when, before leaving Prague in 1914, he spoke to Josef Scheiner, the leader of the national Sokol Organization, about money. Scheiner gave the professor ten thousand crowns, and they discussed whether the Sokol clubs—whose members paid dues to build and maintain gymnasiums and sponsor athletic competitions—could support the movement abroad. Yet this source of funds was soon frozen by the authorities.[18]

The wealthy Czech-American businessman Voska sent a series of checks to Masaryk. One for $1,000 reached Masaryk in Prague in October 1914, payable to Charlotte Masaryk; $3,000 reached the professor on one of his trips to Rotterdam; and another $1,250 awaited him in Geneva in early 1915. Later in 1915 Scheiner and Přemysl Šámal, a successful attorney and politician who took over leadership of the Realist Party from Masaryk, provided an additional eleven thousand crowns of their own. Masaryk kept up a steady demand for more, asking Voska in December 1914 to raise $10,000 among Czech-Americans. By May 1915 he requested $50,000, though only $37,841 reached him by the end of 1915. In 1916 $71,185 was raised and in 1918 $483,438 was raised. All in all, Czech and Slovak-Americans donated at least $1 million to the exiles' independence movement. While advertisements soliciting support in the United States were placed in émigré newspapers, most of the American contributions resulted from fund-raising bazaars in Czech and Slovak communities across the United States. Early in the struggle, one fair in Cedar Rapids, Iowa, raised $25,000; another in New York City netted $22,000; Cleveland raised $30,000; Omaha, Nebraska, topped $70,000; and a whopping $400,000 was raised in Chicago. Finally, a "national tax," or dues, paid by members of the Bohemian National Alliance raised hundreds of thousands of dollars annually.[19]

Another source of support was wealthy American industrialist Charles R. Crane, the oldest child of a self-made Chicago manufacturer of valves, pipes, plumbing fixtures, and elevators. A college dropout, Crane became "a life-long devoted disciple" of Masaryk's, according to Crane's biographer, Norman E. Saul.[20]

At Crane's request, Masaryk had agreed to deliver fifteen or sixteen lectures on Russia in Chicago over six weeks starting in June 1902. Masaryk found a ready audience for his talks in part because, by 1910, the Crane Company employed five thousand people in Chicago alone and Chicago had the second-largest Czech population of any city outside of Prague.[21]

After the war began, at Masaryk's request, Crane wired "a considerable sum" of money to help him launch his campaign-in-exile.[22] Voska later became a conduit for at least some of Crane's support for Masaryk, using Crane's attorney, Roger H. Williams, as an intermediary starting in February 1915. Aside from Crane and the fund-raising among the Czechs and Slovaks in America, "Not a dollar was asked for or accepted from any foreign source. Those were Masaryk's orders," said one supporter, Thomas Čapek, who quoted the professor saying, "This is our revolution, and we must pay for it with our own money."[23] At least initially, this prohibition held, mostly because the exiles' cause had seemed so unpromising. After Voska's intelligence work came to the appreciative attention of Washington and London, Masaryk's efforts were supported by British intelligence.[24] And by late 1917 the French assumed primary responsibility for the finances of the Czecho-Slovak Legion.

Aside from covering the expenses of rent, food, and travel, early fund-raising made it possible for Masaryk and his associates to produce a torrent of what they freely called "propaganda" about the history of the Czechs and Slovaks, their persecution, and how their liberation would cripple Austria-Hungary and, by extension, Germany. Pocket-sized books, pamphlets, leaflets, and maps by the exiles flew off printing presses throughout Europe and North America, with pleading or accusatory titles: *Austrian Terrorism in Bohemia, Bohemia's Case for Independence, Our Fellow Citizens—The Bohemians and Slovaks, Bohemia under Habsburg Misrule,* and *Czech Hatred of Austria Grows.* The activists granted interviews, issued news releases, and wrote articles for publications such as the *Atlantic Monthly,* the *Christian Science Monitor,* the *Edinburgh Review,* *Harper's Magazine,* the *Nation,* the *New Republic,* the *New Statesman,* the *New York Times,* and the *Spectator.* The publicity mill operated by Czech-born Iowa lawyer Charles Pergler regularly sent news releases to five hundred American newspapers.[25]

Beneš and Štefánik honed an approach in Paris in which they drafted "confidential" memoranda for French politicians and journalists, who would then more eagerly share the prized information with their peers, an approach later copied elsewhere. In addition to lobbying political leaders, they reached out to scholars who could trumpet their cause in books, journals, and conferences. Among them was Professor Ernest Denis, who began publishing *La nation tcheque* (The Czech Nation), a periodical for French readers on May 1, 1915, followed by *Le monde slave* (The Slavic World). A Czech-language newspaper, *Československa Samostatnost* (Czechoslovak Independence) appeared in August 1915 in Switzerland, edited by Lev Sychrava, a lawyer and journalist. Sychrava, age twenty-seven, in September 1914 became perhaps the first Czech to leave Austria-Hungary to actively oppose the Habsburg regime. In October 1916 an influential English weekly edited by Seton-Watson, the *New Europe*, appeared, advocating the destruction of Austria-Hungary and the liberation of its peoples. And H. Wickham Steed, too, as foreign editor of the *Times* of London, kept the exile cause in the news.

"Never since the Thirty Years' War have the grievances and political aspirations of the Bohemians been given more widespread publicity," concluded one writer.[26] In addition to purloined government documents, the couriers were now smuggling draft articles and finished periodicals in and out of Austria-Hungary and around the world. While public diplomacy and media campaigns today are common, at the time this was an unusual—yet effective—method of establishing a new nation. "Most states have been fashioned by the sword or have grown out of colonization," says historian H. A. L. Fisher. "Czecho-Slovakia is the child of propaganda."[27]

Police, Spies, Poison, Prison, and Death

BACK IN PRAGUE, the Maffie met for the first time without Masaryk in early March 1915. Present were Beneš, Kramář, Šámal, Scheiner, and Alois Rašín, another journalist and attorney who was once imprisoned for antigovernment activities but who was subsequently elected to the Reichsrat. While supportive of Masaryk's plan to work among the émigrés abroad, Kramář informed Beneš that he would remain in Prague to await the arrival of Russian troops; it was agreed that others should join Masaryk.

Money was needed, as were more allies inside Austria-Hungary and better leadership for the émigrés in Russia and their *družina*. Cipher codes were shared, postal addresses identified, and aliases devised; Beneš alone used at least seven aliases, especially in order to travel, for which his police source provided documents. The police were ever present on the streets, demanding identification and subjecting people to searches. The Maffie hid information inside the covers of books; rolls of paper were inserted into fountain pens, the handles of bags and steamer trunks, the hollow sides of those trunks, and boot heels and coat collars.

While the exiles feared capture and execution by Habsburg authorities, they also had to contend with arrests by the same Allied governments from whom they sought support but who naturally saw them as enemy "Austrians." Beneš was interrogated and jailed three times by the British and twice by the French.[28] It did not help matters that Voska had secretly arranged with British intelligence for his couriers traveling in and out of Germany or Austria-Hungary to use the United Kingdom as a transit point, where they would be openly and ceremoniously arrested by Scotland Yard and then released for lack of evidence, so as to deflect suspicion from them.[29] Steed finally shared with a Scotland Yard inspector the information that Beneš should no longer be arrested. "Before very long, that fellow may be signing passports which you will have to respect; and then he may tell our government that a certain Scotland Yard inspector at Havre is a nuisance and ought to be removed. So treat him kindly," Steed said. "Thereafter, Beneš suffered no more."[30]

Neither could the august Alps of neutral Switzerland protect Masaryk and his coconspirators. "Austrian spies were always at our heels," Masaryk recalled. Pretending to be sympathizers, some of Vienna's agents approached him openly to obtain information on his network. Some got close enough to poison the old man—twice. "In the spring of 1915 one of my arms began to give trouble," Masaryk later recalled. "Small abscesses began to appear on my shoulder. My doctor ascribed them to poisoning and our own people thought the Germans were trying to get at me through my laundry. The matter would not be worth mentioning but for the fact that the same thing happened to me in England, where the doctor also diagnosed poison."[31] The professor not only kept a loaded revolver close at hand, he also practiced his shooting. He wrote to Voska in the United States, "If I were not around, Benes would carry on the cause."[32]

Swiss police occasionally searched the homes of ethnic Czechs and the government forbade anti-Austrian propaganda. Likewise, exile could not keep the war's growing toll of death away from the professor's door. "Hardly had I settled in Geneva when news of my son Herbert's illness came unexpectedly from my family in Prague," he recalled after the war, "and on March 15th, a telegram announcing his death. Thus like thousands of families at home, we were stricken." Masaryk's oldest son, only thirty-five, a gifted artist who was working among refugees in Galicia, died of typhus.[33] In part as a result of this loss, shortly thereafter Beneš for a second time visited Masaryk in Geneva for about a week in early April 1915.

Perhaps moved by the death of his son, Masaryk now told Beneš the time had come to publicly attack Austria-Hungary and advocate their national desires. The activists in Prague worried about Vienna's reaction, but Masaryk insisted the movement was losing valuable time. "Nobody would give us something for nothing," he scolded, "and it would be a great political error to rely only on the Allies and especially on Russia." Masaryk gave Beneš the text of a manifesto he intended to publicize to launch their struggle, and he asked that the Maffie review it and quickly respond. The struggle had to come out into the open, he said, and it must have revolutionary aims. Actions by the émigrés and exiles had to be supported by the Czech leaders in Prague, who *absolutely could not* disavow the independence movement abroad. And, finally, while Masaryk would give the Maffie time to approve the document, "in the end, he would take action on his own account." Meanwhile, he would visit Paris and London to meet Allied leaders.[34]

Later that same April came the encouraging news that Prague's Twenty-Eighth Infantry Regiment of Czechs and Slovaks had defected to the Russian lines.

LATE IN THE evening, on Sunday April 18, 1915, Robert Seton-Watson arrived at Charing Cross Station, the railway station in London. Given the hour and day, Charing Cross was deserted. Reflecting the gloom of a nation at war, it was dreary, unlit, and cavernous, echoing each and every sound. Seton-Watson had no difficulty spotting his visitors, the elderly professor and his daughter, standing on the platform, at a loss as to how to move Masaryk's chest of reports, maps, and intelligence, the essential ammunition of his worldwide propaganda war. Masaryk and Seton-Watson greeted each other warmly and Masaryk introduced his daughter. The two men began hauling the heavy chest and other bags down the dimly lit platform. "Then there were no taxis," Seton-Watson recalled, "and I can still see the two solitary figures standing guard over their luggage while I scoured the neighboring streets for 10 minutes before one of the rare taxis of those early war days could be found."[35] Sometimes, this was what the revolution looked like.

Within days of Masaryk's arrival in London, Seton-Watson introduced him to George R. Clerk, an aide to British foreign secretary Sir Edward Grey, who asked for a brief memorandum, which was titled "Independent Bohemia." Presented to the government on May 3, the document claimed that it represented the views of all Czechs, except the Catholics, which surely was an exaggeration, and that it presented a "program for the restoration of Bohemia as an independent state." At this point, Masaryk still assumed, as did Kramář back in Prague, that Bohemia would be liberated by Russian troops, and that an independent Bohemia would still have a monarch.

Seton-Watson devised a plan that would provide Masaryk with both an income and a platform from which to influence public opinion. In this way, the two men helped to found the School of Slavonic Studies at King's College, University of London, in 1915, only the second such program in Great Britain. Masaryk was known as the author of *Russia and Europe*, which had been published in German in 1913 in two volumes, his greatest scholarly work.[36] In early February 1915 in Geneva, the two men had discussed the possibility of Masaryk's becoming a lecturer in Slavonic History and Literature for one year starting in October 1915.

Seton-Watson made it clear that Masaryk's lectures would be directed to the larger audience of influential adults that Masaryk desperately wished to reach. "I am sure," Seton-Watson said, "it is much the most practical way of arousing interest and sympathy for the cause you have at heart."[37]

Around the time Masaryk was wrapping up his affairs in London, the Treaty of London was signed on April 26, promising Italy the Italian-speaking populations in the city of Trieste, Dalmatia, and other Croat, Serb, and Slovene regions of Austria-Hungary on the Adriatic coast, where many Slavic-speakers resided. Masaryk's Yugoslav allies had aimed to incorporate these regions into a new nation, Yugoslavia. When word of the secret treaty leaked out, the Yugoslavs seethed—yet Italy returned Britain's favor and declared war on Austria-Hungary on May 23.

In Prague, meanwhile, the Maffie read and approved Masaryk's draft manifesto, but asked that it be made public at a strategic moment—at some point in the future. Upon his return to Geneva from Paris and London, Masaryk felt enormous frustration. Even more emphatically, he urged upon his allies in the Maffie the need to act *now* to gain the support of the Allies. But, before they could do so, Habsburg authorities pounced on the small band of conspirators in Prague.

IN A MEETING of the group in Prague on the night of May 20, 1915, Beneš shared copies of *La nation tcheque* and other documents, and Kramář slipped a copy of the French periodical into his breast pocket. Suddenly, Scheiner was called to the telephone—soldiers were searching his home. "It was a critical moment," Beneš said. "If the police knew where Dr. Scheiner was, they would be able to catch us all at one swoop and seize our documents, as well." Šámal thrust a fistful of money into Scheiner's hands and urged him to flee, but authorities grabbed Scheiner at his home the following morning. Kramář was arrested the same day, and the periodical in his jacket was seen as incriminating evidence against him. Beneš spent the evening walking the streets. He watched his house the entire following morning before he entered. The authorities did not come. He cleared his house of all incriminating material. Then, on July 12, Rašín was arrested.

Kramář was accused of the high crime of persuading leading Czechs not to visit Habsburg military headquarters to congratulate the military for the success of the massive Gorlice-Tarnow offensive against the Russians. Just as likely, the arrests of Kramář and Scheiner were designed to avenge the desertion of the Twenty-Eighth Infantry Regiment from Prague during early April, during this successful offensive, which was in fact led by German troops. While Scheiner was released a month later for lack of evidence—the authorities apparently remained unaware of his trip to Russia early in 1914—the Maffie in Prague was forced to burrow further underground.[38]

Declarations of War

AUSTRIA-HUNGARY'S DECLARATIONS OF war in 1914 were issued without legislative approval or input from Vienna's subjects. Martial law descended on Prague. Military courts imprisoned between five and twenty thousand people, many of them under sentence of death, mostly for actions deemed antiwar or treasonous. As historian Josef Kalvoda says, "All opposition activity thus became illegal." A member of the Reichsrat who also led one of the Czech political parties, Václav Klofáč, was arrested September 14, 1914, the first of perhaps seven Reichsrat members who were arrested. In reaction to the distribution of pro-Russian leaflets and other alleged treasonous activities, moreover, police arrests led to eleven trials, where more than twenty death sentences were pronounced.[39]

Field marshal Franz Conrad von Hötzendorf expanded the powers of the War Surveillance Office over schools and curricula, extended the zones under direct military control, and purged the government of allegedly unreliable persons.[40] The governor of Bohemia, the lenient Count Franz Anton von Thun und Hohenstein, was replaced in March 1915 and the military clamped down harder on civilians. Factories supplying the war effort were placed under direct military control. Workers were subject to military discipline. "Trouble-makers" were placed in uniform and marched to the front.[41] Since threatening soldiers with punishment no longer intimidated men who endured combat, authorities turned on their families at home, often threatening them, searching their homes, and investigating family members for antigovernment views. Returning prisoners of war, regardless of their nationality, were placed in detention camps to evaluate their opinions and behavior in the army, which were subject to punishment by military prosecutors. While some reports by the exiles and activists may have succumbed to exaggeration, it is clear that beatings, starvation, disease, and suicide took hundreds, perhaps thousands, of lives among the imprisoned civilians. The persecutions had their intended effect. In June 1915 statements from Czech leaders expressing loyalty to the Habsburgs began appearing in Austria-Hungary's newspapers.

IN GENEVA, MASARYK responded with his first public speech, selecting for this event the date of July 6, 1915, the five hundredth anniversary of the death of Bohemian martyr Jan Hus. Ordained a priest in 1400, Hus had been the rector of Prague's Charles University and an early critic of the established medieval Catholic Church. Hus advocated the use of Czech in the Mass. As a result, he was condemned as a heretic and burned at the stake in 1415. His execution by Catholic rulers sparked a seventeen-year-long Bohemian revolt also known as the Hussite Wars, which turned the Czech lands Protestant. Of perhaps greater inspiration to the exiles was the fact that the Hussite Wars involved small yet zealous Czech armies of perhaps twenty-five thousand that ultimately defeated the much larger armies of the Holy Roman Empire.

To mark the anniversary of Hus's death, two academics appeared at the front of the plain yet cavernous Hall of the Reformation, a monument to Geneva's role as the platform and laboratory of the French Reformation preacher, John Calvin. An audience of twelve thousand Protestants, Czech émigrés, and Masaryk supporters occupied the long wooden desks on the floor and the wooden balconies flanking the rear and sides. They faced a parliamentary-style platform where two speakers sat.[42]

The French scholar Ernest Denis, who had launched *La nation tcheque* two months earlier, spoke first, providing a historical sketch of the life of

Hus. After Denis finished, Masaryk took the podium and launched into a more overtly political speech, demanding the dissolution of Austria-Hungary and the founding of Czecho-Slovakia. In terse remarks labeled "In the Name of Hus, for the Freedom of the Nation," Masaryk drew comparisons between the medieval Hussites and he and his fellow exiles:

> Every Czech must make up his mind either in favor of the reforma-
> tion or of the counter-reformation, for the Czech idea or the Austrian
> idea. . . . Our reformation enjoins this rule upon us—we condemn vio-
> lence. We do not wish to use it, nor shall we do so. But against violence
> we shall defend ourselves, if need be, by iron methods.[43]

His words turned out to be prophetic. Aside from the combat soldiers who were beginning to switch their allegiances on the Eastern Front, the independence movement would not employ violence until Czech and Slovak soldiers came under attack in Russia. Ever the philosopher, Masaryk thought his remarks would show "that, in the spirit of our Hussite ancestors, we were fighting for a moral as well as for a political purpose." Yet the professor remained eager to gain support from Prague by issuing a more "political" manifesto.[44]

Simultaneously, Seton-Watson persuaded two dozen Oxford University scholars to sign a letter about Hus and the plight of Bohemia, which was published July 6 in the *Times* of London. Other lectures and meetings were also held on the subject, and newspapers in Great Britain and France reported on Masaryk's speech in Geneva, bringing the movement valuable publicity. Habsburg authorities correctly perceived the speech as a direct provocation. The Viennese newspaper *Neue Freie Presse* proclaimed it "the first Czech declaration of war against Austria." It wasn't just the speech that caught the eye of the authorities.

SIMULTANEOUSLY WITH DENIS and Masaryk's speeches, sculptor Ladislav Šaloun's large monument to Jan Hus was quietly unveiled in Prague's Old Town Square, unbeknownst to Austrian authorities, by a small group of dissident Czechs who dispersed without public comment. By the end of the day, thousands of flowers and wreaths surrounded the foundation of the sculpture.[45]

To these provocations, Vienna responded with a warrant for Masaryk's arrest on August 4, a warrant extended to all his associates two weeks later. Masaryk's house in Prague was searched on August 30 in High Viennese Official style by an elaborate military-civilian "commission" composed of a colonel, a lieutenant, a magistrate, a superintendent, and a clerk, who together spent two hours ransacking the house—and found nothing. Frustrated, the police took Masaryk's wife, Charlotte, and oldest daughter, Alice, in for questioning.

By August 1915 the police also learned of the anti-Habsburg activities of Edvard Beneš's brother, Vojta, who was raising money for the movement in the United States.[46] "It was high time to get away," Beneš said. Taking his wife Hana aside, he promised her he would be gone no longer than two years, though he could not know how long he would be away. She no doubt would be harassed, cross-examined, maybe even arrested. "Should things become unbearable," he told Hana, "she was to repudiate me. We were ready for whatever might befall us." In the opening days of September 1915 Beneš crossed into Switzerland as "Miroslav Sicha," a traveling salesman whose heavy limp explained why he was not in uniform. Hidden on him were twenty thousand French francs.[47]

A heavy downpour awaited Beneš outside the Des Eaux Vives restaurant in Geneva; awaiting him inside was Masaryk, who wanted Beneš to return to Prague—the link to Prague could not be broken. Beneš explained that associates had twice warned him that he was being watched. Indeed, the two men would soon learn, a criminal indictment had been drawn up against Masaryk the previous month and the noose was tightening around Beneš, almost the only member of the Maffie who had yet to be arrested or indicted.[48] The good news, Beneš said, was that the Maffie had approved Masaryk's draft "manifesto." The professor thought it over. The next day, he decided that he would return to London, Beneš moved to Paris, and Josef Dürich, a powerful pro-Russian Czech political leader who had recently joined Masaryk in Geneva in May 1915, was dispatched to Russia. Sychrava, the lawyer and journalist who had launched the newspaper *Československa Samostatnost* (Czechoslovak Independence), remained in Geneva.[49] Whenever the need arose, Beneš or Štefánik could visit Rome, so that all the major Allied nations would be covered.

Masaryk traveled on a Serbian passport when he made London his base in late September 1915. Publicly, he arrived to accept the lectureship at King's College, which paid him a modest stipend of two hundred pounds annually. His inaugural lecture, "The Problem of Small Nations in the European Crisis," was scheduled for October 19. No less a figure than the British prime minister who took the United Kingdom into the war, H. H. (Herbert Henry) Asquith, agreed to attend. When illness forced Asquith to back out, he sent his undersecretary of state for foreign affairs, Lord Robert Cecil.[50] Asquith released a statement indicating that the Allies were waging war for the protection of small nations, which could have been helpful to the Czech and Slovak cause or seen as a simple restatement of London's defense of Belgium against German invasion. Given the context, however, Asquith was clearly hinting—if *only* hinting—at some vague support for the Czechs and Slovaks. London decided the same day that Czechs and Slovaks would no longer be classified as "enemy aliens."

On December 31, Seton-Watson arranged for Masaryk to meet Sir William Wiseman, who was departing for the United States to lead British intelligence there, saying that Wiseman "might really be able to help the cause." Wiseman would become very close to President Wilson and his chief adviser, Colonel Edward M. House, even vacationing with the two and living with House. Later that month, London agreed to finance Voska's efforts in the United States, which exposed German agents engaged in sabotage and labor actions against ships and cargo bound for England. Voska and Masaryk were now in constant contact with British intelligence.[51] Across the English Channel, Beneš settled in Paris, putting his French to use.

"My beginnings in Paris were difficult. I took up my quarters in the Rue Leopold Robert in a small room on the fifth floor, for which I paid

120 francs a month. The few acquaintances which I had made in France during my first and second stay there," Beneš wrote, "had either forgotten me or else had disappeared in consequence of the war. I was not in touch with official circles."[52] Yet France was from the start the Allied nation most congenial to the aspirations of the Czechs and Slovaks, removing them from the lists of "enemy aliens" on October 2, 1914, for instance, one year before London did so. Beneš made the most of this sympathetic attitude, lobbying scholars, journalists, and government officials, including two former professors of his, historian Ernest Denis and Louis Eisenmann, another specialist on Austria-Hungary now posted to the French Ministry of War. Beneš shared clandestine information he received from Prague with French officials. He bragged to his fellow activists back in Prague, "Every report makes people grateful and puts them under obligation to me."

Beneš also worked feverishly on Masaryk's long-awaited manifesto. He negotiated with exiles and émigrés in America, Europe, and Russia for signatures. Couriers began shuttling drafts from country to country. This effort prompted the creation of an organization purporting to represent all independence-minded Czechs and Slovaks, the Czech Action Committee Abroad, which was established in Paris in July 1915 by Beneš, Dürich, Masaryk, and Štefánik.

The Cleveland Accord

THE SECOND LARGEST Czech and Slovak population outside of Austria-Hungary was in the United States, where estimates placed their number at almost one million on the eve of the Great War.

In the fall of 1914, American Czechs established a pro-independence organization that came to be known as the Bohemian National Alliance, which by January was based in Chicago, with Dr. Ludvik Fisher, a physician, as president.[53] The alliance had issued a manifesto critical of Austria-Hungary long before it made contact with Masaryk, whose first direct communication with the alliance was a letter dated June 10, 1915, that encouraged the organization's activities and made a strong appeal for

funds. Emanuel Voska headed the New York office. The organization became the leading American exponent of independence. By February 1917,
it began publishing a monthly magazine, *The Bohemian Review*. Across
the cover of every issue was the quote from Woodrow Wilson's book, *The
State*: "No lapse of time, no defeat of hopes, seems sufficient to reconcile
the Czechs of Bohemia to incorporation with Austria."[54]

IN SOME WAYS, American Slovaks were earlier organized and better prepared than American Czechs. They had founded the Slovak League of
America in 1907 and had adopted a "Memorandum of the Slovak League
of America" in July 1914. Issued in the name of the American Slovaks
on behalf of the Slovaks of Hungary, the document called for Slovak
cultural and administrative autonomy within Hungary. It did not seek
independence or a union with the Czechs, but the war brought together
Czechs and Slovaks who sought to establish a nation together. A small
number of Lutheran Slovaks—Štefánik was one, Albert P. Mamatey, the
president of the Slovak League, was another—linked the Czechs and
Slovaks in the United States.

Masaryk's suggestion that Czechs link up with the Slovaks was initially met with resistance. In a speech in the Reichsrat in 1907, Masaryk
had staked a claim to Czecho-Slovak brotherhood: "In Hungary we have
two million Slovaks who belong to our nationality. A people of eight million will not, without further ado, leave two million of its co-nationals to
the tender mercies of Magyar jingoism. It is our duty, here and on every
possible occasion, to inform this House, Austria, and the whole of the
general public, that the Magyars are treating our Slovaks in a manner
which is utterly inhuman."[55] Many Slovaks resented the comment that
they "belonged" to the Czechs or that "the Slovaks are Czechs." In his
memorandum to the British government in April 1915, Masaryk had written that "the Slovaks are Bohemians in spite of their using their dialect as
their literary language."[56]

While the Slovak League of America rejected a union with the Czechs
in Europe as late as February 1915, a conference of Czechs and Slovaks

gathered in Cleveland on October 22, 1915, where the Bohemian National Alliance and the Slovak League of America agreed to coordinate their efforts. The conference issued the Cleveland Agreement, the first formal agreement for a union of Europe's Czechs and Slovaks, whose principal Slovak backers were Mamatey and Stefan Osusky, a Slovak-American lawyer from Chicago. The agreement called for "independence" for these peoples and demanded a "union of the Czech and Slovak peoples in a federal union of states with full national autonomy for Slovakia." The Slovaks were specifically promised their own legislative Diet, government, and financial and political administration, and that Slovak would be an official language in the new state.[57] This alliance emboldened the exiles in Europe to throw down a challenge to Vienna.

ON SUNDAY, NOVEMBER 14, 1915, Masaryk finally released his long-awaited manifesto. "The present moment is grave," it began.[58] The inaugural declaration of the Czech Action Committee Abroad was the first public, formal statement of the goals and objectives of the Czecho-Slovak independence movement. It openly called for the dissolution of Austria-Hungary. Recounting recent battlefield losses by Allied Russia, Austria-Hungary's occupation of Serbia and Montenegro, and Germany's seizure of Russian Poland, as well as the strengthening of the Central Powers by new alliances with Bulgaria and the Ottoman Empire, the manifesto declared, "In these tragic days, we feel it our duty to proclaim our absolute confidence in the complete victory of the Allies, and, in the name of the Czech people who we represent, we request the privilege of standing by their side." Among other points it made:

> Before the war, the conflict between the [Habsburg] dynasty and the Czech nation was already sharp. War rendered impossible all attempts at repair. The war was undertaken without the Parliament or the Provincial Diets being consulted. Of all the governments of Europe, only the Austrian government did not dare to ask for the opinion of the representatives of its people; it knew too well their answer. . . .

No more compromise, no more half-measures. Before the war, the various Czech political parties pursued a policy of transforming the Austro-Hungarian dualism into a federalist monarchy which would have guaranteed to the various nations of the state an extended autonomy and respect for their essential rights. Today this spurious solution has become impossible. By causing our children and our brothers to march against our natural allies, by forcing us to carry arms against other Slavs, the Habsburgs have broken the last links which tied us to them. What we demand henceforth is a completely independent Czechoslav state.

Signed by Masaryk and twelve other Czech and Slovak leaders from Allied France, Great Britain, Russia, and neutral United States, the manifesto presented a united front. The signers included Dürich; Bohumil Čermák and Bohdan Pavlů, two of the founding members of the Union of Czecho-Slovak Organizations in Russia; and several Americans, among them Fisher, Voska, and Pergler of the Bohemian National Alliance in the United States and Slovak League president Mamatey and secretary Francis Daxner. "There could not be no turning back," Beneš said. "With this step began the phase of our organized activity abroad."[59]

Following this earlier announcement, most Czech political émigrés in North America and Western Europe recognized and accepted Masaryk's leadership of their independence movement. Yet the situation was very different in Russia, where Masaryk was known as a critic of Russia's tsarist government.

WHILE MASARYK AND Beneš made progress in London and Paris, their allies and family members suffered heavier blows of repression back in Prague. With Beneš in exile, only one of the five core members of the Maffie, Přemysl Šámal, remained free in Prague. The highly capable Šámal was nonetheless alone, which worried the exiles.[60] The detention of a young female courier led to another wave of arrests and the flow of information to and from Prague slowed to a trickle.[61] The tightening surveillance noose prompted Julius Kovanda, the spy, to quit his job as butler to the interior minister, Karl Baron Heinold.[62]

After searching Masaryk's home in Prague, the police released his wife, Charlotte, perhaps due to her heart ailment, perhaps in part because she was a US citizen—but they arrested Alice on October 10 and imprisoned her, first in Prague and later in Vienna. Beneš's wife, Hana, was also arrested. In Vienna, Alice's twelve-by-fourteen-foot cell held twelve prisoners, who slept on the floor. She and Hana were repeatedly told they were to be executed, only to have the punishment postponed. Still mourning the death of her oldest son, Herbert, and suffering from a weak heart, Charlotte Masaryk, who visited Alice in Prague and wrote letters to her in Vienna, experienced "a serious collapse from which she never properly recovered and, which indeed hastened her death."[63] Before the war ended and her husband returned to her, she was committed to a sanatorium.

In December 1915 the espionage trial against Kramář and Rašín opened, drawing even more of the world's attention to the cause of the little-known Czechs. Until its resolution in June 1916, Masaryk and his associates relentlessly publicized the proceedings throughout the Allied nations as solid evidence that Vienna was at war with its subjects. "In fact," says one historian, "the Kramar affair was the first great political event that the Czechs and Slovaks abroad were able to exploit. For a long time, this event was the only proof of the anti-Habsburg attitude of the Czechs at home that the Czecho-Slovak independence movement abroad was able to furnish to foreign publics."[64] Kramář and Rašín (and two other Czech defendants) were sentenced to hang. An appeal was rejected in November 1916, but the hangings were postponed by the emperor's physician, who would not allow the matter to be submitted to Franz Joseph I due to his failing health.

Immediately after Alice Masaryk was jailed, her father wrote to Crane for help. Anxiously awaiting a response, two weeks later, he cabled Crane again, asking him to intervene. Crane contacted the *New York Times* and the *Christian Science Monitor*, reached out to his son, Richard, an aide to US secretary of state Robert Lansing, and even wrote a personal letter to Austria's hard-line premier, Count Karl von Stürgkh, alerting him to the "dynamite" nature of the arrest. Voska and Vojta Beneš also lobbied the Czech American communities, which drew the attention of US congressman Adolph J. Sabath, a Bohemian-born Chicago lawyer, who lobbied the Wilson administration to intervene. Tens of thousands of letters poured into Vienna government offices, and petitions, resolutions, telegrams, and letters likewise flooded the US State Department. The cause célèbre was brought to greater public attention by an erroneous front-page report in the *Chicago Daily Tribune* in April 1916 stating that Alice Masaryk had been executed. She was released in early July, but Vienna waited until August 20 to announce that fact.[65] Hana Beneš, on the other hand, was imprisoned until the end of the war.

"The persecution of our people at home carried conviction that we were rebels in earnest," Masaryk explained. "Martyrdom, and especially blood, win sympathies. The imprisonment, trial and condemnation of Dr. Kramar and Dr. Rasin brought grist to our mill, while the arrest of my daughter, Alice, was of great service to us in England and America. People argued that when even women were imprisoned the movement must be serious. Throughout America, women petitioned the President to intervene and appealed directly to the American ambassador in Vienna. These movements in America and in England made our rebellion better known."[66]

Promising Paris versus Perilous Saint Petersburg

HAVING LEARNED OF Štefánik's offer of high-level French contacts to Beneš, Masaryk arrived in Paris on January 28, 1916, to deliver, with Beneš, twin lectures about the Slavs and the Bohemians at the Sorbonne. Looking for Štefánik, Masaryk said, "I found him lying in a Paris hospital after a severe operation."[67] Even while he recovered from stomach surgery, Štefánik had arranged for Masaryk to be officially received by Aristide Briand, then prime minister and foreign minister of the French Third Republic.[68]

Following their meeting, Briand announced on February 3, 1916:

> We French have always entertained keen sympathies for the Czech na-
> tion, and these sympathies have been strengthened by the war. I assure
> you that France will not forget your aspirations, which we share, and
> we shall do everything in order that the Czechs may obtain their in-
> dependence. We will not speak about the details now, but as far as the
> chief point of your claim is concerned, we are in agreement.[69]

This was the first public Allied expression of sympathy and support
for the aspirations of the Czechs and Slovaks delivered by an Allied government official.

Briand's statement was an enormous advance for the independence
movement and the first confirmation that an exile independence movement whose strategy hinged on winning support among the Western
Allies might actually work. The high-profile meeting and follow-up
communiqué brought worldwide attention to the cause of the Czecho-
Slovak independence movement, especially in Allied capitals, where the
movement's aims would remain an Allied talking point, if not a priority.
As the only exile negotiating with the most senior Allied leaders, Masaryk was now the de facto leader of a global struggle for independence.

Three days later, Masaryk and his associates took another historic step
for their movement. On February 6 they established the Czech National
Council to coordinate communication with the British, French, and Russians in their respective capitals. "The National Council and its Secretar-
iat," its founding statute said, "is the only legitimate organization which
can represent the Czecho-Slovak movement to these governments." The
council, it added, "will thus be a supervisory body, a body of political
and diplomatic action, and a governmental institution."[70] A government-
in-exile, in effect, was taking shape. Masaryk was president, Dürich was
vice president, Štefánik was the "Slovak representative" (later, vice president), and Beneš was secretary general. Except for the divided émigrés in
Russia, Czechs and Slovaks worldwide recognized the council.

Yet Slovaks would encounter episodes when they were not treated as equals. In June 1916, for example, Stefan Osusky, the Slovak-American lawyer, was asked to move to Paris to assist Beneš. In his first meeting with Beneš, Osusky spotted an envelope addressed to the "Czech National Committee." He was surprised. "The Slovaks in America cannot accept this," he said. The two men argued and Osusky threatened to quit, so the organization's name was changed to Czecho-Slovak National Council.[71]

"ABOUT RUSSIA AND her fate I had worried continually," Masaryk said later.[72] The Russian Empire viewed national independence movements with suspicion, and Masaryk wisely followed developments in Russia from a distance. Yet he developed a key relationship with Russian opposition leader Pavel N. Milyukov, one of a handful of State Duma members who visited Masaryk in London in April 1916 and warmed to Masaryk's anti-Habsburg plans. Beneš and Milyukov later met in Paris, and Milyukov returned to Great Britain to lecture at Oxford College, which gave Masaryk, Milyukov, and Beneš more time to talk.

At the end of 1915, the tsarist regime had still failed to induct all the POWs who wanted to join the Česká Družina or to achieve victory on the Eastern Front. This prompted an increasing number of Czech émigrés to divide their loyalties between Russia and Masaryk's independence movement in Europe.

"I had gone abroad in the conviction that we must have an army of our own," Masaryk said. "In Switzerland, France, and England our numbers were small. Few volunteers could therefore be enrolled. In America and in Russia our colonies were stronger; and in Russia there were our prisoners of war, many of whom had given themselves up to the Russians. Hence our army must be formed in Russia." He added, "Unless we had a fighting force, our claim to freedom would hardly be heeded. In a world at war, mere tracts on 'historical and natural rights' would be of little avail."[73] Dürich wrote to the Russian foreign minister, Sergey D. Sazonov, requesting permission to visit Russia, around this time.

THE CZECHS AND Slovaks in Russia were deeply disappointed by the end of 1915, by which time Russian forces had been ejected from Austrian Galicia, Russian Poland, and western Russia. Serbia and Montenegro were also defeated. Disheartening to those émigrés who placed their hopes in Russia, these multiple defeats were exacerbated by the growing realization that the tsar's regime was slowing, if not blocking, the full development of a Czecho-Slovak army.[74] Unknown to them, Russian foreign minister Sazonov had drafted a memo in April 1915 saying that the Czecho-Slovak Union's demand for its own army violated the Hague Convention and could not be granted.

Meanwhile, by the fall of 1915, the émigré newspaper in Kiev, *Čechoslovan*, was referring to Masaryk as the Czecho-Slovak leader and two leaders of the Russian émigré colony had signed Masaryk's "manifesto" in November of that year. Two emissaries of the Union of Czecho-Slovak Organizations in Russia who visited Masaryk in London in January 1916 returned with encouraging news of his progress in London and Paris, especially Masaryk's meeting with French prime minister Briand. Alarmed that Masaryk might pull Eastern Europe under Western European influence if Austria-Hungary did not survive the war, Sazonov also sensed that Saint Petersburg was losing control of the émigré community in Russia. There were only sixteen hundred soldiers in the *družina* by late 1915.[75] While thirteen hundred more volunteers registered by April 1916, only one hundred of them were released from POW camps. Frustrated, about a thousand Czech and Slovak soldiers left their camps with Serbian recruiters instead.

Twenty-five *družina* officers signed a letter in the *Čechoslovan* criticizing the lack of progress in recruiting POWs, and they took their complaints to the Second Congress of the union on April 25, 1916 (OS), in Kiev. The delegates voted to move the union's headquarters from Saint Petersburg to Kiev and—openly aligning themselves with the Czecho-Slovak National Council in Paris—endorse Masaryk as their leader. The congress sent cables expressing confidence in the Paris council to Masaryk, its president, and Dürich, its vice president. Even more vital to the future of the *družina*, the union voted to levy taxes on the wages of Czech and Slovak civilians in Russia, on serving members of the *družina*, and on Czech and Slovak POWs working in Russian industries. Saint Petersburg's influence was now greatly diminished over a *družina* that was better able to support itself financially.

Sazonov responded with a series of moves to gain control of the Czecho-Slovak independence movement. He asked the army chief of staff, Mikhail V. Alekseyev, in February 1916 to permit Dürich, who openly retained his pro-Russian sentiments, to visit Russia and meet members of the *družina*. On April 21 (OS), the tsar followed up with an agreement to liberate all Slavic POWs in Russia—not just the Czechs and Slovaks—and create multiple liberation armies. Yet Dürich in particular would try to wrench the Czech and Slovak émigrés away from Masaryk and his National Council.

"We Shall See if We Can Last Out the Winter"

IN JUNE 1916 Russia came to the rescue of its Allies, then reeling from mounting losses at Verdun, where 160,000 French soldiers perished in the course of the war, and, subsequently, on the Somme River, where the English suffered 57,000 dead, wounded, or missing the first day—the greatest one-day loss by any nation in the war—and 131,000 dead by the end of the battle.[76] While welcomed in the West, Russia's counteroffensive also earned the *družina* a new level of respect within the Russian imperial army.

Launched on June 4, 1916 (NS), an enormous Russian offensive named for Russian General Aleksei A. Brusilov overwhelmed Austro-Hungarian forces along a two-hundred-mile front across western Ukraine, from north of Kiev to Czernowitz (Chernivtsi) in the south. The Russians secretly massed much higher concentrations of men closer to the front and then unleashed innovative artillery barrages designed to create chaos in the enemy lines. German and Austrian commanders ignored the early, alarming reports of forward movement by the Russians—many were busy celebrating Hötzendorf's sixtieth birthday.[77] In many places, the Russians—and thousands of Czechs and Slovaks among them—breached all three enemy lines of barbed wire and trenches. Reports came of massive defections and entire sections of the Austro-Hungarian front began to collapse.

Habsburg soldiers ran in retreat, their officers at times ahead of them. One Slovak officer in a mixed Hungarian unit, Josef Mikolaj, confessed that he and his men ran in panic, especially when Cossack cavalry units overtook them in retreat. After six days on the run, the Cossacks left their horses and chased the exhausted Austro-Hungarian troops on foot toward a small town, Câmpulung (also spelled Cîmpulung, today in Romania). Ahead of them, the Cossacks were already slaughtering Mikolaj's comrades in town, so he and his men took refuge in the surrounding forest. Apprehended by a Cossack the next day, Mikolaj was taken alive in part because he could speak to the Russians in Slovak. He did not regret surrendering, he said, because that evening the Cossacks killed scores of his fellow soldiers in Câmpulung. As he and his fellow prisoners were marched through town the next day, "the ditches of the road were all filled with the corpses of our people. And thus it happened that after an inglorious retreat, our whole brigade was taken into Russian captivity, excepting the commander who, having a car, could run away faster."[78] The fate of the Habsburg Fourth Army illustrates the speed of the losses and the scale of the bloodshed; on June 4, the Fourth stood ready to fight the Russians with 117,800 troops. Four days later, 35,000 men remained.[79] Far behind Habsburg lines, Field Marshal Hötzendorf prepared to evacuate his military headquarters.

Brusilov remarked that the small Czech units under his command not only fought bravely but also heightened the morale of his Russian troops. "They fought magnificently at the front under me and always displayed great bravery," he said. "I posted them at the most dangerous and difficult points, and they always carried out the tasks allotted to them with great gallantry." When they weren't fighting, Czechs entertained the troops, dressing up in costumes, performing in choirs, or erecting circus booths. "They gave us a whole series of plays, dances, fights, farces, songs and balalaika orchestras," he recalled. "The men of the Czech corps played an important part in this entertainment and contributed greatly to its gaiety."[80]

The Russian offensive cost Hötzendorf 475,000 to 750,000 casualties; between 266,000 and 400,000 of them became Russian POWs. More than two-thirds of the total fighting strength of Austria-Hungary of June 1916 was lost, and perhaps 60 percent of the Habsburg casualties were deserters, many Czechs among them.[81] Once again, Germany was forced to rescue its Habsburg ally, laboriously moving at least ten divisions from the Western Front—where the bloodshed of Verdun and the Somme raged on—and turning them eastward. While Brusilov's forces continued to mount attacks through November 1916, the offensive stalled by August.

IN THE WAKE of the surprising power of the Brusilov Offensive, German Kaiser Wilhelm II interceded and imposed an agreement on the Austro-Hungarians under which he became supreme commander of all forces on all fronts, with German field marshal Paul von Hindenburg acting in his name. The Habsburgs "took a clearly subordinate role."[82] If not formally, Hötzendorf was essentially relieved of his duties. In Vienna, Emperor Franz Joseph I, who complained he "had been spared nothing," was humiliated. Deeply pessimistic about the war, the aging monarch told confidants, "We shall see if we can last out the winter, but next spring I shall make peace under any circumstances."[83] Yet the mingling of Austrian and German troops down to the battalion level would make a separate peace all but impossible. That fall, US ambassador Frederick C. Penfield said the mood in Vienna was "describable by no other words than utter and complete despair."[84]

Berlin's militarist leadership, by contrast, no doubt felt vindicated in their martial power, having inflicted enormous losses on the tsar's armed forces, which were now increasingly bruised, bloodied, and battered. The Brusilov Offensive cost Russia at least 1.2 million casualties and 212,000 prisoners, bringing its combined losses since the start of the war to 6,778,000 soldiers—about 4,670,000 dead or wounded and 2,108,000 taken prisoner.[85] Yet all that Saint Petersburg had to show for its losses was increased scarcities of food and fuel in the cities and growing political unrest. Russia did not possess enough healthy, well-trained recruits to replace its losses, and the ill-trained men that filtered into the ranks were poisoned by political unrest behind the lines. Desertions were now remarkably high. "There is a mysterious process in the defeat of any army—the point at which the men give up hope," notes historian Norman Stone. "In the Russian case, the point was reached towards the end of the Brusilov Offensive in September 1916."[86]

The promise and ultimate failure of Russia's boldest offensive had to have been deeply discouraging, and Tsar Nicholas II could not escape responsibility, since he had installed himself as commander in chief the previous year. Austria-Hungary had completely defeated Serbia by the end of 1915. Encouraged by the Brusilov Offensive, Romania had declared war on the Central Powers on August 27, 1916 (NS), but the small nation was unprepared for the conflict. German troops seized two-thirds of its territory by November 1916 and its capital, Bucharest, by December. "A deluge is approaching," Aleksandr I. Guchkov, a reform-minded leader of the Russian Duma and the head of the War Industries Committees, warned army chief of staff Alekseyev in August 1916.[87]

Berlin and Vienna now had enormous supplies of Romanian grain, livestock, timber, and oil without which they might not have survived the winter of 1916–17. Yet Vienna's aging monarch ruled an empire unable to stand on its own at home or at the front. It lost on the battlefields and failed to provide its citizens with the essentials of life at home. "The people in the suburbs of Vienna are starving," Germany's ambassador to Austria-Hungary reported in September 1916. "They are being driven to despair by long waits, often in vain, in queues."[88] Food shortages had begun to appear in the major Habsburg cities by 1915, in part due to the loss of the farmlands of Austrian Galicia, but also due to Hungary's jealous control of its own grain supplies.

On November 21, 1916, Emperor Franz Joseph died. He had been on the throne since 1848, and virtually no one in Austria-Hungary could recall life without him. He had studiously applied bandages of expediency—a patchwork of territories, legislative chambers, parties, ministries, class and ethnic factions, and intergovernmental relationships—to the realm's vexing problems. "No state on the face of the globe," observes historian Arthur J. May, "had a more complicated framework of government than the Habsburg Monarchy."[89]

In response to the growing challenges confronting him—including a war he now knew could destroy his dynasty—he responded with longer hours. Pushing himself harder, as if the elusive answers could be found somewhere among the papers on his desk, Franz Joseph grimly applied himself to a one-man mission to hold together an unraveling mess. "I still have much to do," he said to aides who forced him to bed in his last hours on November 21. "I must get on with my work."[90] Within hours, he was dead.

The new emperor, Karl, only twenty-nine years old, raised high hopes. He "did not have a bad reputation in the Allied countries," admitted Beneš.[91] Karl's wife, Empress Zita, was a strong-willed Bourbon-Parma princess whose two brothers were fighting in the Allied Belgian army. Karl had no role in starting the war and, like his predecessor, could see how it might drag down the monarchy and Austria-Hungary. Yet oppressive measures against Masaryk's national independence movement proceeded. In December 1916 Masaryk himself was sentenced to death.[92]

In Russia, order was crumbling just as quickly as it was in Austria-Hungary. Under withering casualties, material deprivations, and revolutionary propaganda, troops of the Russian imperial army melted away. Anger and resentment grew among the untrained, often illiterate draftees who remained, and inexperienced officers feared their men, especially among the 340,000 troops garrisoned in Saint Petersburg, who were more exposed to revolutionary agitation. "Disgruntled, excitable and armed" was how one historian described the garrison in the winter of 1916–17.[93] Hunger and cold exempted no one, and continued fighting that winter cost the exhausted army another 660,000 dead and wounded and another 96,000 men taken prisoner.[94] The army was a hollowed-out shell whose peasant remnants seethed with anger, confusion, and fear. Indeed, says historian Richard Pipes, "the peasants hurriedly pressed into service in 1915–16 were the mutinous element that would spark the February Revolution."[95]

Masaryk Conquers Russia

DÜRICH ARRIVED IN Russia in the summer of 1916, under Sazonov's wing, and was given a hero's welcome.[96] Despite the fact that Masaryk provided him with six thousand French francs for his work in Russia, Dürich assured the Russians that he represented the Czechs in Prague, had authority to negotiate agreements, that the Czechs wanted the tsar to reign over Prague, and that he would establish a Czecho-Slovak organization separate from Masaryk's. Dürich met with the Russian chief of staff, General Alekseyev, on August 17 (OS). Alekseyev rejected Dürich's request to set up a new organization. Instead, Alekseyev said, the *družina* would remain part of the Russian imperial army under the command of a Czech-born Russian subject, Major General Jaroslav Červinka. Still, Dürich appeared to have won over the Kiev-based civilians leading the Union of Czecho-Slovak Organizations in Russia.

Masaryk believed the Czecho-Slovak forces in Russia must be established not only to support the Russian imperial army, but also to serve as independent units whose aim was national independence for the Czechs and Slovaks. The National Council in Paris was then negotiating an agreement with the French to create an independent army, and most of the available volunteers were in Russia. While some units could remain there, Masaryk felt that most had to be transported to the Western Front. Štefánik, an officer in the French army, planned to travel to Russia to organize the army there.

Štefánik arrived in Russia close on Dürich's heels. While Dürich was close to conservative circles around the tsar, Štefánik, an experienced soldier, quickly won the support of Russia's generals. Štefánik also secured an audience with the tsar in part because, unlike Dürich, he represented an Allied nation. Indeed, French prime minister Briand personally directed Štefánik to represent the French War Ministry and negotiate with the Russians for the transfer of Czecho-Slovak troops to the Western Front. Štefánik and Dürich met on August 28 (OS) at a meeting of the executive committee of the Union of Czecho-Slovak Organization in

Kiev, where again critics complained of the failure to recruit more POWs for the *družina*. The next day, Štefánik and Dürich struck an agreement, the Protocol of Kiev, which recognized Masaryk's Czecho-Slovak National Council in Paris as the supreme authority for the independence movement. Dürich, the vice president of the council, was named its highest representative in Russia, but all financial matters were placed under the control of the council's office in Paris.

Dürich quickly came under censure from the Russian Foreign Ministry, which was angered that Masaryk's council in Paris was again recognized as the leader of the Czecho-Slovak independence movement. The Russian ministry vowed to end the Czecho-Slovak union's role in all military matters, bring the union under the control of the tsarist regime, and ignore any recommendations from the union regarding the release of POWs for service in the *družina*. While tsarist Russia no doubt had an anti-Western bias, the Czecho-Slovak National Council's attempts to raise money through taxes on workers in Russia and create an army on Russian soil violated the sovereignty of Russia, which was also legally responsible for the Czech and Slovak POWs.[97]

Under pressure from Sazonov, Dürich called a meeting of Czech and Slovak leaders in Saint Petersburg in early October 1916, at which he hinted that the Kiev Protocol was not satisfactory and that he no longer wished to be referred to as vice president of the National Council in Paris. Dürich claimed he was unable to cooperate further with Štefánik, and that Masaryk's unpopularity with the Russian government made him an unsuitable leader of their movement. These comments sharply split the exile communities in Russia. "As usually happens in emotionally-charged situations," writes one historian, "slander and gossip began to spread, people began to take sides, and charges and counter-charges were made by both sides."[98]

Dürich proceeded to create a separate Czecho-Slovak National Council in Russia, and he was quickly expelled from the National Council in Paris. Russian officials drafted Dürich's constitution and directed him to introduce it to the émigrés. No pretense was made that the new organization would be independent. It would serve as an arm of the tsarist government, its official business would be conducted in Russian, and it would be funded with Russian rubles. The union was deprived of effective power. In support of this move, Tsar Nicholas II—who in October 1916 at Grigory Rasputin's urging reversed his April 1916 decision to liberate Czech and Slovak POWs for the *družina*—again agreed on January 4, 1917 (OS), to free POWs to join the *družina*. Masaryk noted, "Durich's dependence upon the Russian government made a bad impression in London and Paris, where fear of a pan-Slav Russia was far too general."[99]

In response, on February 7, 1917 (OS), Štefánik presented leaked documents to a confidential meeting of the union's leaders that clearly exposed Dürich as an agent of the Russian government intent on undermining Masaryk. Václav Vondrák, chairman of the union's executive committee and owner of the Prague Hotel in Kiev, promptly withdrew his support of Dürich. In a letter to the Stavka (the Russian high command), French general Maurice J. Janin, head of the French military mission to Russia, fully endorsed Štefánik, who proposed that Dürich be expelled from the Paris-based National Council. Beneš quickly telegraphed his approval and asked the union in Kiev to support Štefánik, actions to which Masaryk later consented. In response, Dürich telegraphed Masaryk, demanding that he disavow Štefánik or accept Dürich's resignation from the Paris council. Masaryk replied that Russian control of Dürich's efforts disqualified him from working for the National Council, but he offered Dürich the opportunity to discuss the issue with him in London.[100] Shortly thereafter, Štefánik replaced Dürich as vice president of the National Council.

But General Alekseyev continued to insist that the *družina* fight only for Russia. As a result, while Štefánik succeeded in undermining Dürich, he felt he had failed in his larger mission to secure troops for the Western Front.[101] Speaking for themselves, the men of the *družina* formally pledged allegiance to Masaryk and his Paris-based National Council. The oath spoke to their very high level of determination:

In the name of human and national honor, in the name of everything that is most sacred to us as human beings and as Czechs and Slavs, in full agreement with our conscience, together with our allies we shall fight to the last drop of blood against all of our enemies until we win for our Czecho-Slovak nation complete freedom. . . . We solemnly pledge . . . never to run away from the battlefield, never to retreat in the face of any danger, to obey the commands of our leaders, to honor our flag and banner, never to beg our enemy for mercy under any circumstances, never to surrender with a weapon in the hand.[102]

Liberation in Paris versus Loyalty in Prague

IN PRAGUE, PRAGMATIC Czech politicians were likewise organizing themselves in opposition to Masaryk and vainly trying to appease their new monarch. In November 1916, in anticipation that the Reichsrat would once again be convened, virtually every Czech deputy joined a single parliamentary club, the Czech Union, except two in exile, Masaryk and Dürich; Šámal in Prague; and seven deputies still imprisoned, including Kramář and Rašín. A Czech National Committee was established in Prague and issued a statement expressing the loyalty of the Czech deputies to the Habsburg dynasty and Austro-Hungarian Empire. Both organizations sent representatives to the somber funeral of Franz Joseph I and to the joyous coronation of Emperor Karl as king of Hungary at Budapest in December 1916. The new emperor responded by commuting the death sentences of Kramář and Rašín to long-term imprisonment and issued an order curtailing some of the army's jurisdiction over civilians. The exiles had clearly not won over a majority of the Czech deputies to the cause of independence.

Following Emperor Karl's accession to the Habsburg throne, Berlin and Vienna signaled their willingness to negotiate an end to the war in a note to neutral parties on December 12. Both French prime minister Briand and British prime minister David Lloyd-George—who had replaced Herbert Asquith days earlier with the promise to prosecute the war more energetically—publicly declined to negotiate.

The leader of the still-neutral United States, however, decided to pursue an end to the war through diplomacy. On December 18, Woodrow Wilson wrote to all the belligerents asking them to state their war aims, opening a door to negotiations.

Berlin and Vienna responded by asking for direct, confidential negotiations, but a startling joint response from the European Allies on January 10, 1917, demanded, among other things, "the liberation of Italians, of Slavs, of Romanians, and of Czecho-Slovaks from foreign domination." While the statement in no way committed the Allies to dismantling the Habsburg empire, one historian says, "the reference to the Czechs and Slovaks represented the first major diplomatic achievement of the Czechs in exile. Despite its vagueness and ambiguity, the Czechs interpreted the statement optimistically—as the announcement of a policy of dismemberment of Austria-Hungary." At the very least, Austria-Hungary would have to restructure its regime and surrender some power to its nationalities. While little known at the time, a furious round of lobbying by Beneš in Paris between December 27, 1916, and January 7, 1917, had led Briand to personally insert the demand for the liberation of the Czecho-Slovaks.[103]

In response to the Allied announcement of their aim to "liberate" the Czecho-Slovaks, the Habsburg foreign minister, Count Ottokar Czernin, summoned the still-docile leaders of the Czech Union and demanded they attach their names to a statement Czernin drafted disavowing the Allied aims. They did so, openly repudiating Masaryk and Beneš and expressing no desire to be liberated from Austria-Hungary.[104] "The split between Masaryk and the Czech leaders at home was complete," notes one historian.[105] This low point for the exiles was about to change, following tsarist Russia's collapse into revolutionary chaos and US entry into the war.

THE SINKING OF the British passenger liner *Lusitania* off the Irish coast by a German submarine in May 1915, in violation of Berlin's pledge to restrict submarine warfare—and shortly after Wilson's own adviser, Edward M. House, himself disembarked from the *Lusitania* in Great

Britain—set in motion the US move toward war. Almost 1,200 passengers were killed in the incident, including 124 Americans.

A month later, Wilson replaced his pacifist secretary of state, William Jennings Bryan, with an experienced diplomat, Robert E. Lansing, whom Wilson and House perceived as a bland, competent clerk who would do their bidding.[106] Within a month of his appointment, however, Lansing began to energetically and persistently urge Wilson to support the Allies.

"What Is This? Stupidity or Treason?"

WORKERS ACROSS RUSSIA had engaged in widespread industrial strikes as early as 1914. The unrest intensified as food and fuel shortages made life increasingly difficult and inflation eroded laborers' salaries. Discontent was especially concentrated among Saint Petersburg's war-industry workers and garrisoned soldiers, whose ranks swelled.[107]

The Duma and the tsar refused to negotiate, while under the influence of the empress, who was under the influence of Rasputin, the tsar hired and fired ministers—from 1914 to 1917, Russia had four prime ministers, five interior ministers, three foreign ministers, four war ministers, and so on. Boris V. Stürmer was named prime minister in February 1916, which increased popular fears of German influence, especially after Stürmer took on the additional titles of interior minister, supreme minister for state defense, and foreign minister—replacing Sazonov.

BY OCTOBER 1916 discontent had reached such intensity that the Department of Police warned that a revolution could be in the offing. By the end of the year, the mood of opposition had spread to the generals, ministerial leaders, and members of the extended Romanov family.

Russian opposition leader Milyukov adopted radical tactics. Anger and desperation swept the ranks of his once moderate Constitutional-Democratic (Kadet) Party. Fearful that the masses would sweep the Duma aside along with the tsar, Milyukov and his fellow Kadets confronted the tsar, demanding Stürmer's dismissal and accusing him of treason.

On November 1, 1916 (OS), the Duma's galleries overflowed with angry crowds, and decorum was the first casualty of the day. When critics of the regime began to speak—there were few defenders—Stürmer and his fellow ministers walked out. Aleksandr F. Kerensky, a rival opposition leader, gave a "hysterical" speech. Pointing to the empty chairs the ministers left behind, he said, "You must annihilate the authority of those who do not acknowledge their duty. They must go." Yet the Duma had heard Kerensky's theatrical performances before. "It was a different matter when Milyukov mounted the rostrum," writes historian Richard Pipes, "for he was widely known as a responsible and level-headed statesman." In a withering speech that listed every failure of the government, interspersing weighty questions with argumentative or hypothetical insinuations, Milyukov thundered: *"Is this stupidity or treason?"*

Unexpectedly for Milyukov, the charge of treason electrified Russia. Despite an official ban on its publication, illicit copies of his speech circulated widely. Lionized by crowds wherever he went, Milyukov found himself at the head of a great mob. "Do you realize that this is the beginning of the revolution?" a colleague asked. Many agreed—including Russia's generals. One who was sympathetic, Lavr G. Kornilov, remembered, "I think that without Milyukov's speech of November 1, 1916, without that manly and daring act, it would not have been possible to arouse the proletariat and the army so unanimously."[108] According to Pipes, "The passions unleashed by Milyukov's speech played a major role in promoting the February Revolution, in which anger over alleged government treason was initially the single most important motive."

Later that November, the tsar capitulated and dismissed Stürmer, yet his replacement, Aleksandr F. Trepov, was abused, loudly and hysterically, when he first appeared in the Duma. In late December Rasputin was lured to the home of an aristocrat and, after a long night of homicidal ineptitude involving one of the Tsar's own nephews, was murdered on December 30, 1916 (OS). His battered corpse, encased in ice, was pulled from a Saint Petersburg canal a few days later. The royal household fell into mourning.

FOUR

RUSSIA UNRAVELS

God, how sad Russia is!

ALEKSANDR S. PUSHKIN[1]

A Revolution in Russia

THE WINTER OF 1916–17 was unusually cold and snowy, even by Russian standards.[2] Through most of February 1917, the average daytime high temperature remained in the single digits (Fahrenheit). Snow drifts blocked rail lines, immobilizing sixty thousand railcars loaded with what little food and fuel existed. This only exacerbated the growing scarcities created by the war, which hit Saint Petersburg hardest. Perhaps thinking his people were frozen into submission, Tsar Nicholas II returned to the front. The day after he left, on February 23 (OS), temperatures rose to the mid-forties, people spewed onto the streets of the capital, and violence quickly followed. For days protesters and striking workers held the streets and skirmishes with the police began to break out, with mobs ransacking and burning police stations.

On Sunday, February 26 (OS), combat units in military gear occupied Saint Petersburg. The soldiers opened fire on the crowds by order of the tsar. Dozens were killed. That night, the city's streets were quiet—chiefly because angry workers and revolutionaries were furiously lobbying garrisoned soldiers to join them. Roughly half of the city's 160,000 troops succumbed, and by Monday, February 27 (OS), workers' protests turned into a soldiers' mutiny that seized power. The unrest was confined to Saint Petersburg, but seizing the tsar's seat of power was enough. Between one and two thousand people were killed and thousands more were injured in Saint Petersburg that day. That evening, the city was under the control of ill-trained soldiers. The tsar's own cabinet of ministers told him that they wished to resign in favor of a Duma-appointed committee, but the tsar refused. Instead, he left to join his family at Tsarskoye Selo (Pushkin), a distant village where the Romanovs had an estate.

At this point, defiant deputies in the Duma and the soldiers and workers in the streets began vying for power. The soldiers and workers created the Petrograd Soviet of Workers' and Soldiers' Deputies, which was led by a member of the Menshevik faction of the Russian Social Democratic Labor Party and made up largely of soldiers. Inviting revolutionaries from other cities to send delegates to Saint Petersburg, the Petrograd Soviet expanded by the end of March into the All-Russian Soviet of Workers' and Soldiers' Deputies. Among the seventy-two members of its executive committee were twenty-three Mensheviks, twenty-two Socialist Revolutionaries, and twelve Bolsheviks. One of the Soviet's first actions was to vote against joining the quasi government then emerging from the Duma.

Ordered to disband by the tsar, members of the Duma instead created a temporary committee composed of twelve members on February 27 (OS). The committee hesitated to proclaim itself a government, but it received many oaths of loyalty from monarchists and socialists alike. The Petrograd Soviet and the temporary committee first met on March 1 (OS) and agreed to release all political prisoners and allow freedom of assembly and speech, which would permit the return of Vladimir Lenin, Leon Trotsky, and Joseph Stalin, all of whom were in exile. More important, the two sides agreed to replace police organs with untrained militias and disband all local governments, destroying any semblance of order. "The result was instant nationwide anarchy," according to historian Richard Pipes. "No revolution anywhere, before or after 1917, wreaked such administrative havoc."

Yet their most promising agreement was to establish a popularly elected parliament, the Constituent Assembly—the revolutionaries were aiming for democracy. On March 2, 1917 (OS), the tsar abdicated. The Duma temporary committee, now known as the Provisional Government, pushed forward with the war, convinced that the tsar's removal solved whatever problems festered in Russian society.

THE FALL OF the imperial regime changed everything for the Czechs and Slovaks in Russia. Josef Dürich's rival Czecho-Slovak National Council in Russia was dissolved. The Third Congress of the Union of Czecho-Slovak Organizations in Russia met in Kiev in late April 1917, refusing seats to Dürich and his followers. The rising number of former prisoners of war in its ranks transformed the union from a mere association of Czech and Slovak emigres into a movement of Habsburg subjects in revolt. The union sent an official message to Prague: "We beg you to sustain your efforts and brush aside promises a thousand times unfulfilled. We must put an end to the second-class status imposed upon our nation by foreign domination. Our people have a historic right to stand in the ranks of free and happy nations. We solemnly promise not to lay down arms until full independence is won for the Czecho-Slovak people."[3] The union established a Russian branch of the Paris-based National Council and appointed Tomáš G. Masaryk its leader.[4]

AT ONE QUIET POW camp, an abandoned, unheated two-story hotel, the Moskovskaia, in Irbit, a small town 125 miles northeast of Yekaterinburg, the joyous news was announced with random gunfire one afternoon. The prisoners were startled by the firing of three shots. The doors of the guardhouse were thrown violently open and out into the snow-covered courtyard stumbled a half-dozen Russian guards, barefooted, carrying their boots, shouting at the sky. The tsar was toppled and under arrest, a people's government was formed—the war would end! Bottles of vodka appeared, strains of the French revolutionary hymn, "The Marseillaise," could be heard, and even the camp's aging, hard-edged Russian military commandant was leading his guards in a celebratory march around the courtyard, at the head of which someone carried a red flag.

Quickly, the barbed wire around the hotel came down, the guards fled, and the prisoners were permitted to wander. "For years we had dreamed of this day, and we were frightened when it came," recalled one young Hungarian POW. "The war was over, but our plight was worse than ever before." The railways were the only way home; trains swarmed with deserting Russians and fleeing POWs clinging to handrails and steps, crowding engines, and lying atop passenger cars. By nightfall, piles of bodies were strewn about the entrances to many tunnels, train hoppers swept off by low ceilings. Other prisoners seized idle locomotives, grabbed the throttles, and sped homeward. Russia was littered with the wrecks of locomotives and passenger cars, the dead scattered about them.[5]

Clearly, getting home might prove difficult.

Woodrow Wilson Goes to War

WOODROW WILSON WAS determined to recognize Russia's new government without delay, which was highly unusual for a stubborn, principled man who evaluated every contingency and struggled with every decision.

SECRETARY OF STATE Robert Lansing informed Wilson on March 15 of Russia's February Revolution, and the news, a Wilson biographer said, "thrilled the President and country." US newspapers cheered a revolution that would allow Russia to be counted among the democracies at war with two German dynasties. "With a single gesture," the *Nation* said, "the Russian people [have] won [their] own freedom and lifted a heavy burden from the shoulders of the Entente. The democratic nations of Western Europe have been emancipated from the handicap of Tsarism and have won a new ally—democratic Russia." The *New York Evening Post* added, "Not since August 1, 1914, has anything come out of Europe to stir the pulse and fire the imagination like the news from Russia."[6] For Wilson, the looming war might finally have a purpose worthy of its price. "The first Russian revolution, which dethroned Nicholas II, had a profound effect upon American willingness to fight on the Allied side," notes diplomatic historian Betty Miller Unterberger. "Wilson was much more willing to fight alongside a young Russian republic rather than one of the most absolute despotisms in Christendom."[7]

Colonel Edward M. House suggested that Wilson recognize the new government in Saint Petersburg only after London and Paris did so, but the US ambassador to Russia, David R. Francis, sent a telegram on March 18 urging its recognition without delay. Wilson issued the recognition order on March 20.[8] Ambassador Francis was able to reach the new Russian foreign minister, Pavel N. Milyukov, with an official letter before noon on March 22 (March 9 in Russia), making the United States the first nation to recognize the new regime.

On March 19, a day after learning that three more US ships had been sunk by the Germans, Wilson and Lansing met to discuss how to respond, but the president continued to resist abandoning neutrality. Instead, Lansing began to use the events taking place in Russia to persuade Wilson to commit to war. In a memo to Wilson the same day, Lansing articulated a theme that resonated with Wilson and would eventually become the best-remembered part of Wilson's war message to Congress. Lansing argued, "the Entente Allies represent the principle of Democracy, and the Central Powers, the principle of Autocracy, and that it is for the welfare of mankind and for the establishment of peace in the world that Democracy should succeed."[9]

A somber cabinet meeting convened on March 20, where Wilson polled his advisers, who unanimously voted for war. Still, Wilson said little. The next day, he issued a call for Congress to meet but revealed nothing of what he would say. What emerged from the cabinet meeting, however, was the very rationale for going to war, which had everything to do with Russia. Alone among the president's official advisers, Lansing made the argument that US entry into the war would transform the conflict into a war on behalf of democracy, linking the effort to Wilson's long-held desire for a League of Nations, then commonly known as a League of Peace. Lansing said, the revolution in Russia, which appeared to be successful, had removed the one objection to affirming that the European War was a war between Democracy and Absolutism; that the only hope of a permanent peace between all nations depended upon the establishment of democratic institutions throughout the world; that no League of Peace would be of value if a powerful autocracy was a member, and that no League of Peace would be necessary if all nations were democratic; and that in going into the war at this time we could do more to advance the cause of Democracy than if we failed to show sympathy with the democratic powers in their struggle against the autocratic government of Germany.[10]

None of the other nine cabinet members present made an argument based on Russia. While the core issue remained Germany, waging a war against autocracy would have been impossible had Russia not had a revolution.

"Nothing, perhaps," Wilson biographer Ray Stannard Baker explains, "better fitted in with Wilson's conviction that war, if it were accepted, must be based upon constructive ideals, than the amazing news that came out of Russia on March 15th—while he was still seeking a decision as to his own course. . . . It is probable indeed that important elements of Wilson's war address on which he was then at work would have been different had there not been a democratic revolution in Russia."[11] Wilson biographer Arthur Link quotes a 1916 statement by Wilson: "I have tried to look at this war 10 years ahead, to be a historian at the same time I was an actor. A hundred years from now it will not be the bloody details that the world will think of in this war; it will be the causes behind it, the readjustments which it will force."[12] Alone, the sinking of ships and killing of Americans did not move Wilson to act. These were the "bloody details" that mattered less than the war's larger causes and consequences. The Russian Revolution, however, allowed Wilson to embark on a course for war based on a long-term cause that he hoped would bring peace to the world via the spread of democracy. "Only the reasonable prospect of redemption—the hope of a league of nations and lasting peace, attainable, now, apparently only through the crucible of war—could permit someone such as Wilson, in whom fate had so mixed the elements, to pronounce the words for belligerency," concludes historian Thomas J. Knock.[13] Wilson himself said, "The Government of the United States is contending for something much greater than mere rights of property or privileges of commerce. It is contending for nothing less high and sacred than the rights of humanity."[14]

Wilson's address to Congress on April 2 made these points with emphasis:

> A steadfast concert for peace can never be maintained except by a partnership of democratic nations. No autocratic government could be trusted to keep faith within it or observe its covenants. . . . Does not every American feel that assurance has been added to our hope for the future peace of the world by the wonderful and heartening things that have been happening within the last few weeks in Russia? . . . [T]he great, generous Russian people have been added in all their naïve majesty and might to the forces that are fighting for freedom in the world, for justice, and for peace. Here is a fit partner for a League of Honor. . . . We are glad . . . to fight thus for the ultimate peace of the world and for the liberation of its peoples, the German peoples included; for the rights of nations great and small and the privilege of men everywhere to choose their way of life and of obedience. The world must be made safe for democracy. Its peace must be planted upon the tested foundations of political liberty. We have no selfish ends to serve. We desire no conquest, no dominion. We seek no indemnities for ourselves, no material compensation for the sacrifices we shall freely make.[15]

That "the world must be made safe for democracy" remains perhaps the most famous of Wilson's utterances, a line that reverberated then, as now, in one of the most highly regarded US presidential speeches of all time. It also elicited one of the most raucous outbreaks of applause in Congress. "Lansing's argument was not lost on the president," says diplomatic historian George F. Kennan. "The view he put forward not only found reflection in the message calling for a declaration of war, but soon became the essence of the official interpretation of the purpose of America's war effort."[16]

ANOTHER FACTOR CONTRIBUTED to the White House's push for a declaration of war: Emanuel Voska's campaign to unearth and publicize the efforts by Austria-Hungary and Germany to finance espionage and sabotage inside the United States. Having returned to the United States, Voska waged a counterespionage campaign against spies and saboteurs of the Central Powers. Known as "Victor," Voska managed eighty-four agents and supplied information to British and US intelligence while also operating a global intelligence and courier service for the Czech and Slovak independence movement. Historian Barbara W. Tuchman calls Voska "the most valuable secret agent of the Allies in the United States."[17] George Creel, the combative propagandist who led Wilson's Committee on Public Information, called Voska "the greatest secret agent of the war."[18]

Vienna's ambassador to the United States, Konstantin T. Dumba, was expelled in September 1915 after British intelligence intercepted—with Voska's help—documents indicating that Dumba was conspiring to foment labor unrest among Habsburg subjects working at US steel and munitions industries. His successor was never formally accredited. German ambassador Johann von Bernstorff and two military aides, Captain Franz von Papen and Captain Karl Boy-Ed, were earlier implicated in schemes to violate American neutrality, including covertly supplying goods to German vessels, which invariably had Czech or Slovak crew members, and the two aides were also expelled.[19] And there was the infamous Zimmerman Telegram, the leaked diplomatic communication named for the German foreign minister who offered Mexico the states of Arizona, New Mexico, and Texas in return for joining the Central

Powers in a declaration of war against Washington. The telegram was given to the US government in late February 1917.

"These great political conspiracies," Vojta Beneš wrote to Masaryk, "by which the official participation of Austria-Hungary and Germany in the crimes against American munition industries [has] been ascertained, have been exposed solely by Mr. Voska." Beneš added, "Mr. Voska's revelations had an immense influence on public opinion in America."[20] Diplomatic historian Betty M. Unterberger confirms this, saying, "During the early years of World War I, the two events which aroused the strongest public opposition to the Austro-Hungarian regime and at the same time engendered the greatest sympathy for the Bohemian liberation movement were the Dumba revelations and the Alice Masaryk affair."[21] The Czech and Slovak exiles exposed both controversies.

ON THE EVENING of April 2, 1917, President Wilson's vehicle, escorted by a troop of cavalry, moved slowly toward the Capitol—its iconic dome's white marble surface aglow in flood lamps against a darkening sky—for the somber mission of asking the US Congress for a declaration of war. Thousands of citizens watched from sidewalks and lawns, waving little American flags, or protest signs. Stopping at the foot of the Capitol building, the president walked quickly past soldiers standing at attention and into the building.

The president entered the House chamber, which one observer called "crowded to suffocation," at 8:32 p.m. "The solemnity of the occasion was evinced by the unbroken silence which prevailed," Lansing said. "Not a whisper was to be heard in all the vast throng."[22] When he finished speaking a few minutes after 9:00 p.m., again a pall of silence descended over the chamber for a few more unbroken moments. "It was the finest tribute ever paid to eloquence," Lansing said. Suddenly, the chamber erupted. Senators, congressmen, the cabinet, even members of the Supreme Court were on their feet, applauding, cheering, and waving little flags.[23] On April 6, the United States officially declared war on Germany. Vienna declared war against the United States on April 8, in slavish devotion to Berlin; however, the United States did not declare against Austria-Hungary until December 7, 1917. The White House was keeping open the possibility of a separate peace with Vienna, Lansing conceded, whose terms would probably spare the existence of the Habsburg realm.[24] This possibility made the exiles extremely nervous.

When President Wilson asked Congress to declare war, the US Army was led by generals who made their reputations fighting Indians. It was ranked by most experts at no better than nineteenth in the world. Few of the army's 5,000 officers and 120,000 soldiers had any combat experience. "They will not even come because our submarines will sink them," German admiral Eduard von Capelle informed the German Reichstag in January 1917. "Thus America from a military point of view means nothing, and again nothing, and for a third time nothing."[25] General John J. Pershing and small units of his First Division arrived in France in June 1917 to the roar of rapturous French crowds, but the first US soldiers did not see combat until October of that year. On December 7, 1917, Austro-Hungarian foreign minister Czernin said in a speech, "It is very easy to speak of transporting an army of millions from America to Europe, but whether such plans can be realized remains to be proved. The military authorities consider it out of the question."[26] By the time of the German offensive in the spring of 1918, the US military presence in France rose to 220,000, but only 139,000 were combatants. Pershing had to recruit and train his own officers and commanders, create an intelligence operation and supply and logistics networks, and organize scores of non-combatants to support the frontline troops, all while relying largely on British shipping, for the United States had few ships, all of which delayed the deployment of US troops. But once the White House, Congress, US industry, and the War Department became fully engaged, they produced and equipped an army large enough to quickly turn the tide of the war.

The Rise and Fall of Milyukov

RUSSIAN FOREIGN MINISTER Milyukov was the real leader of the new Provisional Government in Russia. Fifty-eight years old, he was an adept parliamentarian with the confidence of a schoolmaster but a weak grasp of the passions of the street.

Tension began building between the Petrograd Soviet and the Provisional Government in the Russian capital. On March 1 (OS), the Petrograd Soviet issued "Order No. 1," which placed the capital's military forces under its control and demanded that Grand Duke Nicholas Nikolaevich be removed as commander in chief. While the army could have ended the revolution, Order No. 1 decapitated the army. On March 7 (OS), the Provisional Government issued its first public declaration, stating: "The Government believes that the spirit of lofty patriotism, manifested during the struggle of the people against the old regime, will also inspire our valiant soldiers on the field of battle. For its own part, the Government will make every effort to provide our army with everything necessary to bring the war to a victorious conclusion. The Government will sacredly observe the alliances which bind us to other powers and will unswervingly carry out the agreements entered in with the Allies."[27] "Lofty patriotism," "valiant soldiers," and "sacred" alliances were concepts that did not warm the hearts of the members of the Petrograd Soviet.

In a newspaper interview with Milyukov that appeared on March 23 (OS) that advocated independence for the Czechs and Slovaks, the foreign minister also laid claim to Galicia in Austria-Hungary, the Ottoman capital of Constantinople, and the straits of the Bosporus and the Dardanelles. These acquisitive goals inflamed socialist and antiwar opinion. On March 27 (OS), Milyukov was forced to draft and release a statement saying that Russia did not covet enemy territory but sought "a stable peace on the basis of the self-determination of peoples," a capitulation to the Petrograd Soviet, but one that kept Masaryk's hopes alive.[28] Alone among his colleagues, Milyukov would continue to advocate territorial acquisitions, while the Bolsheviks demanded a "peace without annexation and indemnities." In an April 18 (OS) telegram to the Allies, Milyukov also said Russia would continue to fight "to bring the World War to a decisive victory."[29] In Saint Petersburg, however, people poured into the streets in new antiwar demonstrations. Gunfire erupted, people were killed, and the capital was again in turmoil. The Petrograd

Soviet demanded Milyukov's resignation. The Provisional Government issued an explanation to appease the Petrograd Soviet, which replied by demanding supervisory control of the Provisional Government and its foreign minister.[30] Before a new government took power on May 5 (OS)—the sixth since Russia entered the war—Milyukov resigned.

Russia pushed forward with the war, despite the fact that the war was angering the people, destroying the army, ruining the economy, and feeding the revolution. "Russians, having gotten rid of tsarism, on which they used to blame all their ills, stood bewildered in the midst of their newly gained freedom," says Pipes.[31] The only Russians who knew exactly what they wanted and had a plan were Lenin's Bolsheviks.

Masaryk Slips into Russia

THERE WAS STILL a chill in the air in May 1917 when a "Thomas George Marsden" opened his forged British passport to Russian authorities at the remote northern town and border checkpoint, Haparanda, Sweden, to continue by rail into Russian Finland. So began Masaryk's journey into Russia after he heard of the Russian Revolution. While the revolution moved Wilson in the direction of war, it beckoned Masaryk to Russia itself, a critical turning point in his essential goal of raising an independent Czecho-Slovak army to fight on behalf of the Allies.

By weeks, or even days, Masaryk trailed three other fugitives into Russia. One by one, the men who would create and build the Soviet Union into a totalitarian world power slipped into Saint Petersburg to see the fruits of the February Revolution—for the first time. They were already best known by the aliases they had long used to evade authorities. Joseph Stalin (Josef Dzhugashvili), a loner who looked like a thug even to Leon Trotsky, arrived March 12 (OS), quietly and unnoticed, a fellow exile from Siberia in tow. From Finland, the charismatic Vladimir Lenin (Vladimir Ilyich Ulyanov), in exile abroad for seventeen years except for one six-month stay in Russia in 1905–06, arrived with greater fanfare on April 3 (OS) at the Finland Station, where a small crowd of revolutionaries greeted the famous stranger's train from Switzerland. Finally, on May 4 (OS), Trotsky (Lev Davidovich Bronstein), a Menshevik leader somewhat at odds with Lenin's Bolsheviks, arrived from New York, where he had lived for a few months.[32] Trotsky traveled in the steerage section of a steamship whose first-class compartments held the ubiquitous American industrialist and Masaryk supporter, Charles R. Crane, and his traveling companion, the muckraking journalist Lincoln Steffens, an unlikely pair of unofficial advisers to the White House.[33]

"Halted in the street by a passing carriage," Steffens recalled, "I looked into it, and there was Charles R. Crane. I hailed him. Where was he going? 'To Russia,' he said quietly. 'I am going to the State Department now to get a passport. Get in and come along.'" An ardent advocate of revolution, Steffens was enthralled by the unexpected news from Russia. Aware of Steffens's radical views, but aware also that he and Steffens were among the few people whose opinions Wilson considered, Crane took him along.

In mid-April, Crane and Steffens were among some of the first outsiders to enter Russia after the revolution, where Steffens described a journey through Saint Petersburg's "vacant bumpy streets that felt like a battlefield—to our dark, cautious, whispering hotels."[34] Crane was present as a member of the Root Mission, which was headed by former secretary of war and secretary of state Elihu Root and dispatched by President Wilson to explore how the United States could assist the Provisional Government against its radical adversaries and keep Russia in the war. Crane quickly became pessimistic about what he saw in Russia, and not only because he was robbed of his passport and money amidst the lawlessness there. Unlike the other members of the discredited Root Mission, who returned with optimistic reports, Crane sent Steffens back to Washington with gloomy news.[35] In a meeting with Wilson on June 26 (NS), Steffens explained that the Provisional Government had no power, the Petrograd Soviet ruled, and Russia would not fight. After commiserating with Masaryk in Saint Petersburg, Crane, too, returned home in a dark mood, posing a question in a newspaper article that was destined to be repeated: "What was the world, and in particular America, to do about Russia?"

"WITH OFFICIAL RUSSIA, my relations had not been pleasant," Masaryk said. "Knowing that the Russian reactionaries liked neither me nor the Allies, I did not hasten to Russia during the Tsarist regime. A conflict, which might have arisen with the Russian government, would have encouraged our enemies. But when the revolution had my personal friends and acquaintances in power, some of them being members of the government, I decided to go to Russia and to carry through the creation of an army among our prisoners of war." Unaware when he embarked on the journey that his friend would soon resign, Masaryk said, "Upon Milyukov as Foreign Minister I counted especially."[36]

Masaryk first visited Russia in 1887. [37] He stopped in Saint Petersburg, Moscow, Kiev, and secured the first of three meetings with Count Lev Tolstoy, the author of *War and Peace* and *Anna Karenina*. A year or so later, Masaryk returned to Russia and again visited Tolstoy, having long discussions with him, and the two men met again in 1909 shortly before Tolstoy's death. Following his reelection to the Reichsrat in 1911, Masaryk traveled to the Mediterranean island of Capri for medical reasons, taking with him the unfinished manuscript of what would become his most admired work, *Russia and Europe*, which he discussed with the Russian writer Maxim Gorky, who lived on Capri.[38]

After drafting a "last will and testament" that named Edvard Beneš as executor and leaving it with his daughter, Olga, Masaryk set out for Russia on April 16, 1917 (NS), but his trip was delayed when the ship he planned to take was sunk by a German submarine. He was called back to London to get a fresh report on developments in Russia from Milan R. Štefánik and started again May 5 (NS).[39] From that point forward Beneš and Štefánik led the exile movement in Europe. They did not know that the next time they saw Masaryk, they would call him "Mr. President."

Before he set out, Masaryk had sent a telegram from London on March 18 (NS) to Milyukov welcoming the revolution. Milyukov replied, saying: "I agree entirely with your ideas as to the perspectives which a free Russia is opening to the family of civilized nations as regards the final reshaping of Central and Southeastern Europe."[40] Milyukov followed this with the incendiary newspaper interview of March 23 (OS), in which he embraced Czecho-Slovak independence, going far beyond the Allies in their January 10 statement of war aims. Milyukov called for the dismemberment of Austria-Hungary, becoming the first Allied leader to publically do so. Milyukov said, "our task is the reorganization of Austria-Hungary with the liberation of the nationalities she oppresses. . . . In particular, our tasks include the solution of the Czecho-Slovak question, i.e., the creation of an independent Czecho-Slovakian state that will act as a barrier against the advance of the Germans."[41] Russia thus exceeded France in its support for Czecho-Slovak aspirations, and Masaryk's friendship with the new foreign minister was a key factor in that decision. On March 24 (OS), the Provisional Government confirmed "Regulations for the Organization of the Czecho-Slovak Army," allowing General Jaroslav Červinka to begin building an independent army by May 1917. Yet Masaryk's friend was already gone from the foreign ministry. "I called at once on Milyukov," Masaryk said, "whom I found on the point of resignation—an unpleasant surprise."[42] This was only the first of many unpleasant surprises awaiting him. Indeed, his skeptical views of Russia would be confirmed. When Masaryk arrived in Saint Petersburg late on the night of May 2 (OS), the streets in the city's working-class districts were empty and menacing amidst the damp chill, while wealthier residents crowded theaters and restaurants, their entertainments not much disturbed by the occasional outbreaks of violence. Masaryk and his allies were in control of the Union of Czecho-Slovak Organizations and the small Czecho-Slovak *družina* in the Russia armed forces, but demonstrations, strikes, and street violence plagued the major cities, the Russian army was in disarray, and the new liberal Provisional Government was stumbling badly. Masaryk was even more determined to gain access to Russia's three hundred or so POW camps, but he also dispatched Štefánik to try to recruit volunteers in the United States.

The original Czecho-Slovak *družina*, which comprised a mere twenty-three hundred men in March 1916—with only 343 former prisoners of war—was now becoming a majority-POW unit. By May 1917 the unit recruited 9,249 men, 7,273 of whom were former POWs.[43] Reaching Saint Petersburg shortly before Masaryk, a visiting French minister of armaments and munitions, Albert Thomas, renewed Paris's formal request that the *družina* be transported to France, and Russia's new regime approved the request on May 14 (OS). Masaryk quickly reached agreement with the French military mission to transfer thirty thousand Czech and Slovak soldiers to France. Masaryk called this agreement "the first treaty to be concluded by our National Council with a state."[44] As a result, twenty thousand more POWs would need to be recruited. Beneš began negotiating with Paris for concrete commitments that would support an Allied Czecho-Slovak army.

Despite this activity, Russia hesitated to support Masaryk's recruiting efforts. The Provisional Government feared that the *družina* would encourage Russia's ethnic nationalities—such as the Ukrainians or Poles—to demand independence also, especially since the *družina* and its supporters were based in Kiev. War minister Aleksandr I. Guchkov wanted Czech and Slovak POWs already assigned to labor duties to remain working, as labor shortages were among Russia's many problems. And the more radical Aleksandr F. Kerensky, a member of the Socialist-Revolutionary Party, was deeply suspicious of the *družina*'s service in the tsar's army; he had even considered disbanding the unit in the spring of 1917.[45]

The Battle of Zborov

THE RUSSIAN ARMY was dying. Of the more than 15 million Russians mobilized for the entire war, about 55 percent were wounded, captured, or killed by the summer of 1917. About 1.3 million men were dead and 4.2 million wounded. A total of 2,417,000 were taken prisoner, bringing total losses to almost 8 million.[46] What was left was a mass of armed peasants, untrained, badly led, and demoralized. As a result, control of the army by the antiwar Petrograd Soviet was almost a moot point. By April 1917 two Duma deputies visiting troops far from Saint Petersburg found them unwilling to fight. "Everyone is weary *of fighting*, and the Bolsheviks insist on the immediate ending of active military operations," they reported.[47] The new Russian commander in chief, General Mikhail V. Alekseyev, together with his front commanders, traveled to Saint Petersburg on May 2, 1917 (OS), to inform both the Provisional Government and the Petrograd Soviet that the army was finished.[48]

The Provisional Government desperately hoped that the disintegration of the Russian army, which lay behind the disintegration of Russia, would be halted by a success on the battlefield. It also hoped that Russian soldiers would fight more eagerly for their new, more democratic government than they had for the tsar. As an old Russian proverb says, "Hope dies last." An emotional lawyer who served as a cheerleader for the revolution, Kerensky was always ready to impersonate a leader for the anxious crowds he loved to address. By spring, he was appointed minister of war, which required that he impersonate a military leader. He ordered Russia's defeated army to launch one more offensive—its last. Yet the *družina* pulled a modest victory from the resulting disaster, energizing the liberation movement.

ON MAY 22 (OS), Kerensky removed General Alekseyev as commander in chief and replaced him with Aleksei A. Brusilov. Despite numerous threats from his own men that they would kill him if he launched another offensive, the general organized the Kerensky Offensive. The attack began in western Ukraine on June 18 (OS), with the main thrust aimed at Lemberg (Lviv, Ukraine). Somehow, more artillery had been found to support this offensive and the barrage was unusually effective in smashing the Austrian and German trenches. Leading the attack were new "shock battalions," volunteer units of still-loyal soldiers plucked from regiments decimated by death and desertion, a novelty introduced by Brusilov to get around the fact that the majority of soldiers in the Russian army were now openly defying their officers.[49]

One of these shock battalions consisted of the newly enlarged *družina*—now fighting for the first time in three rifle regiments composed solely of Czechs and Slovaks under the command of Colonel Vaclav Troyanovsky.[50] Although hungry and having an insufficient number of weapons, the Czecho-Slovaks were elated at their chance to fight together. Numbering between three thousand and seven thousand, the Czecho-Slovaks occupied a position in Austrian Galicia between two Russian divisions near Zborov (Zboriv, Ukraine), a small town of about six thousand between the larger cities of Lemberg and Tarnopol (Ternopil, Ukraine). Russian troops on either side of them were refusing to fight, but the Austro-Hungarian forces facing them included two Bohemian infantry regiments, the Thirty-Fifth from Pilsen (Plzen, Czech Republic), which was 60 percent Czech and 40 percent German; the Seventy-Fifth from Neuhaus (Jindřichův Hradec, Czech Republic), which was 80 percent Czech and 20 percent German; and the First Infantry Regiment from Sarajevo, which was mostly Serbo-Croatian.[51]

On July 2 (OS), after a severe, stubborn battle between the opposing lines in the vicinity of Zborov, Russian-uniformed Czechs leapt out of their positions and attacked the enemy with unexpected ferocity and vigor. "I approached the enemy with 10 grenades, and my first rifle came from the Austrian I took it from," recalled one veteran of the battle, Alois Vocásek.[52] The Czecho-Slovaks broke through three successive, fortified enemy lines of trenches and barbed wire on the heights to the west and southwest of the village. Within a few hours, they captured sixty-two officers, 3,150 soldiers, fifteen artillery pieces, and many machine guns, according to the Russian army report, "and many of the captured guns were turned against the enemy." The Czecho-Slovak regiments suffered fairly heavy casualties—almost two hundred dead or missing and seven to eight hundred wounded. No sooner had the men caught their breath than they were forced to flee a larger and stronger German counterattack; the legionnaires retreated with the Russians.

Masaryk said, "Our legionnaires actually met their fellow-countrymen in battle. In some cases, brother fought against brother, father against son, though as a rule they recognized each other, those on the Austrian side coming over to our Legion."[53] Indeed, among the Austro-Hungarian troops taken prisoner at Zborov were many Czechs who then joined the legion, placing the Czecho-Slovak red-and-white ribbons on their caps. Marching toward Tarnopol, Vaclav Koucký and his fellow prisoners encountered men in Russian uniforms shouting questions at them in Czech. "Is somebody here from Prague? Who is from Pardubice, who from Brno, from Tabor?" In this way, Koucký and his fellow POWs confirmed rumors that a Czecho-Slovak unit was taking shape behind the Russian lines. After a two-day rail journey to a POW camp outside of Kiev, the Slavic prisoners were called together and told about the émigré campaign to undermine Austria-Hungary and free its Slavs. "When the speeches ended," Koucký said, "applications of volunteers were being accepted, and I was one of those who applied."[54]

The Czecho-Slovaks were cited for bravery in a Russian report of July 3 (OS). Desperate to recognize troops that fought well, Kerensky dropped his objections and on July 17 (OS) allowed recruiting POWs for the *družina*. He visited the men and promoted their commander at Zborov, Colonel Troyanovsky, to the rank of general. In late July, Masaryk met with General Brusilov, who said the legion "fought in such a way that the world ought to fall on its knees before them."[55] Brusilov agreed to Masaryk's plans to transform the *družina* into an independent Czecho-Slovak corps that would remain militarily under Russian command but politically under the Czecho-Slovak National Council. He agreed to their departure for France and to Masaryk's demand that his men maintain neutrality inside Russia.[56] Masaryk traveled constantly among Kiev, Moscow, and Saint Petersburg, giving speeches to his troops, attending parades, and visiting POW camps to recruit more men. To pro-Russian Czechs and Slovaks suspicious of his ties to the Allies, he explained, "If I say that we must not bet everything on one card, it is because Russia herself is weak, and perhaps others will decide her fate."[57] Given the extreme turmoil in Russia, this was becoming an ever more persuasive argument.

The success at Zborov, combined with the recruiting drive, drove enlistments up. "Militarily," Masaryk said, "things grew better after the Battle of Zborov, where our Legion showed both bravery and strategic skill. Our lads were officially commended, the name of the Czech Legion became known throughout Russia and, as a recompense, the [Russian] Supreme Command ordered the formation of a second division."[58] And the independence movement's "propaganda" machinery made sure the entire world learned of the victory. Ludvik Fisher, president of the Bohemian National Alliance, wrote to President Wilson, "May I be permitted to call your attention to the fact that in the recent successful Russian offensive the most signal services were rendered by the Czecho-Slovak soldiers fighting alongside of the Russians?"[59]

ON DECEMBER 2, 1916, Austrian Emperor Karl had assumed supreme command of the military and, by March 1, 1917, finally relieved Field Marshal Franz Conrad von Hötzendorf of his duties, replacing him with General Arthur Arz von Straussenburg.[60] The military's control of civilian life was eased, yet the emperor seemed not to appreciate that the dynasty—having waged war against its subjects as well as against the Allies—would not earn much gratitude among cold and hungry subjects. "Intelligent persons assure me," reported US ambassador Frederick C. Penfield early in 1917, "Monarchy has food but for two or three months. Nearly every street in Vienna has bread lines, and misery and destitution visible everywhere. People all classes praying for peace."[61] Easing up on oppressive measures did not provide food or fuel, but it did release pent-up anger in Hapsburg subjects. Pressure to end the war was mounting; the emperor's new foreign minister, Count Ottokar Czernin, drafted a highly confidential memo for Berlin in April, painting a very dark picture. "It is quite obvious that our military strength is coming to an end. . . . Any further endurance of the sufferings of the war is impossible . . . in the late summer or in the autumn *an end must be put to the war at all costs.*" In vain, Czernin begged Berlin to announce peace terms.[62] The emperor was equally candid in a May 1917 confidential memo to Czernin about Vienna's prospects under continued German domination, saying, "A brilliant German victory would be our ruin."[63] Admitting such problems, however, would not resolve them.

Good-natured and well-meaning, the emperor's every concession looked like appeasement and smelled of fear. Trapped between a suspicious and powerful Berlin, and increasingly angry subjects, the emperor merely reacted. Shaken by the speedy collapse of tsarist rule in Russia, for instance, he permitted the Reichsrat to reconvene for the first time since the war began. Yet doing so allowed the exiles to resume plotting with the Czechs in Prague, an option that had hardly been possible after Beneš left Prague and communication between the two groups withered. Urgent messages from Beneš and Masaryk now insisted that the Czech members stand firmly in opposition. "Austria is exerting every effort to save herself. Intrigues are of daily occurrence, and they are a source of much danger. We are almost powerless against them," Beneš wrote. "It is only your opposition which can save us, as the formula concerning the self-determination of nations cannot be abandoned." He urged the deputies not to vote with the government "on any point," not to be present for any manifestations of loyalty and, above all, "not to disavow us."[64]

The Russian Revolution, America's entry into the war, and growing Allied support for the Czecho-Slovaks confirmed that aligning with the West had been a smart play for the exiles. They continued to win friends and supporters. The suspicious American Slovaks warmed to the idea of a union with the Czechs as a result of the movement's successes, in particular the Allied demand on January 10 for the liberation of "the Czecho-Slovaks." On February 22, 1917, the Slovak League of America for the first time called for the destruction of Austria-Hungary and the creation of a Czecho-Slovak state.[65] In June and September 1917 the exiles also received declarations of support from the Czech Social Democratic Party.

YET VIENNA'S DARKENING public mood, a new emperor, and the spreading hunger and other depredations of war throughout Austria-Hungary escalated the chances that Vienna would sue for peace, undermine the independence movement, and condemn the activists to a life in exile. By now, 200,000 refugees, deserters, and fugitives crowded Vienna's streets, competing for space with wounded and ill veterans. Before the end of the war, one-half of the realm's physicians were serving with the fighting forces and women were performing one-half of all labor on Austrian farms. During Europe's harsh winter of 1916–17, Viennese homes were allowed to heat only one room and water pipes burst all around, forcing people into the cold streets to fetch water.[66] The emperor furtively pursued a negotiated peace with the Allies, with secret communications about possible terms for peace continuing through March 1918.

Alerted, the exiles began to urge the Czechs in Prague to demand independence. "Any compromise with Vienna in the summer of 1917 would have been an unmitigated disaster to us," said Beneš. "By that time we had a political and military movement organized on a large scale, and as its leaders we had committed hundreds of thousands of our people and their families to a life-and-death struggle."[67]

Thanks to the efforts of the exiles and their supporters in Prague, 222 Czech intellectuals and artists signed the Manifesto of Czech Writers on May 17, urging the new Czech Union in the Reichsrat to stand up for the Czech nation. Though no Slovaks signed the manifesto, it made the first passing reference inside Austria-Hungary to the "Czecho-Slovak nation."[68] When Emperor Karl reopened the Reichsrat on May 30, 1917, the Czech Union indeed demanded a "transformation of the monarchy into a federal state consisting of free and equal national states," as well as a union of the Czechs and Slovaks. Notably, the resolution would have preserved the monarchy.[69] Yet mass rioting due to reduced food rations broke out just as the parliament convened and Czech metalworkers launched a strike that turned political. For the first time, crowds started to shout, "Long Live Masaryk!"[70] The Southern Slavs likewise demanded an autonomous state. The opening of the Reichsrat and its debates revealed how unpopular the war and the Habsburg regime were. "For the general public," according to scholar Joseph Redlich, "these debates proved something of a revelation."[71]

The emperor responded with an amnesty manifesto on July 2 that pardoned political prisoners and asked for all his subjects to join him in an effort to heal the empire's wounds. While more than seven hundred

Czechs were released, it took a special demand from the new Czech Union to gain the release of Karel Kramář and Alois Rašin (Josef Scheiner had been released earlier for lack of evidence), and still the authorities refused to restore their Reichsrat offices and privileges since they were convicted felons. Also released was Václav Klofáč, the Czech deputy who was arrested back in 1914 and not even charged with a crime until the eve of the reopening of the Reichsrat. Masaryk and Dürich were deemed to have lost their seats because they failed to attend the session or seek an excuse for their absence. As a result, Prague's leaders were still effectively banned from the Reichsrat.

Vienna's position was untenable: Hungarian leaders began to speak openly of breaking with Austria in order to keep their Slovak province, while Germans were increasingly angry at the emperor's conciliatory approach to Czecho-Slovak "traitors." "For the first time in Austria's history," historian C. A. Macartney notes, "a proportion of German nationalist feeling began seriously to turn against the existence of the Monarchy."[72]

From this point forward—perhaps emboldened by the electrifying news of the Battle of Zborov, which occurred on the same day that the emperor released his amnesty manifesto—the Czechs in the Reichsrat stopped making efforts to appease the Habsburgs. They devoted themselves to aiding the exile independence movement, as well as working closely with Croat, Serb, and Slovene deputies who sought independence for a Yugoslav state.[73] Kramář and other Czech activists released from prison were met with wildly enthusiastic mass demonstrations in Prague and Kramář publically announced that Czecho-Slovak independence was his aim.

Oddly, the collapsing authority of the Habsburgs went largely unnoticed by a world that watched quite another story unfold on the battlefields in late 1917 and early 1918. At the Battle of Caporetto (Kobarid, Slovenia), combined German and Austrian armies delivered a stunning loss to the Italian army, halting fighting on that front. German submarines were strangling Great Britain's ports, the Allies had lost Russia,

Serbia, and Romania—all now defeated—and they now feared that Italy, like Russia, would sign a separate peace and leave the war, according to US secretary of state Lansing.[74] At the very least, Berlin and Vienna had pacified the entire Eastern and Southern Fronts. All that was left for the Central Powers was to assault the Western Front, where the Allies barely hung on. Austria-Hungary appeared strong and the Allies braced for the worst.

On the Eastern Front, despite the heroism of the Czecho-Slovaks at Zborov, the Russian army was defeated. Another 170,000 soldiers were dead or wounded, bringing total battlefield casualties to between 1.6 and 1.85 million. In the Kerensky Offensive in the summer of 1917 another 213,000 Russians had been taken prisoner—the first time prisoners outnumbered casualties.[75] The once-high ratio of casualties to prisoners—61 to 39 percent in the first year's campaigns and 87 to 13 percent as late as the campaigns of 1916–17—plummeted. By summer, 55 percent of the Russian losses were prisoners and "only" 45 percent were dead or wounded. The numbers reporting sick increased by about 250 percent in 1917, a year without major epidemics.[76] Hundreds of thousands of Russian soldiers deserted, wreaking havoc behind the lines in criminal gangs and crowds that engaged in violent street crimes and demonstrations. Many more draftees simply refused to report for duty. "More than anything else, the summer offensive swung the soldiers to the Bolsheviks," says historian Orlando Figes, "the only major party which stood uncompromisingly for an immediate end to the war."[77]

The Germans pushed back on July 6, 1917 (OS), forcing the Russian front to buckle and the Russian army to retreat. Reeling backward in panic from advancing German troops, Russian army deserters crowded the roads. They murdered officers and robbed and assaulted civilians in their path. Even the Bolsheviks in one unit expressed alarm, sending a telegraph to the Provisional Government that said:

A sudden and disastrous change occurred in the attitude of the troops, who had recently advanced under the heroic leadership of a few units.

Their zeal soon spent itself. The majority are in a state of growing disintegration. Authority and obedience exist no longer. Persuasion and admonition produce no effect; threats and sometimes shots are the answer. . . . For hundreds of miles one can see lines of deserters, armed and unarmed, in good health and high spirits, certain they will not be punished.[78]

Not yet in total control of the Petrograd Soviet, the Bolsheviks responded to the Kerensky Offensive with public demonstrations against the Provisional Government. More than thirty thousand soldiers, sailors, and workers launched the raucous July Demonstrations in Saint Petersburg. Kerensky responded by raiding Bolshevik headquarters and closing the Bolshevik newspapers. He released information claiming that Lenin and his allies were German agents, and warrants were issued for their arrest. Lenin fled to Finland; Trotsky was among eight hundred Bolsheviks who were arrested; and Stalin remained in hiding in Saint Petersburg. The prime minister, Prince Georgy Y. Lvov, his hair turned white, resigned, and Kerensky replaced him on July 8 while remaining minister of war and the navy. A virtual Russian dictator, Kerensky moved into the tsar's Winter Palace, now an armed camp, with soldiers in the hallways and ballrooms, and wet towels, caps, tunics, and gunbelts hanging from statues.

In late August, Kerensky and his new commander in chief, Lavr G. Kornilov, agreed that Kornilov would move on Saint Petersburg with loyal army units and subdue the capital's garrison, which was the backbone of the Petrograd Soviet, now openly at war with the government. Yet at the last minute, Kerensky demanded dictatorial powers, government ministers resigned, and Kerensky fired Kornilov by telegram. In large part because German troops had taken Riga (Latvia) by August 21 and advanced further toward Saint Petersburg, Kornilov refused to obey and appealed to the army to rise up against a regime he saw as under Bolshevik control. Kerensky in turn labeled the general a rebel bent on a coup d'état. While Kornilov was likely trying to save the government from the Petrograd Soviet and the Germans, one historian says, "having been denounced as a rebel, Kornilov chose to rebel." But the troops did not respond. Kornilov and his aides surrendered on September 1. Kerensky named himself commander in chief, with General Alekseyev (who privately referred to Kerensky as "a nincompoop, buffoon, and charlatan") as chief of staff.[79]

To the Allies, the fall of Kornilov "ended any chance of sustaining the fiction that Russia was still fighting a war."[80] The Mensheviks and Socialist Revolutionaries who supported Kerensky began to lose faith in his regime, which had become a one-man show, and the Bolsheviks were able to take majority control of the Saint Petersburg and Moscow soviets by September.

"My Name Is Legion, for We Are Many"

THE CZECHO-SLOVAK NATIONAL Committee, meanwhile, dispatched three hundred recruiters to POW camps around the country. With Masaryk in Russia to lead it and the Battle of Zborov to inspire it, the recruitment drive was hugely successful despite objections from local soviets. Masaryk visited eager prisoners in camps and cheering legionnaires throughout August 1917.[81] On December 1 (OS), volunteers gathered in Kiev and swore their oath of allegiance to Masaryk. The professor delivered multiple speeches on the war, Allied aims, and the need to fight in the west. "A Czech army must know clearly what political aims it was fighting for, and why," he said. "It must swear allegiance to our nation; in a word, it must be our own army."[82]

Since recruiting relied on getting information into POW camps, the main *Čechoslovak* newspaper was enlarged with a Slovak-language supplement, *Slovenské Hlasy* (Slovakia Report) in May 1917. In recognition of the quasi-independent status of the Czecho-Slovak Corps, a new monthly journal, *Československy Vojak* (The Czecho-Slovak Soldier), began publication in early October 1917, edited by Rudolf Medek. A new daily, *Československy Denik* (Czecho-Slovak Daily), was launched by Masaryk in Kiev to replace the *Čechoslovak* in December 1917 following the Bolshevik coup. It became the central organ of the Union of Czecho-Slovak

Organizations in Russia and was edited by a union founder, Bohdan Pavlů. The first issue thanked President Wilson for the US declaration of war against Austria-Hungary. The *Denik's* printing presses followed the Czecho-Slovak Legion to Vladivostok and continued to be published there until July 1920.[83]

From May through September 1917 scores of recruiters visited POW locations throughout Russia and Central Asia—including the Czech-American Voska—and convinced 21,670 prisoners to take up arms again. In the last four months of 1917 an additional 9,780 men signed up. Before May 1918—when the infamous incident at Chelyabinsk occurred—another 6,631 men volunteered, for a total force of 47,420 soldiers, all but 1,976 of them former POWs.[84]

While often extolling the legion, Masaryk remained clear-eyed regarding its composition—the recruits were not all of the same quality. Not all were committed to the independence movement, nor were all of them brave. "Naturally, too," he noted, "not all of them had been prompted to join us by patriotic enthusiasm." Service in the legion offered a release from POW camps, as well as some protection in a foreign country in chaos. About a hundred Russian members of the original *družina* disappeared before the Battle of Zborov, he said, "but the great majority of our men were good, trustworthy fellows who did their hard job honorably and well."[85]

The collapse of the Russian army showed the Czechs and Slovaks how dangerous their world was becoming, but it also presented the legion with an opportunity to arm itself. The Czechs and Slovaks raided Russian armories. "We had to take what we wanted," Masaryk said, "for it was out of the question to make arrangements with the authorities, so great was the prevailing uncertainty and so rapidly did the authorities change."[86] Indeed, in September 1917, in Ukraine, the legion came to possess three artillery batteries when Russian troops simply deserted their posts.[87]

No doubt, many men joined the legion at this time because it offered the protection of armed brethren amidst the chaos of a revolution that caused basic services in POW camps to fall into disarray. Joining the legion may have also seemed the only way out of Russia, and it offered the chance to do so in the company of one's fellow Czechs and Slovaks. Despite the alternatives, it still took courage to join the legionnaires. Not only did the volunteers agree to leave POW camps or their POW jobs in factories and farms to return to combat and possible death, but they did so without a government to supply them or a famous general to lead them. They also knew that joining the legion was a treasonous act, a crime punishable by death, and that reentering combat placed them within the grasp of Austro-Hungarian or German soldiers who could turn them in. Even if they were to survive combat, all of them could be executed should their unlikely, ill-equipped, ad hoc army fail to achieve its wildly audacious goal. In light of these facts, it is surprising that as many as 25 to 30 percent of the estimated 210,000–250,000 Czech and Slovak prisoners joined at all.[88]

Lenin's Coup d'État

IN 1917, RUDDERLESS and nearly in ruins, Russia had lost a dynasty that reigned for more than three hundred years, an imperial army that had kept order, and the food and fuel needed to keep hunger and cold at bay. Virtually no one defended what little was left.

At a secret nighttime meeting of the Bolsheviks on October 10 (OS), with Lenin present, they voted 10 to 2 to seize power through an armed uprising. While worried predictions of a threatened Bolshevik "move" began to appear in newspapers, the Bolshevik-controlled Petrograd Soviet created a Military Revolutionary Committee (MRC). Directed by Trotsky, the committee issued a decree that all military orders must be countersigned by the MRC. In his usual brutal elegance, Lenin urged on his fellow revolutionaries: "Hunger does not wait. The peasant uprising did not wait. The war does not wait."[89] On October 20 (OS), the Bolsheviks began dispatching "commissars" to all military units in and around the capital. Kerensky demanded that the MRC decree be retracted and asked loyal troops to converge on Saint Petersburg to defend the Provisional Government.

On the night of October 24–25 (OS), loyalist troops occupied key points in the capital and shuttered Bolshevik newspapers. Making up his mind to arrest the members of the MRC, Kerensky ordered their commissars ejected from Stavka (the Russian high command) and all military units. The Bolsheviks reacted decisively the same night. The Bolsheviks fielded perhaps twenty thousand Red Guards—a militia of untrained, yet armed, workers—who were able to fan out across Saint Petersburg and seize key sites, meeting little resistance, less violence, and relatively few casualties.[90] Amidst occasional small-arms fire and infrequent cannon fire, the Red Guards grabbed telegraph and telephone exchanges, post offices, the state bank, utilities, bridges, and railroad stations. On the morning of October 25 (OS), Lenin declared the Provisional Government overthrown, then made it real by ordering Red Guards to seize the Winter Palace. Hours earlier, Kerensky had fled the capital to find loyal troops, without much success, yet by nightfall the Bolsheviks surrounded the largely undefended palace and arrested the officials inside. "The legendary 'storming' of the Winter Palace, where Kerensky's cabinet held its final session, was more like a routine house arrest," says historian Orlando Figes.[91]

A Council of People's Commissars (Sovnarkom) was immediately created, with Lenin as chairman, Trotsky as commissar for foreign affairs, and Stalin as chairman for nationality affairs. The Sovnarkom was formed, its creators said, to govern the country only until the Constituent Assembly was convened, and elections for the parliamentary body were scheduled for November 12 (OS). Indeed, convening the assembly, securing peace, and giving land to the peasants were the new regime's first three promises.

Outside the city limits of Saint Petersburg, now in Bolshevik hands, more violent armed clashes ensued. On October 27 (OS), a Cossack army of perhaps six hundred moved on the capital at Kerensky's urging but was defeated at Pulkovo Heights, south of the city, four days later by a larger force of about six thousand Red Guards. The Cossacks signed an armistice on November 1, the same day that Kerensky went into hiding. In Moscow, back-and-forth pitched battles between thirty thousand Red Guards and loyalist troops ended with the Bolshevik seizure of the Kremlin on November 2 (OS).

As it happened, Masaryk was in Saint Petersburg, Moscow, and Kiev as the Bolsheviks battled their way into power in each city. "By some strange chance, I found myself in each of those cities, in the thick of the Bolshevist fighting," he said. In Saint Petersburg, a shell hit his hotel, which was opposite the Telegraph and Telephone Office. He dodged bullets in daily runs between his hotel and the offices of the Czecho-Slovak National Council. He fled to Moscow to avoid the fighting—and arrived in time to find himself in the midst of the pitched battle for the city and the Kremlin. Loyalist troops seized the Hotel Metropole, where Masaryk was staying. "There I spent six days, hotly besieged by the Bolshevists," he said, before the loyalist troops withdrew. In Kiev, he found himself in yet another downtown hotel that was caught in the crossfire. "While we were conferring there, a huge shell fell into an adjoining room but, luckily, did not explode." After the fighting in Moscow, the dead were thrown onto horse-drawn carts. "The stiffened bodies were thrown like logs into the little vehicles, the legs sticking out on one side and the head or, sometimes, a hand on the other," he recalled.[92] Masaryk was as surprised as anyone that a handful of obscure fugitives had seized control of the largest country in the world.

THE VIRTUAL DISSOLUTION of the Russian army enabled the Bolsheviks to leave the war without fear of resistance from the armed forces. "'October' may have been a '*coup*' in the capital," says historian Allan K. Wildman, "but at the front it was a revolution."[93] On October 26 (OS), the Bolsheviks transmitted a Decree on Peace, offering an armistice and negotiations for "an immediate peace without annexations (that is, without the seizure of foreign territory and the forcible annexation of foreign nationalities) and without indemnities."[94] The Allies rejected Moscow's request, but armistice talks were accepted by the Germans on November 14.

Having secured an armistice, the Bolsheviks entered protracted negotiations at German army headquarters in Brest Litovsk (Brest, Belarus), which extended into March 1918. Significant combat between Germany and Russia had long since ceased—but that would change, in part because the Brest Litovsk Treaty would betray the legionnaires to the hated regimes in Berlin and Vienna.

FIVE

THE ODYSSEY BEGINS

*At each step I here take, I see rising before me the phantom of Siberia,
and I think of all that is implied in the name of that political desert,
that abyss of misery, that tomb of living men—a land peopled with
infamous criminals and sublime heroes, a colony without which this
empire would be as incomplete as a palace without cellars.*

ASTOLPHE, MARQUIS DE CUSTINE, *Empire of the Czar: A
Journey Through Eternal Russia*[1]

THE BOLSHEVIK COUP in October 1917 (OS) and the continued chaos
in Russia threatened Allied military supplies there. At the start of the
war, the German navy closed Russia's Baltic Sea ports and Turkey followed by closing the Dardanelles, the channel to Russia's Black Sea ports.
As a result, few ports were available to Russia. Vladivostok offered access
to the Pacific, was ice-free most of the year, and was safe from German
submarines, but it was connected to European Russia only by a journey thousands of miles long on the Trans-Siberian Railway, which in
places had only a single track. Less useful was Archangel, on the White
Sea, which was icebound six months of the year and accessible only by
a single-track railway line. Murmansk, further north on the Arctic Sea,
was ice-free year-round, but the single-track line leading to it was not
completed until January 1917. Because of this diminished port access,
large quantities of Allied military supplies piled up. Some 662,000 tons
were being held at Vladivostok by July 1917 and 162,495 tons at Archangel
by the end of 1917, much of it sitting outdoors.[2]

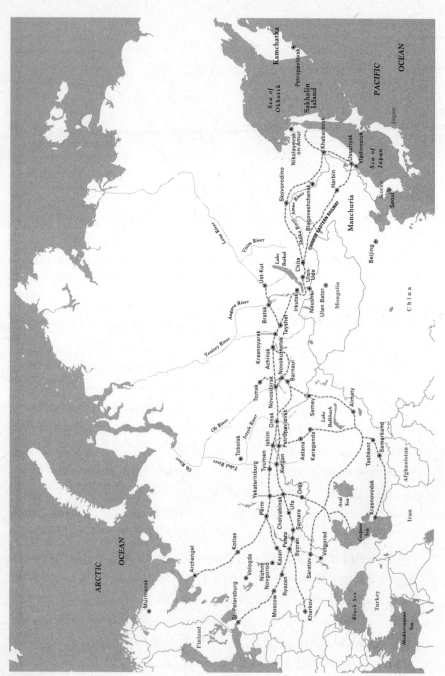

Trans-Siberian Railway, Europe & Asia

Admiral Austin M. Knight, US commander in chief of the Asiatic Fleet, was quickly ordered to pay a visit to Vladivostok. His flagship, the USS *Brooklyn*, arrived on November 25 and remained in port until December 11 (NS).[3] As early as December 21 (NS), US secretary of state Robert Lansing heard that the British and French were considering landing troops at Vladivostok in cooperation with the Japanese. Lansing told Tokyo's ambassador on December 27 (NS) that it would be unwise for US or Japanese troops to enter Russia, yet London's ambassador to Washington, Cecil Spring Rice, wrote President Woodrow Wilson a secret letter the same day recounting a conversation he had with the same Japanese ambassador, who indicated Tokyo was making military preparations for a move into Siberia.[4]

On January 1, 1918, Wilson received another secret cable from the war cabinet in London, urging that Japanese and American troops land in Vladivostok to guard the military supplies.[5] On January 10, the French government made "the first overt and formal appeal for a full-fledged military intervention in Siberia," embodied in a letter from the French ambassador to Washington, Jean-Jules Jusserand, to Lansing.[6] Even Washington's own ambassador to Russia, David R. Francis, joined in. As German forces occupied much of western Russia early in 1918, Francis wired a warning to Lansing on February 21 that Russia was about to become a German province. "I earnestly urge that we assume control Vladivostok and the British and French control Murmansk and Archangel in order to prevent supplies . . . falling into German hands." He renewed this request with greater urgency three days later.[7]

Bolshevik authorities in Archangel began removing the Allied supplies in March 1918, shipping three thousand tons per week into the Russian interior. Given that the new regime had repudiated all tsarist debts to the Allies, Moscow was effectively stealing war supplies for a war it would not fight, which fed suspicions that the supplies were destined for German hands. On the other hand, the Allies also feared a German occupation of the northern ports, even after the Treaty of Brest-Litovsk took Russia out of the war. French and British warships arrived in Murmansk by mid-March, putting a few hundred soldiers ashore, but taking no action, and London and Paris began to urge an American naval presence in Murmansk.[8]

The "Greatest Onslaught" Begins

RUSSIA'S MILITARY COLLAPSE breathed new life into Berlin's Schlieffen Plan, which had been adopted in 1905 and which foresaw a two-front war. With both Russia and Serbia defeated and Allied Italy struggling to hold a defensive line, Germany swung forty divisions to the west. While 178 French and British divisions had barely been able to hold off Germany's initial 147 divisions, they now faced 191 German divisions.[9] Yet Field Marshal Erich Ludendorff, the de facto German commander in chief, knew that he had to defeat the French and British before the bulk of US troops landed in Europe. What Winston Churchill called the "greatest onslaught in the history of the world," launched on March 21, 1918, was under way.[10]

Four days into the offensive, the Germans broke through the juncture of the French and British armies. On March 26, the Allied Supreme War Council placed all Allied forces under the strategic direction of French marshal Ferdinand Foch, leaving "tactical" decisions to individual British, French, and American commanders. The American Expeditionary Force commander, US general John J. Pershing, continued to resist demands to insert his arriving soldiers into British and French lines. The generals argued, the politicians grew doubtful of their generals, the Allies grew distrustful of one another, and tough German soldiers kept coming. Foch aptly observed that he had been awarded "a poisoned chalice."

By the end of the first week, by one count, the Germans had advanced forty miles across a fifty-mile-wide front, inflicting 300,000 casualties, one-third of them as prisoners.[11] Within seventeen days, they broke through the British lines and pushed to within twelve miles of the railroad center of Amiens, while also advancing toward the English Channel ports, intending to cut off supplies of men and matériel from Great

Britain, as well as to doom any hope of a British escape. The Germans advanced more quickly and with greater ease than at any time in the war. The British war cabinet was "unanimously aghast." All the British commander in France, Douglas Haig, could say was that he was doing his best.[12]

He offered to resign, which the war cabinet discussed, then rejected. During this stage of the fighting, only twenty-two hundred US combat troops were fighting with the Allies. The second German attack commenced on April 9. By that date, only sixteen French divisions were defending Paris. Germany held sixty-four divisions in reserve—and the position of forty-nine of them was unknown. "Haig warned London that without reinforcements he would face a very serious manpower crisis even in the absence of the heavy fighting that everyone expected," says historian John Keegan. The German offensive shocked London into shipping more (and younger) men to the front. Yet the war's slaughter saw British infantry forces rapidly shrink in absolute numbers from 754,000 in July 1917 to 543,000 in June 1918.[13] French casualties were twice that and French soldiers had famously mutinied the previous year.

The British and French insisted that American soldiers be inserted into their lines as reinforcements, while Pershing was under orders to create an independent US army, which would take time. Yet the endless slaughter now approached the point where—among men of a certain age who were fit for military service—the dying were beginning to outnumber the living. The Allied commanders met in Abbeville, France, on May 1 and 2. British prime minister David Lloyd-George and Foch pummeled Pershing with accusations and histrionics. A tall man with a trim mustache, sharp eyes, and the confidence to spar with presidents and prime ministers, Pershing stood his ground. His orders required that he create a "separate and distinct" army.[14]

On the second day of the Abbeville conference, Pershing relented. He offered at least 120,000 soldiers in May for the British and French lines, another 120,000 in June, and possibly the same number in July, after which all arriving US troops would be assembled, trained, and organized into an independent US army. Despite the concession, Allied leaders remained bitterly disappointed. Lloyd-George wrote to the British ambassador in Washington, Lord Reading, "It is maddening to think that though the men are there, the issue may be endangered because of the short-sightedness of one General and the failure of his Government to order him to carry out their undertakings."[15] In rare agreement with his prime minister, Haig called Pershing "very obstinate, and stupid."[16]

A decision was also hastily made at Abbeville to deploy an unlikely volunteer army inside Russia. Paris and London agreed to ask the Czecho-Slovak Legion to resurrect an Eastern Front inside Russia, with or without the approval of the revolutionary regime trying to establish itself in Moscow. A more serious problem was that the plan required the legion to split its forces, sending half northwest toward Russia's Arctic port of Archangel and shipping the rest through the eastern port of Vladivostok. Worse, the Allies did not quickly communicate the plan to the legionnaires, who first heard of it from hostile Bolshevik sources.

The Enemy Advances

"To GO FROM Kiev to France by way of Siberia—a fantastical plan, I sometimes said to myself," Tomáš G. Masaryk conceded, but it was the only escape from a Russia on its knees and the German armies closing in on it.[17] Even with its diminished forces in the east, German troops swarmed into Ukraine. The Germans and Austrians took special pride in hunting down legionnaires, who might be killed in combat or handed over by the Russians for execution or imprisonment. The Czechs and Slovaks were doomed unless Austria-Hungary was destroyed.

Masaryk continued his barnstorming campaign to recruit POWs for the legion in Ukraine, warning the Czechs and Slovaks that returning to Austria-Hungary meant a return to combat on behalf of the Habsburgs.[18] The Bolshevik coup also made it more likely that POWs would join the legion. Moscow classified all POWs as "free citizens" and opened the gates of the camps, which separated rank-and-file Czechs and Slovaks from their officers. Russian sentries fled their posts and food and fuel were cut off, leaving the men hungry, cold, and on their own. Finally, as Russian soldiers returned from the front, POWs employed outside the camps were resented. The result of these changes, said one POW nurse, was that "hundreds of thousands of starving unemployed prisoners wandered about the country without the right to return home, since peace was not yet concluded."[19] The Czechs and Slovaks among them sought refuge in the legion.

Once the Bolsheviks opened peace negotiations with the Central Powers, the legion perceived that its obligations to Russia were terminated, since the legion was officially a French military unit and thus remained at war. In the meantime, Bolshevik agents began trying to recruit Masaryk's legionnaires to join the revolution and, with a growing sense of chaos surrounding Masaryk's otherwise idle soldiers, morale plummeted.

Masaryk and his generals issued multiple orders to the troops in the fall and winter of 1917–18, demanding that they remain neutral. Masaryk worked furiously to maneuver through a treacherous and shifting political-military landscape, changing negotiating partners almost constantly. It did not help that—with utter insincerity—the Soviet regime on November 2, 1917 (OS), issued a Declaration of the Rights of the Nations of Russia, signed by Vladimir Lenin and Joseph Stalin, granting the peoples of Russia "free self-determination, including the right of separation and the formation of an independent state." Russian Finland was the first to declare independence, followed quickly by Lithuania, Latvia, Ukraine, Estonia, Georgia, Armenia, Azerbaijan, and Russian Poland. Yet it was the shifting fortunes of a Ukraine struggling to become free that most challenged Masaryk and his men.

Despite promising "self-determination," Moscow feared Kiev's independence and objected to its formation of Ukrainian military units independent from Russian armed forces. The Bolsheviks demanded on December 4 (OS) that Ukraine recognize Soviet authority, while a Bolshevik cell seized control of the eastern city of Kharkov and proclaimed itself Ukraine's government on December 12 (OS).

Masaryk quickly negotiated an agreement that allowed him to evacuate the legionnaires from Ukraine. Yet Moscow had already dispatched a small army under the command of Lieutenant Colonel Mikhail A. Muravyov to take Kiev, and Soviet uprisings began toppling cities across Ukraine. Kiev came under fire by January 15, 1918 (OS). Despite Masaryk's orders, and not for the first time, small units of legionnaires stationed there engaged in the fighting, at least in part on orders from one of their Russian commanders. As many as a dozen were killed or wounded fighting for or against the Bolsheviks, Ukrainian nationalists, or Russians. One of Masaryk's two military liaisons, Prokop Maxa, ordered the legionnaires off the streets and Masaryk fired at least one of his Russian commanders, Colonel M. P. Mamontov.[20] A motley force of six hundred to eight hundred Red Guards led by Muravyov took Kiev on January 26 (OS).

By December 16, 1917 (NS), Paris issued a decree making the Czecho-Slovak Legion a part of the French Army. The decree was signed by French president Raymond Poincaré, minister of foreign affairs Stéphen-Jean-Marie Pichon, and the fiery new prime minister, Georges Clemenceau, who had replaced Briand with promises to fight the war even more vigorously. The details were further itemized in an agreement signed by Clemenceau and Edvard Beneš on February 7, 1918. The Czecho-Slovak Corps recognized the supreme authority of the French army and was legally French, but would fight under a Czecho-Slovak flag and remain politically under the control of the Czecho-Slovak National Council in Paris. Importantly, recruits were to swear allegiance to a Czecho-Slovak nation that did not yet exist.

On December 22, 1917, France and Great Britain signed a formal plan to support any and all anti-German forces in Russia without, it was hoped, antagonizing the Bolsheviks. While Paris urged that the legionnaires be shipped to France, London increasingly saw them in terms of what they could do in Russia.

General Maurice J. Janin, the head of the French military mission to Russia since 1916, was appointed commander in chief of all Czecho-Slovak troops in the French army, including the legionnaires in Russia.

Janin was familiar with the Czecho-Slovaks in the Russian Army and Masaryk backed him. "He had learned Russian, knew Russian military conditions, and had seen our men," Masaryk said.[21] The rest of the officers were to be appointed by the National Council in accord with the French, and Czechs and Slovaks would be given preference. This provided some protection to the legion, though the Allies wielded little power in Russia. "The Soviet government at once recognized the international character of these troops," Beneš said.[22] Although now formally an Allied force, the legionnaires remained subject to Allied disagreements, which saw London, Paris, Washington, and Tokyo pursue competing policies in regard to the emerging assortment of left-wing and right-wing opponents to Bolshevik rule.

THE FRENCH CONNECTION strengthened Masaryk's hand in his approach to General Muravyov in Kiev. Masaryk agreed to have his legionnaires temporarily guard select public buildings and strategic sites, but Muravyov failed to persuade Masaryk to have his troops remain in Ukraine to fight the Germans. After consulting his bosses, Muravyov agreed on February 16[23] to recognize the corps' armed neutrality, promised not to hinder its departure, and agreed to supply it. Muravyov advanced the legion 3 million rubles, debiting French bank accounts. On the copy of Muravyov's letter to Masaryk, which he forwarded to Paris, Masaryk wrote, "A proof that it is possible to do business with the Bolsheviks." He said, "We will be completely loyal to the Bolsheviks and honest with them. However, we will not promise any collaboration with them that would not be practicable."[24] Having negotiated a neutral exit with a second regime in Kiev, Masaryk believed his men were ready to depart Ukraine for their journey across Siberia.

Masaryk's agreement with the Soviets came just in time. As head of the Soviet delegation at Brest-Litovsk since December 27, 1917 (OS), Leon Trotsky debated, hectored, and lectured the Germans—all designed to delay the talks until revolutionary uprisings could occur in Berlin and Vienna, forcing the Central Powers to end the war. This was a genuine anticipation and abiding hope of Lenin, Trotsky, and their colleagues. Dodging this Bolshevik obstruction, with their eyes on the scarce fuel and grain available in Ukraine, German commanders quickly negotiated a separate peace treaty with the anti-Bolshevik government in Kiev on January 27, 1918 (OS), the day after Soviet troops took the city. Trotsky broke off negotiations, insisting that there would be "neither war nor peace." German major general Max Hoffman, who was present, said, "We were all dumbfounded." While his colleagues scratched their heads, Hoffman argued that Trotsky had denounced the armistice—the peace—and hostilities must recommence.[25] Berlin agreed, ordering 600,000 troops to advance into Ukraine, its new ally, on February 18.

The German move forced the Bolsheviks to capitulate—and the Czecho-Slovaks to scramble for safety. The legionnaires fled eastward into Ukraine, often on foot. "The Germans were constantly on our heels," said one legionnaire, Frank Jelinek, who was one of many who fled the Germans through snow, ice, and mud on foot. Jelinek and his group covered ninety-three miles in six days to reach Kiev.[26] In the midst of this bedlam, Muravyov's Soviet forces panicked, pleading with the Czecho-Slovaks for help, but the Russian branch of the National Council of Czechs and Slovaks ordered the legion to evacuate Ukraine entirely by February 21. Bolsheviks and legionnaires together fled Kiev, and the National Council scheduled a long-awaited conference of all legionnaires to discuss their long-range plans.[27] About March 1 the legionnaires were barely across the bridges of the Dnieper River, which bisects Kiev north to south, when enemy troops attacked. A brief but fierce fight over the main bridge in Kiev resulted in five dead legionnaires and fourteen wounded.[28] Further east, their brother soldiers scrambled furiously to obtain dozens of locomotives and passenger and freight cars—seizing at gunpoint what they could not purchase—in order to quickly evacuate the men and their supplies, including legionnaires still fleeing Kiev.

As German troops drove deeply into Ukraine and Russia, Berlin increased its territorial demands on Moscow. By March 1 humiliated Russian negotiators returned to Brest-Litovsk.[29]

A Cynical Peace

TROTSKY REFUSED TO return to the negotiating table to sign a treaty that ratified Germany's looting of 34 percent of Russia's population—54 million people—32 percent of its farmland, 54 percent of its industrial plants and equipment, and 89 percent of its coal.[30] Having no intention of honoring the very terms it dictated, Germany immediately attacked again, pushing beyond the troop demarcation lines in the treaty. Berlin's armies advanced deep into Russia, chasing what was left of its army from the Black and Baltic Seas, seizing Ukraine and the Crimea, Finland, Russian Poland, and Russia's Stavka (high command) headquarters at Mogilev, as well as what are now the nations of Estonia, Latvia, and Lithuania. While fuel resources were tapped, however, Ukraine's farmers did not easily surrender their foodstuffs. German planes had already dropped bombs on Saint Petersburg, which was highly vulnerable to occupation from German troops occupying Finland. Following Allied diplomats, who fled Saint Petersburg for Vologda on February 27, on the night of March 10–11 Lenin moved to Moscow and took an apartment in the Kremlin. By March 12 the Soviet government had officially moved to Moscow, the new seat of Russian power.

While Russia and Germany exchanged diplomats, some Bolsheviks resigned from the government and Lenin was bitterly condemned as a "traitor." One important consequence was that the Left Socialist Revolutionary (LSR) Party quit the government, putting itself in opposition. Trotsky resigned as foreign affairs commissar and prepared to replace Nikolai V. Krylenko as commissar for war and chairman of the Supreme Military Council. Georgy V. Chicherin succeeded Trotsky in the foreign affairs post. And to distance the regime itself from the wildly unpopular "Bolshevik" peace treaty, within days of the signing of the treaty Soviet leaders changed the name of their party, Russian Social Democratic Labor Party (Bolshevik), to Russian Communist Party.

Having allowed Lenin and his fellow revolutionaries to return to Russia, having spent great sums of money to prop up the Soviets, and having signed the Brest-Litovsk Treaty, Berlin and Vienna expected Moscow to return their POWs. At least two telegrams between German diplomats discussing Lenin's return to Russia said that the émigrés would work for "the release of a number of German prisoners."[31] Article 8 of the Brest-Litovsk Treaty that officially ended the war for Russia on March 3, 1918, stated, "The prisoners of war of both parties will be released to return to their homeland."[32] International law was also on the side of the Central Powers. The 1907 Hague Convention stated, "After the conclusion of peace, the repatriation of prisoners of war shall be carried out as quickly as possible." Contrary to its position with regard to the Soviets, Berlin was still using Russian POWs in labor-intensive work needed to free Germans for fighting, while Moscow was recruiting German, Austrian, and Hungarian POWs for the Red Army. As a result, serious negotiations regarding the POWs did not get under way until April 1918.[33]

Moscow returned POWs but was less eager to hand the Czecho-Slovak legionnaires over in part because the German threat might force Russia to accept military assistance from any Allied quarter. Also, under the influence of passionate Czech communists who were trying to recruit the legionnaires, Soviet officials came under the impression the legionnaires were revolutionary socialists—as well as anti-German nationalists—who might defend Moscow's new regime.

INDEED, A STRANGELY cooperative spirit emanating from Moscow allowed the legion's trains to enter Russian territory. The Soviet regime was aware that the legionnaires and the Red Army fought the Germans side by side, and it harbored a desperate hope that the legion—or any Allied force—might yet provide military aid to it. On February 21 Trotsky asked the French for help in stopping the German offensive; the answer from French ambassador Joseph Noulens was affirmative. Late into the next night, Trotsky secured a one-vote margin of approval from the Party Central Committee to accept Allied aid. Lenin concurred: "I ask to add my vote in favor of taking potatoes and arms from the bandits of

Anglo-French imperialism."[34] Unofficial British, French, and US liaisons began urgent discussions with Lenin and Trotsky on military aid.

While Paris promised aid, the Allies were still smarting from Russia's withdrawal from the war and its repudiation of all external debts, much of it owed to them. A top Bolshevik, Lev B. Kamenev, was sent on a secret mission to London and Paris to seek military aid. Kamenev was denied permission to land in France and was manhandled like a burglar in London. Allied capitals had been listening to Moscow's unfriendly speeches and proclamations. "I cannot see," Lansing wrote to Wilson about the new rulers, "how this element which is hostile to the very idea of nationality can claim that they are the government of a nation or expect to be recognized as such. They are avowedly opposed to every government on earth; they openly propose to excite revolutions in all countries against existing governments; they are as hostile to democracy as they are to autocracy. If we should recognize them in Russia, we would encourage them and their followers in other lands. That would be a serious error."[35] Among the Allies, says historian John W. Wheeler-Bennett, "Official opinion was divided between a horrified distrust of the Bolsheviks and a sublime conviction that they would be swept away from power in a few weeks."[36] Initially, Masaryk was also unimpressed with the Bolsheviks, assuming that they would not long remain in power.

Advancing German troops had also struck fear into French and British military representatives in Murmansk. By chance, on March 1, the day when Moscow feared that the talks at Brest-Litovsk had collapsed and the Germans would resume their invasion, Trotsky approved a landing of British troops at Murmansk, which the Murmansk soviet had requested earlier the same day. Desperate for any help, Trotsky replied that evening, "You must accept any and all assistance from the Allied missions and use every means to obstruct the advance of the plunderers." It so happened that the 150 to 200 British sailors sent ashore quickly crossed paths with about 500 Czecho-Slovaks on their way to France and the Western Front. Had the request from Murmansk arrived even hours later, Wheeler-Bennett notes, the answer might have been different.[37] Trotsky sent additional requests for Allied support on March 5 and 21, which encouraged more Allied landings in Russia. Indeed, President Wilson approved on April 4 the dispatch of the USS *Olympia* to Murmansk, but with orders to not be drawn into Russia's internal affairs without prior approval.[38]

At least one rising British leader had also not closed the door on Allied support for Russia. In a secret note to the war cabinet on April 7, Winston Churchill—who would later be accused of rabid anticommunism—urged London to support the Soviet regime if it would resume fighting Germany. Having recovered politically from the Dardanelles disaster—the failed Anglo-French effort to break Turkey's blockade of the Black Sea, which took 250,000 Allied lives, mostly on the Gallipoli peninsula—Churchill had been appointed minister of munitions by Lloyd-George in July 1917. "Not allowed to make the plans," he said, "I was set to make the weapons."[39] Churchill suggested a distinguished Allied leader, perhaps former US president Theodore Roosevelt, be sent to Russia to persuade the Bolsheviks to reopen the Eastern Front as a way to safeguard their revolution. "Let us never forget," he wrote, "that Lenin and Trotsky are fighting with ropes round their necks. They will leave office for the grave. Show them any real chance of consolidating their power, of getting some kind of protection against the vengeance of a counter-revolution, and they would be non-human not to embrace it." The Allies should offer the Soviet regime aid and support, he added, as an effort "must be made to re-build some kind of anti-German power in the East."[40]

To such hopes were added two friendly messages to Moscow from President Wilson. In his January 8, 1918, Fourteen Points speech, Wilson encouraged the Soviets to resist German demands at Brest-Litovsk, asking for "the evacuation of all Russian territory" and the provision of "assistance also of every kind that she may need and may herself desire. The treatment accorded Russia by her sister nations in the months to come will be the acid test of their goodwill."[41] More concretely, Allied ambassadors in Russia proposed on April 3 that they (without the United

States) would help Moscow organize its Red Army, Moscow would assent to Japanese landings on Russian soil, Allied forces would occupy Archangel and Murmansk, but they would otherwise refrain from interfering in Russia's internal affairs.

THE DAY AFTER the Russian branch of the Czecho-Slovak National Council ordered the legionnaires to evacuate Ukraine entirely in late February, Masaryk departed Ukraine for Moscow in the company of British and French diplomats. In Moscow, Masaryk concluded arrangements for Allied financing of the legion, which would eventually total about 15 million rubles; Masaryk was given eighty thousand pounds in Moscow. More important, at Lenin's personal request, Moscow on March 15 gave its official blessing to allow the legion to depart Russia by embarking on ships at Vladivostok. Moscow wanted to rid itself of an Allied army striving to fight a war from which Russia had withdrawn. Just as he did when he departed Prague in December 1914, Masaryk left written instructions for any scenario. While the legionnaires were *not* to interfere in Russia's domestic conflicts, in response to an armed attack, he said, the legion was to "defend itself vigorously."[42] On March 7, 1918, Masaryk's sixty-eighth birthday, he boarded the Trans-Siberian Railway in Moscow, headed for Vladivostok, and from there to Washington, DC, by steamer, leaving his soldiers in the hands of Maxa, Jiří Klecanda, and František Šip.[43]

The Battle of Bakhmach

WITHIN HOURS OF Masaryk's departure from Moscow, advancing German troops rendered his agreements with Kiev and Moscow irrelevant. The legionnaires were split into two groups, one of them west of Kiev, in the vicinity of Zhitomir, and the other east of Kiev, in the vicinity of Borispol. From the west, the Germans moved rapidly on Kiev while also advancing from the north to a point further east, behind Kiev, that would cut off the legion's escape route toward Russia.[44] On the western outskirts of Kiev, men fleeing Germans behind them at times encountered

German units in front of them; at least one firefight resulted in three legionnaires killed and five wounded.[45] "We had no lines of communication behind us, no stores of material, and no reserves," said legionnaire captain Vladimir S. Hurban. "Everywhere there was disorganization and anarchy, and the Bolshevik Red Guards seized locomotives and were fleeing east in panic."[46]

The Sixth and Seventh Regiments of the legion's First Division were ordered immediately to the crucial railway junction of Bakhmach, about ninety miles northeast of Kiev, which an advance unit of Germans had already reached in hopes of blocking the legion's escape. The weather darkened and the clouds hung low amidst wind and rain as the legionnaires boarded their trains, but their excitement was palpable. "At last," said legionnaire Sergeant Gustav Becvar, "we were to have the chance of action against our enemies, the Germans. For years, we had stagnated, idle and restless. Now our chance had come, and against the people with whom we most wished to fight."[47]

After furiously attacking and scattering the small German unit holding the train station, the legionnaires reached agreement with Red Army troops to allow the legion to occupy Bakhmach on March 5. Patrols were dispatched to occupy the three main rail lines approaching the town from the north, west, and south—one or more of them lifelines to the legionnaires still fleeing Kiev—and the men were ordered to seize as many engines and railcars as they could. The Germans approached quickly from all directions and fighting erupted on March 8. The legionnaires stopped the Germans about thirty miles north of Bakhmach and sixteen miles south. By March 10, enemy troops pushed to within seven miles of Bakhmach from the north and five miles from the west. The legionnaires repulsed German attacks for several days straight to defend Bakhmach, keep open the lines from Kiev for retreating comrades, and then to evacuate toward Kursk, over the Russian border. Under fire, they acquired, connected, and organized seventy to eighty trains, each with forty or forty-five passenger or freight cars, boarded the men, and began moving them through Bakhmach.

At one point, when Red Army soldiers joined them, the legionnaires found themselves fighting alongside the Bolsheviks. If nothing else, this cooperation would later help ease suspicions about the legion's ultimate aims. The untrained Red Army soldiers quickly fled, however, most of them leaving behind weapons, which the legionnaires collected. The defensive circle the legionnaires held around Bakhmach was getting ever smaller until the rest of the legion's troop trains began arriving from Kiev. Fresh troops jumped from arriving trains, their machine guns ablaze. Small artillery rounds began pounding the enemy, who began retreating in the face of the kind of resistance the Germans had not seen on the Eastern Front for a long time.

These trains finally brought the legion together: tens of thousands of men, thousands of horses, a dozen vehicles, artillery pieces, four airplanes, and an arsenal of rifles, machine guns, sidearms, and ammunition—"everything we could carry," Hurban said. During the night of March 14, the final shots petered out as the last few legionnaires hustled onto the last trains rolling eastward into the darkness. While Hurban estimated two thousand Germans were killed, the legionnaires suffered almost six hundred dead, wounded, or missing.[48] Another account said the legionnaires suffered 145 dead or missing and almost three hundred wounded.[49] "Now there could be no turning back," recalled Becvar. "France was our goal. The great march of the Legion had begun."[50] The next day, the Germans closed in on Bakhmach, but the station was deserted.

The first legion trains departing Bakhmach for Vladivostok were crowded and had no working stoves, and food was at first limited to weak soup and stale bread. On the other hand, discipline improved as the men realized—with the loss of the Russian army, the Provisional Government, independent Ukraine, and their base of operations in Kiev—that they were virtually alone. They would have to rely on themselves to get to France. "The discipline, so lax during the difficult retreat, had quickly and automatically strengthened," said legionnaire Josef Kyncl. "Everyone felt it was necessary to pull together if we wanted to get out of this bloody chaos."[51] The men began to better provision and organize themselves;

they distributed weapons they had gathered in Ukraine. Occupying two or three cars were the writers, editors, and printing shop for one of their newspapers, *Československy Denik* (Czecho-Slovak Daily), which began appearing every day. The men started to paint and otherwise decorate their cars with leaves, bark, moss, ribbons, and little flags, as well as images of Masaryk and Hus. Slogans included, "Vive la France," "Better Death Than Life as a Slave," "Farewell Brotherly Russia," "Victory or Death!" In another sign of their rising esprit de corps, the legionnaires started to teach each other French.

They would commence their journey against a tidal wave of POWs—their former non–Czech and Slovak comrades in the Habsburg armies—moving in the opposite direction. Despite the Brest-Litovsk Treaty, Germany, Austria-Hungary, and Russia did not sign an agreement to exchange POWs until June 24, 1918, "six months after POWs had actually begun returning from captivity," according to scholar Alon Rachamimov. By October 18, 1918, 670,508 Habsburg prisoners had found their way home from Russia, only 28 percent of whom returned with the aid of repatriation commissions in Kiev and Moscow. Instead, swarms of men with hollow eye sockets, clothed in rags, hungry, sick, injured—perhaps all three—surged westward. By early 1918 an average of four thousand such men appeared each day at Austria-Hungary's borders. On one day alone, May 12, more than ten thousand swarmed across the frontier.[52]

Russia's Thin Metal Spine

A LITTLE MORE than one hundred years ago, two elements were introduced into Russia without which the Russian Civil War would not have been so consequential or so deadly. One element was the Czecho-Slovak Legion, which quickly emerged as the most disciplined fighting force in that conflict. The other was the Trans-Siberian Railway. According to Harmon Tupper's history of the railway, "The Trans-Siberian is inseparable from the history of this bloodshed."[53]

Virtually completed as the war dawned over the neighboring continent of Europe, the Trans-Siberian was designed chiefly to move settlers and soldiers across distant lands Russia first claimed in 1582, when Vasily Timofeyevich, the Cossack known as Yermak, embarked on an expedition beyond the Urals with an army of 840 men. Although Yermak was paid by the wealthy Stroganov family, he claimed Siberia for Tsar Ivan the Terrible, with whom he hoped to make amends for past crimes.[54] Siberia gave the tsarist kingdom at Moscow the world's largest land empire and the reach and resources of a great power, without which she would have remained just another European power on a par with France or Italy.

The Trans-Siberian infused this empire with a thin metal spine that extends from the Ural Mountains to the edge of the Pacific, stretching almost five thousand miles. Siberia's 5 million square miles are bounded by the Urals in the west and the Bering Sea, the Sea of Okhotsk, and the Sea of Japan in the east. To provide perspective, Siberia could contain the United States (including Alaska) and all of Europe (excepting Russia) and still have 300,000 square miles to spare.

In 1891 Tsar Alexander III's ministers announced their intention to build the Trans-Siberian Railway, and the heir apparent, Grand Duke Nicholas—the future Tsar Nicholas II—broke ground for the rail line at Vladivostok on May 19, 1891 (OS). The line would connect Vladivostok with Chelyabinsk, the frontier town on the eastern slopes of the Urals, which was already connected with European Russia's rail network. To save money, the designers adopted building standards far below those used elsewhere. Plans called for only a single track of lightweight rails laid on fewer, and smaller, ties and a narrow, thinly ballasted roadbed, while timber was used for bridges crossing three-quarters of the streams. All this parsimoniousness raised safety concerns, though Italian stonemasons built the massive stone piers supporting the steel bridges over Siberia's widest rivers, most of which still stand. While most Siberian towns and cities were built on rivers, further cost saving dictated that the Trans-Siberian cross those rivers at their narrowest point, which placed most train stations one to fourteen miles from towns. Three miles outside of Chelyabinsk, construction of the eastbound route was begun on July 19, 1892, eventually linking the city with the cities (west to east) of Omsk, Novosibirsk, Tomsk, Krasnoyarsk, and Irkutsk.

Discouraged by the rough terrain between Sretensk and Khabarovsk—where steamships along the Shilka and Amur rivers filled a gap in the railway, but frequently ran aground—the Russians in 1896 negotiated a loan and treaty of alliance with China to build a line from Chita to Vladivostok across Manchurian China, reducing the length of the rail journey by 341 miles. China surrendered a strip of land more than nine hundred miles long to the Russian-controlled Chinese Eastern Railway Company and construction began in 1897. The Chinese Eastern lines connecting Chita with Vladivostok, through the city of Harbin, and a branch line south from Harbin to Port Arthur, opened in 1901. With the start of regular traffic on the line in 1903, the Trans-Siberian Railway was complete—except for a 162-mile missing link around the southern tip of Lake Baikal.

Russia was still putting the finishing touches on that link on February 8, 1904, when Japan opened a torpedo-boat attack on Russia's naval squadron at Port Arthur. Competing with Russia to dominate Manchuria and the Korean peninsula, Japan decided to strike at Russia before the completion of the Trans-Siberian would allow for easier shipment of Russian troops into China—due to the gap at Lake Baikal that was not yet closed. In the peace treaty signed on September 5, 1905—mediated by US president Theodore Roosevelt, who won the Nobel Peace Prize for his efforts—Russia had to surrender to Japan its lease of the Chinese Eastern's branch line south from Harbin to Port Arthur; the southern half of Russia's Sakhalin Island, which sits north of Japan; and an exclusive sphere of influence in Korea. Fearful that Tokyo might one day seize the Chinese Eastern Railway, Russia later built the stretch of the Trans-Siberian between Sretensk and Khabarovsk. The five-thousand-foot-long bridge across the Amur at Khabarovsk completed this stretch in October 1916, as well as the original dream of a railway crossing Russia entirely on Russian soil.

THE TRANS-SIBERIAN WAS an indispensable link between Saint Petersburg and Vladivostok, which lies one-third of a world and ten times zones to the east, so that midmorning in Vladivostok was still evening of the previous day in Saint Petersburg. Even after the Bolsheviks moved the capital to Moscow, Vladivostok remained about 5,800 miles away. During the revolution, Russia's railways quickly began to collapse, in tandem with the collapse of the tsarist regime and its imperial army. Shortages of available locomotives, fuel, and railcars persisted due to poor maintenance, equipment failures, lack of spare parts, unskilled workers, and labor unrest.[55] Fifty percent of all locomotives were out of service on January 1, 1918.[56] The civil war inflicted even further damage.

It was along this long, thin line that the trains carrying the legionnaires began to roll in March 1918, fitfully and with great difficulty, toward the languid port of Vladivostok.

Twilight In Vienna

ACROSS EUROPE, THE winter of 1917–18 came early and stayed cold. Long reliant on foodstuffs from Hungary, Austria had a disappointing fall harvest and Hungary, always difficult, now openly defied Habsburg rule, refusing to share its agricultural products with Austria. The Allied blockade of European ports exacerbated the problem. "The feeding of the army and of the civilian population," one scholar said, "became a question of survival for Austria-Hungary." In April 1918 the army command informed Vienna that "the minimum that the army can ask for is to be saved from famine by the hinterland." On the other hand, "The food supply of the hinterland was on the verge of collapse."[57] By January 1918 Vienna's ministers were warning each other of a "catastrophe," while urgent pleas for food came from the governor of Bohemia, the archbishop of Cracow, and the governor of Trieste. The invasion of Ukraine failed to provide many foodstuffs. "Only 42,000 truck-loads in all were exported from the Ukraine during the whole period of German and Austrian occupation (March-December 1918)," says Wheeler-Bennett.[58] Everything was scarce. Officials appealed for donations of used underwear for soldiers and suggested the dead be buried naked in order to preserve clothing.

Power shortages spread, and hospitals were among many buildings that were no longer entirely heated. Metal shortages forced the government to requisition household utensils and door latches for arms makers. Aristocrats exchanged their luxury items for food supplies; thefts and other crimes against persons and property escalated.[59]

Strikes started to break out in January 1918 in Vienna, then spread to Bohemia, Moravia, and Hungary. Strikers repeated Bolshevik slogans and formed councils, like the Russian soviets, to represent them. After March 1918 returning Austro-Hungarian POWs, combat veterans all, many of them radicalized inside Russia, spread real fear, roaming the countryside in armed bands, looting as they went. The authorities were forced to retain seven combat divisions for internal security duties.[60]

That winter and spring almost half a dozen navy and army units, comprising many nationalities, mutinied, most of them prompted by the hunger that gnawed at the men, rather than because of political grievances. In April Emperor Karl and his foreign minister, Count Ottokar Czernin, warned Berlin in a memorandum that Austria-Hungary faced "collapse." By August 1918 Italian planes were dropping thousands of leaflets on Vienna, stating, "People of Vienna . . . the whole world has turned against you. . . . To continue the war is suicide for you. . . . A decisive victory is like bread from the Ukraine; one dies while waiting for it."[61] Czechs in Prague began to lose their inhibitions about demanding independence.

Despite their efforts to weaken Vienna, Allied leaders throughout early 1918 still denied any wish to alter the makeup of the Habsburg realm. Wilson himself was caught between a sincere desire to promote national self-determination for all peoples against his Realpolitik wish to negotiate a separate peace with Austria-Hungary. As early as May 27, 1916, in a speech to the League to Enforce Peace, Wilson had said, "We believe these fundamental things: first, that every people has a right to choose the sovereignty under which they shall live."[62] In remarks to the US Senate on January 22, 1917, Wilson had argued "that no nation should seek to extend its polity over any other nation or people, but that every people should be left free to determine its own polity, its own way of development, unhindered, unthreatened, unafraid, the little along with the great and powerful." Yet the president informed the French two weeks later that he did not intend the destruction of Austria-Hungary. "All that he had had in mind," a biographer wrote, "was a grant of broad autonomy to the Empire's subject nationalities."[63] Nearly a year later, in his December 4, 1917, request to Congress for a declaration of war on Vienna, Wilson said, "we do not wish in any way to impair or to re-arrange the Austro-Hungarian Empire. It is no affairs of ours what they do with their own life, either industrially or politically. We do not propose or desire to dictate to them in any way."[64]

The Allies agreed. In a speech on January 5, 1918, British prime minister Lloyd-George said that "a break-up of Austria-Hungary is no part of our war aims," and French prime minister Clemenceau publicly endorsed this position. And when Wilson put forth his Fourteen Points on January 8, 1918, as conditions for a general peace, he demanded independence for Poland, but said only that, "the peoples of Austria-Hungary . . . should be accorded the freest opportunity of autonomous development," without a hint that independent states such as Czecho-Slovakia and Yugoslavia might be established.[65] Wilson remained unmoved by the subsequent arrival of a letter from the Bohemian National Alliance, as well as a telegram from Masaryk, welcoming Washington's declaration of war against Austria-Hungary the previous month but insisting on Czecho-Slovak independence.[66] The threat of a separate Allied peace with Vienna loomed darkly over the exiles.

IN PRAGUE, KAREL Kramář, released from prison, became the local leader of the independence movement under the aegis of a new party, the Czech State-Right Democracy. About 150 people signed the Epiphany Declaration on January 6, 1918, which demanded independence and condemned Austrian foreign minister Czernin, who on Christmas Day 1917 had accepted the Bolshevik peace formula—peace without annexations or indemnities on the basis of self-determination of peoples—at

Brest-Litovsk. The Czechs in Prague responded with a demand for representation at Brest-Litovsk, and workers organized a general strike against rationing that quickly turned to political demands. Czernin, an impulsive aristocrat whose temper was easily ruffled, especially by those he saw as his social inferiors, retorted that peoples who had *not* been independent before the war would have to seek any changes to their status within existing constitutional frameworks; in effect, the Czechs and Slovaks would have to negotiate with their rulers in Vienna and Budapest. The Epiphany Declaration demanded instead that "all nations, including therefore the Czecho-Slovaks, be guaranteed participation and full freedom of defending their rights at the Peace Conference."[67] The declaration was confirmation that the Czechs in Prague and the exiles abroad were now united in their demand for independence and no longer satisfied with a federalized "autonomy."

In Hungary, even the oppressed Slovaks began to stir. On May 1, 1918, Slovak Social Democratic Party members gathered in secret in the town of Liptovsky Mikulas (Liptószentmiklos; Liptovsky Svaty Mikulas, Slovakia) and adopted a resolution demanding the right of self-determination for the Slovaks. One Slovak leader allied with the exile independence movement, Vavro Šrobár, called for a union of the Czechs and Slovaks in such a way as to publicly support Masaryk. The resolution was followed on May 24 with a secret gathering of the nonsocialists in Turciansky Svaty Martin (Martin, Slovakia), in particular, the followers of Andrej Hlinka, a Catholic priest, fiery orator, and tireless organizer of Slovak Catholics. Agreeing to a union with the Czechs, Hlinka declared, "Our thousand-year marriage with the Hungarians has failed. We must part ways."[68] Yet at that meeting, and for the rest of his life, Hlinka insisted on autonomy for "the Slovak nation." Across the Atlantic, a Slovak legionnaire reached American shores in January 1918 to consolidate Slovak support. Jan Jancek persuaded Czechs and Slovaks to establish a US branch of the Czecho-Slovak National Council, which would be loyal to the Paris National Council. It was led by eight Czechs and eight Slovaks.[69]

IN RESPONSE TO the unrest in Prague—and perhaps emboldened by the German offensive just then smashing the Western Front—Czernin lashed out April 2, 1918, at "certain leaders of the people" who "find no words of blame for Czech troops which criminally fight against their own native land. . . . The wretched Masaryk is not unique in his kind. There are also Masaryks within the boundaries of the monarchy."[70] Angered by the intransigence, but also emboldened by the apparent weakness revealed in Czernin's outburst, activists responded with a large rally at Smetana Hall in Prague on April 13, at which hundreds raised their hands and swore a public oath to fight for an independent state. Kramář spoke, but the Union of Czechs in the Reichsrat was now unified behind Masaryk's independence agenda.

On the same day that he condemned Masaryk, Czernin publicly claimed that France had initiated separate peace talks with Vienna. This was not true. Emperor Karl had kept hidden moves *he* had made to initiate the talks the previous year. The bellicose French prime minister, Clemenceau, publicly and angrily refuted Czernin's accusation. When Czernin repeated the assertion, Clemenceau released the documents proving that Vienna had sought the talks with his predecessor, Aristide Briand. The public claims, counterclaims, and denunciations created a worldwide cause célèbre. Now Karl was openly suspected in Berlin of betraying Germany and condemned even among his own Austrian subjects as faithless to their German ally; a separate peace with the Allies was now impossible. Cutting his losses, the emperor forced Czernin to resign on April 15. Yet Prague was not pacified. On May 1, 1918, seventy thousand people loudly demonstrated in Prague, demanding more food, independence, and peace, and chanting "Hang the Kaiser." On May 15, Czechs again gathered, ostensibly to celebrate the fiftieth anniversary of the Czech National Theater, but instead joined other Slavic subjects in a loud demonstration of solidarity. Kramář was the principal speaker, the Czech national anthem was sung, and the names of Masaryk and Wilson again were cheered. Before police dispersed the crowds, a secretive revolutionary committee was established, with Kramář as chair.[71]

Karl was forced to travel to German military headquarters at Spa, Belgium, to sign a humiliating agreement on May 12, which ceded effective control of the Habsburg armed forces, defense industries, and railroads to Berlin by transforming an alliance of nominal peers into a military union, as well as an economic and customs union. A separate directive drove home Vienna's subservience by requiring uniform military training and organization; standardized arms and ammunition; coordinated railway construction; and even exchanges of officers.[72] Allied opinion was summed up by the London *Spectator*: "Prussia has annexed Austria."[73]

In retrospect, this accord resembled a suicide pact. That same month, May 1918, the Allied armies began to push back against the Germans in the west and the Czechs and Slovaks ignited a rebellion in the east. With the opportunity of a separate peace with Vienna now off the table, the Allies no longer had any reason to care about Austria-Hungary. When Vienna's subjects demanded its dismemberment, the Allies no longer objected. "The fact remained," historian Gunther E. Rothenberg notes, "that no matter how much the emperor desired peace, the preservation of his dynasty and empire depended, as it had done so often in the past, on the strength of his army."[74] Yet tens of thousands of Karl's troops were turning against him despite threats of courts-martial and death sentences. The emperor was a figurehead, the war on the Western Front only intensified, and a band of deserters and former POWs was coming together in Siberia.

Dancing with Dismemberment

WHILE MANY ALLIED leaders objected to the dismemberment of Austria-Hungary, Lansing had begun sending Wilson memoranda arguing for its dissolution. As early as January 10, 1918, he wondered whether Wilson would have to reconsider preserving the Habsburg realm, which was implied by the Fourteen Points address of January 8, and had been more bluntly stated a month earlier in his December 4, 1917, war message to Congress. "I think that the President will have to abandon this idea and favor the erection of new states out of the [Habsburg's] imperial territory and require the separation of Austria-Hungary. This is the only certain means of ending German power in Europe."[75] On May 29, Wilson decided to support the independence of the Czecho-Slovaks and other Habsburg subjects. British intelligence liaison William Wiseman met with Wilson for an hour on that date and recalled Wilson's thoughts:

> Now we had no chance of making a separate peace with Austria, and must look to the other way—the way which he disliked most intensely—of setting the Austrian people against their own Government by plots and intrigues. We were not good at that work, and generally made a failure of it, but he saw no other way. He intended to support the Czechs, Poles, and Yugoslavs.[76]

Recognition of the independence aims of the Czecho-Slovaks, therefore, had been decided before news of the legion's revolt in Siberia reached Washington and other Allied capitals. It is highly unlikely Wilson was even aware of the initial fighting, which began on May 25. Allied newspapers didn't carry reports on the outbreak of hostilities between the legionnaires and the Soviet regime until June 3, and they were very brief.[77] In a note to Lansing dated June 26, Wilson—now aware of the fighting—said, "I agree with you that we can no longer respect or regard the integrity of the artificial Austrian Empire." Lansing noted, "From the moment that the President adopted and made known this policy, the future continuance of Austria-Hungary as a great European power was doomed."[78] Despite his slow journey to this position, the peoples of Austria-Hungary had long since read their own hopes into Wilson's many speeches about self-determination. "Long before the President knew it," says historian Victor S. Mamatey, "he was in the eyes of the subject peoples their particular champion."[79]

British policy on the Habsburg nationalities was also undergoing a shift. In London in February 1918, *Times* foreign editor H. Wickham Steed, now an adviser to Alfred Lord Northcliffe, director of propaganda in enemy countries, had drafted a memorandum which said, in essence, that there were only two policies London could pursue vis-à-vis Austria-Hungary: negotiations for a separate peace or efforts to "break the power" of the Habsburg regime. The first policy had failed, so it remained to try the second. After describing the ethnic composition of the Habsburg empire, Steed issued a powerful—if very simplistic—conclusion: "There are thus in Austria-Hungary as a whole some 31 million anti-Germans and some 21 million pro-Germans. The pro-German minority rules the anti-German majority. Apart from questions of democratic principle, the policy of the Allies should evidently be to help and encourage the anti-Germans." He urged London to use the Czecho-Slovak exile movement as a vehicle to break the Habsburg regime.[80] Northcliffe forwarded Steed's memorandum to the war cabinet on February 24, just before German armies began pummeling the Western Front. To undermine Vienna's morale, London authorized a massive propaganda blitz. Airplanes, balloons, loudspeakers, and rockets showered Vienna's soldiers and civilians with defeatist news, revolutionary pamphlets, and manifestos. London's Department of Propaganda in Enemy Countries had an Austro-Hungarian section—and the principal directors were Steed and R. W. Seton-Watson. As part of this work, the two departed for Rome in the spring of 1918 to organize a gathering of Habsburg nationalities, the Congress of Oppressed Nationalities.[81]

In early April 1918, Poles, Romanians, Serbs, Croats, Slovenes, Czechs, Slovaks, and Italians gathered in Rome for the congress, pledged their cooperation in opposing Austria-Hungary as an "instrument of German domination," and promised to each seek "complete liberation and complete national unity as a single free state." The Czechs were led by Beneš and Milan R. Štefánik and fraternal greetings were telegraphed to Masaryk in Russia. After the congress, Štefánik persuaded Rome to create Czecho-Slovak units in the Italian Army. Like the accord signed by Clemenceau and Beneš on February 7, 1918, the Italian accord of April 21 was a formal agreement between Rome and the Czecho-Slovak National Council, again giving the exile organization de facto diplomatic recognition. At a ceremony for the Czecho-Slovak troops on May 24, Italian prime minister Vittorio Orlando declared, "Long live free Bohemia!" US ambassador Thomas Nelson Page warmly addressed the legionnaires, making it seem as if Washington had decided to recognize the Czecho-Slovaks. In Paris, Clemenceau had privately assured Beneš on April 20 that he was preparing to recognize the National Council and after the congress publicly welcomed a delegation from it.[82]

Lansing issued a statement on May 29 that said, "The Secretary of State desires to announce that the proceedings of the Congress of Oppressed [Nationalities] of Austria-Hungary, which was held in Rome in April, have been followed with great interest by the Government of the United States, and that the nationalistic aspirations of the Czecho-Slovaks and Yugoslavs for freedom have the earnest sympathy of this Government."[83] The term "nationalistic" went beyond the "autonomous development" phrase Wilson used in his Fourteen Points speech, but still fell short of declaring support for national independence.

Beneš traveled to London on May 7, by which time London and Washington were already discussing the possibility of Czecho-Slovak independence, perhaps in part to persuade Masaryk and Beneš to leave the legion in Russia. The legion's ability to fend off the Germans at the Battle of Bakhmach had sparked London's interest. In a meeting on May 10, Beneš asked Foreign Secretary Arthur J. Balfour for recognition of the National Council. Balfour said that he was "personally" in favor of an anti-Habsburg policy and promised a more official response. Balfour asked Beneš to see Robert Cecil, the British undersecretary of state who had attended Masaryk's first public lecture at King's College in October 1915.

In their first meeting, discussing the Allied need for assistance on the Russian front, Beneš recalled, "Lord Robert Cecil asked me direct whether we would not prefer to leave our troops in Siberia for these purposes. I answered him by explaining our point of view: We wanted to arrange the transport of at least 30,000 of our troops to France in accordance with our original agreement. We had, of course, no objection to an arrangement by which our troops in the East would, jointly with the Allies, renew the Eastern Front against Germany, if any such Allied action was really to be reckoned with." More to the point, the exiles had no leverage with the Allies, whom they vowed to support militarily. In their second meeting, Cecil expressed even greater enthusiasm for Czecho-Slovak aspirations. Then, on May 22, Cecil made a public speech lauding the work of the Congress of Oppressed Nationalities and expressing support for the "liberation" of Habsburg subjects.[84] Still, the French and British met in London and reaffirmed the Abbeville decision to split the legion's forces.[85] In other words, shipping the men to the northern ports was a short-term compromise between getting them to France and, in the interim, joining them with British troops in Archangel and Murmansk to protect Allied supplies and, perhaps, either to support or to pressure Moscow.

Moscow's Opponents Take Up Arms

IN RUSSIA, LONG-AWAITED elections to the Constituent Assembly began on November 12, 1917 (OS), and continued through the end of November. The Bolsheviks were trounced. The Socialist Revolutionary Party won most of the 707 seats, electing 410 representatives (58 percent) to 175 for the Bolsheviks (25 percent). The Mensheviks elected only sixteen members. Out of 36 million individual votes cast, the Bolsheviks received 9 million while the Socialist Revolutionaries won an absolute majority of almost 21 million. In response, Bolshevik Moisey S. Uritsky arrested the members of the electoral commission. Uritsky's attitude was typical of the Bolsheviks: "Shall we convene the Constituent Assembly? Yes. Shall we disperse it? Perhaps; it depends on circumstances."[86] On December 7, the Soviet regime established the Cheka, forerunner of the KGB, which was intended to rule Russia with different means. On January 5, 1918 (OS), the first freely elected representative body in Russian history was called into session. Soviet authorities declared martial law and ordered troops to surround the Tauride Palace, where the assembly was to meet. The Bolshevik delegation, led by Lenin, walked out, the signal for the sailors and soldiers who were "guarding" the assembly to shout abuse at the speakers for several hours before ordering them to disperse. Outside, troops were ordered to fire at a raucous demonstration in support of the parliament. The assembly, the first and only constitutional convention in Russian history, was formally closed on January 6 (OS). Within days, the Bolsheviks officially declared the founding of the Soviet Russian Republic.

Now that the political opposition was defeated, remnants of Russia's armed forces began to reorganize. The Volunteer Army, which would become known as the White army, began to gather in Russia's southern provinces under the protection of Cossack leader Aleksey M. Kaledin. General Mikhail V. Alekseyev arrived to organize it in early November, and generals Lavr G. Kornilov and Anton Denikin, who both escaped from Bolshevik custody at Stavka, joined him. Kornilov served as commander of offensive military forces, Alekseyev was in charge of political and financial matters, and Kaledin was charged with the defense of the territory they held. Milyukov joined them, as did members of his Kadet Party and the Socialist Revolutionary Party, Cossacks, and imperial army officers.[87]

Initially, this White army attracted few rank-and-file troops. Instead, notes historian William Henry Chamberlin, "it attracted into its ranks, in the main, only the bravest, the most reckless, and the most embittered officers and aristocrats." By February 1918 it counted, at most, only three or four thousand men. "The fighting quality of the troops," on the other hand, "was very high; there was a large proportion of veteran officers, and many of the recruits came from families which had suffered very much at the hands of riotous mobs in city or village and were filled with a burning spirit of vengeance."[88] Yet basic food and military supplies were scarce. In late January 1918 (OS) Alekseyev appealed to the French to divert some of the Czecho-Slovak legionnaires to his White army.[89] Masaryk refused this request, although a few hundred Czechs or Slovaks were allowed to join the White army.[90] Under an early Red Army onslaught, Kaledin resigned on February 12 at a meeting in Novocherkassk. He then excused himself, entered an adjacent room and shot himself dead.[91] In one of the Volunteer Army's first offensives in April 1918, Kornilov was killed at his headquarters by a stray Bolshevik shell. As his successor, Alekseyev appointed Denikin. Exhausted and ill, Alekseyev died of a heart attack in the fall of 1918, leaving Denikin in charge.

As MASARYK'S TRAIN was nearing Vladivostok on the Trans-Siberian, Emanuel Voska was summoned to meet President Wilson in New York. Now a US Army captain serving in America's somewhat informal intelligence service and in regular contact with Colonel Edward M. House, Voska was asked about a proposal sanctioned by Habsburg emperor Karl and drafted by Austrian professor Heinrich Lammasch. The proposal called for a federated Austria-Hungary, but retained the Habsburg dynasty and kept both the armed forces and the finances of the empire in central hands, all which would leave the "autonomous" Czechs and Slovaks vulnerable to oppression. "What do you think of it? And what do you know about Lammasch?" Wilson asked. Not much and nothing, Voska thought, but he maintained the united front behind Masaryk that had served the émigrés so well. "No one has the right to pass on such an important proposal except Professor Masaryk." Wilson asked Voska to get Masaryk's opinion.[92]

On April 1, Masaryk departed from Vladivostok for Tokyo, where he was met by US ambassador Roland S. Morris, who had been given the task by Lansing to ask Masaryk about the possibilities of organizing armed resistance to Germany in Russia. Masaryk drafted a fourteen-point memorandum by April 10, urging the Allies to recognize the Soviets and try to influence them to resist Germany. Prophetically, he now believed, "the Bolsheviks will maintain their power longer than their adversaries suppose." While he was aware of the weakness of the Soviet regime, he said—again, prophetically—that its domestic opponents were weaker. He made the long-term argument that if Russia were lost, Germany would dominate both Eastern and Western Europe.[93] Keeping in mind the trains of the legionnaires that were coming up behind him, he said, "Everywhere I raised the question of getting ships."[94]

Masaryk's memorandum angered American, British, and French leaders, who blamed the Bolshevik exit from the war for the German onslaught on the Western Front. French ambassador to Russia Noulens, in an April 23 message to Lansing, argued for an intervention in Russia and, for the first time, suggested including the legionnaires.[95] This was significant, given that the legion was a French army unit. On April 30, French foreign minister Pichon asked his ambassador in Washington to urge Masaryk to be more cooperative. It did not help matters that an American consular agent mistakenly communicated to Washington that Masaryk "wishes to visit Washington in the interest of the Russian Bolshevik government," identifying him as "Professor Masaryk, alias Marsden, of the Bolshevik government in Russia."[96]

"FOR ALL WE care, you can cut each other's throats for as long as you like, but let us through," barked Czech lieutenant Jiří Cehovsky. He was speaking to a rough-looking group of Red Guards who had seized the finest home on the square in the center of the Russian town of Balashov, about 350 miles east of Kursk, and made it their headquarters. The unshaven, smoking Bolshevik commanders wore black-leather jackets without signs of rank or position and carried revolvers in their belts.

Earlier that day, as a train carrying legionnaires pulled into town, the station was already an armed camp of Socialist Revolutionaries fighting the Reds for control of the town. The fighters asked for help against an expected Bolshevik attack. The legionnaires refused, as usual, but they needed to speak to the Red Guards, which prompted Cehovsky to lead three other armed legionnaires to the former home of the town's wealthiest man. Brushing past clumsy guards, the legionnaires entered the house, where revolvers and knives lay about, rifles were stacked in a corner, and several sabers hung from coat hooks. "We have come to give you plain warning," Cehovsky said. "It is true that we have been ordered not to intervene in any way in your internal affairs but, on the other hand, we cannot allow our lives or property to be hazarded by anybody else's actions." Cehovsky's tough talk was persuasive. "All right," replied the Red commander. "We will delay our attack on the station, but do not fail to go quickly. We cannot have you here."[97]

This sort of exchange proved to be unusual. Delays and confrontations frequently cropped up as Red Army officers in each city, town, or train station made impossible demands or issued contradictory orders, openly contemptuous of orders from Moscow's Soviet authorities that the legionnaires be allowed to proceed. Waiting trains were swarmed with Bolshevik agents tempting men with good money to join the Red Army, promises of safety, arguments to remain in Russia and support the new Soviet regime, or threats of what would happen if they continued to Vladivostok.

The Allies made no serious effort to remove the Soviet regime from power in the closing months of the war, when their only interest was whether the regime would reopen the Eastern Front. Despite Moscow's open hostility, the Allies took no significant steps to intervene in Russia until an Allied army headed for France—the legion—came under attack in Siberia. Even then, the Allies responded under the duress of the German assaults in the west in mid-1918. Restoring an Eastern Front was a mirage the Allies could not help chasing that fateful year.

SIX

THE SEIZURE OF SIBERIA

And we are here as on a darkling plain
Swept with confused alarms of struggle and flight,
Where ignorant armies clash by night.
MATTHEW ARNOLD, *Dover Beach*[1]

Revolutions are not about trifles, but they spring from trifles.
ARISTOTLE[2]

WHEN THE TRAINS swayed on the curves, the cars groaned like the bowels of a wooden ship in a storm. The clackety-clack of metal wheels on metal tracks competed with the muffled grinding, snapping, thumping, crunching sounds as the Czecho-Slovak Legion's wooden cars wrestled with their steel couplings. Rolling eastward in March 1918, the men passed through rolling hills, dense forests, and a countryside that turned misty green on wet mornings. Primitive homes of peasant families dotted the lonely landscape, surrounded by endless green or golden fields hosting mounds of hay, men slicing the golden shoots with long wooden scythes, and smoke from crumpled chimneys slowly curling upward to meet the soft white mist descending from low mountains. Such idyllic scenes provided a rare respite as fear mounted among them.

"We are afraid of all that is going on around us," confessed one Czech, František Langer, in a letter to the *Čechoslovak* newspaper on June 23, 1917. "We are afraid for our freedom, because it seems to us that Russia

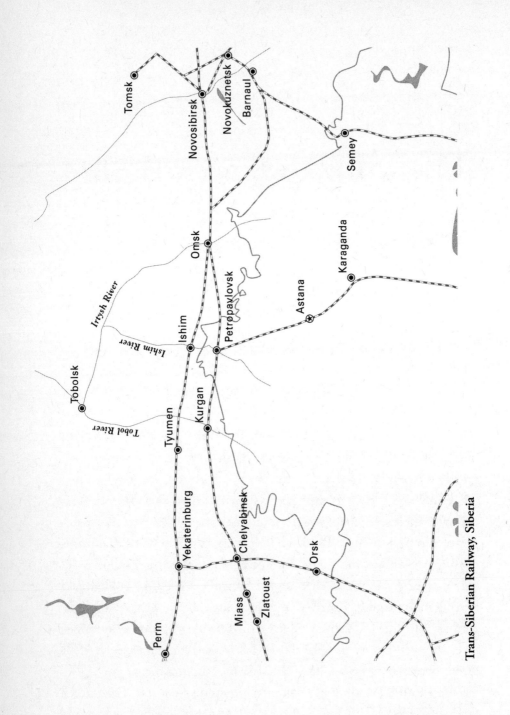

Trans-Siberian Railway, Siberia

is weakening and falling apart."[3] "Good God, how different is this country which our Slavophile hearts once dreamed of," said another, Rudolf Medek, about Soviet Russia. "In the soul of these people we saw heaven and hell. Love without measure or bounds—and the hatred and savagery of an animal devouring its own young."[4] They passed scores of armed Hungarian and Austrian POWs, many of whom were especially angry at the "traitorous" legionnaires. Indeed, the Czecho-Slovak revolt happened, in part, as a result of the Hungarians and Austrians who seemed to threaten the legionnaires at every step. That and a clumsy misstep by the Allies, who mistook the legionnaires for pawns on the Great War's chessboard.

The Unsung Internationalists

WHILE SOVIET LEADERS long complained about Allied intervention in the Russian Civil War, the Soviets themselves deployed many foreign troops in the conflict in the form of ex-POWs of the Central Powers who were persuaded or coerced into joining the Red Army. This phenomenon was a key to the Allied intervention—but it was entirely confused with baseless rumors that the Central Powers were arming German and Austro-Hungarian POWs in Russia.

The tsarist regime's efforts to provide better treatment for Slavic POWs and to recruit Czechs and Slovaks into the *družina*, as well as the Provisional Government's support for Czecho-Slovak independence, angered Austrian, German, and Hungarian POWs, many of whom saw in the Bolshevik coup a welcome change, a shared desire to end the war, and, for POWs working in factories, a new advocate for their rights. As a result, many of them fought alongside the Bolsheviks in the November 1917 coup. In its wake, Red Guard units made up of freed POWs (at least in part) were established in more than four hundred cities and towns, with units of one hundred or more in seventy-six cities. The vast majority of these POWs were Austrians or Hungarians, natural enemies of the "traitorous" Czecho-Slovaks.[5] Several hundred Hungarian POWs helped the Bolsheviks seize

Moscow, Kiev, and the cities of Irkutsk, Khabarovsk, Krasnoyarsk, and Omsk along the Trans-Siberian Railway.[6] Scholar Arnold Krammer says that these POWs helped establish Soviet rule in sixteen cities.[7]

POWs succumbed to an array of inducements to join these so-called Internationalist Brigades. Ideological sympathy was a factor for some, but fatter salaries (recruits got 150 to 200 rubles per month), food and shelter, physical protection, escape from the camps, and promises that they could go home—once Soviet rule was secured—were other reasons.[8] "Men who had been exposed to socialist agitation for two or three years in prison camps," historian Rudolf L. Tokes says, "found it difficult to resist the incentives of food, drink, warm clothing, a new pair of boots, and freedom of movement within the confines of a city or district, especially with such incentives reinforced by popular political slogans."[9] Moscow issued leaflets and newspapers in the languages of the POWs.[10] Those who resisted could face reprisals, especially at camps where Internationalists served as commandants or guards. "Here the Hungarians in particular inaugurated a sheer reign of terror," said a nurse. "By humiliations of all kinds, by starvation and ill-treatment they tried to force their comrades to adopt Bolshevism."[11] The Internationalists also threatened the legionnaires with the notion that Moscow might disarm them and repatriate them to Austria-Hungary, where they would face death or imprisonment.[12] Sometimes, the choices were presented starkly to POWs; one German prisoner who knew Russian and sometimes served as an interpreter, Edwin Dwinger, recounted an exchange with the new Bolshevik commander of his Siberian POW camp somewhere between Chita and Khabarovsk:

> You understand Russian? Good, write as follows. Whoever supports the White troops will be shot. Have you got that? Whoever gives information to the White troops will be shot. Have you got that? Whoever among the prisoners of war will enter our ranks at once becomes a free Russian citizen and will be given pay and arms—have you got that also?—like our soldiers. Commandant Pastuchow. Finished.[13]

MOSCOW SPONSORED MANY conferences to recruit Internationalists in early 1918, including the Conference of International Social Democratic Prisoners of War on March 14, which was attended by Vladimir Lenin. Other than Russian, the official languages of the All-Russian Congress of Prisoners of War in Moscow on April 13, 1918, were German and Hungarian—which must have sounded ominous to Czech and Slovak ears, as the vast majority of German-speaking POWs in Russia were from Austria-Hungary. Recruitment of POWs was directed by the Federation of Foreign Groups of the Russian Community Party—forerunner of the Communist International—whose 1,791 delegates included 724 Hungarians, 400 Germans, and 438 Czechs and Slovaks.[14]

Three scholars conclude that 80,000 to 100,000 Hungarians fought for the Red Army in the Russian Civil War, and they lean toward the higher figure.[15] Yet if the representation of Hungarians among the Internationalists reflected the same proportion of elected delegates to the Federation of Foreign Groups of the Russian Community Party—724 out of 1,791 delegates, or 40 percent—then the total number of Internationalists could easily have been 200,000. Indeed, two scholars peg the number of Internationalists at 180,000 to 190,000 armed POWs. Krammer says that "the accepted number" of German, Austrian, and Hungarian POWs joining the Red Army or its Internationalist Brigades was 190,000, approximately 100,000 Hungarians and 90,000 Austrians and other Germans. "Most eventually fought," he says, "on all of the internal fronts during the civil war."[16] Historian John Bradley says that the Internationalists included twelve nationalities and 182,000 men.[17] This estimate confirms that these POWs constituted a force at least 50 percent larger than the Czecho-Slovak Legion. The legionnaires encountered these POWs as their trains moved through Siberia.

The presence of Austrian and Hungarian soldiers gave rise to reasonable fears among the legionnaires of collusion between Moscow and the Central Powers, who would execute the legionnaires if they were captured. After all, Soviet Moscow had signed a peace treaty with the Central Powers and both sides quickly exchanged diplomats, the Bolsheviks' first diplomatic relations. The Czecho-Slovaks, notes John Erickson, "were increasingly convinced of German-Bolshevik collusion. Conspiracy theories were given added weight by the Bolshevik arming of prisoners of war in Siberia."[18] The Internationalist Brigades posed a clear and present danger to the legionnaires, especially if they resisted the Soviet regime.

PERHAPS WORSE, MOSCOW was also recruiting Czechs and Slovaks, and these men would bear a large share of the responsibility for the legion's revolt, as they represented the greatest threat to the legion's unity in a hostile environment. Hundreds if not thousands of Czechs and Slovaks supported the Bolsheviks and even fought and killed fellow Czechs and Slovaks in the streets of Kiev in the fighting for Ukraine. After the Red Army seized Kiev on January 26, 1918 (OS), Soviet general Mikhail A. Muravyov encouraged a campaign to recruit more Czechs and Slovaks. A few more than two hundred signed up from among the legionnaires, Masaryk said, "and several of them came back the next day."[19] Muravyov's own chief of staff was a Czech, one of about five to ten thousand Czech and Slovak POWs throughout Russia who eventually joined the Reds, which was particularly threatening to the legion's stability.[20] What was galling to still-loyal legionnaires was that most of these Czechs, according to the legion's leadership, "were bad soldiers and men of weak character. They went over to the Soviet army for mercenary reasons, the munificent salaries, the opportunity to at once assume a position of high rank, fear of the French front, petty personal spite—these were the motives that led these men to desert their comrades."[21] Some of these men were placed in charge of Moscow's decisions regarding all Czecho-Slovaks and began advising Trotsky that there were 15,000 Bolshevik sympathizers in the legion.[22] "The indignation against the Czech Red Guards grew a hundred times," said Czech legionnaire Josef Kyncl as the legionnaires' trains entered Russia. "Everyone knew that it was mainly them who set the soviets against us."[23]

One Czech recruited by the Soviets was Jaroslav Hašek, who after the war achieved acclaim as author of the classic antiwar novel, *The Good*

Soldier Švejk.[24] Born the son of an alcoholic father who died when Hašek was thirteen, Hašek was inducted into the Ninety-First Regiment from Budweis (České Budějovice) in Bohemia in early 1915 and left for the front on June 30. Hašek quickly saw intense fighting, his battalion was decimated, and he was taken prisoner. Wallowing in a disease-ridden Russian POW camp near Samara, he was visited by recruiters for the *družina* in early 1916. Hašek quickly volunteered, becoming a recruiter and a writer for the *Čechoslovan*.

Hašek leaned leftward in politics but had a weakness for anarchism and thus could not keep to a consistent course. The Russian Revolution threw him into a tailspin of political intrigues aimed against the *družina*, where he became a pariah. Hašek redeemed himself by fighting bravely in the Battle of Zborov, after which he was awarded a medal, promoted to lance corporal, and rejoined the staff of the *Čechoslovan*—where he quickly turned his pen against the Bolsheviks. Yet as the legion evacuated Ukraine, Hašek performed another about-face and fell in with the pro-Bolshevik Czechs, called for the arrest of the legion's leaders, and became involved in an attempted putsch against those leaders. The putsch failed, but there were thousands of Czechs like Hašek.

IN THE WAKE of the Bolshevik coup in late October 1917 (OS), a conference of Social Democrats was held in November in Kiev, where the legion was represented by twenty-seven of the seventy-one delegates.[25] However, twenty-five of the twenty-seven legion delegates walked out of the conference in opposition to Bolshevik influence. Tomáš G. Masaryk himself acknowledged that at least some of his soldiers in Russia were at each other's political throats. In an article in *Československy Vojak* (The Czecho-Slovak Soldier) on December 6, 1917, he said, "the Bolsheviks have attacked us and by organizing their hostile activities declared war on us. We have the right to defend ourselves." Masaryk's commander in chief, General Vladimir N. Shokorov, and his chief of staff, Mikhail K. Diterikhs, were angered by Bolshevik agitation and deeply worried about morale. "The confusion and the class hatred that had ruled all around us began to seep even into our military, in which one could detect some seething," said legionnaire Josef Kohák.[26] Events came to a head on February 17 at a meeting demanded by the radicals, who suggested amidst the fighting in Kiev that the leaders of the Russian branch of the National Council resign and new leaders be elected, an election the radicals hoped to win. Mounting the rostrum at the assembly and speaking with great passion and conviction, Masaryk won over most of the participants. While joining the Bolsheviks and remaining in Russia might never have been all that attractive to most legionnaires, what no doubt swayed a few votes were the advancing German troops, which prompted the urgent order for the legion to evacuate Ukraine by February 21.

Czech and Slovak communists continued their campaign by, among other actions, writing articles for *Pravda* criticizing Masaryk, the legion, and the National Council in Paris, labeling them counterrevolutionaries. On February 20, a Congress of Prisoners of War Internationalists was held in Saint Petersburg, which established the first Internationalist Brigade that included Czechs and Slovaks. Along with the entire Soviet regime, radical Czechs and Slovaks moved to Moscow in March, where they began publishing a periodical, *Prukopnik* (The Pioneer). The first issue contained an article by the former legionnaire, Jaroslav Hašek, who declared:

> We shall not betray Russia. We shall not serve the imperialists. Nor shall we go to France. We are convinced that if each man in the Czecho-Slovak Army were informed about our attitudes, the whole army, as one man, would rise up against its treacherous leadership. We are sure that the army would then declare its readiness to fight on the side of the Russian revolution under all circumstances and to the very last man.

Not the most stalwart colleague, Hašek soon ran afoul of the Bolsheviks in Moscow, too. "His criticism of its unfulfilled promises, brutal despotism, and wanton destruction and bloodshed made him a candidate for a purge," says historian Victor M. Fic. Hašek was suspended from the party at the First Congress of the Czecho-Slovak Bolsheviks in Moscow in May 1918.[27]

The heated arguments that divided the legionnaires created anxiety and fear among them, which were exacerbated by the fact that most of their experienced Russian officers had been dismissed or had departed voluntarily when it became apparent that they were suspected—by the Bolsheviks, if not always the legionnaires—of holding counterrevolutionary ideas. Although the Russians Diterikhs and Shokorov remained the top two commanders, the legion was slowly coming under the leadership of Czechs in their late twenties or early thirties, such as Lieutenant Stanislav Čeček; Lieutenant Jan Syrový, who wore an eye patch to cover the eye he lost in the Battle of Zborov; and Captain Radola Gajda, the youngest and most daring of the three young officers. While these youthful men would distinguish themselves in the fighting to come, they initially lacked command experience. "There was," according to Josef Kalvoda, "a serious morale problem in the Legion."[28] Still, growing numbers of Czechs and Slovaks were joining the legion as its trains crossed western Ukraine and entered Russia and as news of its existence was still just reaching some POWs.

Fleeing the advancing Germans in Ukraine, the Internationalists moved their operations to Penza, a Russian city just west of Ukraine and a key junction through which the trains of the legion would have to pass. By March the legion's seventy to eighty trains were moving through western Ukraine toward Russia, while the Internationalist Brigades, including Czech and Slovak members, were organizing in Penza, one said, "to prevent the 50,000 men from being dragged against their will, as cannon fodder, to France to be slaughtered in defending the interests of imperialists."[29]

THIS UNDERLYING, MULTILAYERED hostility led to a pronounced difference in how the legionnaires treated the Internationalists and the Russians they encountered in combat; Internationalists who actually fought the legionnaires were executed.

"The facts are these," said Czech captain Vladimir S. Hurban, the officer aboard the first train to cross Russia,

> Russian Bolsheviks taken by our troops were disarmed and sent home, but the Magyars and German prisoners, taken with arms in hand, were killed. Our purpose was made known to them beforehand. The Austrians hanged all of our wounded whom they captured on the Italian Front, and they attacked one of our trains of wounded in Siberia. Four years of a struggle for life have taught us to be on guard. We did no harm to German or Magyar prisoners who did not oppose us. Although they were our enemies; we could have killed thousands and thousands of them, but we allowed them to leave Siberia in peace, if they desired to go home. When, however, they treacherously attacked us, they were of necessity made harmless. We made an official announcement that every German and Magyar caught by us with arms in hand would be given no quarter. On the contrary, we could cite many instances of unprecedented brutalities committed on our wounded by the German and, especially, the Magyar prisoners.[30]

Gajda likewise singled out the Internationalists in his instructions for possible military operations in May 1918: "If possible, the entire operation will be carried out without bloodshed [but] . . . resisting armed German and Austrian prisoners of war will be shot on the spot."[31] A Swedish nurse in Siberia, Elsa Brändström, confirmed that Internationalist fighters were often executed, as did the US vice consul at Samara, who reported that the legionnaires executed about fifty Austrian prisoners who were captured fighting against them in the June 1918 battle for Samara, while they released virtually all the Russian Red Army troops from that conflict.[32] The US consul at Irkutsk, Ernest L. Harris, also confirmed this practice: "Austrian and German prisoners caught by the Czechs with arms in their possession are immediately shot, while all Red Guard prisoners of Russian nationality are handed over to the Cossacks and White Guard for such treatment as their case may require. The fate of most of the commissars thus far caught has been hanging, especially those in the large cities."[33]

A Little-Known Note

IF ALLIED LEADERS had grasped the real aspirations of the legionnaires, they might not have entertained the idea they began considering early in 1918. Without enough ships to collect the troops, they began to discuss splitting the corps in two, sending legionnaires west of Omsk to the northern ports of Archangel and Murmansk and letting units east of Omsk continue to Vladivostok. Leon Trotsky, Lenin, and Joseph Stalin gave explicit consent to negotiations by the chairman of the Murmansk soviet, Aleksey M. Yuriev, with British and French officials in late March and early April for Allied troop landings at Murmansk.[34] On the other hand, British ships were not more readily available in Archangel and Murmansk than were US ships in Vladivostok; none of the Allies had enough ships and northern shipping was vulnerable to German submarines. Still, the Allied Supreme War Council fatefully approved splitting the corps at a meeting in Abbeville, France, on May 2. "Moscow did not object," says historian Richard Pipes, "but the decision caused great unhappiness among the Czecho-Slovaks."[35]

Small numbers of legionnaires had already been sent to France from the northern ports, but the British in particular were starting to consider using the legion inside Russia—instead of in France—as was Trotsky, who continued negotiating with Allied representatives about using the legionnaires to protect Archangel and Murmansk. Even the French warmed to the idea, with General Jean Guillaume Lavergne suggesting use of the northern ports on April 9, and French military aides discussing with their British counterparts shipping the legionnaires through Archangel.[36]

In fact, reestablishing an Eastern Front inside Russia never received the consideration that such an enormous undertaking required. The British and French did not have the men and matériel to spare and the

White House was firmly opposed to armed intervention. As a result, the French and British began to encourage Japan to intervene against the Germans, but Japan would send troops only as far west as Irkutsk. It was unclear how this would expel Germans from Ukraine and western Russia. Yet London and Paris continued to urge that either Japanese troops or the Czecho-Slovak legionnaires somehow reopen an Eastern Front in Russia, persistently negotiating, pleading, and arguing their way toward military half measures.

The initial deliberations about the legionnaires and their ability to reopen an Eastern Front took place through the Supreme War Council.[37] Woodrow Wilson did not attend its meetings and Colonel Edward M. House attended only the first and last of the council's sessions, but US general Tasker H. Bliss was permanently stationed at the council's offices at Versailles. As early as December 24, 1917, the council addressed the situation in Russia. The council's Joint Note No. 5 proposed support for anti-German groups in Russia to circumvent German military acquisition of food and fuel inside Russia.

In Versailles, the French feared that Germany might obtain release of their POWs in Russia and either move them to the Western Front or organize them into a force capable of seizing Siberia, as reports emerged of the more than 100,000 Austrian and Hungarian POWs fighting—but not for Berlin or Vienna—in the Internationalist Brigades. This led some to think the legionnaires could counter them. French marshal Ferdinand Foch suggested on March 21—mere days before he was named supreme Allied military leader—that there might be merit in leaving the legionnaires inside Russia. On the same day, the British Foreign Office prepared an analysis for the War Office on the potential utility of the legionnaires inside Russia. As a result, the British drafted Joint Note No. 20 for the council's military representatives early in April 1918. Entitled "The Situation in the Eastern Theater," it pulled together arguments in favor of intervention. Support would be given to any elements willing to resist Germany. "In Siberia," it said, "that support can only be given effectively by the Japanese, with the eventual assistance of Czech and other elements which can be organized on the spot." Reflecting Washington's opposition to intervention, Bliss refused to sign the note, which killed the idea momentarily.

Yet US resistance to intervention only encouraged Paris and London to focus on the legionnaires. Edvard Beneš was handed a communication from the British War Office on April 1 expressing doubt that the legionnaires could be shipped to France and asking instead whether they could be deployed in Siberia or perhaps at Archangel. Beneš immediately replied to the French and British that the legionnaires could be shipped to Archangel only to expedite their transport to Europe. "By the terms of our agreement with the French government," Beneš said, "the Allies were not allowed to make use of our army without our consent." By April 27, aboard a steamer crossing the Pacific, Masaryk, too, learned of the plans to use Russia's northern ports, but he saw this as simply another way to ship the legionnaires to France.[38] Paris responded by asking the United States to provide ships at Vladivostok and also began exploring the availability of additional Allied vessels at Archangel.[39]

On April 27, the Allied military aides working for the Supreme War Council approved Joint Note No. 25, "Transportation of Czech Troops from Siberia." It included an Allied-Russian agreement to transport half of the legion to Russia's northern ports and, despite its title, vaguely envisioned employing the legionnaires to defend Siberia against German penetration. No final agreement was reached on whether the legionnaires would indeed ever serve on the Western Front. "The note proposed that the Czechs leave Russia by way of both eastern and north Russia. The concentration of Czechs at Murmansk and Vladivostok would provide troops for use in a possible intervention. Thus the note concerned itself more with using the legionnaires for military purposes in Russia than with their transport to France. When the Supreme War Council met at Abbeville on May 1–12, it approved Joint Note No. 25." Thus did the Allies precipitate a crisis. The legionnaires were not quickly informed of these discussions, even though the Allies sought Trotsky's approval, which they received by May 7. Worse, the legionnaires first learned of this plan from Soviet authorities amidst hostile encounters with their agents in Siberia.[40] "It was certainly a tactical and political blunder that the Allied plan was not communicated in time and in sufficient detail either to the Czech military leaders or [to] the branch of the National Council in Moscow," Beneš said.[41]

The Railway Platform

CHELYABINSK WAS AN unlikely place to make history. Then again, the sequence of events set in motion there on May 14, 1918—which prompted one of the wildest misadventures in the annals of modern history—were equally improbable.

Chelyabinsk was a frontier outpost on the edge of Siberia, a remote, isolated landscape almost beyond the reach of civilization. Indeed, one would have to cross three "Europes"—Western, Eastern, and Russian—and then cross her fabled border with Asia, to find Chelyabinsk, nestled on the steeper, more fractured, eastern slopes of the Ural Mountains. The Urals divided two continents and Russia from many of her penal colonies, making the modest mountains a convenience for cartographers and a fig leaf behind which Russia hid her unsightly Siberia. Outside of town, a beautiful green valley sheltered salt-and-pepper birch trees and small, sparkling lakes. Fields of corn or wheat shared the landscape with dense forests of spruce, pine, or fir. Dark even at noon, the forests sheltered wolves, bears, and the occasional runaway convict, yet this was where Russians found their beloved mushrooms. Swift, wild creeks ran toward Siberia's rivers, most of them larger and stronger than the Mississippi.

Until 1892, when the tentacles of the Trans-Siberian Railway first reached the town, Chelyabinsk had few visitors, and early visitors were not impressed. "Conceive a field in which a cattle show has been held for a week, and it has been raining all the week," said a British traveler in 1901. "That will give you some idea of Chelyabinsk. The buildings were sheds, and the roadways mire."[42] Even an official guide of 1900, promoting travel, admitted, "The hotels are very bad."[43]

Begun as a wooden fort planted on the banks of the Miass River to protect fur traders from indigenous tribes, the town remained rough looking in 1918, despite a few onion-domed Orthodox church towers piercing the air. Wide dirt streets lined with weeds hosted a few hulking stone edifices that housed government officials or wealthy merchants, the mortar cracked and broken by Russia's hard winters. More common were simple, wooden-frame homes, stores, and warehouses, their unpainted planks all turned slate gray, and the occasional Siberian log home, squatting heavily in the soil. Windows in every building had cotton or rags stuffed between double panes of smoky, dirty glass. When summer rains turned the town's dirt roads into rivers of rich Russian mud, the "better" townsfolk stepped carefully along sagging wooden planks that had thin strips of bark visible along the edges. The town's quiet was broken only by an occasional trade fair on Cathedral Square, a periodic religious procession, when clergy would carry an icon of the Virgin Mary through town, or a blast from a train's whistle.

The Trans-Siberian's cattle-car-like efficiency began in the 1890s to deposit successive waves of peasants at the station outside of town. And in the same way that the majestic Romanov dynasty seemed out of place in a poor nation, the station it built at Chelyabinsk was a dash of splendor amidst the squalor and bucolic indifference of rural Russia. Like the dynasty and its entourage, the station seemed larger and more elaborate than necessary, and it sat somewhat distant from the people it was meant to serve. Yet the growing numbers of Russians seeking land and a freer climate meant that, by 1914, a migrant village was erected around the station, with barracks for railway and telegraph workers, warehouses, bath houses, a small infirmary, and a wooden church.

A village of only five thousand in 1861, Chelyabinsk's population quadrupled to about twenty thousand by 1900, in the wake of the arrival of the Trans-Siberian. By 1914 the town's population reached as high as seventy thousand.[44] The town quickly became a busy transit point for agricultural goods moving westward to feed European Russia, where famine was not unknown. Eastward came the hardened criminals and political exiles, but also millions of land-hungry immigrants seeking cheap land or jobs. Many Chelyabinsk residents were first-generation town dwellers of peasant stock; they were largely illiterate. They worked in flour mills, slaughterhouses, tanneries, distilleries, or nearby gold mines. A total of 5.7 million migrants poured into Siberia between 1891 and 1914, and the Trans-Siberian funneled most of them through Chelyabinsk, which saw 242,000 transients in 1914 alone. The tide ebbed early in the war but redoubled by 1918, when 175,000 soldiers, deserters, or refugees fleeing hard-pressed cities crossed the Urals in the first four months of 1918.[45]

By May 1918 a global war, a turbulent revolution, the collapse of the government and its entire armed forces amidst persistent hunger, spreading disease, strikes, demonstrations and riots forced an ailing fleet of steam locomotives to push or pull mobs of soldiers, deserters, refugees, and freed POWs through the Chelyabinsk station.

Incident at Chelyabinsk

THEIR PAST SERVICE in Russia's armed forces differentiated the Czechs and Slovaks from other enemy POWs. It enabled Masaryk to negotiate the Kiev agreement on February 16 with Red Army general Muravyov that allowed the legion to depart Ukraine—and even be supplied and financed by Moscow—as well as the March 15 agreement with the Soviet government, which had Lenin's personal support, permitting the legion's trains to roll into southern Russia and toward Vladivostok. Yet chaos, fear, suspicion, and poor communication unraveled these accords.

The Soviet cabinet, the Sovnarkom, which Lenin chaired, on March 14 had approved the legion's departure from Russia, but Trotsky objected. Having previously secured a one-vote margin of approval from the Party Central Committee to accept Allied support on February 22, Trotsky hoped to use this approval to persuade or force the legionnaires to join the Red Army to help protect Russia against the Germans—*or* the Allies—depending on whether he believed they were anti-German nationalists or Bolshevik sympathizers. Complicating the situation even further was the fact that Moscow did not yet fully control its local soviets.

The two leaders of the Russian branch of the Czecho-Slovak National Council, appointed by Masaryk to serve as liaisons to Moscow, appeared not to be in close communication, which was unsurprising given the chaotic state of Russia at this time. Jiří Klecanda negotiated the March 14 agreement with the Soviet regime in Moscow, but Prokop Maxa was in the vicinity of Kursk as the legion's first trains reached the southern Russian city around the same time.

The Kursk soviet was more truculent than Moscow, demanding the legion's weapons. Holding true to Masaryk's neutrality policy, and thus wishing to avoid a confrontation, Maxa agreed on March 16 to hand over an arsenal of 21,000 rifles, 1,080,000 ammunition cartridges, 216 machine guns, forty-four artillery pieces, five trucks, six automobiles, four airplanes, and 3,500 horses, which Czech captain Hurban valued at more than 1 billion rubles. The legion retained only ten rifles for every hundred men.[46] Receiving this bounty was Red Army general Vladimir A. Antonov-Ovseyenko, a leading Bolshevik who had directed the capture of the Winter Palace and the arrest of the Provisional Government. The general announced, "The revolutionary troops will never forget the fraternal help which the Czecho-Slovak Corps has rendered the working people of the Ukraine in their struggle against the imperialist looters." He ordered local soviets to allow the legion to pass.[47]

Absent from the Sovnarkom meeting, Trotsky arrived in Moscow on March 17 to assume his new duties as commissar for war, which is when the difficulties began.[48] Five days later, the Omsk soviet ordered that all the legion's trains be stopped and redirected to Archangel. This would be the first time the legion heard of the plan to split its forces.[49] The Omsk soviet cited fears "that the Czecho-Slovaks might be used by counterrevolutionists and imperialists against the Soviet Government." This news bred even higher levels of fear and mistrust among the legionnaires. Klecanda communicated to the men along the Trans-Siberian that they should retain as many weapons as possible.[50]

The decision to divert the trains to Archangel was reversed March 26 by a telegram from Soviet commissar for nationality affairs, Joseph Stalin, directed to the Czecho-Slovak National Council in Moscow when its trains were stopped at Penza. Stating that their journey to Vladivostok is "just and fully acceptable," Stalin added, "The Czecho-Slovaks shall proceed not as fighting units but as a group of free citizens, taking with them a certain quantity of arms for self-defense against the attacks of counter-revolutionists." The telegram ordered the removal of the legion's "counter-revolutionary commanders," which eliminated a number of Russian officers, and demanded that each train accept a Bolshevik commissar provided by the Penza soviet. The National Council and Moscow agreed that the legionnaires could retain 168 rifles and one machine gun for each train of six hundred men. All other weapons would be surrendered at Penza. This became known as the Penza Agreement.[51] Weapons were handed over and trains were searched, but some men hid small numbers of rifles and hand grenades in the coaches. "We gave up our weapons with a profound inner protest, trying to look calm," said legionnaire Josef Kyncl, who said only one-quarter of the men had rifles.[52] Meanwhile, the Reds kept recruiting, demanding the legionnaires join them. "As soon as we arrived," said legionnaire Jan Cinert, "the Czech Bolsheviks were doing their agitation, wanting to recruit our brethren for the Communist army. They were promising all kinds of possible and impossible things, only to prevent us from serving in the 'bourgeois' army, as they put it, in order not to leave for France and fight for 'foreign capital.' . . . The mood against them was such that only a small spark was needed to ignite a fight."[53]

Yet trains that surrendered weapons at Penza were stopped at Samara, where Bolsheviks demanded yet more weapons. "We want an engine," a handful of legionnaires announced bluntly as they walked into the Samara soviet headquarters, according to one of them, Sergeant Becvar. Just as blunt was the reply: "You won't get an engine unless you pay for it, and the payment we want is 30 rifles." The legionnaires countered, "By agreement in Moscow we are to be given free passage to Vladivostok. In return for this concession, we surrendered our arms in Penza." The Russians replied, "This is Samara. We don't care what you arranged in Moscow or what further arrangements you make in Siberia. This is Samara and we in Samara need 30 rifles. Give them to us now or we shall demand twice as many." After a huddle, the legionnaires produced the rifles, but their growing anger led to hushed, angry debates about whether or not the group should start seizing engines, or entire stations. This scene repeated itself in Ufa, Zlatoust, Omsk, Irkutsk, Chita, all along the line.[54]

Local soviets viewed the legionnaires with suspicion, coveted their weapons and trains, feared their strength and discipline, and demanded that they join the revolution. Trains were stopped, moved onto sidings, and their departures delayed as each soviet demanded its pound of flesh, typically weapons in exchange for locomotives. Meanwhile, Czech Bolsheviks, especially, subjected the legionnaires to ham-handed recruitment campaigns at every station, swarming the legion's trains, arguing, bribing, or threatening in their efforts to persuade the legionnaires to join the soviets. Some infiltrated the legion. More fearful were the Austrian and Hungarian POWs, hardened combat veterans all, who were serving the Bolshevik regime. All the while, the men saw westbound locomotives returning POWs still loyal to Germany and Austria-Hungary, which angered the legionnaires and reinforced the reasonable suspicion that the Bolsheviks might turn them over to the military authorities in Vienna or Berlin.

Ordinary legionnaires soon began giving—rather than taking—orders. Having been victimized as Austro-Hungarian soldiers and again as Russian prisoners, they refused to become victims again. Plans began to be hatched without regard to the Czecho-Slovak National Council or the Allies. While the order to halt the legion's trains was reversed on April 12, the leaders of the First Division of the Czecho-Slovak Corps convened a secret meeting on April 13 at a small town, Kirsanov, about one hundred miles short of Penza, where they adopted the Kirsanov Resolution, a private agreement among the men that was grounded in fears they would be stopped and disarmed, leaving them defenseless against the Bolsheviks and the Austrian and Hungarian POWs opposed to Czecho-Slovak independence. The resolution made several "final and irrevocable" demands: refusing to surrender more weapons, recovering the arms and ammunition given up at Penza, obtaining additional ammunition, and securing all locomotives and fuel depots along those rail lines hosting the legion's trains.[55]

A few days later the Kremlin heard reports of an anti-Bolshevik Cossack army under Grigory M. Semyonov moving north along the Chinese Eastern Railway toward Russia. In response, the Bolsheviks declared martial law throughout Siberia on April 17 and four days later the legion was again stopped. The newspaper of the communist Czechs and Slovaks, *Prukopnik*, which was hostile to the legionnaires, reported on April 18 that they would have to be shipped to Archangel, in part to avoid the Internationalists. A telegram from Georgy V. Chicherin, the Soviet commissar for foreign affairs, announced the Archangel plan to the legion on April 21.[56] On May 22, on the eve of the revolt, the legion's own newspaper, *Československy Denik*, confirmed a similar plan to ship some legionnaires through Archangel. The legionnaires suspected a conspiracy.

When all seventy to eighty trains had stopped, the legionnaires were stretched almost five thousand miles from Penza, which lay west of the Urals and just a few hundred miles south of Moscow, to Vladivostok—roughly the distance between New York and Honolulu. Although the total strength of the legion may have risen to 50,000 by this time, there were concentrations of 8,000 legionnaires near Penza (with some still west of that western city), another 8,800 around Chelyabinsk, 3,830 near Novosibirsk, and 15,000 in or near Vladivostok.[57] If, in fact, the legion fielded 50,000 men at this time, it had only ten men for every linear mile of the Trans-Siberian Railway.

The legionnaires desperately wanted answers, needed weapons, and hungered to flee Russia. While they shared only a smattering of pistols, rifles, and grenades, morale was high. The men drilled and did calisthenics; their discipline, constant preparations, and fierce loyalty to one another were fearsome qualities. In his diary, Edward T. Heald, an employee of the YMCA—whose efforts to care for the war's prisoners and refugees included staff, like Heald, who traveled with the Czecho-Slovaks—wrote, "The undaunted, confident, enthusiastic spirit of the Czechs, their disdain of danger, and their wonderful morale strike you with admiration from the first."[58]

At the stations, however, the legionnaires noticed scores of trains chugging westward, toward the Western Front, full of men who would one day fight them. "While the troop trains were standing at Chelyabinsk, I saw train after train of German and Austrian prisoners of war pass *en route* from prison camps in Siberia for home," another American YMCA employee, Kenneth D. Miller, noted in his diary. Miller added, "As this was the time (May 1918) of the great German offensive on the Western Front, it was obvious that these prisoners were being sent home with the consent of the Soviets, to strengthen the armies of the Central Powers. It was a galling thought for the Czecho-Slovaks. While they were held up, impotent, and *hors de combat*, enemy troops were being hurried past them to fight against the Allies. Every such train meant added strength to Germany and danger to the Allies and to the Czech cause."[59]

ON MAY 14, 1918, in Chelyabinsk, an angry, Hungarian-speaking POW threw a chunk of iron from his train, delivering a serious head wound to a legionnaire. After a furious series of scuffles, threats, arguments, and one violent assault, the assailant was dead, killed by the legionnaires. The legion's officers managed to identify the victim, and their hearts sank further.

"The name of the culprit was Malik," noted Sergeant Becvar, "which is a pure Czech name meaning 'small finger.' This was the irony of the tragic incident. The man was of Czech descent, but a renegade." When the Czech guards marched Malik's Hungarian comrades to the office of the Bolshevik commissar in Chelyabinsk, the Hungarians conceded Malik's guilt. He had, his former comrades confessed, vowed to kill a Czech before their train left Chelyabinsk.

"What had turned him so violently against his blood brethren is not known," Becvar said, "but it occasionally happened that by means of promises, bribery or force, weak Czechs and Slovaks were seduced from their natural allegiance to become mere creatures of the Austrians. Doubtless Malik had become one of these, or at least the son of such a man who, perhaps, had been compelled to send the unfortunate lad to a German school where he had learned to forget his Czech ancestry. The Austrian habit of Germanizing in this manner their Czech subjects was one of the reasons which caused us to rise up against the Empire."[60]

The Reaction in Moscow

LIKE EVERY TOWN or city, Chelyabinsk was ruled by a committee, or soviet, usually comprising rare literate townsfolk, POWs who joined the International Brigades, or factory workers with little or no experience of government. Their powers not widely understood, even by their members, and, lacking formal recognition, traditional legal authority, or established structures, the soviets improvised, often relying on secrecy, promises, threats, or violence. As it happened, the Chelyabinsk soviet also included a large number of Hungarian POWs among its members.

The soviet held a tenuous grip on power, but this did not prohibit it from taking action. It would perhaps follow orders from Moscow, but Moscow was 1,363 miles away by train, and the trains were moving only slowly and fitfully. Orders were received via the telegraph line that ran mostly parallel to the Trans-Siberian Railway. The telegraph agents were housed in the stations along the line, and most railroad workers, including the telegraph operators, would happily oblige whatever army was in charge; many were, in fact, anti-Bolshevik. As a result, whoever controlled the Trans-Siberian controlled the telegraph. And whoever controlled both controlled the breadth of Siberia, which had virtually no passable highways.[61]

The Soviet regime in Moscow was in a constant frenzy, preoccupied with holding on to the power it had seized. Russia was coming apart at its imperial seams. As a result of signing the Brest-Litovsk Treaty, the country lost one-third of its population, one-third of its farmland, one-half of its industrial plant, and almost 90 percent of its coal mines. Many Russian provinces—from Finland in the north, down through Ukraine and into Georgia, Armenia, Azerbaijan—declared independence under German protection or were incorporated into Germany. As well, the slogan, "All power to the soviets," encouraged every factory, village, or city to create its own ruling bodies. Moscow's authority was even more unclear following the Bolshevik loss in the elections to the Constituent Assembly, which they disbanded. By one count, there existed thirty-three "governments" in Russia in June 1918.[62]

In the wake of an assassination attempt on Lenin on January 1 (OS), both Lenin and Trotsky had reason to fear for their lives. Widespread hunger had emptied the larger cities, reducing the labor force, and unrest mounted among those left behind. On May 9, 1918, in an echo of tsarist rule, the regime again fired on demonstrators near Saint Petersburg. "The spring and summer of 1918 were unusually hard," confessed Trotsky. "There was no food. There was no army. The railways were completely disorganized. The machinery of state was just beginning to take shape. Conspiracies were being hatched everywhere."[63] Into such an atmosphere would come news of the Czecho-Slovak revolt in Chelyabinsk.

RESPONDING TO THE deadly fracas at the station, the Chelyabinsk soviet quickly established a three-man commission to determine what had happened and who should be held accountable. The soviet, however, was dominated by Hungarian Internationalists, who, despite their newfound socialist ideology, may not have been unbiased regarding a conflict between fellow Hungarians and the Czecho-Slovaks.[64] The soviet listened to the Hungarian POWs confess that one of their own had initiated the altercation and they were promptly released. The Hungarians returned to the station and their train departed by nightfall.

The commission now turned its attention to the Czechs, specifically the ten guards who had marched the Hungarian POWs into town. Called to appear as witnesses before the commission, the men were instead arrested. When the guards did not return to the station after many hours, two Czech officers were dispatched to the town to demand their release. Word reached the station later that day or the next that these two had also been arrested. Moscow's failure to honor its promise to the legionnaires and the repeated efforts to disarm them and recruit them into the Red Army angered the men. When the Chelyabinsk soviet, under Hungarian influence, arrested the Czechs but not the Hungarians, however, there was no turning back. A ragtag collection of refugees and deserters was about to become this era's most fearsome army.

"The troops were thoroughly roused and demanded prompt action," Sergeant Becvar said. Yet it fell to a young Russian officer, Lieutenant Colonel Sergey N. Voitsekhovsky, commander of the Chelyabinsk legionnaires, to lead them. One of a handful of Russian officers still with the legionnaires, Voitsekhovsky was described by YMCA employee Heald, who met him in December 1918, as having the same laudable characteristics that were often used to describe the Czechs and Slovaks; he was "an approachable, direct, forceful, clean-cut young man of something like 35 years."[65]

In response to the unwarranted arrests, Voitsekhovsky mobilized three thousand of the legionnaires on May 17 and led them to capture the telegraph office. An assortment of rifles and pistols were handed out to the men on the train platform late in the afternoon. Their orders clear, the two battalions departed from the station, marching quickly along the dirt road toward the town. They arrived inside the city limits at about 6:00 p.m. Spreading out amidst scuffles and small-arms fire, they quickly took control of key intersections, cut telephone lines, disarmed surprised Russian sentries, and broke into the town's armory, taking about eight hundred rifles and two machine guns. As many as three Czechs were shot and killed and two wounded, but since the legionnaires were under strict orders not to shoot, there were no Bolshevik casualties, according to the official report of the city's top Bolshevik, Commissar Sadlucky. In a further sign that discipline had returned to the ranks of the legionnaires, the building that housed the executive committee of the Chelyabinsk soviet was left untouched and Sadlucky was permitted to walk about.

The legionnaires, moreover, tried to reason with Sadlucky in regard to the imprisoned legionnaires. On May 18 the legionnaires returned the rifles and machine guns they had seized in Chelyabinsk, despite the fact that the eight thousand legionnaires in the vicinity of Chelyabinsk were sharing only fifteen hundred weapons. They also posted declarations in the town that they were not opposing Soviet rule either in Chelyabinsk or Moscow.[66]

"The demonstrating Czechs demanded an immediate release of their imprisoned comrades and pressed me for action," Sadlucky later telegraphed to Moscow. "I argued that I could not release the imprisoned men because what was happening then in the streets amounted to an armed action against the Soviet Government. But the Czechs assured me of their loyalty to the Soviet Government and declared that the release of the imprisoned was their only concern. To avoid bloodshed, I categorically demanded that the Czechs evacuate the city at once, warning that we could not restrain our men for long. Then," he concluded, "seeing the discipline of the Czechs, and considering the lack of readiness on our part, I decided to let the imprisoned go. As soon as we released these men, the Czechs left the city for their trains, singing folk songs."[67]

So ended, on May 18, an incident that could easily have gotten out of hand. Only then it did. As military historian John Keegan says, "A war entirely subsidiary to the Great War ensued."[68]

NEWS OF THE incident at Chelyabinsk produced a hysterical, bloodthirsty reaction in Moscow. On May 20, an assistant to Trotsky, P. V. Aralov, telegraphed an order from Trotsky to all soviets along the railway instructing them to forcibly remove the legionnaires from their trains and place them in labor battalions or the Red Army. The next day, two officials of the Russian branch of the Czecho-Slovak National Council, Prokop Maxa and Bohumil Čermák, were arrested in Moscow (although this was not widely known) and forced that day to order the men to surrender their weapons. "Anyone not complying with this order," they said, "will be considered a traitor and declared outside the law."[69]

While Trotsky would quickly earn a reputation as a ruthless and effective military leader of the Red Army, his initial anger got the best
of him. He may have failed to appreciate that, having taken control of
the Chelyabinsk train station, the Czecho-Slovaks also controlled the
telegraph. Quite literally, Trotsky was telegraphing his moves to his new
adversaries. This precluded any hopes of a peaceful resolution to the
situation.

Unbeknownst to the legionnaires, the Czecho-Slovak communists had
confiscated the offices and seized the assets of the Russian branch of the
National Council on May 9 in Moscow, where at the end of May fully 101
Czecho-Slovak communists convened a congress claiming to represent
7,450 fellow Czechs and Slovaks in the Red Army and its Internationalist Brigades, triumphantly declaring a victory over the legionnaires and
inviting any socialists among them to join their ranks.[70] Yet, simultaneously, about 120 legionnaires were arriving in Chelyabinsk as delegates
for the long-planned legion conference. At the decisive meeting on May
23, the chairman, František Richter, the secretary of the Russian branch
of Czecho-Slovak National Council, was addressing the delegates when
a messenger quickly entered the room, handed him some papers, and
whispered something to him excitedly. First reading the words in silence,
Richter then stood and read aloud Trotsky's May 20 telegram to the men.

> There was a dead silence when I finished, and the delegates were wait-
> ing for my comments in regard to the telegram. This is what I said:
> "Brethren, we have only one response to this command—we will not
> turn over our weapons! If you want them, come and get them!" An in-
> describable roar filled the room amid shouts of "Come and get them!"[71]

The legionnaires grew louder and louder, Richter recalled, until they
rose from their seats, shouting and swearing. Then—the room hushed
into silence. Without embarrassment, the men began to sing. Their eyes
wet, their fists clenched, the roomful of men began to emit a low rumble
of the sad strains of a song they would sing throughout their Siberian

epic, later to become the national anthem of Czecho-Slovakia: "Where Is My Homeland?" It so happened the date was May 23, 1918, the three hundredth anniversary of the Defenestration of Prague.

THE CONGRESS OF the Czecho-Slovak Army Corps voted to publicly repudiate the Russian branch of the Czecho-Slovak National Council. The council's representatives had lost the men's trust by their willingness to disarm the troops, as well as by the many broken promises from Moscow. In a resolution telegraphed May 23, the congress said the corps would be led by a new Provisional Executive Committee, which nonetheless included a few trusted National Council officials who were present and supportive, such as Richter and Bohdan Pavlů. The new leaders vowed to ignore orders from "any other Czecho-Slovak organization" and refused to surrender any more weapons. Yet the resolution said that the corps still "entertains the hope that the Soviet government will place no obstacles in the way of the departing Czecho-Slovak revolutionary troops."[72] These decisions were taken over the vocal objections of the two French military liaisons who were also present, Major Alphonse Guinet and Captain Pierre Pascal.[73] Any of the remaining Russian officers who expressed hesitation were dismissed or even arrested.[74]

Trotsky slammed the door on a negotiated settlement on May 25 with a drastic order:

> Every armed Czecho-Slovak found on the railway is to be shot on the spot, every troop train in which even one armed man is found shall be unloaded, and its soldiers shall be interned in a war prisoners' camp. Local war commissars must proceed at once to carry out this order; every delay will be considered treason and will bring the offender severe punishment.[75]

The Russian officer who led the Czecho-Slovak force that liberated the men at Chelyabinsk, Lieutenant Colonel Voitsekhovsky, was placed in charge of the 8,800 troops there. Younger Czechs were appointed to three other commands. Lieutenant Jan Syrový was given command of the legionnaires just west of Omsk. Thirty years old at the time of the rebellion, Syrový had been a Czech émigré working in Warsaw when the Great War broke out; he joined the *družina* when it was part of the Russian imperial army.

East of Omsk, Captain Radola Gajda was given command of the longest stretch of the Trans-Siberian, occupied by almost 18,000 legionnaires from Novosibirsk—through Tomsk, Krasnoyarsk, Irkutsk, Chita, and Khabarovsk—to Vladivostok, where the largest concentration of about 15,000 legionnaires was located. About twenty-six years old, Gajda had been a medical assistant in the Austro-Hungarian army on the Serbian front when he was taken prisoner. In 1915 he joined about a thousand Czech and Slovak POWs who, frustrated that the Russian imperial army did not enroll them in the *družina*, left their POW camps to fight for Serbia in the Balkans. When Serbia was defeated, Gajda managed to make his way back to Russia. He returned to the Czecho-Slovak Corps in time for the Battle of Zborov and rose to the rank of captain.

Lieutenant Stanislav Čeček was given command of about 8,000 legionnaires marooned on the other side of the Ural Mountains in the vicinity of Penza, the furthest troops from Vladivostok. In his early thirties, Čeček was a lieutenant in the Austro-Hungarian Army when he was taken prisoner by the Russians early in the war; he volunteered for the *družina* in 1914. As commander of the last units fleeing Bakhmach, Čeček now found his position at the rear equally perilous.[76]

The Seizure of Siberia

THE SAME DAY that Trotsky issued his threatening order, the legionnaires attacked. Their first priority was to link all the legionnaires in a single chain—especially those around Penza, who were furthest from Vladivostok and the most vulnerable. From Chelyabinsk, Novosibirsk, and Penza, commandeered trains were directed east and west under full steam to rescue their brothers and defeat the Reds all along the Trans-Siberian. They often ran into Red Army units much larger and better armed than they were.

Two eastbound trains approaching Omsk suffered a surprise attack on the evening of May 25 at the small town of Maryanovka, about twenty-five miles west of Omsk, when a Red train equipped with two machine guns and carrying hundreds of Bolsheviks approached from Omsk. The Bolsheviks opened fire. The legionnaires had few rifles but used the hand grenades they had hidden in their trains with deadly effect. Suffering six to ten dead and eight to ten seriously wounded, they still managed to kill or wound two hundred of the enemy and force their train back toward Omsk. The next day, legionnaires aboard a train outside the town of Zlatoust, about a hundred miles west of Chelyabinsk, jumped from their seats when they watched their carriages being slowly moved in front of a line of armed Reds. Piling out of the train and attacking the enemy's two flanks in some cases only with rocks, they captured machine guns and rifles and quickly turned them on the other Bolsheviks, causing them to flee. The legionnaires reportedly suffered six dead and ten severely wounded. Trapped by tracks damaged by the retreating Reds, the legionnaires circled Zlatoust on foot and returned to Chelyabinsk.

Defeating Bolshevik forces in almost every encounter, the legionnaires began building an arsenal with captured weapons and trains. At Chelyabinsk, they overpowered Bolshevik guards and seized two improvised flatcars with artillery pieces mounted on them and two freight cars full of Russian rifles and ammunition. Success in combat also brought them weaponry. "Due to our commander's inexperience," one Bolshevik said after a defeat, "the retreat was effected in a disorderly fashion. . . . Everything was abandoned to the Czechs."[77] Most railway and telegraph workers cooperated with the legionnaires, giving the Czecho-Slovaks access to all communications between Moscow and its many soviets, none of which realized the fact. The legionnaires were thus able to learn where Reds were concentrated, what their orders were, and when to anticipate attacks.

A series of firefights exploded along the Trans-Siberian across Russia throughout that summer—from Penza in European Russia, to Vladivostok on the Pacific coast, and then back westward again to Kazan in European Russia. Day by day, week by week, one city after another fell to the Czecho-Slovaks along the Trans-Siberian Railway and its tributaries:

May 26—Novosibirsk[78]

May 27—Chelyabinsk

May 29—Penza

May 29—Syzran

June 4—Tomsk

June 7—Omsk

June 8—Samara

June 20—Krasnoyarsk

June 24—Nizhneudinsk

June 29—Vladivostok

July 4—Ufa

July 5—Ussuriysk[79]

July 11—Irkutsk

July 22—Ulyanovsk[80]

July 25—Yekaterinburg

August 6—Kazan

August 24—Ulan-Ude[81]

August 27—Chita

September 5—Khabarovsk

WHILE THE LEGIONNAIRES would soon rivet the world's attention with their conquest of Siberia, they initially did not try to seize and hold cities or territory, contrary to Soviet claims of an Allied conspiracy to topple the Bolshevik regime. A Soviet attack on the legionnaires at Irkutsk on May 26 illustrates this. The first train shuttling four to six hundred legionnaires to Vladivostok approached Irkutsk, unaware of the revolt, at about 3:00 p.m. The men aboard had only ten rifles and twenty hand grenades, according to an officer present, Captain Hurban. At the station, Hurban said, the train "was surrounded by a few thousand Red Guards armed with machine guns and cannon. Their commander gave our men 10 minutes to surrender their arms or be shot. According to their habit, ours began negotiations. Suddenly there was heard the German command, 'Schiessen!' ['Fire!'] and the Red Guards began firing at the train. Our men jumped off the train and in five minutes all of the machine guns were in their possession, the Russian Bolsheviks disarmed, and the Germans and Hungarians done away with."[82] Fifteen legionnaires were killed and forty-one wounded, said the US consul general at Irkutsk, Ernest L. Harris, who witnessed the attack.[83] Wishing to avoid further bloodshed, the legionnaires again negotiated an armistice with the Irkutsk soviet, surrendered the arms they had just captured, and proceeded onward.[84]

At about midnight, two more trains with about a thousand legionnaires approaching Irkutsk from the west became engaged in an hours-long battle with Red Guards and POWs three miles west of the city, opposite a POW camp. The legionnaires eventually defeated their attackers, killing four Austrians and one German, and wounding a larger number. They also captured twenty-two Austrians, nine Russians, and four Germans, according to Harris, who said that these "Red" troops were still wearing their original Austro-Hungarian or German uniforms. While the fighting was still going on, two soviet officials approached Harris and asked for his intervention. Harris, the city's French consul general, Gaston Bourgeois, and the two Bolsheviks proceeded by special train—French and American flags fluttering alongside a large white bedsheet—to the scene of the battle. After several hours of negotiations, the legionnaires surrendered all weapons in excess of thirty rifles per train and twenty rounds of ammunition per rifle, in return for which Soviet officials promised them safe passage toward Vladivostok. The trains proceeded without further difficulty, and a fourth train that agreed to the same terms at Irkutsk also moved on peacefully.[85]

Unaware of the legion's larger revolt against the Soviet regime, Harris did not realize he was essentially violating US policy by intervening in

Russia's internal affairs. Harris thought the skirmish at Irkutsk was an isolated incident that arose from a misunderstanding, but, when he learned
by June 8 of the wider revolt, he abandoned all further mediation. Three
trains of legionnaires had defeated Red forces on two occasions, suffering
thirty dead and sixty-three wounded, yet returned all of their captured
weapons.[86] The legion was not happy that mediation efforts allowed Soviet authorities to remain in power in Irkutsk long after entire sections of
the Trans-Siberian had fallen into the legion's hands. Legionnaire captain
Gajda was reportedly furious at what had happened, vowing to court-
martial the officers who consented to surrender their weapons there.[87]

Sources reported that many POWs of the Central Powers participated
in the Irkutsk battles. An Austrian officer accompanied Harris to a POW
camp, where he saw the dead and wounded, and the rest of the prisoners,
wearing Austro-Hungarian uniforms. "This seems to establish beyond
doubt the question that a large number of the prisoners in Irkutsk are
armed," said Harris.[88]

The forces of Gajda, who commanded the stretch of the Trans-Siberian
from a point east of Omsk to Vladivostok, quickly occupied the railroad
junction at Novosibirsk, the first large city east of Omsk, on May 26,
and then launched counterattacks both westward toward Omsk and eastward toward Irkutsk on May 27 and 28. Eastbound legionnaires seized
the town of Mariinsk, halfway to Krasnoyarsk, while those hurtling westward seized the town of Chulym. At Chulym, the men learned that a
large Red Army unit was moving toward them from Omsk. About four
hundred legionnaires were assembled at the station—with just forty rifles.
The other 360 armed themselves with wooden clubs and other improvised
weapons.[89] "They were indeed a motley crew," said Sergeant Becvar, "and
gazing upon their eager enthusiasm, it was heart-rending to recall the
quantities of good arms we had been forced to surrender through the
trickery and false dealing of local soviets." The enemy approached in and
around an armored train, its engine flanked by flatcars front and back,
both of them walled in timber and sandbags. The first car bristled with
several machine guns and an artillery piece. Aboard and flanking the

train were about twenty-four hundred soldiers. A small unit of legionnaires advanced and destroyed a wooden railroad bridge, which stopped the train. That first night, thirty legionnaires crawled away from the railway to circle to the rear of the train and tear up the tracks behind it, but the men were spotted and retreated under enemy fire. The Reds attacked the main legion unit, pushing them back to allow the Reds to repair the bridge and move forward. "Rifle fire was useless against the train," said Becvar, "which advanced inexorably, no matter what we attempted against it." The legionnaires retreated for days, falling back toward Novosibirsk, giving ground to the armored train flanked by Red Army troops.

Without apparent reason, one day an order was passed among the legionnaires to lie down in the tall grass along the banks of a river that the enemy was approaching. The legionnaires waited and at two hundred yards opened fire. The train's machine guns responded with deadly effect until, suddenly, a single artillery piece from behind the legionnaires opened fire on the train; its second shot was a direct hit and the armored train began limping away. The legionnaires rose from the tall grass and began charging. The enemy fled, and the legionnaires gave chase, and after a brief firefight, they captured two hundred prisoners, four artillery pieces, three hundred shells, and twenty-four machine guns.

Advancing again to within 120 miles of Omsk, the legionnaires approached Red forces at Tatarsk, whose commander telegraphed urgent requests to Omsk for more troops; he was promised immediate help. This cheered the Bolsheviks—until they realized they had communicated with a legionnaire. Omsk had just fallen to Czecho-Slovaks advancing from the west. As the legionnaires approached from both sides of the city, the railway employees and other workers, despite being armed by the Omsk soviet, threw their support to the legionnaires. Soviet leaders abandoned the city, along with their allied POWs. Anti-Bolshevik Russians publicized the surrender on June 7, while the legionnaires were still several miles outside of the city.[90]

Similar victories were reported all along the Trans-Siberian. Voitsek-hovsky's forces had reoccupied Chelyabinsk on May 27, where they took three thousand Hungarians and two thousand Russians as prisoners, releasing the Russians and sending the Hungarians back to the POW camps. The entire line from Chelyabinsk to Novosibirsk—stretching hundreds of miles on either side of Omsk—was in their hands. Voitse-khovsky's troops began moving westward from Chelyabinsk, more deeply into Russia, to link up with Čeček's forces beyond the Ural Mountains.[91]

FURTHEST FROM VLADIVOSTOK when the revolt erupted, Čeček's le-gionnaires near Penza were still armed. They had not yet reached Penza station, where they would have surrendered their weapons under the terms of the Penza Agreement. Most affected by the delays, and most vulnerable in regard to their position deep inside European Russia, these legionnaires were also the most agitated. The Penza soviet advised Trotsky on May 26 that it could not disarm them, to which Trotsky replied the same day: "Comrades! Military orders . . . should not be discussed but obeyed."[92] The legionnaires who had attended the Chel-yabinsk meeting did not return to Penza until May 28, when they be-came aware of Trotsky's orders and received the same response. "We will break through!" yelled one legionnaire who jumped to his feet. "We will not surrender our weapons." Čeček shouted, "If there are 8,000 of us, there is nobody to match us!"

That same day, the legionnaires in Penza seized three armored cars sent from Moscow, a firefight broke out, and the legionnaires found themselves up against a large contingent of Czecho-Slovak Internation-alists. By the next day, the legionnaires had won, killing 128 Interna-tionalists and taking three of their leaders as prisoners. As they did in Chelyabinsk, they posted flyers throughout the town stating they had no wish to change the governments of Penza or Russia. On the same day the legionnaires took Penza, however, sixty-five miles southeast at a station near Serdobsk, a unit of legionnaires was ordered to turn back a few miles further west to confiscate six locomotives. As they fired up the engines at a station at Rtishchevo, 125 legionnaires were surrounded and attacked by Red Guards and a Latvian Rifles unit. Eleven legionnaires were killed, nineteen wounded, and the rest taken captive; a handful of escapees did not reach their units in the east until August.[93] Čeček's forces continued eastward toward the Volga River, attacking and occupying Syzran, a small town on the western banks of the Volga, on May 29. The legionnaires evacuated Penza entirely by June 2, once again showing that they had no plans to seize and hold Russian territory.

With Syzran in their possession, Čeček's men set their sights on a bigger target, Samara, a large city and transit hub on the opposite banks of the Volga, just north of Syzran.[94] The legionnaires attacked on June 8, and the battle for Samara, which was defended by two thousand Red Guards, was brief but intense, according to the US consul at Samara, George W. Williams, who was forced to evacuate his office. Launched at 2:30 a.m., the attack was led by fifty legionnaires throwing hand grenades, and forces on both sides employed everything from small artillery to revolvers. In five hours it was over. Revealing the common fear of combat among fleeing Red Guards, only six legionnaires and thirty Red Guards had been killed.[95] "In a moment," Williams said, "it was evident that the Czechs had no hostile feeling against the inhabitants, and . . . were received like conquering heroes. . . . The Czechs went about their task of restoring order with intelligence; within three hours men were removing the broken wires and repairing the telephone lines, and within 12 hours the streets were clear. Their courtesy and good nature were infectious. Soon the streets were thronged with people who celebrated a holiday." The legionnaires executed fifty members of Internationalist Brigades, Williams said, most of them Austrian-Hungarian POWs, including two fellow Czechs. In a more lenient approach to prisoners than is normal, he added, "They are for the most part releasing the Bolsheviks after disarming them."[96] With Samara in their possession, the legionnaires held one of Russia's largest cities on the eastern banks of the Volga River.

Disgrace, Acclaim, and Confusion

HAVING LOST EFFECTIVE control of the legionnaires, Masaryk and Beneš were completely at the mercy of the Allies in the summer of 1918. For instance, they depended completely on the Allies to ship the legionnaires

from Vladivostok—and at least some of the Allies now looked upon the
legionnaires as a potential army for a renewed Eastern Front in Russia.
Yet more than that, the legionnaires seized the attention of the Allies,
helping to focus a spotlight on the Czecho-Slovak aspirations for national independence. On July 28, 1918, Beneš wrote to Masaryk in the
United States that General Maurice Janin, head of the French military
mission to Russia, should arrange for the earliest departure of the legion
from Russia. "We shall win only on European battlefields, especially in
France," he said. "If we have 20,000–25,000 troops here we shall achieve
everything in politics we want." Around the same time, however, Beneš
told British foreign secretary Arthur Balfour that while the National
Council wanted the legion in France, he understood that the legion "can,
for the time being, be of great service for the Allies and for England if it
facilitates intervention in Russia."[97] Underneath these considerations was
the hard fact that none of the Allies could readily ship the legionnaires
from Vladivostok.

The panicked tone in Trotsky's hysterical telegrams was real. "I found
Moscow in a state of siege," said Bruce Lockhart, a British intelligence
agent who met frequently with Trotsky and Lenin, in the wake of the
Czecho-Slovak revolt. High-ranking officials urgently sought Lockhart's
help, including Chicherin, the Soviet commissar for foreign affairs, "begging me to use my influence to settle the Czech incident amicably."[98]
What the Soviet regime did not appreciate was that the legion's own
leaders and French commanders were also frightened.

One of the legion's principal French liaisons, Guinet, flew into action
up and down the Trans-Siberian, threatening, ordering, and pleading
with the men to obey Allied orders and cease fighting. In an interview
with the legionnaire newspaper, *Československý Deník*, on May 25, Guinet
insisted that at least some of the legionnaires would be going to Archangel.[99] On May 31 in Omsk—as armed legionnaires approached the city
from both east and west—he took part in a hasty meeting with Soviet,
Czech, French, and American officials. The Soviet officials waved a copy
of an intercepted Czech telegram advising the legionnaires to disregard

French orders. At that, Guinet issued a telegram to a unit of legionnaires based in Isil Kul, a town seventy-five miles west of Omsk, which had already defeated Soviet forces at the battle for Maryanovka:

> Your action forces the French Mission to wash its hands of this affair. It will be a disgrace for the Czechs to become involved in Russian difficulties. If the Czechs persist in their activities, everything must end between them and the French Government. The Czechs must take no action whatever until the French Mission . . . arrives in Isil Kul.[100]

Making no progress, Guinet left Omsk for Chelyabinsk on June 1 to speak directly to the legion's leaders. Guinet's message was one of at least two telegrams from the French to reach Gajda by June 3, urging him to stand down. Gajda was also by now informed that Marshal Foch had ordered the legionnaires to Archangel and that he was threatened with a court-martial. Unaware of what had transpired between local soviets and the legion, one Frenchman argued, "Soviet organs enlist all of their strength to make possible the speeding of the transports." Gajda stuck to his position and directed his men to disregard French orders. Meanwhile, Maxa, who was being held prisoner in Moscow, was forced to sign flyers dropped from aircraft as the legionnaires approached Syzran at the end of May. It said, "Wake up from this grave misunderstanding that threatens to destroy our sacred cause. . . . Immediately stop all operations . . . and send delegates to negotiations. To continue the hostile behavior would mean, inevitably, to create animosity between ourselves and the brotherly Russian people. That you must not allow to happen! . . . Send delegates with a white flag unarmed along the railway tracks to Syzran."[101]

THE CONFLICT THAT erupted at Chelyabinsk illuminated the stunning weakness of the Red Army, on which the Bolsheviks relied to remain in power, according to historian Victor M. Fic, who says that it "showed that they could have been defeated had a march against Moscow and St. Petersburg been ordered in January–March 1918."[102] This persuaded the

Allies to see in the legionnaires their hope to reopen the Eastern Front, just as the Western Front was buckling. Yet throughout the summer of 1918, the legionnaires acted at all times in their own self-interest, fighting only to defend themselves from hostile local soviets and aggressive Bolshevik agitators—who did not always follow Moscow's orders. In their determination to leave Russia, they defied the military plans of the Allies and even the pleas of the French government and their own Czecho-Slovak National Council. If the legionnaires had wanted to march on Moscow, they could have readily allowed units west of Omsk to remain in Russia or move northward, in Moscow's direction. In fact, the entire legion could have moved west, instead of clinging as it did to reaching Vladivostok.

While the legionnaires were being scolded and threatened by their leaders in Siberia, newspaper coverage of their exploits was brought into countless homes and offices in the United States and Europe. These accounts illuminated the aims of an obscure clique of exiles with strange accents and funny names, but the speed with which the legionnaires conquered much of Eurasia amazed diplomats, prime ministers, and the US president. US consul Harris shared with Secretary of State Robert Lansing this assessment:

> A handful of Czecho-Slovak soldiers, men of unparalleled courage, trained in the school of adversity, having always in mind the oppression of their own country, after fighting their way out of the hands of their Austro-Hungarian pursuers, after fighting their way out of the Ukraine, after being completely disarmed in the city of Penza, realizing that the time had come for action, which meant to them liberty or death, they have, unaided by the assistance of the outside world, entirely dependent upon their own resources in the heart of a vast continent, and surrounded by enemies whose every act toward them meant ruin, performed a deed which will live in history as long as the deeds of mankind shall be worthy of chronicling.[103]

The legionnaires always made an impression on persons not easy to impress. While based in Russia, the British writer and spy W. Somerset Maugham said, "My work throws me in close contact with the Czechs, and here I see a patriotism that fills me with amazement. It is a passion so single and so devouring that it leaves room for no others. . . . They are organized like a department store, disciplined like a Prussian regiment."[104] British prime minister David Lloyd-George wrote to Masaryk on September 11, 1918, to say, "The story of the adventures and triumphs of this small army is, indeed, one of the greatest epics of history."[105] While he often disagreed with the prime minister he served, Winston Churchill agreed with Lloyd-George about the legionnaires: "The pages of history recall scarcely any parallel episode at once so romantic in character and so extensive in scale," he said. "Thus, through a treacherous breach of faith, by a series of accidents and chances which no one in the world had foreseen, the whole of Russia from the Volga River to the Pacific Ocean, a region almost as large as the continent of Africa, had passed as if by magic into the control of the Allies."[106] Former US president Theodore Roosevelt, long out of office and grieving over the death of his own son in the war, was nonetheless inspired by reports of the legion's achievements in Siberia. He donated one thousand dollars of the cash award he had received from his 1906 Nobel Peace Prize to the legionnaires, "the extraordinary nature of whose great and heroic feat is literally unparalleled, so far as I know, in ancient or modern warfare."[107] His mortal enemy, Wilson, would agree.

YET ALLIED LEADERS struggled to agree on a common and coherent policy regarding Russia, in part because they could not obtain accurate, comprehensive, or timely information about the developments in a constantly changing and vast Russian landscape.

Communications between Russia, and particularly locales across Siberia, and the Western capitals after the February Revolution were so delayed and confused as to be a serious detriment to understanding or

planning. An entirely chaotic environment, moreover, saw rapidly changing political and military developments. For weeks, if not months, at a
time, there were no communications between cities within Russia and
both official and private telegrams were often garbled. In a letter home
from Russia in May 1917, Charles Crane said, "Things are moving so
rapidly here that it seems impossible to chronicle anything of value by
the time a message reaches its destination."[108] While he was in Russia,
Masaryk said, "there was no connection between Russia and the West.
News passed very slowly and incompletely."[109] British propaganda agent
R. W. Seton-Watson said, "Communications between London and Moscow were virtually impossible."[110] Beneš conceded, "This inadequacy of
communication was a great handicap."[111]

Indeed, one of the first official reports to Washington about the revolt
of the legionnaires did not reach its recipients for more than two months;
the telegram from US consul Harris in Irkutsk dated May 26, which concerned the first day's fighting in that city, reached the State Department
on July 30.[112]

SEVEN

The Ambivalent Intervention

I was in command of the United States troops sent to Siberia and, I must admit, I do not know what the United States was trying to accomplish by military intervention.

WILLIAM S. GRAVES
MAJOR GENERAL, US ARMY (RET.)[1]

IN MAY 1918 Tomáš G. Masaryk was still unaware that a war had broken out between Moscow and his legionnaires. He was touring the United States, being hailed as a hero, seeking out US officials, and telling major newspapers that the Allies should recognize the Soviets, negotiate with them, and avoid intervening in Russia.

His efforts to get the legionnaires out of Russia, which had resulted in toppling Soviet power across Siberia, was about to be complicated by the French and British, who were coming to a decision to use the legionnaires as a reason to get *into* Russia. Their aims of intervention, too, began to shift from reestablishing an Eastern Front to, perhaps, toppling the Soviet regime.

Vladivostok in the Cross-Hairs

ISOLATED AS ON an island, the fifteen thousand legionnaires in and around Vladivostok were not involved in the conflict; indeed, it took

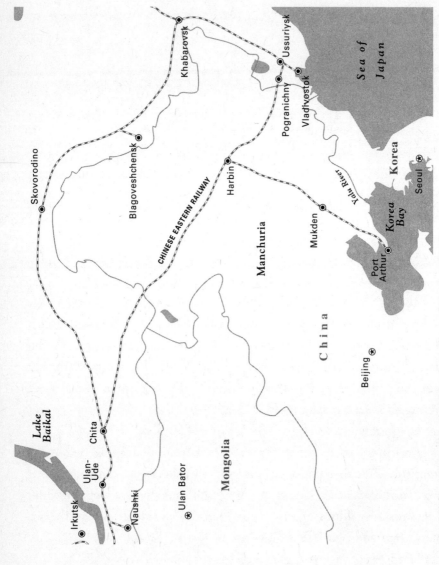

Trans-Siberian & Chinese Eastern Railways, Russian Far East

them several weeks to learn the full extent of what was happening in the west beyond Lake Baikal. Reflecting their isolation from timely and accurate information, officials of the Czecho-Slovak National Council and General Mikhail Diterikhs, Masaryk's chief of staff, as late as June 16, 1918, ordered the legionnaires engaged in combat to observe "complete neutrality in Russian affairs" and to reach agreements with local soviets to move their trains along.[2] No mention was made of the repeated stopping of trains or of Leon Trotsky's threatening orders to pull the legionnaires off the trains, disarm them, and force them into labor battalions or the Red Army. Yet they eventually saw the June 11 issue of *Československy Denik*, which called upon the Vladivostok troops to turn back to rescue their brothers to the west. Emphasizing the break with Moscow, Radola Gajda on June 12 announced that "any negotiations with the Bolsheviks or conclusion of peace with them is ruled out; we are now in a life-or-death struggle with them; we must destroy the Bolsheviks at any price. According to the reports I have received, we will, most likely, not travel to France."

Meanwhile, with the legionnaires in control of about twenty-five hundred miles of the Trans-Siberian Railway from Penza to a point just west of Irkutsk, Gajda's focus now swiveled to the east, where the Trans-Siberian stretched eastward from Irkutsk to Vladivostok, along which substantial Red forces stood ready, already devising a bold scheme to trap all the legionnaires who were located west of Irkutsk.

Small numbers of Czecho-Slovaks were holding off enemy forces at Mariinsk, a small town about two hundred miles east of Novosibirsk, and, further east, another group of legionnaires was besieged on two sides outside of Nizhneudinsk, three hundred miles west of Irkutsk. Gajda's troops advanced from Novosibirsk toward Mariinsk, where battle-hardened Austrian and Hungarian Internationalists reinforced a line of Red Army soldiers. Gajda's boldness gave his men confidence. "Gajda was a leader whose belief it was to strike at once, to strike often, and with determination," recalled Sergeant Gustav Becvar. "In those days, he seemed never to hesitate in his course of action."[3]

Just before Mariinsk, the legionnaires employed the first of many flanking movements. At nightfall, one thousand legionnaires marched away from the rail line southward into the chilly darkness. After trekking seventeen miles, they came to the Kiji River, where the men used a handful of rowboats to cross the river through the rest of the night. At daybreak, they resumed their march until they heard distant field guns off to their left, where the comrades they left behind were drawing fire from the Reds. Coming over the crest of a ridge, the legionnaires found themselves behind Mariinsk—and behind the enemy. As they swept down the mountain slope toward the rail line, the Reds opened fire with machine guns, some of them on a Bolshevik armored train. While most of the legionnaires dug in and returned fire, small numbers ran or crawled furiously forward to destroy the tracks and trap the train. Sensing their vulnerability, the train sped away toward the east—which allowed the legionnaires to commence attacks on Mariinsk from two directions. The Red Guard soldiers fled, leaving behind two hundred dead and six hundred prisoners.[4]

Gajda refused to rest, ordering the men to continue moving east at once. They fought scattered enemy units for days and captured small stations, all the while fearing to approach Krasnoyarsk, a large city and a Bolshevik stronghold. On the evening of the third day, friendly railroad workers ran toward them with good news, "Krasnoyarsk is in Czech hands!" The Krasnoyarsk Bolsheviks panicked at the news from Mariinsk, and the legionnaires outside of Nizhneudinsk took advantage of the situation and attacked from the east, taking Krasnoyarsk on June 20. The combined forces turned again toward the east and finally captured Nizhneudinsk itself on June 24. In celebration, the legionnaires adopted a stray bear cub, whom they called Misha, as a mascot that traveled with them in his own cage all the way to Vladivostok.[5]

In July 1918, despite these successes, the Czecho-Slovak Legion remained divided. While about 40 percent of the men were at Vladivostok, awaiting Allied ships, most of them were still trapped west of Irkutsk, a city just west of Lake Baikal. When news of the Chelyabinsk revolt finally reached them, the troops at Vladivostok knew they had to turn back to aid their brothers by clearing the Trans-Siberian of enemy forces. The US consul at Vladivostok, John K. Caldwell, US admiral Austin M. Knight, and legionnaire general Diterikhs variously estimated that there were between twenty and fifty-two thousand Red Army and Internationalist troops between Vladivostok and Irkutsk, with concentrations at Ussuriysk, Khabarovsk, and Chita.[6]

Caldwell reported on June 25 that leaders of the Czecho-Slovak National Council had formally requested arms, ammunition, and as many as 100,000 Allied troops to support them as they prepared to rescue their brothers farther west. Caldwell said that the Allied consuls agreed that arms, supplies, and troops should be sent to Vladivostok to assist them.[7] The next day, Admiral Knight aboard the USS *Brooklyn* forwarded a similar plea from the legion's leadership. The Japanese agreed to provide six artillery pieces, forty machine guns, ten thousand rifles, and ammunition.[8] The legionnaires first had to gain control of the teeming and contested port city, which was crowded with Cossacks, Bolsheviks, anti-Bolshevik socialists, former tsarist officers, Siberian independence advocates, Chinese Eastern Railway guards, and soldiers, sailors, and officials that came to number seventy-three thousand Japanese, twelve thousand Poles, nine thousand Americans, five thousand Chinese, four thousand Serbs, four thousand Romanians, four thousand Canadians, two thousand Italians, sixteen hundred British, and seven hundred French.[9]

The legionnaires decided to make their move on June 29, in part based on reports that the Vladivostok soviet was shipping some of the Allied arms and ammunition to Red forces west of the city. After quietly disarming Bolshevik sentries the night before and assuming positions on the hills overlooking the city, at 10:00 a.m. the legionnaires presented an ultimatum to the soviet to surrender, demanding a reply in thirty minutes. Hearing no answer, the legionnaires forcibly entered the soviet's headquarters, disarmed guards without shooting, and occupied the building. At a fortresslike structure near the railway station, however, fighting broke out with rifle and machine-gun fire and hand grenades.

Legionnaires closed in and threw four grenades into the first floor of the building, which caught fire. Its occupants surrendered at 6:00 p.m. While the British and Japanese landed troops as a precaution, they did not participate. Four legionnaires died and twenty-one to twenty-five were wounded, while sixty to eighty Reds were killed, including an unspecified number of Hungarian Internationalists. The five members of the soviet were detained in the legion's barracks, but they were permitted to speak at the mass funeral for the Red Guards, which was attended by five to six thousand people. A much smaller crowd attended the funeral for the legionnaires, according to Caldwell, who reported, "I regret that Admiral Knight and Secretary of State [Robert Lansing have] so far been able to offer them less encouragement and assistance [than] representatives of Japan and Great Britain."[10]

On July 2 the legionnaires at Vladivostok finally started moving west. On July 11 their eastbound comrades marched into Irkutsk, happy to find that the Red Guards had evacuated the city—until they learned a perilous trap was being set further east. It was in between these two dates that President Woodrow Wilson finally relented on the issue of an intervention in Russia. He ordered US troops to Vladivostok, principally to rescue the Czecho-Slovak legionnaires, just as they entered upon their most serious battles with enemy forces around Lake Baikal.

After thirteen thousand Czecho-Slovaks moved out of Vladivostok on July 2, British and French soldiers and sailors began guarding and patrolling the city. On July 6 the Allied representatives in Vladivostok proclaimed a "protectorate" over the city.[11] Even then, however, according to Edvard Beneš, French foreign minister Stéphan Pichon informed London that the real purpose of putting French troops ashore was to secure the port for the evacuation of the legionnaires, not to launch a larger intervention in Russia.[12] Closely following the exploits of the legionnaires, the New York Times reported that "the small force under General Dieterichs might well be annihilated" and urged the Allies to support them.[13]

Within days the legionnaires launched an all-out attack on Ussuriysk, a city just eighty miles north of Vladivostok where the Trans-Siberian and the Chinese Eastern Railways linked up and which was defended by artillery, an armored train, and at least two thousand enemy soldiers. On July 5, the legionnaires routed Soviet forces, which retreated in eight trains, blowing up at least one bridge and destroying three miles of track as they fled north toward Khabarovsk. The legionnaires suffered about eighty dead and at least 170 wounded, but captured six hundred Hungarian Internationalists.[14] At Ussuriysk, the legion split its forces. One group advanced north along the Trans-Siberian toward Khabarovsk—supported by US and Japanese troops in some of the only combat to involve American soldiers in Siberia—from whence they moved westward toward Chita, a city east of Irkutsk. The rest took the Chinese Eastern Railway from Ussuriysk northwest across Manchuria, which reconnected with the Trans-Siberian at Chita.

By September 1, the legion had secured the entire Trans-Siberian from the European border to the Pacific Ocean.[15] Given the lack of passable roads, this gave it control of most of Siberia, more than five million square miles or almost 10 percent of the earth's land surface. Along with the Trans-Siberian went control over virtually all communication between Moscow and Vladivostok.

Birth of the Soviet Camps

THE BRITISH AND French had, throughout the summer, continued to push for the legion to move west, in the hopes of reopening the Eastern Front against the Central Powers. As a result, the Soviet regime came to suspect an Allied conspiracy behind the Czecho-Slovak revolt, just as the legionnaires saw the hands of Berlin and Vienna behind every Bolshevik approach to them. Willing from day one to employ violence against any opponent, Moscow nonetheless began to construct vast institutions of detention and punishment chiefly as a result of the revolt of the legionnaires.

Historian Richard Pipes reports that "talk of concentration camps was first heard in Soviet Russia in the spring of 1918 in connection with the Czech uprising." He calls the camps "an institution which the Bolsheviks did not quite invent but which they gave a novel and most sinister meaning."[16] Historian Arno J. Mayer likewise concedes that "it was also in this mood of systemic ruthlessness, and at the high point of the crisis in the Civil War during the summer of 1918, that the Bolsheviks took the first steps toward establishing a system of labor camps."[17] Mayer continues, "When and why was the idea for concentration camps first raised? [Vladimir] Lenin himself had repeatedly invoked the use of forced social labor for penal purposes . . . but it was the acute perils of the summer of 1918 that turned general proposals into practice."

On several occasions, Trotsky himself linked the establishment of concentration camps and the Czecho-Slovak rebellion. Within days of the revolt, Trotsky issued his inflammatory telegram of May 25 ordering authorities to shoot or disarm the Czecho-Slovaks and place them in camps. Further confirming his intention to establish a network of concentration camps in response to the Czecho-Slovak revolt was a May 31 message that Trotsky personally handed to a representative of the legion, Václav Neubert, which said, "The order for shooting Czecho-Slovaks found armed and refusing to hand over their arms is to remain in full force; also to remain in full force is the order that any unit in which a weapon is found is to be confined in a concentration camp."[18] A few days later, Trotsky issued a similar order "to all units fighting against the counter-revolutionary Czecho-Slovak mutineers." This order of June 4, 1918, boldly and erroneously discussed possible negotiations with the legionnaires, then added, "An obligatory condition for negotiations is surrender of all arms by the Czecho-Slovaks. Those who do not voluntarily hand over their arms are to be shot on the spot, in accordance with the order previously given. Echelons which have been forcibly disarmed are to be confined in concentration camps."[19]

"Though the fact is little-known," reports Pipes, "it was Trotsky, not [Joseph] Stalin, who introduced into Soviet Russia the concentration camp, an institution that under Stalin developed into the monstrous Gulag empire."[20] That was because Stalin was in rare perfect agreement with Trotsky on the utility of the camps. When Bolsheviks in Estonia telegraphed him about "counter-revolutionaries and traitors," Stalin replied, "The idea of a concentration camp is excellent."[21] The camps were turned over to the Cheka, the Soviet security organization, in July 1918. Fueled in part by the official Red Terror launched on September 5, in the wake of a second, more serious, attempt to assassinate Lenin, and mentioned in the very first decree on Red Terror, the number of such camps grew. By the end of 1919 there were 21 registered camps; by the end of 1920 there were 107.[22]

The Pittsburgh Pact

LOOKING BACK YEARS later, R. W. Seton-Watson credited three tactical achievements for the success of the Czecho-Slovak independence movement. The first was Masaryk's decision to go to Russia in May 1917 to organize the legionnaires. The second was the work of Beneš and Milan R. Štefánik in promoting the Italian-Yugoslav rapprochement after the Battle of Caporetto and the holding of the Congress of Oppressed Nationalities in Rome in April 1918. The third achievement, he said, was Masaryk's ability to reach Washington in time to influence President Wilson's relations with Austria-Hungary, modifying his peace terms.[23] "That America might help did not occur to me," Masaryk said of his thinking as he left Prague in 1914.[24] Now in America, Masaryk gave a face to the exploits of the legionnaires, which were jumping off the pages of American newspapers just as the professor began making speeches, granting interviews, and, especially, lobbying the White House. Once again, he was in the right place at the right time.

Masaryk arrived in Vancouver aboard the *Empress of Asia* on April 29, 1918, where he was met by Charles Pergler, the Czech-born Iowa lawyer who generated much of the exile movement's publicity in America. Based in Washington, DC, Pergler was vice president of the United States branch of the Czecho-Slovak National Council. "During my whole stay in America he was with me, working indefatigably," Masaryk said.[25] The presidency of the US council was reserved for a visiting member of the

Paris National Council, in this case Masaryk. While the efforts of the exiles in Europe was limited to one-on-one meetings with key officials, American democracy and the size of the Czech and Slovak communities in the United States enabled Masaryk to launch a public-speaking campaign to thank his American brethren for their financial support, raise additional funds, and show US politicians how popular the Czecho-Slovak cause was.[26] His efforts were immeasurably aided by the generous and positive coverage in American newspapers of the emerging epic of the legionnaires battling their way across Siberia. "The effect in America was astonishing and almost incredible," said Masaryk. "All at once the Czechs and Czecho-Slovaks were known to everybody. Interest in our army in Russia and Siberia became general and its advance aroused enthusiasm. As often happens in such cases, the less the knowledge the greater the enthusiasm; but the enthusiasm of the American public was real."[27]

EVEN WITH NEWSPAPERS trumpeting the exploits of the Czecho-Slovak legionnaires in Russia, Masaryk was not entirely prepared for the tumultuous welcome he received when he arrived in Chicago. Pergler said, "A welcome was accorded to him which in American history is probably without a parallel." More than a hundred thousand Czechs and Slovaks greeted him at the railway station on May 5. "From the railway station to the hotel, there was a huge procession; the city was beflagged with Czech and Slav colors," Masaryk said.[28] When the professor stopped to speak outside the Blackstone Hotel, "an enthusiastic and stormy ovation" filled Michigan Avenue. Speaking in Czech, Masaryk again credited his soldiers. "After the outbreak of the war I returned to Prague and the first thing I saw was the opposition of the Czech soldiers to military service. They resented going to war against the Slavs, they protested. They did that of their own will, without leaders, without any agitation, just by themselves. When I saw it I said to myself: you, as a Representative, cannot do less."[29]

When on May 9 he arrived at Union Station in Washington, DC, twenty-seven senators and congressmen greeted him. "It took me a while to get used to my American fame," he confessed.[30] However, Masaryk's eagerly awaited meeting with President Wilson would be delayed, in part because in interviews with the *Washington Post* on May 12 and the *New York Times* on May 27, Masaryk again urged the Allies to recognize the Soviets, negotiate with Moscow, and avoid intervening in Russia.[31] At the same time the White House was also wrestling with the issue of whether to recognize the independence of the Czecho-Slovaks and other Habsburg nationalities, and a meeting with Masaryk would have forced Wilson's hand on either (or both) of these issues.

Awaiting a summons to the White House, Masaryk continued speaking and granting interviews in Baltimore, Boston, Cleveland, New York, and Pittsburgh. In New York on May 25—the day Trotsky issued his violent ultimatum and fighting broke out between his legionnaires and the Soviets—Masaryk addressed a packed Carnegie Hall, though he stuck to his usually thoughtful, direct, and low-key manner of speaking. "Evidently he was not striving for oratorical effect," reported the *New York Tribune*. "In fact, what he said smacked of the scholar in the study." That is, until he sternly emphasized the need to break up Austria-Hungary, which brought the audience to its feet.[32] In an interview with the *New York Times*, he said:

> Think of your time of struggle, when Washington was hard-pressed. Think what it meant to you when France came to your aid. That is what we ask of you today, to come to our help, and at the same time to take a step that will lead to the defeat of Germany. . . . Now is the greatest time in the history of the world to make a stroke for democracy and against imperialism by freeing the peoples of Austria-Hungary and of Eastern Europe from domination by foreign races. A peace aimed to give these peoples their long-sought rights is the only one that can endure, because it will rest on justice. It is an opportunity to duplicate your own great Revolution and its benefits many times over.[33]

On May 28, he spoke to another large audience in Chicago, where he gave the legionnaires primary credit for advancing their cause: "Having no arms whatsoever, who could make a revolution? And yet we started a revolution and our soldiers did it in the first place. They realized that the hour of final decision had come. In this I see the great discipline and strength of our people and an assurance for the future."[34] Everything was finally falling into place; the next day, Secretary of State Robert Lansing issued his May 29 statement, in the wake of the Congress of Oppressed Nationalities of Austria-Hungary in Rome, "that the nationalistic aspirations of the Czecho-Slovaks and Yugoslavs for freedom have the earnest sympathy of this Government."[35]

Perhaps the most significant accomplishment of his American tour occurred on May 31, 1918, the day after Masaryk attended a large public meeting in Pittsburgh, home to many Slovaks, some of whose members worried about Czech domination of the independence movement and Masaryk's anti-Catholic reputation. While many Slovaks were aware of how solicitous of Slovak welfare Masaryk had shown himself to be, Slovak Catholic leader Josef Hušek was particularly assertive in demanding a signed agreement guaranteeing Slovak autonomy in any new state. Given the formidable obstacles to negotiating with the Slovaks in Hungary for a mandate, Slovak American scholar M. Mark Stolarik says, "the Czechs in exile who advocated a union of Czechs and Slovaks had to depend on American Slovaks to provide this mandate."[36] So it happened that Masaryk felt obliged to sign the Pittsburgh Agreement in a meeting with leaders of the Slovak League of America, the Bohemian National Alliance, and the National Union of Czech Catholics on the thirty-first. Appearing to reinforce the Cleveland Agreement of 1915, it used somewhat different language. Its promises to the Slovaks yet seemed clear and strong:

> We approve of the political program which aims at the union of the Czechs and Slovaks in an independent state composed of the Czech lands and Slovakia. Slovakia shall have her own administrative system, her own [legislative] Diet, and her own courts. The Slovak language shall be the official language in the schools, in the public offices, and in public affairs generally. The Czecho-Slovak state shall be a republic, and its constitution a democratic one.

It added, "Detailed provisions relating to the organization of the Czecho-Slovak State shall be left to the liberated Czechs and Slovaks and their duly accredited representatives."[37] All sixteen members of the American branch of the Czecho-Slovak National Council—eight Slovaks and eight Czechs—signed the document.

One of the strangest qualities of the agreement, however, was that it was done on the fly—and written only in pencil. Another oddity was that most of the signers were Americans, who were effectively making decisions for the Slovaks in Hungary. A final oddity was that the Hungarian Slovaks did not learn about the Pittsburgh Agreement until 1919.

On the same day, May 31, 1918, Senator W. H. King of Utah, introduced a resolution promoting the cause of Czech and Slovak independence, similar to the ones introduced the previous year by Senator William S. Kenyon and Congressman Adolph J. Sabath. And the fund-raising continued in Czech and Slovak communities across the United States, with fairs or bazaars in the fall of 1918 that netted $65,109 in Omaha; $50,000 to 60,000 in Taylor, Texas; and $25,000 in Cedar Rapids, Iowa. A nationwide fund-raising campaign linked to the 1918 Thanksgiving holiday raised another $320,000. And grassroots organizers were on fire with enthusiasm for the independence movement. "At times," one Czech American participant said, "it seemed that every Czech living in the United States had constituted himself a committee of one for the purpose of convincing his fellow citizens, of other origins, and particularly the White House, of the justice of the Czech cause and the propriety of aiding it." The White House was once so deluged with telegrams from Czech Americans that the Associated Press bureau in Washington, DC, filed a story about it.[38]

These political victories aside, Beneš, like Masaryk, remained skeptical of the emerging plans to use the legionnaires to reopen an Eastern Front. "I could have seen some point in a united intervention on a large scale with definite political aims, directed towards the construction of an Eastern Front," he said. "I knew, however, that for a scheme of this kind there was neither the determination nor the resources, and I feared the effects of any vague and half-hearted action for the Allies and for Russia, to say nothing of ourselves, since our troops would fall a victim to it."[39] Which, of course, is exactly what happened to the legionnaires.

The Intervention Chorus

THE LEGION'S SURPRISING revolt occurred against a background of Washington's firm opposition to pleas from London, Paris, and Tokyo for a major intervention in Russia from Vladivostok. Wilson and his advisers saw this approach as far too remote from the theater of war, and the expected role for Japan was problematic. "The only thing on which everybody agrees," said British foreign minister Arthur Balfour, "is that without the active participation of America nothing effective can be accomplished through Siberia."[40] Yet throughout the first half of 1918, Wilson or Lansing had drafted negative replies to such requests on January 16, February 8, February 13, March 5, March 18, and May 7.[41] Despite their opposition, Lansing and Wilson were more open to limited Allied landings in Russia's northern ports to safeguard military supplies. They were also slowly inching toward the idea of doing *something* in Siberia, if only to appease the Allies, who were not yet seeing many US troops on the Western Front, which was under a series of horrendous German assaults that spring and summer.

In the wake of the Czecho-Slovak revolt, urgent pleas for intervention from US diplomats joined the chorus from the Allies. David R. Francis, US ambassador to Russia, met with French, British, and Italian representatives on May 29, where they agreed that all would urge their governments to intervene.[42] Francis had already advocated intervention in a May 2 telegram to Lansing, prompted by the arrival of German ambassador Wilhelm von Mirbach in Moscow and perceived German threats to Murmansk and Archangel, but also half expecting Russia to welcome the Allies.[43] French ambassador Joseph Noulens sent a similar recommendation to Paris on May 14.[44] The US minister to China, Paul S. Reinsch, now joined Francis with telegrams urging intervention on May 30 and June 5. On June 13, he urged a specific response to the Czecho-Slovak revolt: "It is the general opinion of Allied representatives here in which I concur that it would be a serious mistake to remove the Czecho-Slovak troops from Siberia. With only slight countenance and support, they could control all of Siberia against the Germans. They are sympathetic to the Russian population, eager to be accessories to the Allied cause, the most serious menace to extension of German influence in Russia."[45] While his argument had one significant weakness—the legion would actually require considerable military support to hang on, let alone reopen the Eastern Front—it may have tipped the scales for President Wilson.

Allied diplomats in Russia also began to strongly defend the legionnaires, with the French in particular reversing their position. On May 31 Noulens telegraphed French general Jean Guillaume Lavergne, ordering him and other commanders not to follow Moscow's orders to disarm the legionnaires. Accordingly, French liaison officer Major Alphonse Guinet began adjusting his stance. On June 4, having reached Chelyabinsk, he denounced the Czecho-Slovak revolt at a meeting of the legion's new Provisional Executive Committee. By June 6, however, he began asserting that French commanders never considered disarming the legionnaires and that the revolt may have been justified. Also on June 4, the Allied ambassadors to Russia submitted a formal protest of Trotsky's disarmament orders to Commissar for Foreign Affairs Georgy V. Chicherin and demanded a meeting with Trotsky.[46] Masaryk, too, got involved. Although Washington did not recognize the Soviet regime, Lansing forwarded a private message from Masaryk to Chicherin on June 25 protesting the efforts to disarm, imprison, or kill the legionnaires and Moscow's failure to keep its promises to allow the men transit across Siberia. "I can prove," Masaryk said, "by incontrovertible documents that I rejected every plan directed against your government submitted to me by your political adversaries, even of such adversaries who justly could not be called counter-revolutionary. I can prove that, until lately, I recommended to the Allied statesmen to be on good terms with your government. We Czecho-Slovaks love Russia, and we wish her to be a strong and free democracy."[47]

UNTIL THE CZECHO-SLOVAK revolt in Siberia, it remained bedrock US policy not to intervene in Russia's internal affairs. US Army Chief of Staff Peyton C. March reiterated this policy as late as May 28 in response to a request for instructions from General Tasker H. Bliss at the Supreme War Council, saying, "The President's attitude is that Russia's misfortune imposes upon us at this time the obligation of unswerving fidelity to the principles of Russian territorial integrity and political independence."[48] The Czech uprising was getting under way, of course, and Paris and London seized on the legion's uprising as another reason for intervention. "From this point on," historian David F. Trask notes, "the absolute character of American resistance to intervention began to crumble." By June 1, General Bliss informed the Allies that Wilson had withdrawn objections to a limited intervention in Russia's north, adding, "but such efforts should proceed, if at all, upon the sure sympathy of the Russian people and should not have as their ultimate objects any restoration of the ancient regime or any other interference with the political liberty of the Russian people."

When the Supreme War Council met at Versailles from June 1 to June 3, German artillery could be heard in the distance and preparations were under way for the evacuation of Paris; military planners clung to vague hopes for some kind of salvation to emerge from Russia. The council approved Joint Note No. 31, entitled "Allied Intervention at Allied Russian Ports," which envisioned the Czechs moving to Russia's northern ports to help the Allies and remaining there to cooperate in some vague fashion with other Allied forces. This never happened, of course, due to the revolt then under way. The idea, according to noted historian George F. Kennan, "never at any time had reality outside the minds of the Allied military planners themselves."[49]

Yet with Wilson no longer objecting to limited Allied landings in Russia's northern ports, the council also decided to send reinforcements to

Murmansk, where small Allied forces landed in early March, as well as to occupy Archangel. The council's biggest decision, however, was an agreement to request Japanese troops land at Vladivostok and advance as far west as possible "for the purpose of encountering the Germans," yet respect Russia's territorial integrity and take no sides in Russia's internal politics.[50] Still wanting to see the legionnaires in France, French prime minister Georges Clemenceau pushed for an agreement to ask Tokyo to ship as many legionnaires to his country as they could.[51] Back in Paris on May 22, Clemenceau had reassured Beneš, "I want to have all of your troops in France. I consider them first-rate soldiers," he said. "We will give you a declaration and will acknowledge your independence. You must be independent because you deserve it. You can rely on me not to leave you in the lurch."[52] Wilson remained the obstacle to a large-scale intervention in Russia. Instead, he and his aides debated sending a relief commission, which Lansing said, "would, for the time being, dispose of the proposal for armed intervention." Wilson's adviser Colonel Edward House agreed.[53]

Also at work amidst the urgent discussions concerning Russia was the fact that virtually every Allied diplomatic or military official in Russia suspected that Berlin was behind Trotsky's orders to disarm the legionnaires—which allowed Allied leaders back home to believe that supporting the legionnaires was crucial to fighting the Central Powers in Russia. To what extent Moscow was influenced by Berlin is open to endless debate, in large part because neither side was transparent about its real aims. Yet Berlin and Moscow did share diplomatic relations and often walked in lockstep. Soviet commissar for foreign affairs Chicherin in mid-June, for example, demanded that the Allies evacuate Russia's northern ports, which German ambassador Mirbach had demanded in early May.[54]

US ambassador Francis wired Lansing on June 3 that the legionnaires should not be disarmed, adding that he warned Moscow that "the Allies would consider disarmament and severe treatment as inspired by Germany or certainly by hostile sentiment toward the Allies."[55] In another telegram to Washington on June 7, he said that US consul general

DeWitt C. Poole in Moscow "advises that Soviet order to disarm [the legionnaires] was dictated by Germans."[56] Masaryk's own June 25 telegram to Chicherin said, "It seems that some local soviet yielded to the Austrian and German intrigue and attacked our troops." Representatives of the Czecho-Slovaks accepted these claims. US consul Alfred R. Thomson at Omsk forwarded an official statement from the new Provisional Executive Committee leading the Czech-Slovak Corps on July 4 that said, "The Czecho-Slovaks are convinced that the action taken against them by the Soviet government was dictated from Berlin by [ambassador to Russia] von Mirbach."[57]

In addition to the fact that German, Austrian, and Hungarian POWs were fighting for Moscow and that Germany had diplomatic relations with Moscow, Berlin was financially backing the Bolsheviks. The first German ambassador to Russia, Mirbach, was instructed to support the Bolsheviks; he cabled Berlin on June 3, 1918, saying that doing so would cost 3 million marks per month. The German Foreign Ministry set aside 40 million marks to support operations in Russia, and Moscow received monthly subsidies from Berlin of 3 million marks in June, July, and August.[58] Kaiser Wilhelm II decided on June 28 to rescue Moscow again—by vowing not to conduct further military operations against Russia. This allowed Trotsky to move reliable Latvian units eastward to the Czecho-Slovak front where, by the end of July, they started to engage the legion near Kazan, attack legionnaires at Yekaterinburg, and suppress the anti-Bolshevik uprising in Izhevsk and its environs. "These operations turned the tide of battle in the Bolsheviks' favor," says Pipes. "The long-term effect of the Kaiser's verdict was to enable the Bolsheviks to weather the most critical period in their history."[59] As documents from Soviet archives confirm, Lenin demanded more funds from Berlin as late as August 1918 to support propaganda in Western Europe.[60] "In truth," says historian John Keegan, "the Allies, desperate for any diversion of German effort from their climatic offensive in France, did not become committedly anti-Bolshevik until the mid-summer of 1918 and then because the signs indicated, correctly, that the Bolsheviks had strayed from their own initially anti-German policy towards one of accepting German indulgence of their survival."[61]

Paris, which lost considerable Russian investments as a result of the Soviet takeover, was most threatened by the prospect of an alliance between Berlin and Moscow. "There is no question that of all the Allied governments it was the French which reacted most violently to Russia's departure from the war," says Kennan, and as a result, "the French became the unswerving, enthusiastic, and undiscriminating partisans of any Far Eastern intervention, anywhere, by anyone, and at any time."[62] The fact that the legionnaires were formally members of the French armed forces thus made their dilemma in Siberia especially acute. Kennan notes, "There was nothing in the code of Bolshevik ethics to inhibit the acceptance of [German] subsidies, and nothing that would have caused the Bolshevik leaders to feel the slightest sense of moral obligation to the Germans by virtue of having accepted them."[63]

Wilson Turns to Masaryk

AMERICAN INDUSTRIALIST CHARLES R. Crane's closeness to both Wilson and Masaryk made him a natural intermediary. On May 8, 1918, the day before Masaryk arrived in Washington, Crane wrote to Wilson, "I hope you can set aside a little time with Professor Masaryk."[64] On May 16, Masaryk had dinner at the home of Crane's son, Richard, who was an aide of Lansing, with a handful of subcabinet officials.[65] One of the diners, third assistant secretary of state Breckinridge Long, wrote a memorandum that evening that oddly disparaged the independence movement: "Masaryk is particularly interested in spreading propaganda amongst the Czecho-Slovaks and fomenting them to revolt against Austria. The scheme seems to me impractical."[66] Masaryk clearly had work to do.

When European and American newspapers carried the first news of the Czecho-Slovak revolt on June 3, 1918, Lansing summoned Masaryk to a meeting the same day.[67] Although Lansing had warmed to the Czecho-Slovak independence movement, Masaryk repeated to Lansing his objections to an Allied intervention in Russia, urged recognition of the Soviets, and pointed out that the legionnaires wished to fight in France, not Russia. Lansing told Masaryk there were no Allied ships available to move his men from Vladivostok. Masaryk and the White House were somewhat at odds.

Despite these disagreements, the news of the legion's revolt that emerged in June and persistent lobbying by distinguished advisers to President Wilson finally gained an audience with the president for Masaryk. On June 9, the elder Crane wrote again to ask Wilson to see Masaryk: "I believe no one else in Europe could make so valuable a contribution as he." Wilson responded on June 11, "Of course, I will try to see Professor Masaryk."[68] On June 12, Masaryk called on Wilson's other foreign policy adviser, Colonel House, in Massachusetts.[69] Finally, another presidential confidant, Dr. John R. Mott, the head of the American YMCA and member of the Root Mission, which had been sent to Russia in April 1917, urged Wilson in a White House meeting on June 18 to see Masaryk.[70]

The first meeting between the two men occurred at 5:00 p.m. the next day and lasted forty-five minutes. Masaryk told the president that "I am not in favor of a so-called intervention, because I do not see what it would bring about. But I would be in favor of renewing the war upon Germany by the whole Japanese army." The men discussed how Japan would be compensated, whether Tokyo would seek Russian territory in return, and whether its forces were prepared.[71] Japan's reasons for wanting to become involved were difficult to decipher, or accept. "To the Japanese mind," concludes Kennan, "the advantage to Japan of participation in the European war had always been seen largely in the prospect of putting the western Entente powers under obligation to Japan, and then exacting a price in the form of concessions to Japanese aspirations on the Asiatic mainland."[72] Interestingly, Masaryk pointed out that he thought it would take 1 million soldiers to resurrect the Eastern Front, an astute observation that was oddly overlooked by Allied officials, who did not appear to appreciate such details. "The President was told that it would not be practical at the present time to send an army into Russia unless it could be one of overwhelming numbers," reported the *New York Times*.[73] With Wilson, Masaryk repeated his arguments for shipping his legionnaires to France. While the meeting was friendly, if formal, Wilson closed by saying he was bound to support the Allies on intervention.[74] While Masaryk and Beneš were throwing cold water on plans for an Allied intervention, the legion's revolt had the countervailing effect of making their Czecho-Slovak independence movement important to Allied plans.

A FLOOD TIDE of publicity about the legion's exploits in Siberia, moreover, was raising the stakes. The twin events of May 1918—the Czecho-Slovak Legion's revolt in Siberia and the hero's welcome accorded Masaryk—spawned an avalanche of American newspaper coverage favorable to the Czecho-Slovaks, starting in June. Up until May, for example, the *New York Times* had not carried a single editorial about the Czecho-Slovaks and news reports always subsumed "Czech" and "Czecho-Slovak" stories under the "Austria-Hungary" heading, but *Times* indexes for July and September 1918 list two and a half pages of articles about the Czecho-Slovaks and their national aspirations. The legionnaires in Russia grabbed by far most of this attention.

"In fact," said one observer who helped Masaryk in the United States, "for most Americans the Czecho-Slovaks as a people existed only through the army in Siberia. Many Americans could not pronounce their name nor visualize a location for them."[75] The reporting also spawned a wave of editorial opinion favorable to an intervention in Russia, with the Czecho-Slovak Legion at the leading edge. The *Chicago Herald-Examiner*, the *New York Times*, and the *Washington Post*, among other papers, argued for Allied assistance to those Russians who might naturally oppose both Soviet tyranny and German influence inside Russia.

The united chorus of American diplomats, Allied leaders, and American newspapers bore down upon Wilson.[76] The tipping point for American intervention was the president's meeting with Masaryk and the

Czecho-Slovak revolt, whose magnitude and significance became clear during June. "It was not until after the middle of the month that there was any reasonably intelligible picture of what had occurred, and even this was spotty and in many respects confusing," says Kennan. "But in Washington, as in the Allied community in Russia, the dawning realization that the Czechs were in possession of a large portion of Siberia aroused a host of speculations as to their possible role in solving the dilemmas of Allied policy."[77] On June 16, the *Washington Post* quoted French general Henri M. Berthelot, who had arrived in Washington to urge the White House to join the Allies in intervening in Russia.[78] On June 17, the British ambassador, Lord Reading, handed Colonel House an ominous new cable from London: "Unless Allied intervention is undertaken in Siberia forthwith we have no chance of being ultimately victorious, and shall incur serious risk of defeat in the meantime."[79]

Despite the fact that they did not see eye to eye, Wilson was preparing to hitch US policy to Masaryk and his legionnaires. Lansing weighed in on June 23 with a request to meet with Wilson to discuss the Czecho-Slovak Legion. "As these troops are most loyal to our cause and have been most unjustly treated by the various soviets," he said, "ought we not to consider whether something can be done to support them?"[80] And intervention in Russia wasn't the only issue on the table. Supporting independence for the peoples of Austria-Hungary was also in play; it was unlikely to have been a coincidence that it was in the wake of mid-June's news of the revolt that Wilson sent the note to Lansing on June 26 that said, "I agree with you that we can no longer respect or regard the integrity of the artificial Austrian Empire." Concludes Kennan, "It was the reports concerning the Czecho-Slovaks, not the arguments of the Allied chanceries, that were now determining Wilson's decision."[81]

At the same time that the White House was beginning to rethink its resistance to an Allied intervention in Siberia, Allied commander Ferdinand Foch approved the dispatch of US troops to Russia's northern ports in a note to Wilson on June 27 that said, "I consider the expedition to Siberia as a very important factor for victory, provided action be immediate, on account of the season being already advanced." British ambassador Reading personally delivered a message from Prime Minister David Lloyd-George and his war cabinet to Wilson on June 28 asking him to refrain from making a decision until he heard from the Allied Supreme War Council.[82]

On July 2, Tokyo agreed with the war council to put troops ashore at Vladivostok, but only if Washington approved, and it agreed to send troops into the interior, but only as far as Irkutsk, very far from areas of German troop activity. Turning to Wilson, the council drafted what David F. Trask calls "the most powerful and urgent plea for intervention yet propounded by the Allies," their formal proposal for an Allied intervention in Russia. It envisioned deploying at least 100,000 soldiers, stating that it was "imperative that the force shall be considerable in number," and assumed that the vast majority of them would be Japanese.[83] By this time, even Beneš had given in to the inevitable, writing to Prague from Paris on July 8 that "military negotiations are being conducted here about intervention in Russia, which is now bound to take place and in which we shall play a certain role."[84]

LIKE EVERY PLAN to intervene in Russia, this one was deeply flawed. It proposed insufficient forces that were expected to reopen an Eastern Front and it disregarded Moscow's likely response. Most plans acknowledged, but ultimately ignored, Russian hatred and fear of the Japanese. They all overestimated how any army traveling from Vladivostok could engage the Germans in European Russia, five thousand miles away, without Moscow's approval or support. In his May 28 memo to General Bliss in Versailles, General March wrote, "Intervention via Vladivostok is deemed impractical because of the vast distance involved, the size of the force necessary to be effective, and financing. . . . Such an intervening expedition would have to penetrate into European Russia. . . . Its appearance would be such that German propagandists would be able to persuade the Russian people that compensation at their expense and out of their territory was ultimately to be exacted."[85] Colonel House's biographer, Charles Seymour, says, "Plans for an effective expeditionary force to Siberia and one capable of redressing the military balance in Europe would have required something like a miracle to assist them to success. It was a practical impossibility to send a large American Army across the Pacific and far into Siberia, with only a single line of communication to Vladivostok. The shipping necessary to carry supplies for such a force was lacking. In the spring of 1918 all available American troops and every American ship was demanded for the reinforcement of France." Colonel House said, "The Japanese told me it would take their entire army to keep the Siberian Railway open."[86]

Clearly, the ability of the legionnaires to seize all of Siberia played a decisive role on behalf of intervention, yet Kennan says, "It is idle to seek any single source for this suggestion. It arose—if the preponderance of evidence may be believed—in a thousand minds at once: some of them Czech, some of them Allied, most of them Russian. . . . In Allied circles, as we shall see shortly, the news of the uprising decisively tipped the scales in favor of those who desired intervention. All sorts of schemes at once arose in the minds of Allied officials for combining the now-proven fighting power of the Czechs with that of the Allied forces whose intervention was now expected at an early date."[87] What did not arise was an actual Allied intervention equal to the gargantuan task of reopening the Eastern Front or, even if desired, toppling the Soviet regime.

Lenin and Trotsky, however, spoke openly of the threat the legionnaires posed to the Soviet regime at an "extraordinary joint session" of Soviet leaders in late July. On July 28, Lenin urged upon the leadership the necessity of

> crushing the Czecho-Slovaks and their counter-revolutionary partisans on the Volga, in the Urals, and in Siberia. This is the most urgent task of the Russian Revolution, and all other tasks must be relegated to background for the present. All forces must be devoted to war.[88]

Commissar for War Trotsky followed with equally pointed remarks on July 29:

What is now happening on the Volga, in the shape of the Czecho-Slovak mutiny, puts Soviet Russia in danger and therefore also endangers the international revolution. At first sight it seems incomprehensible that some Czecho-Slovak Corps, which has found itself here in Russia through the tortuous ways of the world war, should at the given moment prove to be almost the chief factor in deciding the questions of the Russian revolution. Nevertheless, that is the case.[89]

Wilson Turns to Russia

ON A STEAMY Thursday, July 4, 1918, Wilson and Lansing were aboard the White House yacht, the *Mayflower*, floating down the languid Potomac River toward Mount Vernon, where Wilson was to give a patriotic speech about George Washington and independence. Yet their thoughts were on Siberia. Wilson had only recently been handed the plea for help from the Supreme War Council; the president was now convinced that, finally, he had to bend. Lansing drafted a key memorandum for the president regarding Russia, which he sent to Wilson the next day. The legion's seizure of Siberia, Lansing wrote, had "materially changed the situation by introducing a sentimental element into the question of our duty."[90] Lansing considered aid to the legionnaires a humanitarian effort, which was more easily defended than any other scenario for intervening.

Wilson summoned Lansing, Secretary of War Newton D. Baker, Army Chief of Staff March, and Secretary of the Navy Josephus Daniels to the White House on Saturday, July 6. Joined by Admiral W. S. Benson, chief of naval operations, the men watched as Wilson entered the room with a pad in his hand and then stood in front of them and read from his notes. The president told his advisers that he had made a few decisions. His first: "That the establishment of an Eastern Front through a military expedition, even if it was wise to employ a large Japanese force, is physically impossible [if] the front was established east of the Ural Mountains." This point was lost on the Allies, who approved a Japanese advance that would stop at Irkutsk. A related decision: "That under present circumstances, any advance westward of Irkutsk does not seem possible and needs no further consideration." Instead, the president announced that US and Japanese forces would enter Russia to rescue the Czecho-Slovaks—and for no other reason. Wilson was proposing a mission to rescue the legionnaires only, which was far less than what the Allies desired.

He said, "The present situation of the Czecho-Slovaks requires this Government and other governments to make an effort to aid those at Vladivostok in forming a junction with their compatriots in western Siberia; and that this Government on sentimental grounds and because of the effect upon the friendly Slavs everywhere would be subject to criticism if it did not make this effort and would doubtless be held responsible if they were defeated for lack of such effort." A series of military steps would be required: (1) furnishing small arms, machine guns, and ammunition to the Czecho-Slovaks at Vladivostok, (2) landing 7,000 Japanese and 7,000 American troops "to guard the line of communication" of the legionnaires advancing toward Irkutsk and hold the port, and (3) a "public announcement by this and Japanese Governments that the purpose of landing troops is to aid Czecho-Slovaks against German and Austrian prisoners, that there is no purpose to interfere with internal affairs of Russia, and that they guarantee not to impair the political or territorial sovereignty of Russia."[91]

After his presentation, Wilson retired to his Hammond typewriter with furrowed brow; he needed to make his notes official. Two days later, Wilson wrote to Colonel House, "I have not written recently because I have been sweating blood over the question what is right and feasible (possible) to do in Russia. It goes to pieces like quick-silver under my touch, but I hope I see and can report some progress presently, along the double line of economic assistance and aid to the Czecho-Slovaks."[92] In the meantime, Tokyo's ambassador was briefed and only then were the British, French, and Italian ambassadors informed that Tokyo and Washington were discussing an intervention that did not seem to require their participation. London quickly ordered the Twenty-Fifth Middlesex Regiment to Vladivostok and appointed Major General Alfred W. F.

Knox to head a British military mission to Siberia. The State Department informed Tokyo on July 16 that it could command the Allied troops, without asking the War Department. The next day, Wilson's labors at the typewriter came to an end; over Lansing's name, an aide-mémoire was presented to the Allied ambassadors on July 17. It was the one justification for landing US troops on Russia soil.[93]

The aide-mémoire seemed to expand on possible uses of the US and Japanese troops with vague language about helping "Russians," without specifying *which* Russians Wilson proposed to aid. In addition to helping the legionnaires consolidate their forces, the document said, "Military action is admissible in Russia . . . to steady any efforts at self-government or self-defense in which the Russians themselves may be willing to accept assistance. Whether from Vladivostok, or from Murmansk and Archangel, the only legitimate object for which American or Allied troops can be employed, it submits, is to guard military stores which may subsequently be needed by Russian forces and to render such aid as may be acceptable to the Russians in the organization of their own self-defense." A subsequent passage said, "each of the associated [Allied] powers has the single object of affording such aid as shall be acceptable, and only such aid as shall be acceptable, to the Russian people in their endeavor to regain control of their own affairs, their own territory, and their own destiny."[94] The document mentioned the possibility of sending an American economic relief commission to Russia, but nothing ever came of that.

Any scenario in which Allied soldiers helped or supported "Russians" would of course necessitate many hundreds of thousands of soldiers, if not a million or more. Yet Wilson was limiting US troop levels to seven thousand, which the legionnaires may have perceived as simply a first step; it was not. It was instead a firm and nonnegotiable ceiling.

Also strange was that Russia's Soviet regime was not mentioned once, nor even alluded to, in the aide-mémoire, despite the fact that the legionnaires were engaged in a continent-wide, life-and-death war with that very regime. Fatal to Wilson's persistent desire not to "interfere" in Russia's internal affairs was the new language endorsing aid to generic "Russians," which opened a loophole for support of the White Russians.

Also left unsaid was the purpose of helping the legionnaires consolidate their forces. Was it Wilson's intention to help them get to France, for which US officials knew there were no ships, or was it to help them fight in the Russian Civil War, in which they were already engaged? The aide-mémoire's stance was *against* intervention, which was odd too. "Superficially friendly in tone, the statement expressed American distrust of intervention in unmistakable terms," says Trask. "The *aide-memoire* specifically or inferentially refuted all of the arguments advanced by the prime ministers in their message to the President. The document was a firm and unmistakable rebuff to the Entente and the Supreme War Council."[95] This no doubt explains why neither London nor Paris was consulted, which highlights yet another defect in the document. The aide-mémoire stipulated demands on Allied behavior in Russia without even consulting the Allies, let alone winning their agreement to the terms of this document. By July 17, the day it was drafted, the French and British were already implementing completely different plans for the legionnaires.

On July 24 Tokyo responded to Wilson's offer. The Japanese ambassador informed State Department counselor Frank L. Polk that Tokyo would not limit its forces to the suggested seven thousand but would instead send a full division—numbering perhaps twelve thousand—and reserved the right to send more. Wilson was said to be "shocked," and further discussions ensued, until Tokyo issued a unilateral declaration of its intentions on August 2. The White House was now forced to make public its own decisions of July 6, as well as the aide-mémoire of July 17 regarding its plans for Russia.[96] Having already committed the United States in the aide-mémoire handed to the Allied ambassadors, Wilson had no choice but to appoint a commander for the US forces in Russia.

UNDER GERMAN PRESSURE as early as May, Trotsky began warning the Murmansk soviet to cease cooperating with Allied military officials. The German ambassador at Moscow, Count Mirbach, lodged a formal protest on June 8 and on June 12 Soviet foreign minister Chicherin informed the Allies that the legionnaires threatened Russia's neutrality, necessitating that they be disarmed.[97] Berlin clearly viewed the legionnaires with apprehension. The German minister of foreign affairs, Richard von Kuhlmann, had warned Moscow on June 1 that Berlin "cannot stand by and watch" Czecho-Slovak troops depart Russia for the Western Front. He specifically demanded that a legionnaire troop train that had passed through Khabarovsk to Vladivostok be stopped. A few days later, General Erich Ludendorff, the German commander in chief, had written to Kuhlmann to complain that the Soviet regime's initial failure to disarm the Czecho-Slovaks was "especially annoying."[98] The Soviet regime was also becoming more alarmed as it learned of the furtive desire of the British and French to link their forces in the north with the legionnaires. Moscow issued harsher directives to the Murmansk soviet, demanding that it expel token Allied military forces there; soviet leader Aleksey M. Yuriev refused, in part because he could not physically expel the larger and more professional Allied military formations.[99] Tensions between Moscow and the Murmansk soviet rose sharply and Yuriev was proclaimed an enemy of the people in a decree signed by Lenin and Trotsky on June 31. That evening, Yuriev and Chicherin hurled insults at each other, but nothing changed. S. P. Natsarenus, the Kremlin agent in Murmansk, abruptly departed, cutting telegraph lines and blowing up railroad bridges in his wake, isolating Murmansk from the rest of Russia.[100] Coming two days after the legionnaires deposed Soviet rule in Vladivostok, Natsarenus's actions left Moscow cut off from the only ports not closed by the German navy. Allied forces now controlled Siberia and Russia's major ports, east and west.

A Gauntlet of Tunnels

HAVING BY NOW taken control of the two strongholds of Bolshevik power in the Russian Far East, Irkutsk and Vladivostok—but still separated—the legionnaires moving eastward from Irkutsk faced a dangerous gauntlet and a harrowing challenge—the thirty-nine tunnels that

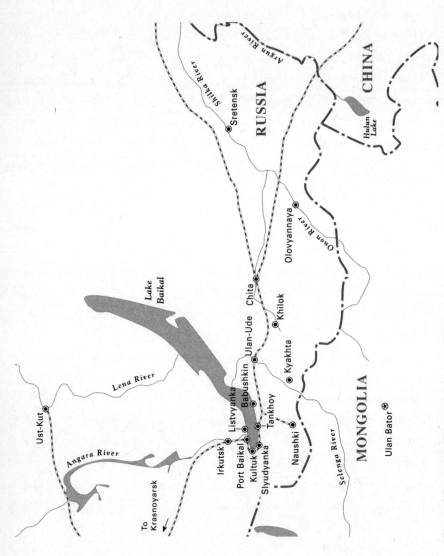

Trans-Siberian Railway in Vicinity of Lake Baikal

carried the railway through the sheer cliffs along the southern shores of Lake Baikal. The opening of the Chinese Eastern Railway to traffic in 1903 completed the original Trans-Siberian, but it relied on ice-breaking ferries to cross Lake Baikal until the rail line was extended through the mountainous 162 miles around the southern tip of the lake.

A 25-million-year-old scar on Russia's backside, Baikal's four-hundred-mile-long, crescent-shaped gash in the earth's tectonic plates holds a lake so large that locals call it a sea. Its surface is larger than Belgium and its depths hold one-fifth of the world's fresh water. Razor-sharp edges line the cliffs that wall the southern rim of the lake, rocketing toward the sky and plummeting into Baikal's uncharted depths. Baikal drains the Russian heartland, swallowing all the 336 rivers and streams that feed it, from which only the Angara River sends Baikal's waters roaring westward into the interior. Raw and unspoiled, the lake's placid surface hides enormous depths. While transparent as a fishbowl in summer, in winter it freezes to a depth of up to six feet. Faced with endless mountain ridges and river gorges around the lake, the builders of the Trans-Siberian around the lake's southern tip had to dynamite cuttings into the sides of sheer mountains; build more than two hundred bridges and trestles to span river gorges, inlets, and Baikal tributaries; shore up miles of embankments; and bore through rock to create the tunnels, some of them very long.[101]

Spooked by the legion's growing power across the middle of Siberia, Soviet armed forces abandoned Irkutsk just before the legionnaires marched into the city on July 11. By the end of their first day in Irkutsk, the legionnaires learned that the retreating Bolsheviks had taken with them an entire train loaded with explosives. They would blow up one or more of the tunnels, trapping all the legionnaires west of Lake Baikal. Radola Gajda appreciated the fact that he and his men had to get to the tunnels as soon as possible to prevent their destruction.

Yet Gustav Becvar, now a second lieutenant, had an experience in Irkutsk that exposed the political weakness of the legion's position in Russia, while the world marveled at its military prowess. The legionnaires were warmly welcomed by the Russian residents. US consul Ernest L. Harris said, "As if by magic, law and order were established, and the streets became crowded with every class of society exceedingly happy at having been rescued from Bolshevik rule."[102] At a warm welcoming reception for the legionnaires, sponsored by and attended by the leading Russians of Irkutsk, Becvar spoke. "I began by thanking the people for the wonderful reception they had given us, saying how much we appreciated their goodwill. These remarks went down well," he said, "but when I proceeded to warn them that we had no intention of interfering in any way in the internal affairs of their country, that any fighting we had done had been undertaken solely to secure our passage to Vladivostok, and that therefore we could not be relied upon to stay in the neighborhood of Irkutsk, they were less pleased. After this announcement, much of the joy occasioned by our arrival evaporated."[103] Like the Russians, the Allies would also be disappointed when the Czecho-Slovaks showed little enthusiasm for remaining in Siberia.

AT IRKUTSK, THE Trans-Siberian Railway was built opposite the Angara River from the city. The tracks originally ran eastward along the Angara for about forty miles until they reached Lake Baikal at the village of Port Baikal, where the ice-breaking ferries *Baikal* and *Angara* shuttled passengers, trains, and freight across the lake to the town of Babushkin, where the Trans-Siberian Railway resumed.[104] Port Baikal, from which the railway now extended south along the shores of the lake through thirty-nine tunnels, was also where, the legionnaires learned, the Bolsheviks had parked an explosives-laden train. The station and its tracks sat between the steep cliffs above Port Baikal and the mouth of the Angara River at the lake.

Gajda dispatched three parties in the direction of the enemy on July 15. One unit of five hundred men hiked cross-country and quietly approached another lakeside village, Kultuk, south of Port Baikal. A second party followed the Trans-Siberian down the Angara valley toward Baikal but kept to the hills above the valley to avoid detection. An armored train the legionnaires had captured from the Red Army followed slowly behind these men. On the Irkutsk side of the valley, a third unit followed the old Moscow post road from the city to the lakeside village of Listvyanka, north of Port Baikal. This third unit turned and left the road as it approached Listvyanka and climbed into the hills above the village. After a few hours, the men reached a ridge and crawled to its edge, looking below in wonder at the enormous sparkling lake spread out beneath them, ringed with stone cliffs and dense woods. Off to their right in the distance sat Port Baikal station. "We stared silently at the indescribable loveliness of the view. Men drew their breath quickly, but few broke the silence," recalled Becvar. "Suddenly, there came a crashing explosion which seemed to shake the very hills. The sound came from the direction of Baikal station. The air trembled, and our ears rang, and the sound and its many echoes went crashing through the mountains like thunder, gradually fading away in the distance. A huge column of thick, black smoke rose from the place where, until a moment before, we had seen the station. The smoke rose and spread in leisurely fashion, masking a long stretch of the shore." Assuming this signaled their attack, Becvar and his brothers ran toward Listvyanka, firing at enemy troops who scrambled aboard two steamers that vanished across the lake. When the legionnaires explored the devastation at Port Baikal, they saw buildings leveled, tracks twisted, shattered coaches, rockslides, and human body parts everywhere. Their comrades who earlier reached the cliffs above the station confessed that when they engaged in a firefight with the enemy train, some of their rounds probably hit dynamite.[105]

Gajda ordered most of the men to pursue the Bolsheviks through the tunnels on foot. A small detachment remained behind to repair the tracks and allow the legion's armored train through. Early the next morning, numerous troop trains began moving through the tunnels toward Kultuk, while other troops were dispatched into the hills above the tunnels. After five days of fighting, the combined three units of legionnaires took Kultuk. The soldiers then advanced toward Slyudyanka, a town on the southern tip of Lake Baikal, beyond which lay the last of the thirty-nine tunnels. As the men advanced the day after they took Kultuk, they heard another booming explosion ahead that echoed through the tunnels and across the lake to their left. The men ran ahead until the tracks in front of them disappeared under a pile of stone and earth.[106]

Working day and night, the legionnaires required three weeks to clear the massive stones and earthy mess from the tracks. Once finished, they boarded their one armored train and several passenger trains and rounded the southern cone of Lake Baikal in the direction of a town on the eastern shore, Tankhoy. "The Bolsheviks were entrenched strongly in front of this station, and not even our newly arrived armored train could shell them out of their fortified nests," said Becvar. Scouts spotted about sixty Red Army troop trains crowding the line between Tankhoy and the station at Babushkin, which was further north along the shore. Gajda briefed the men: legionnaires left behind at Listvyanka on the opposite side of the lake acquired simple barges that they fortified with timber, as well as steamboats that could tow the barges. The boats started across the lake that night, landing at yet another lakeside village, Posolska, north of Babushkin, behind the Red Army forces. At the same time, another battalion marched east into the taiga and, in a wide flanking move, approached the enemy from the east. The remainder of the troops advanced north along the tracks behind the legion's armored train.

"The enemy fought hard and well," said Becvar, who said that the legion's armored train backed off more than once. By about noon, however, enemy soldiers began bolting from their lines. "Others followed. Then the whole front retreated." The enemy no doubt got wind of the legionnaires approaching from their rear. "Then the retreat turned into a positive rout. The Bolsheviks were given no time or opportunity to use their trains. They were driven in a panic-stricken mass along the line towards Posolska." What awaited them was a massacre. "Rifle and machine-gun fire raked the driven mob until they scattered into the hills," said Becvar. Red casualties numbered in the hundreds; the legion gained countless trains and a larger arsenal.

The Red Guards never recovered from their defeats in the battles on Lake Baikal's eastern shores. Baikal's thirty-nine tunnels behind them, the legion's trains started eastward again. On August 24 they reached Ulan-Ude, a city sixty-two miles east of Lake Baikal.[107] A week later, the men who had been trapped west of Lake Baikal finally reunited with their brothers from Vladivostok.

EIGHT

THE MOMENT
OF TRUTH

There's a Legion that never was 'listed,
That carries no colours or crest,
But, split in a thousand detachments,
Is breaking the road for the rest.
Our fathers they left us their blessing—
They taught us, and groomed us, and crammed;
But we've shaken the Clubs and the Messes
To go and find out and be damned
(Dear boys!),
To go and get shot and be damned.

RUDYARD KIPLING, *The Lost Legion*[1]

The Murder of the Romanovs

THE MEMBERS OF the Czecho-Slovak Legion moved on Yekaterinburg in early July in order to take control of the principal rail line that connected the Trans-Siberian Railway to the northern port of Archangel. Two armies of legionnaires approached Yekaterinburg, one from Chelyabinsk in the south, the other from Omsk in the east. The men could not know what their attack on the city would mean for the Romanovs.

In the late summer of 1917, fearing a German drive on Saint Petersburg and spooked by the Bolshevik's aborted July uprising, also in the capital, Russian prime minister Aleksandr Kerensky moved the former tsar and his family from Tsarskoe Selo, their estate outside Saint Petersburg, where they were being held under house arrest, to an isolated town just beyond the Urals, Tobolsk, where the family remained in custody.[2] But the regime began to fear that pro-tsarist forces might free the Romanovs. As a result, the family was moved at the end of April 1918 a few hundred miles west to Yekaterinburg in the Urals, about 120 miles north of Chelyabinsk. Here the Bolsheviks took over the house of a retired engineer, Nikolay Ipatiev, at No. 49 Voznesensky Prospekt, built a stockade around the property, and gave it a code name, "The House of Special Purpose." There, about three dozen courtiers and servants were dismissed; the Romanovs were joined only by the family physician, Dr. Yevgeny Botkin, and three servants. Fifty-six combat-tested Bolsheviks guarded the exterior of the property, and sixteen men were stationed inside the house. Security was especially tight, since the Bolsheviks had failed to keep secret the identity of their captives.

By June the faint explosions of distant artillery fire could be heard on the streets of Yekaterinburg. After the Czecho-Slovaks conquered Omsk on June 7, fear, anger, and paranoia gripped the hardened Bolsheviks, who were surrounded and increasingly cut off from Moscow. They turned to violence, killing more than two hundred peasants, forty-five Orthodox priests, and eighteen of Yekaterinburg's most prominent citizens. By July four detachments of ten thousand legionnaires led by Lieutenant Colonel Sergey N. Voitsekhovsky began closing in on Yekaterinburg, heartened by news that the United States had agreed to land troops in Siberia to support them. The Bolsheviks placed the city under martial law. Some residents tried to flee and panic gripped those who remained. The roster of guards around the House of Special Purpose was increased to three hundred. The city was swamped with troops, many of them Austro-Hungarian Internationalists, moving to the front. Wounded soldiers also littered the city. In Moscow, Vladimir Lenin and his aides urgently discussed what to do with the Romanovs, but they were very careful not to keep written records or to allow evidence of their deliberations to survive.

According to historian Helen Rappaport, "it was the pressing argument of the Czech advance that won the day and the sanctioning of this ultimate act of political expediency. It was not just a matter of preventing the Romanovs falling into enemy hands but also a response to continuing pressure from Germany: if the Tsar fell into Czech hands and became a rallying point for an anti-German resurgence in Russia, then the Brest-Litovsk Treaty, and with it the bolstering-up of the Soviet government, would be dead in the water."[3] By the time Yakov Yurovsky arrived on July 4 as the new commandant of Ipatiev House, the decision to liquidate the entire family and their servants had been made by Lenin in Moscow. Yurovsky was entrusted with the preparations for the execution, code-named "Chimney Sweep." While the house remained quiet, by the evening of July 16, the sound of artillery fire grew louder; the legionnaires were twenty miles south on the rail line connecting Chelyabinsk to Yekaterinburg.

At 1:30 a.m. on July 17, Yurovsky awakened the Romanov family, Dr. Botkin, and three servants, and led them to the basement, ostensibly for their own safety. They were lined up at one end of a room, some seated, the rest standing; they appeared to believe they were waiting for transportation out of Yekaterinburg. Yurovsky and perhaps eight others walked into the room, standing opposite the family. Yurovsky asked them to stand. He stepped forward, brandishing a sheet of paper and read out the sentence of death, announcing, in part, "in view of the fact that the Czecho-Slovaks are threatening the red capital of the Urals—Yekaterinburg—and in view of the fact that the crowned executioner might escape the people's court, the presidium of the Regional Soviet, fulfilling the will of the Revolution, has decreed that the former Tsar Nicholas Romanov, guilty of countless bloody crimes against the people, should be shot." Yurovsky pulled a Colt revolver from his pocket and shot the tsar in the chest at point-blank range. The other eight men opened up with their own weapons in a furious round of shooting that filled the room with acrid smoke. The loud gunfire drowned out much of the initial screaming and moaning of their victims.

Even here, the deadly hand of the Hungarian Internationalists was felt. While it is often said that the assassins, all members of the Cheka, who repeatedly shot and stabbed the members of the royal family, were Latvians, in fact five were Hungarian, former prisoners of war who were recruited into the Cheka.[4] A coded telegram was sent to Moscow on the evening of July 17 by the Ural regional soviet confirming that "the entire family suffered the same fate as its head." While news of the tsar's execution quickly spread across the globe, however, the Soviet regime insisted that his wife and children had been spared and "sent to a place of safety." The Czecho-Slovaks finally took Yekaterinburg on the night of July 25–26 after a brief battle at the train station. The next day the legionnaires paraded along the city's streets, greeted by grateful Russians waving flags and throwing flowers at their feet to the pealing of church bells.

Taking a Stand on the Volga

BY THE END of July 1918 a few things were clear—the Soviet regime and the Western Allies saw each other as implacable enemies, Moscow did not control even most of Russia, and the Czecho-Slovak Legion appeared to be the strongest armed force between Berlin and Tokyo. All of this further encouraged the Allies to flex their muscles in and around Russia. The legionnaires were asked to oppose hundreds of thousands of Hungarian and German POWs who were thought—incorrectly—to be fighting for Berlin and Vienna. In fact, the POWs were fighting in support of the Soviet regime in Moscow. As the exile movement made gains toward an independent Czecho-Slovakia and an Allied victory on the Western Front started to look possible, the legionnaires began to ask why they remained fighting anyone in Russia.

Samara, a major Volga River port city and transit hub, had been taken by the legionnaires on June 8. Lieutenant Stanislav Čeček's soldiers had pushed ahead eastward to clear a path toward their comrades at Chelyabinsk. The city of Ufa had been conquered on July 4, making it possible for the Penza and Chelyabinsk forces to finally link up on July 6. To the south, meanwhile, local Cossacks rebelled against the Soviets and seized the town of Orenburg. The Volga cities of Syrzan and Samara now in hand, the legionnaires came into possession of several barges-turned-gunboats, which they used to ply the Volga north and south, launching attacks on cities from both land and water. On July 22, they took another Volga city, Ulyanovsk,[5] birthplace of both Vladimir Lenin and Aleksandr Kerensky, north of Samara.[6] This handed them control of three cities or towns on both sides of the Volga within a day's travel time of each other, creating a formidable north-south front in the heart of Russia.

With the approval of Edvard Beneš and General Maurice Janin, the French Ministry of War on June 20 instructed General Jean Guillaume Lavergne to order the legionnaires to hold their positions along the Trans-Siberian and to refuse to surrender more weapons, in the event the Allies decided to intervene in Russia.[7] This was the first official indication Beneš had that the plan to evacuate the legionnaires from Russia was on hold.[8] Predicting an Allied intervention was Joseph Noulens, the French ambassador, who was at Vologda, Russia. On June 18, Noulens had dispatched the first of two telegrams that French and American diplomats sent that day that implied strong Allied support for the legionnaires. Noulens's message to Major Alphonse Guinet, the French liaison in Chelyabinsk, said, "The French Ambassador informs Major Guinet he can thank the Czecho-Slovaks for their action, this in the name of all the Allies, who have decided to intervene [at] the end of June, and the Czech army and French Mission form the advance guard of the Allied army. Recommendations will follow concerning political and military points with respect to occupation and organization."[9] In Moscow, US consul general DeWitt C. Poole, unaware of US policy, had sent a similar message the same day to a colleague at Samara: "You may inform the Czecho-Slovak leaders confidentially that pending further notice the Allies will be glad from a political point of view to have them hold their present positions. On the other hand, they should not be hampered in meeting the military exigencies of the situation. It is desirable first of all that they should secure control of the Trans-Siberian Railway and, second, if this is assumed at the same time possible, retain control over the territory where they now dominate."[10] This controversial message made the legionnaires believe that Washington had decided to intervene in Russia to assist them in their growing armed conflict with the Soviets and that reinforcements were coming.

Lacking any other guidance from Washington, which was a chronic problem for US diplomats in Russia, Poole and Ambassador David R. Francis interpreted the decisions of June 1–3 by the Allied Supreme War Council as a decision for all the legionnaires to remain in Russia and for some to be transported to Russia's northern ports to work in tandem with other Allied forces. Confronted with then-exaggerated rumors of a full-fledged Allied intervention that was said to be in the works, Poole and Francis assumed that the legionnaires were to hold their positions.[11] Francis had sent a telegram to US secretary of state Robert E. Lansing on June 14, in which he referenced the Supreme War Council meeting: "Paris conference also decided to hold Czech detachments in Russia for the present."[12]

On June 22, Čeček, commander of the most westward legionnaires now in Samara, had received a message from the French consul at Samara that read: "The French Government notifies the Czech detachments concentrated in Samara that without express and authenticated instructions from the authorities of the Allied armies, they should not leave any of the positions held. On the contrary, they should fortify them. . . . The aim of the Czech detachments is no longer to transport themselves by train via Vladivostok to France, but to prepare the Eastern Front on the Volga River."[13] That same day, *Československý Denik* (Czecho-Slovak Daily) duly described the legion as the "advance guard" of the Allies. Historian J. F. N. Bradley says, "These announcements were taken extremely seriously by the Czechs and no one questioned their feasibility."[14] Accordingly, the Czecho-Slovak National Council's officials in Russia on June 25 asked the Allies for fifty to a hundred thousand soldiers, as well as arms and ammunition, "to establish permanent front against Germany," a request that was at this time endorsed by the US consul at Vladivostok, John K. Caldwell.[15]

Reversing himself entirely, Guinet had met with the legion's leaders on June 29 to tell them, "I have been authorized to express the thanks of the Allies to the Czecho-Slovak Corps for their action in Russia. The behavior of the Czecho-Slovaks, arising out of a clear understanding of the situation, is to the greater honor of the whole Czech-Slovak Corps." Promising Allied support, he said, "From now on you will see us straining every effort to support . . . the Czecho-Slovak Corps. It is to you that we owe the re-establishment of the Russian front."[16] The same day the legionnaires had seized Vladivostok. Guinet had been ordered on July 2 to complete the takeover of the Trans-Siberian and to prepare for an Allied intervention from the east.[17] The new Provisional Executive Committee of the Czecho-Slovak Corps followed up on July 6 with a decision to remain in Russia at the request of the Allies, and the next day Čeček publicly announced that "our Corps has been made a vanguard of the Allied forces" for "the establishment of an anti-German front in Russia in conjunction with the whole Russian nation and our allies."[18] Now in command of the legion's Volga front, Čeček would soon be promoted to general.

To DEPLOY TROOPS into northern Russia in order to link up with the legionnaires holding the Volga River, the French and British military began to occupy Archangel. Assuming, incorrectly, that this effort was designed only to guard Allied military supplies, Woodrow Wilson agreed to send three US battalions to Archangel, against the advice of Secretary of War Newton D. Baker and Army Chief of Staff Peyton C. March.

Led by Lieutenant Colonel George E. Stewart, the Americans were under strict orders to avoid any involvement in Russia's conflicts. Yet Stewart's orders were mysteriously delayed in transmission. So it was that five thousand American soldiers went ashore on September 4, 1918, to join seventeen hundred English soldiers—under British command and a cloud of confusion. Anti-Bolshevik Russians overthrew the Archangel soviet on August 2, without casualties, and pro-soviet forces evacuated the city.[19] The French and British wanted to base themselves at

Archangel—further south than Murmansk—because it offered a direct rail line south toward the legionnaires holding the northern reaches of the Volga River. A British officer traveled south on July 27 to Vologda, meanwhile, where the Allied ambassadors were holed up, to say that British general Frederick C. Poole requested they leave Vologda for Archangel, removing them from harm's way. Ambassador Francis relented and headed north. In less than twenty-four hours, the US troops were fighting Red forces a hundred miles away. Not having received orders to the contrary, Stewart felt compelled to obey Allied commander Poole.[20]

By late August, Francis reported from Murmansk that Allied soldiers were advancing one hundred miles south toward Vologda and Kotlas, which were only about 350 miles north of Moscow. On August 27, largely cut off from outside communications, including those of the White House, and not comprehending the intended limits on US troops under British command, Francis wrote to Lansing, "I shall encourage American troops to obey the commands of General Poole in his effort to effect a junction with the Czecho-Slovaks and to relieve them from the menace which surrounds them." Francis said the troops had ventured 360 miles south by September 6.[21] Yet these Allied troops numbered no more than a few thousand and they were stretched very thinly. "To have intervened at all was a mistake," said Bruce Lockhart, the British intelligence agent in Russia. "To have intervened with hopelessly inadequate forces was an example of spineless half-measures which, in the circumstances, amounted to a crime."[22] US Army chief of staff March felt the same way about the number of US troops dispatched by Wilson, saying, "it is self-evident that that in an enormous territory like Siberia, then populated by armed bands of Cossacks, bandits, Czechs, German and Austrian prisoners of war, Russians for and against their own provisional governments; and with all law and order gone with the Tsarist debacle, the sending of a little handful of men like our expedition was a military crime."[23]

FURTHER SOUTH, THE legionnaires were expecting Allied forces to come to their aid. On July 31 they had written to Tomáš G. Masaryk, asking him to inquire about Allied reinforcements and supplies, as well as, they said, "the need for expediting military support, which Japan would have already given if they had obtained the official concurrence of the United States. This point is an essential one for us."[24] For their part, Beneš and Masaryk clung to the hope the Allies would still ship the legionnaires to France as soon as possible. In July Beneš told British foreign secretary Arthur J. Balfour that the Czecho-Slovak National Council still insisted on the shipment of the legionnaires to France, but conceded that the corps "can, for the time being, be of great service for the Allies and for England if it facilitates intervention in Russia."[25]

THE LEGIONNAIRES ADVANCED strongly toward their comrades in the west and on August 7 seized the city of Kazan, which lies on the Volga River in European Russia, about two hundred miles north of Samara and northeast of Penza; it was widely considered a gateway to Moscow. Kazan was also the hiding place for about one-half of Russia's fabled gold reserves.

At the outbreak of the war, the tsar's gold holdings were enormous.[26] "Russian bank notes were 98 percent backed by gold," says historian Richard Pipes. "At the time, Russia had the largest gold reserve in Europe."[27] Somewhat depleted to finance the war, the reserves were still valued at $613 million (plus about 5 million rubles' worth of securities) in November 1917. The Bolsheviks aimed to possess it, along with all other Romanov or state property, sparking multiple confrontations between the staff of the Russian State Bank and armed Red Guards. Only $308 million of the gold was housed in Saint Petersburg and Moscow, however; the balance had been moved to a branch of the Russian State Bank in Samara when German forces advanced in 1917. After signing the Brest-Litovsk Treaty, the Soviet regime was forced to ship $160 million in gold to Berlin, more than one-half of what it had on hand. The Bolsheviks moved the Samara gold north along the Volga on barges to Kazan, where it was combined with another $25 million in gold, bringing the total value of the Siberian gold to $332 million. Over the next eighteen months, $120 million was dispensed; most was spent to finance the White Russian regime of Admiral Aleksandr V. Kolchak and small amounts may have been stolen. When the legionnaires seized Samara in early June 1918 and Kazan in early August, the gold came into the possession of the regional Socialist Revolutionary government, Komuch, at Samara.

Kazan fell to the legionnaires on August 7. Two days later munitions workers in Izhevsk and Votkinsk, neighboring cities about 150 miles north of Kazan, led spontaneous rebellions that overthrew soviet power and declared their sympathy for Komuch. It was the largest workers' uprising against the Bolsheviks.[28] In control of Kazan, the legionnaires could storm across the Volga River and make a dash toward Moscow. Assuming that sufficient Allied reinforcements and supplies would be delivered without delay, no one involved on either side of this conflict doubted that Moscow could have been conquered.

With Samara, Yekaterinburg, and Kazan in their possession, the legionnaires and the People's Army of Komuch paused, believing that Allied troops would move south from the northern ports of Archangel and Murmansk, as well as from Vladivostok in the east. Even before Kazan was taken on August 7, the People's Army quartermaster general, P. K. Popov, reported, "Several Frenchmen who had come to Samara via Simbirsk stated positively that Allied forces were soon to appear." Confessed another officer in the People's Army, V. I. Lebedev, "All of our calculations rested on this."[29] "Stand firm, the Allies are sending troops to your assistance," Becvar said his men were told.[30] The dashing of these hopes granted a final reprieve for Soviet rule, but it embittered the legionnaires, who, it must be remembered, agreed to fight Russians only because the British and French governments asked them to do so.

Flaws behind the Fanfare

"THE DECISION OF the Executive Committee of the army on July 7, 1918, to set up an anti-Bolshevik front in the Volga area, to begin an advance against the Soviets, and to proceed further into central Russia, seemed to me a political and military blunder, and I still think so," Beneš recalled years later. He and Masaryk only reluctantly accepted the vague Allied plans to use the legionnaires inside Russia. "It counted upon Allied help which could not be given, and was stimulated partly by the insistence of the anti-Bolshevik elements in Russia, partly by unfounded reports about Allied intervention which was alleged to be already in progress."[31]

The legionnaires' revolt had both positive and negative results for Masaryk and Beneš. On one hand, the rebellion had the clear benefit of bringing their independence movement riveting global press attention, which helped the exiles gain the attention of Allied leaders. At the same time, it made the Czech-Slovak National Council and its representatives appear somewhat irrelevant. As a result, Masaryk and Beneš were now able to communicate with Allied leaders, but those same Allied leaders did not much listen to them and often ignored their concerns.

Among those concerns were the many warnings that the legionnaires did not want to fight Russians—they wanted to fight only their Austro-Hungarian and German enemies. In the very first days of the revolt, on May 27, US admiral Austin M. Knight, aboard the USS *Brooklyn* at Vladivostok, had reported, "Ten thousand Czechs are now here. Have been informed they have been approached as to willingness to conduct military operations in Siberia and Russia and they are positively opposed to this. . . . They are unwilling to fight any Slavic race or faction, but enthusiastically eager [to] fight against Germany."[32] In his June 3 meeting with Lansing, Masaryk had explained that the legionnaires wanted to fight in France. While Masaryk seemed slow to realize how the legion's seizure of Siberia would alter his plans for them, he understood that his men had taken dramatic steps in Siberia only to hasten their exit from Russia. On June 23, 1918, Lansing had written to Wilson, "Professor Masaryk assured me that these rebels against Austria-Hungary, collected from the Russian prison camps and from deserters, would not fight against the Russians, but only sought to pass via Vladivostok to the Western Front."[33] On June 10, meanwhile, the British ambassador to the United States, Lord Reading, had reported to Lansing, "These troops desire above all things to be transported to France, being unwilling either to remain in Russia or to take any part in the internal struggles which are taking place there, and their wishes are fully supported by their national representatives."[34]

What the Allies also failed to notice was that the legion—at most sixty-five thousand men defending an expanse the size of the continental United States—was stretched to the breaking point. Throughout that summer, while newspapers were heralding their military prowess, the legionnaires were taking a pounding, holding on to Siberia unassisted. Northwest of Yekaterinburg in October 1918, Becvar said that the constant fighting, without fresh troops, winter clothing, or other supplies, was depleting his unit. At an early-morning roll call, he was surprised to see that only half of his six hundred brothers could stand to fight. "Were we to be left fighting without rest until all of us had been gradually killed?" he wondered.[35]

As early as June 30, the US consul general at Moscow, DeWitt C. Poole, had advised Lansing, "If Czechs are not supported, there is danger that they may be overthrown by Bolsheviks and prisoners of war."[36] On July 2 the US liaison to the Allied Supreme War Council in Versailles, Arthur H. Frazier, had reported, "The Allies are under the responsibility of taking immediate action, if these gallant allies are not to be overwhelmed."[37] On July 7, the US consul at Vladivostok, John K. Caldwell, had cabled, "Very necessary I have immediate reply, indicating attitude of Allied governments toward Czechs. We are waiting for this. For them, delay is very serious and may even prove fatal, if Allied support denied."[38] On August 9 a British consul at Vladivostok, Robert Hodgson, had related, "There are now only two months before the beginning of winter and the Czech troops in central Siberia will be lost unless help can reach them by then." Hodgson continued that they needed reinforcements and weapons and that "the forces so far proposed to be sent by the Allies are certainly inadequate."[39] On August 13 Ernest L. Harris, the US consul at Irkutsk, had reported from Vladivostok that the legionnaires were taking "heavy" losses along the Volga front, where they were bearing "all the burden," and he urgently requested Allied troop reinforcements.[40]

As early as the end of June, however, another factor became increasingly problematic—morale among the legionnaires had plummeted after the men achieved their objective of clearing a path toward Vladivostok. "The cohesion collapsed as soon as Vladivostok was reached," says historian J. F. N. Bradley. "There were no other aims, there was no common plan, no appreciation of the political implications of the revolt, no anticipation of the next step."[41]

Also unappreciated was how Russia's many anti-Bolshevik "governments" refused to cooperate with one another. Although the Socialist Revolutionaries enjoyed more support in rural areas, Bolshevik cells were stronger in the cities and larger towns, while most of Russia's White military leaders detested all socialists and saw no distinctions among them. The two largest so-called anti-Soviet governments, at Samara and Omsk, failed to work together, largely because of their selfish desires to become the only government.

Amidst persistent fighting between the governments in Samara and Omsk, the Czecho-Slovaks issued an appeal for cooperation on August 20, 1918: "Three months have passed since the Czecho-Slovak Army rose against the Bolshevik usurpers," said the appeal. "At first we had to defend our own freedom, but very soon we decided to . . . come to the rescue of the Russian people. . . . We hoped that the Russians themselves would make an effort to establish their military and political organization. . . . Instead of a national government being established, we witness strife among the different parts of Russia." Despite the fact that the legionnaires "were known to be in sympathy with the Socialist-Revolutionists," these anti-Bolsheviks were increasingly persecuted by the White Russians who were assuming more power in Siberia.[42]

ON FRIDAY, AUGUST 2, 1918, newly minted Major General William S. Graves, who had assumed command of the Eighth Army Division at Camp Fremont, in Palo Alto, California, only fifteen days earlier, was handed a coded message from Washington. "You will not tell any member of your staff or anybody else of the contents of this message," it said, ordering him to take the first train from San Francisco to Kansas City, proceed to the Baltimore Hotel, and ask for the secretary of war. General Graves arrived at 10:00 p.m. the following day at the Kansas City railway station, where Secretary of War Baker awaited him. After the two men exchanged the usual pleasantries, Baker apologized for some last-minute orders—Graves and his men were being sent to Siberia.

Baker handed Graves a sealed envelope and said, "This contains the policy of the United States in Russia which you are to follow. Watch your step; you will be walking on eggs loaded with dynamite. God bless you and good-bye." When he got to the hotel, Graves opened the envelope and found a copy of the aide-mémoire President Wilson had typed on his Hammond.[43] "From that hour until the Siberian Expedition returned to the United States," Baker said, "General Graves carried out the policy of his Government without deviation, under circumstances always perplexing and often irritating."[44] Indeed, virtually every person or nation involved in Russia's affairs, including US diplomats, came to strongly resent Graves—except Wilson and Baker, who interpreted the vagueness of the aide-mémoire as an order to Graves to do nothing except facilitate the retreat and evacuation of the legionnaires through the port of Vladivostok. Graves, unhappily, became the perfect soldier for Wilson's imperfect Russian policy.

Also on August 2, State Department counselor Frank L. Polk secured several personal assurances from the Japanese ambassador that Tokyo would not send more than ten to twelve thousand troops into Siberia.[45] The same day, the White House finally announced its plans for sending troops into Russia. The US War Department ordered about two thousand soldiers from the Philippines to Vladivostok, where they would meet Graves and five thousand troops under his command sailing from San Francisco. The first American soldiers began arriving at Vladivostok on August 16.[46] Also traveling with the legionnaires were the American military engineers of the Russian Railway Service Corps, who rebuilt more than one hundred bridges, stations, depots, and water towers that were destroyed by the retreating Red Army. Still, the engineers endeavored to remain neutral.

On September 1 the legionnaires celebrated their final juncture in Olovyannaya, a small Russian town south of Chita, a city east of Lake Baikal and just north of Russia's border with Mongolia.[47] In an ironic coincidence, on that same day, Graves came ashore at Vladivostok to rescue the legionnaires. Graves learned on his first day there that US soldiers were already engaging Red Army troops north of Vladivostok and helping to clear a path of retreat for the legionnaires, in accord with Washington's orders.[48] On top of that, the Allies by now had abandoned their faint hopes of providing ships to take the legionnaires from Vladivostok. This raised serious challenges for Graves—what was he to do with the legionnaires, or with his own troops? Meanwhile, various factions, chief among them the US State Department, tried to drag Graves into conflicts that roiled the Russian Far East.

Having no choice but to go along with the new policy, on August 5 Masaryk wrote to Wilson, "With the deepest satisfaction, I thank you for your decision to help our Czecho-Slovak Army in Russia. . . . Your name, Mr. President, as you have no doubt read, is openly cheered in the streets of Prague—our nation will forever be grateful to you and to the people of the United States. And we know how to be grateful." With surprising candor, on August 7 Wilson replied, "Your letter of August 5th is greatly appreciated. I have felt no confidence in my personal judgement about the complicated situation in Russia, and am reassured that you should approve of what I have done."[49]

The Unseen Enemy

WELL BEFORE THE revolt of the Czecho-Slovak Legion, on March 24, 1918, Secretary of State Lansing had warned Wilson that if reports of "German" POWs taking control of Irkutsk and other cities in Siberia are true, "we will have a new situation in Siberia which may cause a revision of our policy. . . . With the actual control by the Germans of so important a place as Irkutsk, the question of the moral effect upon the Russian people of an expedition against the Germans is a very different thing from the occupation of the Siberian Railway in order to keep order between contending Russian factions. It would seem to be a legitimate operation against the common enemy. I do not see how we could refuse to sanction such a military step."[50] Seen only as German or Hungarian, these POWS were believed to be affiliated with the Central Powers. Of course, the POWs were actually serving the Bolsheviks.

The size, composition, and combat role of the Internationalists were underestimated not only by contemporary observers in Siberia, but even later by scholars like George F. Kennan. His otherwise highly valuable work on revolutionary Russia downplays the role of the hundreds of thousands of Austrian, Hungarian, and German POWs fighting for Moscow, a result of his effort to dispel rumors that the POWs were being armed by Berlin.[51] Kennan says, "there could not have been more than 10,000" armed Central Powers POWs and makes much of the fact that "there were relatively few Germans." Basing his assessment on a flawed report by two hapless officers given the task of assessing the extent of the POW threat, British captain W. L. Hicks and American captain William B. Webster, Kennan concludes that "relatively few of these prisoners were ever armed and used," which has since been disproven by much original documentation and by numerous other scholars.[52]

The presence and influence of the German, Austrian, and Hungarian POWs astounded even high-level German officials in Berlin. In a December 5, 1917, report to Kaiser Wilhelm II, a German agent reported on the situation in Siberia following the Bolshevik coup:

> Quite a number of different, independent republics have been formed. The latest of these, however, are the *German Prisoners' Republics*. In various places where there are large prisoner-of-war camps, the German prisoners, finding that all order had broken down around them, took the business of feeding and administration into their own hands and now feed not only themselves, but also the villages around. The villagers are extremely satisfied with this state of affairs and, together with the prisoners, have formed something like a republican administration, which is directed by the German prisoners. This could surely be called a new phenomenon in the history of the world. Russia, even more than America, is the land of unlimited possibilities.[53]

Captain Vladimir S. Hurban, an officer on the first legion train to cross Siberia, observed: "In every Soviet, there was a German who exercised a great influence over all its members."[54] On July 4, 1918, the US consul at Omsk, Alfred R. Thomson, had reported to Lansing, "In most places the chief strength of [Soviet] armed forces consisted in armed German and Magyar prisoners," citing Soviet military leaders or entire Red units that were, in fact, Austro-Hungarian or German POWs in Omsk, Ishim, Petropavlovsk, and Irkutsk.[55] Large Internationalist Brigades were established throughout Russia, particularly along the Trans-Siberian Railway.

The Danish ambassador was quoted in a Russian newspaper on April 19, 1918, saying, "The report that war prisoners in Siberia are being supplied with arms is not subject to doubt. The number of men thus armed is very considerable and the Siberian authorities compel them to go into action."[56] The many congresses of Internationalist POWs that were held in cities across Russia might have provided additional evidence of a mass movement of prisoners enlisting in the Red Army.

Admiral Knight at Vladivostok reported on June 26 that Major W. S. Drysdale, US military attaché in Peking (Beijing), "fully confirmed" reports of twenty to thirty thousand armed POWS fighting the legionnaires on behalf of soviets in Siberia. "Drysdale, who has heretofore minimized danger from war prisoners admits they have now gone beyond [the] control [of the] Soviets," Knight telegraphed Washington.[57] The threat posed by the POWs was relayed to Lansing by William G. Sharp, US ambassador to France, as early as April 11, 1918. However, historian Donald F. Trask notes, "The United States government tended to discount this argument after receiving reports from American observers in Russia which indicated no immediate threat of such activity."[58]

To the legionnaires it made no difference whether Berlin, Vienna, or Moscow was somehow arming the POWS. The hostility that Austrian and Hungarian POWs felt toward the Czechs and Slovaks preceded— by centuries—the hostilities that broke out between Moscow and the legionnaires. While the Internationalists were not under Berlin's command, there were significant numbers of German, Austrian, and Hungarian POWs that did not merely menace the legionnaires, but actually fought and killed them. By May 1918 it hardly mattered to the legionnaires which government was arming their avowed enemies.

The Intervention Snare

ON AUGUST 7, before Graves arrived on Russian soil to rescue the legionnaires, the French Ministry of War ordered the legionnaires—who were officially a unit of the French army—to consolidate their forces and advance deeper into Russia to link up with Allied forces in the north, as well as with the White Volunteer Army in southern Russia, creating a north-south front of Allied or friendly armies.[59] "The battalion's train seemed to go mad. It raced back across the Trans-Siberian line like a scared horse," said Sergeant Becvar, who was among a trainload of legionnaires at Ulan-Ude who reversed course and headed into the interior of Russia. "For days and nights we sped toward the west." Becvar nonetheless said the legionnaires were not at all happy to be entering a conflict that wasn't theirs. "To have fought and struggled to the east, merely to be sent back to the west in the very hour when we thought we had won our purpose, was hard, and few of us could prevent feeling an occasional twinge of resentment at our lot. We experienced little enthusiasm for the coming fighting."[60]

Lansing told Wilson on August 18 that "the situation is developing in a way which differs considerably from the plan originally determined upon."[61] Waging war on Moscow was indeed different. "In endeavoring to carry out this plan, Czechs are meeting unexpected and strong resistance. . . . Taking of Perm will be delayed indefinitely and in all probability will be impossible without reinforcements from Allies in Siberia," US consul at Irkutsk Harris said in a message that reached Washington on September 1.[62] Wilson was furious. "This illustrates in the most striking way the utter disregard of [British] General [Frederick C.] Poole and of all the Allied governments (at any rate of all who are acting for them) of the policy to which we expressly confined ourselves in our statement about our action in Siberia," Wilson told Lansing on September 5. "It is out of the question to send reinforcements from eastern Siberia (I presume they mean from the forces recently landed at Vladivostok) to Perm; and we have expressly notified those in charge of those forces that the Czecho-Slovaks must (so far as our aid was to be used) be brought out eastward, not go out westward. Is there no way—no form of expression—by which we can get this comprehended?"[63] Isolated near the Arctic Circle, US soldiers could not readily be ordered to stand down.

It was not until September 8 that Graves first learned that the legionnaires, the British, and the French—supported by Japanese troops in eastern Siberia—were extending operations to the Volga River. Under British and French influence, the Czecho-Slovaks had been enlisted in the Allied intervention. An aide to General Radola Gajda arrived in Vladivostok on September 9 to demand immediate aid from the Allies. Graves said he could not help, other than to protect the Trans-Siberian as far as Lake Baikal.[64]

Wilson criticized Allied policy in Russia severely and vowed not to have anything more to do with it. However, by September 23, US ambassador Francis, now a witness to US soldiers fighting the Soviet regime in Russia's north, felt compelled to telegram Lansing an obvious query: "Can Department advise me whether a state of war exists between the United States and Bolshevik government?"[65] Two days later, French ambassador to the United States Jean-Jules Jusserand requested on orders from Paris that more US battalions be sent to the Russian north to join more British battalions. While Jusserand said that Paris was "entirely giving up every idea of reorganizing an Eastern Front," troops were needed to prevent the foodstuffs and raw materials of Siberia "from reaching the Bolsheviks and, through them, the Germans." While defending Murmansk, the new troops would also "advance from Archangel to give a hand to the Czechs" near Vologda and Perm.

Lansing responded the next day to Francis and every Allied government that US troops were to be limited to guarding the northern ports and that no more troops would go to Russia. As late as October 10, Francis, clearly isolated for too long, continued to urge an intervention by

100,000 US troops.[66] The impending end of the war soon took the wind from such arguments, and Allied forces were never dispatched to Russia's northern ports in numbers sufficient even to ponder a march on Moscow or to link up with the legionnaires. General Poole was subsequently dispatched to southern Russia to assist the White Volunteer Army under General Anton Denikin. Francis eventually sailed home aboard the USS *Olympia*; it was fifteen years before another US ambassador set foot in Russia. Allied forces were evacuated from the northern ports in the fall of 1919.[67]

By SEPTEMBER 1, 1918, the day all the legionnaires in Siberia finally linked up together near the city of Chita, it was apparent that they had valiantly tried, and failed, to expand their front along the Volga River and satisfy British and French ambitions to link up with Allied forces that were supposed to drive south from Archangel toward Yaroslav and Vologda. Having taken Samara, Yekaterinburg, and Kazan, the legionnaires were awaiting reinforcements. But Washington made it clear on August 20 that any reinforcements would not be wearing US uniforms. Lansing announced that the United States would neither provide nor support any troops beyond the seven thousand or so it had already committed and would also not support the legionnaires in western Siberia, urging them to retire eastward as rapidly as possible.[68]

Washington was prepared to offer only bare sustenance. On August 2 the State Department had cabled Caldwell, the US consul at Vladivostok, that "inquiries are now being made as to whether warm clothing can be provided for the men."[69] And on August 29 Lansing had informed Wilson that the Red Cross was sending clothes and shoes and asked him whether US military supplies could be sent. Wilson directed Lansing to Bernard Baruch, chairman of the War Industries Board, who in turn asked to see Masaryk.[70] Yet the reports of the dire combat conditions of the legionnaires led even Lansing and Masaryk to confront Wilson in September on whether it was wise or just to ask the legionnaires to abandon their Russian allies, and whether it was wise or just to abandon the legionnaires without supplies.

The legionnaires might have been physically united for the first time since they had crossed Ukraine, yet they were getting their noses bloodied by a quickly growing Red Army. As a result, some political divisions resurfaced within the legion. Small numbers of the more fervent socialists defected to the Red Army. The morale of others weakened, something that Allied leaders in distant cities remained largely unaware of.

A Red Army Rears Its Head

IN AUGUST 1918, like a strong yet inexperienced prizefighter stepping into a boxing ring, ready to size up his new opponent, a formidable armored train rumbled to a stop at Sviyazhsk. This was the last station before a bridge that carried the Trans-Siberian Railway over the Volga River to the larger city of Kazan, which had fallen to the Czecho-Slovak Legion on August 7. Traveling from Moscow to what was called the "Czecho-Slovak Front," Leon Trotsky emerged from the train to take personal command of the Red Army and lead the attack on the legionnaires. "There," he said, "for a whole month, the fate of the revolution hung again in the balance. That month was a great training-school for me." His beleaguered soldiers had shared "only a readiness to retreat—so superior were the enemy in both organization and experience." Russia "had hardly any army . . . after Kazan would have come the turn of Nizhny Novgorod, from which a practically unobstructed road lay open to Moscow," Trotsky added. "The situation seemed hopeless."[71]

While the birth of the Red Army formally dated to January 1918, Trotsky appreciated that it had been formed as a response to Moscow's combat with the Czecho-Slovak legionnaires. Soon after the collapse of the tsarist regime, the Bolsheviks organized the Red Guards, a group of about twenty thousand armed and politically reliable workers and peasants, in Saint Petersburg. Similar Red Guard militias were thrown together in other cities and towns, but under fire the largely untrained guards could be highly unreliable.

On January 15, 1918 (OS), the Bolsheviks had issued a decree calling for the formation of a Workers' and Peasants' Red Army, reestablishing a standing army for Russia, but one composed of volunteers.[72] Yet the decree was largely symbolic; nothing much was done to create an army. The Red Guards remained as Soviet Russia's largely untrained militia, commanded by elected, inexperienced "officers" leading small units of seven hundred to a thousand volunteers who often hailed from the same factory or small town. But volunteers had failed to materialize, desertions were rampant, and discipline was lax in the Workers' and Peasants' Red Army. Distrustful of professional soldiers, on April 8, the Bolsheviks inserted a network of overtly political "commissars" into all military units to supervise the commanders. By that date, Trotsky was commissar for war and chairman of the Supreme Military Council, and he personally credited the Czecho-Slovak revolt for spurring the creation of a genuine Red Army.

"Hitherto," says Red Army specialist John Erickson, "Red units in the interior had grappled in clumsy style with hostile forces as weak and as poorly organized as themselves." No more. Red Army divisional leaders scrambled to meet the threat from the Czecho-Slovaks. On May 29, mere days after the Czecho-Slovak revolt was launched, Moscow introduced compulsory military service. Fifteen mobilization drives were organized through August 1918, which inducted 540,123 men and 17,700 noncommissioned officers. By the end of June, Moscow deployed fifty thousand men across what it called the Czecho-Slovak front, but they were as yet no match for the legionnaires. Under fire, Red Army units dispensed with the famous soviets (committees), voting by soldiers was set aside, incompetent commanders who had been elected by the rank and file were replaced, and, after much debate, the first mobilization of former imperial officers took place on July 4. By the end of the year, twenty-two thousand former tsarist officers were serving. By the end of the civil war, there were seventy-five thousand.[73]

Packed into Trotsky's armored train were fifty young Bolsheviks in trademark black-leather jackets. His heavily armored train included a telegraph station, telephones (including spares), a printing press, a radio station, an electric-power generator, a library, a garage holding several semiarmored vehicles, a bath, and a fuel reserve. As a result of its weight, the train required two engines, one of which was always under steam— just in case. The entire train bristled with sharpshooters and machine guns, and two men with handheld machine guns squeezed into Trotsky's own passenger car. At times, the train, speeding at more than forty-five miles per hour, so shook the tracks "that the maps that hung from the ceiling of the car would rock like a swing," Trotsky said. "During the most strenuous years of the revolution, my own personal life was bound up inseparably with the life of that train," he said. "The train," on which Trotsky lived for two and a half years and traveled 65,244 miles, "linked the front with the base, solved urgent problems on the spot, educated, appealed, supplied, rewarded, and punished."[74]

Arriving at the front in the wake of the retreat from Kazan, Trotsky issued his first orders to the commanders, political commissars, and soldiers: "I give warning that if any unit retreats without orders, the first to be shot down will be the commissar of the unit, and next the commander. Brave and gallant soldiers will be appointed in their places. Cowards, dastards, and traitors will not escape the bullet. This I solemnly promise in the presence of the entire Red Army."[75]

White Russian soldiers under Commander Vladimir O. Kappel, a cavalry officer who had helped lead the People's Army in Samara, crossed the Volga under cover of darkness and seized a small railway station behind Trotsky's train, destroyed the tracks, and cut the telegraph lines to Moscow. After an eight-hour battle, Kappel's forces retreated. The cut in the telegraph link to Moscow, however, prompted the dispatch of fresh reinforcements for Trotsky. Small Soviet airplanes dropped primitive explosives on Kazan, gunboats fired at the city's waterfront, and a Red Army detachment pressed it from the northeast—all prompting townspeople to flee the city and pro-Bolshevik workers to rise up again.[76]

Kazan fell to the Red Army on September 10—a little more than thirty days after it was captured by the legion—and Ulyanovsk fell two days later. These were the first indications that the Red Army might win the struggle. "We are now forging on the anvil of war an army of first-class quality," Trotsky said after Kazan. "It can be said that if the Czecho-Slovaks had not existed, they would have had to be invented, for under peacetime conditions we should never have succeeded in forming, within a short time, a close-knit, disciplined, heroic army. But now this army is being formed before our eyes."[77]

Subsequent historians also credit the Czecho-Slovak Legion with providing the impetus that led to the formation of the Red Army. Richard Pipes writes that "it was the Czecho-Slovak rebellion that finally forced the Bolsheviks to tackle the formation of an army in earnest."[78] By July the Red Army and its Internationalist Brigades of Austrian and Hungarian POWs already consisted of three armies deploying 27,130 infantry, 835 cavalry troops, five hundred machine guns, twelve heavy artillery, three armored trains, thirteen armored automobiles, and eleven airplanes, according to US consul Harris at Irkutsk.[79] Trotsky confirmed that the initial battles along the Volga River involved twenty-five to thirty thousand Red Army troops.[80]

"There Is Limit to Human Endurance"

THE LEGIONNAIRES WERE stretched to capacity to take and hold Siberia against even weaker forces and could not, alone, withstand the growing Red Army across a front that extended for eight hundred miles. By the time General Graves landed at Vladivostok on September 1, historian George F. Kennan writes, the legionnaires "had actually over-extended themselves in relation to the growing strength of their opponents."[81] The next day, US consul Harris said, "the Czechs are not strong enough to hold their grip on such a large territory and will be destroyed unless Allies hurry to their assistance. [White] Russian army not progressing as it should and cannot be depended on to materially assist Czechs."[82] By September 9, Gajda organized thousands of the men and led them westward to help their brothers hold Kazan and their front along the Volga River.[83] On September 10, Harris reported, "Losses heavier than in other fighting and Czechs weary from constant fighting at most difficult points with minimum of rest."[84] From this date forward—the date the Red Army recaptured Kazan—the legion began to retreat. From Irkutsk came desperate requests for rifles and ammunition—"They must have them at once"—and a report that twelve thousand legionnaires and White Russians were trying to defend Yekaterinburg against thirty to forty thousand enemy troops.[85] The *New York Times* correspondent reported on September 11, "It is astounding, in these circumstances, that every Allied unit in the Far East has not immediately been sent by railway to the critical point in support of the Czechs."[86]

"Our situation on Volga is critical," telegraphed Jan Syrový, now commander in chief of the entire Czecho-Slovak Corps, on September 12 from Chelyabinsk. "Our troops, wearied by three months' uninterrupted fighting, tire incredibly fast, and transfer of [legionnaires] from east will only delay catastrophe temporarily. It is impossible to continue to operate without immediate assistance of strong Allied force. Demand from Allies immediate and categorical reply following questions, if our common cause is dear to them: (1) Is it their intention to participate in any way in operations supporting us on Volga front; (2) If so, do they intend to start at once an extraordinary transfer of troops and in what numbers?"[87] Three days later, Bohdan Pavlů, the president of the Russian branch of the Czecho-Slovak National Council, telegraphed a similar plea for assistance from Irkutsk.[88] In Washington, DC, Masaryk visited Breckinridge Long, the US third assistant secretary of state, at his home on the evening of September 17 and told him about "the state of physical exhaustion of the Czechs and their need for moral and physical report."[89] With widespread publicity about the legionnaires now common, even the newspapers were reporting by September on their dire struggles with headlines such as "the czechoslovak legion in danger" and "czech setback in russia." According to the second of these two stories from the *Times* of London, "The Czechs are very tired, and lack munitions, equipment, and stores—the fall of Kazan, indeed, appears to have been entirely due to want of ammunition." It reported that Soviet armed forces had swelled to more than 100,000.[90]

Both the British and French appealed simultaneously for help from Tokyo. British major general Alfred W. F. Knox and French prime minister Georges Clemenceau made "separate urgent appeals for a massive Japanese intervention." There was no immediate response. "Reports from the Volga region all agree that the Czech forces there are seriously menaced from various directions," wrote the US ambassador to Japan, Roland S. Morris. "The single question which confronts the Czech leaders is whether they can make some arrangement with the Allies which will permit them to hold the Volga region or, failing that, the line of the Urals during the coming winter and thus keep the door open into European Russia. They are clear that this cannot be done unless reinforcements are sent to them promptly."[91] Morris was advocating a holding action at Omsk in support of a holding action by the legionnaires further west—to "keep the door open," but for what purpose? Lansing urged approval of Morris's plan the very next day, warning Wilson that the legionnaires faced "annihilation" unless they were reinforced, and adding that the Japanese, British, and French were unable or unwilling to provide the troops.[92] Masaryk weighed in with a similar plea on September 27. "But here again," he said, "I am touching a sore point—the lack of a uniform and clear plan of the Allies and the United States concerning Russia."[93]

Wilson, however, would not hear of changing his policies regarding the legionnaires or Russia. On September 26, Lansing reiterated US policy that "it is the unqualified judgement of our military authorities that to attempt military activities west of the Urals is to attempt the impossible. We mean to send all available supplies that we can spare from the Western Front as fast as possible for the use of the Czecho-Slovak forces," he added, but urged the legion again to retreat eastward. "This Government cannot cooperate in an effort to establish lines of operation and defense through Siberia to Archangel."[94]

Meanwhile, on October 2 British foreign secretary Balfour directed his embassy in Washington, DC, to make the case for supporting the

White forces—and for keeping the legionnaires in Russia. "If we were now to ask the Czechs to withdraw to the east of the Urals, that would be to cut off from [Russian general Mikhail V.] Alekseyev and those with him their last hope of Allied assistance," Balfour said, indicating that London would approach the French and Japanese for support. Regarding the White House, he added, "if they feel unable to assist us beyond the point indicated, we hope they will not discourage our other Allies from helping us."[95] On October 23, Tokyo responded to the French and British requests to come to the aid of the legionnaires that it was not interested in helping Russia, had its own interests in Siberia, and would not act according to Allied wishes.[96]

In one final appeal for help, Václav Girsa, a leader of the Russian branch of the National Council, had written an open letter to the Allies on September 29 from Vladivostok. Pointing out that the men were not only outnumbered and lacking arms and ammunition, but also short on decent food, clothing, and basic medical care, Girsa wrote what reads like a suicide note: "Their utter exhaustion has led them to communicate to me through their commander-in-chief that they will do their duty to the very last in spite of everything, and they beg me to inform Professor Masaryk that all of them to the last man will prefer to die rather than tarnish the honor and glory of the Czecho-Slovaks. For my part, I will say it is plain and indisputable that fate of our troops is determined; one cannot but expect their loss. There is limit to human endurance."[97]

While diplomats, soldiers, and politicians in the West made what looked like good-faith efforts to at least reach a consensus, the men in Siberia knew little about such affairs. As they faced more than another year of Siberian combat, for no very good reasons, a bitter sense of betrayal took hold and spilled out of them.

As the Red Army pummeled the legionnaires and pushed into Siberia, a former tsarist naval officer journeyed into the eye of the storm. Dispirited by a pointless visit to Washington, DC, in 1917, Admiral Aleksandr V. Kolchak was further disheartened at learning the Bolsheviks had overthrown

Kerensky on the day his ship left San Francisco for Vladivostok in late October 1917. By the time he reached Tokyo, he concluded that the new Soviet regime, the armistice, and the peace negotiations with Berlin represented the complete subjugation of Russia to Germany; he could not serve Russia. In Japan, Kolchak approached the British ambassador and offered his services to the Allies, but little came of that. The admiral decided to cross Siberia in the direction of Crimea, where his wife and son resided, and where he could volunteer with anti-Bolshevik forces.[98]

On his way through Vladivostok, now under control of the Czecho-Slovak legionnaires, Kolchak felt sick at the spectacle of the city. "Vladivostok made an exceedingly painful impression on me—I could not forget that I had been there in the times of the Empire. Then, we were masters." Now, Vladivostok's streets were crowded with almost a dozen nationalities among the soldiers, refugees, and former POWs, and circulating among them were a half-dozen currencies, foreign newspapers, and at least a dozen competing political factions. To all of this, Kolchak felt a profound humiliation, and the legionnaires were at the center of it all. "It was my belief that, after all, this intervention would end in the occupation and seizure of our Far East by alien hands. . . . Besides, the very purpose and character of the intervention were profoundly insulting. It was not to help Russia—it was all being advocated as assistance to the Czechs, assistance to their safe return home, and in this connection everything assumed a character deeply humiliating and profoundly painful for the Russians."[99]

Having never received the reinforcements and supplies that they needed, the legion began to retreat in significant numbers no later than September.[100] Falling back first from Syzran, then Kazan, then Samara, the legionnaires were heartened only by news of Allied victories in Europe and reports of the growing success of the independence movement.

The Allies Recognize Czecho-Slovakia

IT IS HARD to avoid the conclusion that both the legion's fanciful potential to support the White forces in Russia, which London especially desired, and the very real beating it was then taking in combat against the Red Army, which Washington no doubt regretted, combined to encourage the United Kingdom and United States to join the French in recognizing Czech-Slovak sovereignty.

Following the agreements that Paris and Rome signed with the Czecho-Slovak National Council on February 7 and April 21, 1918, respectively—giving the exile organization de facto diplomatic recognition, largely as a result of the Czech and Slovak soldiers serving in their armies—in a May 10 meeting with British foreign secretary Balfour, Beneš asked for London's recognition of the National Council. Whether it was a coincidence, or not, it was on June 3—the day news broke in Europe and North America about the legion's revolt in Siberia—that Balfour replied in the affirmative. He said, "I have the honor to assure you that His Majesty's Government, who have every possible sympathy with the Czecho-Slovak movement, will be glad to give the same recognition to this movement as has been granted by the Governments of France and Italy."[101] This did not, however, amount to recognition of an independent state, nor even recognition of the National Council as a government-in-exile. Yet Balfour later confided to an Italian diplomat that Czecho-Slovak independence "means the destruction of Austria-Hungary."[102] On the same day, US secretary of state Lansing had met with Masaryk for the first time, Masaryk's first significant meeting with a US official, just days after Lansing issued his own statement "that the nationalistic aspirations of the Czecho-Slovaks . . . have the earnest sympathy of this Government."[103]

Lansing sharpened this point of view on June 28, saying: "all branches of the Slav race should be completely freed from German and Austrian rule."[104] That same day, French foreign minister Stéphen Pichon informed Beneš that Paris would soon recognize the independence of the Czecho-Slovaks and recognize the National Council as a provisional government.[105] On June 29 Lansing received a statement that Pichon planned to read the next day, with Beneš at his side, at a ceremony at which the first Czecho-Slovak unit in the French Army would receive its colors. Pichon's remarks recognized the council only "as the supreme organization of the Czecho-Slovak movement in the Entente countries," and not a "government," but added that Paris would support "the aspirations to independence for which its soldiers are fighting in the ranks of the Allies."[106] On the same day, in Siberia, Major Alphonse Guinet told the legionnaires, "I have been authorized to express the thanks of the Allies to the Czecho-Slovak Corps for their action in Russia."

Meanwhile, the Czechs in Prague continued their public campaign for independence. On July 13, they founded their own Czecho-Slovak National Committee, whose ranks included members of Masaryk and Beneš's Maffie. Their principal demand was the "right of self-determination in a fully independent Czecho-Slovak State with its own administration within its own borders and under its own sovereignty."[107]

By midsummer 1918 Masaryk was lobbying the White House for recognition. He submitted a formal request for recognition to the US State Department on July 20 that relied heavily on arguments related to the Czecho-Slovak troops in Russia, France, and Italy:

> I think that this recognition has become practically necessary: I dispose of three armies (in Russia, France, and Italy), I am, as a wit said, the master of Siberia and half Russia, and yet I am in the United States formally a private man. . . . We have an army, the most essential attribute of sovereignty according to international views, not having a territory—yet the French Republic by her recognition has solved the question and created a precedent. I hope the United States will join France. This recognition has for us a great practical value: we can more effectively protect our soldiers who are taken prisoner by the Austrians, etc.[108]

Masaryk again urged that the legionnaires be shipped to France, yet conceded that "our army can be used with advantage in Russia." He criticized the plans for intervention as inadequate and vague, and concluded, "I therefore propose that after Siberia is put into order, and that should be accomplished before winter, half of our army be transported to France; the other half could in the meantime remain in Russia."[109]

On September 3, Lansing announced US recognition of the Czecho-Slovak National Council as a de facto "government." Making clear that the legionnaires deserved credit for the looming independence of the Czechs and Slovaks, he said:

> The Czecho-Slovak peoples, having taken up arms against the German and Austro-Hungarian Empires, and having placed organized armies in the field which are waging war against those Empires under officers of their own nationality and in accordance with the rules and practices of civilized nations; and
>
> The Czecho-Slovaks having, in prosecution of their independent purposes in the present war, confided supreme political authority to the Czecho-Slovak National Council;
>
> The Government of the United States recognizes that a state of belligerency exists between the Czecho-Slovaks thus organized and the German and Austro-Hungarian Empires.
>
> It also recognizes the Czecho-Slovak National Council as a de facto belligerent government clothed with proper authority to direct the military and political affairs of the Czecho-Slovaks.
>
> The Government of the United States further declares that it is prepared to enter formally into relations with the de facto government thus recognized for the purpose of prosecuting the war against the common enemy, the Empires of Germany and Austria-Hungary.[110]

On September 7 Masaryk wrote to Wilson: "Allow me to express the feeling of profound gratitude for the recognition of our Army, the National Council, and the nation. . . . America's recognition will strengthen our armies and our whole nation in their unshakable decision to sacrifice everything for the liberation of Europe and of mankind." Wilson's reply of September 10 again drew attention to his doubts about the course he had followed in regard to the Czecho-Slovaks: "It reassures me to know that you think that I have followed the right course in my earnest endeavor to be of as much service as possible to the Czecho-Slovak peoples."[111] The United States made a loan of $7 million to the Czecho-Slovak National Council to help it get established, and Wilson received the first Czecho-Slovak ambassador, Charles Pergler, on September 9. Wilson's brief remarks to Pergler underlined the role of the legionnaires: "By your conduct throughout the war, especially by your armies, you have demonstrated that you insist on complete independence. We have merely recognized an accomplished fact."[112] London, Paris, and Rome quickly moved to formalize relations with the exiles. Beneš wrote another urgent letter to Prague on September 11, beseeching the Czechs not to create a separate government body and to prepare themselves to leave the Reichsrat and disavow Vienna.[113]

Masaryk next turned his feverish activity on two ambitious projects—drafting a declaration of independence for his Czecho-Slovaks and organizing another conference of delegates of Europe's peoples seeking independence, much like the Rome Congress.[114]

"All along, my object was to show the Allies by practical demonstration, as it were, that the object of the war was and must be the political transformation of Central and Eastern Europe in particular, and the liberation of a whole series of peoples whom the Central Powers oppressed," he said.[115] On Sunday, September 15, 1918, representatives of the oppressed peoples of Austria-Hungary once again gathered at Carnegie Hall in New York to make their voices heard. In a sign of the growing influence of the European exiles, presiding over the meeting of four thousand participants was US senator Gilbert M. Hitchcock, the chairman of the Senate Foreign Relations Committee. Meanwhile, Masaryk and Wilson met on September 11 and again on September 20, when Masaryk and about a dozen other Habsburg empire dissidents presented Wilson with resolutions they had adopted at the conference in New York. Wilson's warm embrace of their aims made a strong impression. Masaryk confided to their escort, George Creel, the leader of the White House Committee on Public Information, after the meeting, "Why, your president is the most intensely human man I have ever met! He's actually incandescent with feeling!"[116]

WHILE THE EXILE movement made progress in world capitals and the Allies began to push the Germans back along the Western Front, the situation in Siberia remained confused and contentious among the Whites, the Reds, the Americans, the Japanese, and the legionnaires.

The end of the Great War, on November 11, 1918, moreover, did not change US policy toward Russia, such as it was, consigning US general Graves to his hellish neutrality and the legionnaires to another Russian winter. "The armistice had absolutely no effect in Siberia," said Graves.[117] As President Wilson began to prepare for the Paris Peace Conference, he was certainly aware of the plight of the Czecho-Slovaks, but no doubt held the British and French responsible for drawing them into the Russian Civil War. "I hope before you go away you can give me a suggestion with regard to the Russian situation and your view of what we should do with regard to Siberia," Secretary of War Baker wrote to Wilson in a letter on November 27, 1918. "The presence of our troops in Siberia is being used by the Japanese as a cloak for their own presence and operations there, and the Czecho-Slovak people are quite lost sight of in any of the operations now taking place."[118] On December 4, the day Wilson and Lansing sailed for France aboard the *George Washington*, however, State Department counselor Polk said that US policy would remain unchanged until "the question of how to further assist Russia, particularly after the withdrawal of German troops from Russian occupied territory, is determined by discussion with the Allied governments at Paris."[119] The legionnaires would have to wait yet longer, this time to allow for Allied leaders to gather at Versailles and rearrange the world.

NINE

THE VIEW FROM SIBERIA

Altruistic passion is sluiced into the reservoirs of nationalism with great ease, and is made to flow beyond them with great difficulty.

REINHOLD NIEBUHR,
Moral Man and Immoral Society[1]

The Other October Revolution

GERMAN AND AUSTRO-HUNGARIAN armies began a final retreat along the Western Front in the fall of 1918, and on October 1 the German high command admitted that the war was lost and suggested an armistice. The new German chancellor, Prince Max of Baden, appealed to President Woodrow Wilson on October 4 for a peace based on his Fourteen Points, as did Austria-Hungary the same day. Wilson began exchanging notes with Berlin—but not with Vienna. Meanwhile, Tomáš G. Masaryk and his associates learned that Habsburg Emperor Karl was at the same time preparing a bold, if desperate, Federalization Manifesto to transform half his kingdom into a league of autonomous peoples.

Things were moving quickly, forcing Masaryk and Edvard Beneš to work at a furious pace. On September 29, the members of Prague's Czecho-Slovak National Committee, which had been founded in July, together with the Czech deputies in the Austro-Hungarian Reichsrat, had met to demand full independence, rejecting any constitutional reforms of Austria-Hungary. On October 2, according to Beneš, the chairman of the new Czech parliamentary club in the Reichsrat, the Czech Union, František Staněk, declared its recognition of the Czecho-Slovak National Council in Paris as a de facto government. Another Czech deputy announced the following week that all 150 Czechs in the Reichsrat were leaving the parliament.[2] Perhaps underestimating their position, Masaryk and Beneš remained anxious that emboldened Czechs in Prague might announce their own provisional government or strike a deal with the Habsburgs. Beneš consulted with Masaryk.

"Benes and I had often thought of this so as not to be caught napping when the time came," Masaryk said. "Now the time had come."[3] Beneš dashed off a message to the French Foreign Ministry on the evening of October 14, announcing the formation of a provisional government. Masaryk was named president, prime minister, and finance minister; Beneš was named minister of both foreign affairs and the interior; and Milan R. Štefánik was named minister of war. The Slovak-American lawyer Stefan Osusky, who helped Masaryk and Beneš in Europe—and who insisted on Slovak equality—was named ambassador to London. Lev Sychrava, the lawyer and journalist who edited *Československa Samostatnost* (Czecho-Slovak Independence), which he moved to France after his expulsion from Switzerland, was made ambassador to France. Bohdan Pavlů, one of the founders of the Union of Czecho-Slovak Organizations in Russia and editor of the legionnaire newspaper, *Československy Denik* (Czecho-Slovak Daily), who was then in Omsk, was made ambassador to Russia. Iowa lawyer Charles Pergler became ambassador to the United States, while Lev Borský was posted to Italy.

Because the emperor's Federalization Manifesto threatened all these plans, Masaryk quickly began drafting a Czecho-Slovak declaration of independence. What became known as the Washington Declaration was drafted in Czech over long days in hotel rooms and rented apartments in Washington, DC—but it first appeared in English.[4] Among those who advised Masaryk were Supreme Court justice Louis D. Brandeis, the son of Czech immigrants; Ira E. Bennett, the editorial page editor of the

Washington Post, which was then publishing editorials in support of Masaryk; and Interior Secretary Franklin K. Lane. Finally, at about 4:00 p.m. on October 16, Jaroslav Císař, an aide to Masaryk, raced toward the Powhatan Hotel two blocks west of the White House on Pennsylvania Avenue. Taking an elevator to an upper floor, Císař knocked on the door of Herbert A. Miller, an Oberlin College specialist on nationalities who had volunteered to assist Masaryk.[5] "This is the Czecho-Slovak Declaration of Independence," Císař said. "The professor wants you to put it into good English."

Having begun that same day speaking at the funeral of a friend at Arlington National Cemetery, Miller was tired. He walked into Lafayette Park and sat down on a bench. He thought the draft would not appeal "to the American public which it, in part, sought to influence, and that it needed complete revision." A friend, sculptor Gutzon Borglum, who sculpted the Mount Rushmore National Memorial, happened to walk by with Charles W. Nichols, an employee of the American Agricultural Association. It so happened that Borglum had earlier allowed Štefánik to establish a training camp on his estate in Stamford, Connecticut, for Czecho-Slovak volunteers for the French army. The two men offered to help edit the constitution and agreed to meet at Nichols's office, where they were joined by Císař and three others. "The original typewritten copy was cut into more than 100 pieces and pasted together in different order and then revised again and again," Miller said. The group worked from 7:30 in the evening until 1:30 the following morning. Later on October 17, Miller took the draft to Masaryk, where it again underwent revisions into the morning hours of October 18.[6]

While Masaryk and Beneš were long criticized by some for purporting to speak for the Czechs and Slovaks of Europe without their complete, or informed, consent, Masaryk's declaration expressly cited the Epiphany Declaration that the Czech deputies in the Reichsrat had adopted on January 6, 1918, which demanded complete independence and rejected "autonomy." The opening words of the new declaration of independence emphasized the context of this moment and the practical, yet pressing, motivations of the National Council:

> At this grave moment, when the Hohenzollerns are offering peace to stop
> the victorious advance of the Allies armies and to prevent the dismem-
> berment of Austria-Hungary and Turkey, and when the Habsburgs are
> promising the federalization of the Empire and autonomy to the dissat-
> isfied nationalities committed to their rule, we, the Czecho-Slovak Na-
> tional Council, recognized by the Allies and American Governments as
> the Provisional Government of the Czecho-Slovak State and Nation, in
> complete accord with the Declaration of the Czech Deputies, made in
> Prague on January 6th, 1918, and realizing that federalization, and, still
> more, autonomy, mean nothing under a Habsburg dynasty, do hereby
> declare this our Declaration of Independence.

Masaryk made it public in every Allied country on October 18. In a
cover note to Wilson, he said, "The National Council was compelled to
make this declaration now because of the Austrian moves for peace and
toward a mock-federation calculated to deceive the world."[7]

That same day, news arrived in Washington of the emperor's manifesto, which had been published two days earlier. Clearly trying to leverage Wilson's own Fourteen Points of January 8, when Wilson had urged
that Habsburg subjects be given "the freest opportunity of autonomous
development," the emperor declared, "I have decided to undertake this
work with the free collaboration of my peoples in the spirit of those prin-
cipals which the Allied monarchs in their peace offer have adopted. Following the desires of her peoples, Austria must become a federated state
in which every race will form its own state commonwealth in the districts
inhabited by it." Except, he might have added, for the Slovaks and the
Yugoslavs, since Hungary refused to agree with him and since Budapest
controlled their lands. "He was a drowning man clutching at a straw,"
thought Masaryk. The legionnaires and exiles were demanding independence, and Masaryk added, "it must be said that the Siberian Anabasis of
our troops had attracted his attention and had awakened his goodwill."[8]

On October 19, Secretary of State Robert E. Lansing signed for Wilson a direct response to the emperor that was, in a word, devastating:

The President deems it his duty to say to the Austro-Hungarian Government that he cannot entertain the present suggestions of that Government because of certain events of utmost importance which, occurring since the delivery of his address of the 8th of January last, have necessarily altered the attitude and responsibility of the Government of the United States. Among the fourteen terms of peace which the President formulated at that time occurred the following: "The peoples of Austria-Hungary, whose place among the nations we wish to see safeguarded and assured, should be accorded the freest opportunity for autonomous development." Since that sentence was written and uttered to the Congress of the United States, the Government of the United States has recognized that a state of belligerency exists between the Czecho-Slovaks and the German and Austro-Hungarian Empires and that the Czecho-Slovak National Council is a *de facto* belligerent Government clothed with proper authority to direct the military and political affairs of the Czecho-Slovaks.

The response concluded:

The President is, therefore, no longer at liberty to accept the mere "autonomy" of these peoples as a basis for peace, but is obliged to insist that they, and not he, shall be the judges of what action on the part of the Austro-Hungarian Government will satisfy their aspirations and their conception of their rights and destiny as members of the family of nations.[9]

Wilson's famous Fourteen Points were amended—by the deft moves of the exiles. "The Emperor Karl's manifesto came too late," Masaryk said, adding, "Wilson's answer to Austria struck Vienna like lightning."[10] The leading newspaper of Austria-Hungary, the *Neue Freie Presse*, described the note as a "blow at the heart." The editorial added, "Austria-Hungary has a Premier whose seat is at Washington; his name is Wilson."[11] A US diplomat said that the effect within Austria-Hungary "has been to complete the demoralization of the country."[12] Wilson wrote to Masaryk on October 21, "I need not tell you with what emotion I read the Declaration of Independence put out by the National Council of the Czecho-Slovaks, and I think that my recent reply to Austria will apprise you very fully of my own attitude in the matter."[13]

Beneš remained anxious about the Czechs in Prague, with whom communication was difficult. Perceiving no further relaxation of military rule in Prague, Czechs had launched a general strike on October 14, aimed in particular at ending exports of scarce food to Vienna. The demonstrators in the city were quickly confronted by armed soldiers.[14] Beneš sent Prague's leaders the announcement of a provisional government on October 17 but expressed a willingness to negotiate and compromise. Significantly, he offered to allow Prague to make the appointment to the post of prime minister so long as Masaryk remained "at the head of the government." A leader of the Czechs in Prague promptly announced that the Paris-based exiles would handle all international negotiations.

SEEKING ALLIES BEYOND the Habsburg lands, Masaryk next helped to organize the Mid-European Union to foster dialogue among Central Europe's nations—in this case Albania, Armenia, Estonia, Greece, Italy, Latvia, Lithuania, Poland, Romania, Ukraine, and Yugoslavia—to encourage them to resolve major disputes or misunderstandings, especially in regard to territorial claims, before the larger powers began formulating postwar settlements. Masaryk embraced the idea that the group should hold a public meeting at Independence Hall in Philadelphia to draw publicity to their aims.[15] Masaryk was made chairman; Herbert A. Miller was named executive director.

Eleven nationalities were represented by delegates to the Mid-European Union meeting in Philadelphia in late October, which met for several days of intense negotiations regarding a new map of Europe. Italians hotly argued with the Yugoslavs over disputed borders. News of armed clashes between Ukrainians and Poles in Austrian Galicia were being reported. After differences were aired and some agreements reached, the delegates gathered at noon on Saturday, October 26, in the courtyard behind Independence Hall. On a platform flanked by new flags and aspiring leaders of European peoples, Masaryk read the union's Declaration of Common Aims, which they had all signed. The document agreed on government by consent and self-determination, promised civil rights to all citizens, and endorsed the idea of a League of Nations. The four-year-old child of a Czech immigrant unveiled a replica of the original Liberty Bell, which other children attired in Old World costumes tolled as each speaker expressed his gratitude to the United States and President Wilson for putting their nationalist aims on the postwar agenda. The entire crowd then retired to the nearby Bellevue-Stratford Hotel, where Masaryk received a telegram—confirming that he would be appointed president of Czecho-Slovakia.[16] Two days after the meeting in Philadelphia, an independent nation for the Czechs and Slovaks was born.

"Dear God, We'd Actually Done It!"

ACCOMPANIED BY OSUSKY, the Slovak-American lawyer, and a few others, Beneš met a delegation of key Prague Czechs in Switzerland on October 28 at the Hotel Beau Rivage on Lake Geneva, close to the pier where Habsburg Empress Elizabeth was stabbed to death in 1898 and not far from the café where Masaryk and Beneš joined forces in exile on a rainy night in 1915.[17] The men were nervous, fearing another wave of arrests and executions by Vienna or even an invasion of Austria-Hungary by German troops. With very little dissent, they agreed that Karel Kramář would become prime minister and they approved the earlier appointments announced as the Provisional Government: Masaryk as president, Štefánik as minister of war, and Beneš as foreign minister. Alois Rašin, another one of the core members of the Prague Maffie, was named minister of finance. Kramář and Beneš were to represent the country at the Paris peace talks. A Revolutionary National Assembly would be created from the elected Czech members of the Reichsrat in Vienna and the legislative Diets of Bohemia and Moravia. A Slovak who had been close to Masaryk since his student days at Charles University, Vavro Šrobár, one of three Slovaks who was appointed to the new cabinet, was given the important task of identifying a number of Slovaks to serve in the National Assembly, when few Slovaks held elective office.

That same day, the new republic was declared when the Czecho-Slovak National Council formally proclaimed independence. "Czecho-Slovak people! Your ancient dream has been realized," it announced, hailing "our liberators, Masaryk and Wilson" and citing "the glorious pages of your history, to which have been added the immortal exploits of the Czecho-Slovak Legions on the Western Front and in Siberia."[18] In Prague, people spilled out of offices, factories, and homes, and large crowds filled Wenceslas Square, where the proclamation was read aloud amidst cheering, flag-waving crowds.

By October 30, the last Austrian-allied Hungarian government was deposed in what resembled a coup, which emboldened about three hundred Slovaks to gather again at Turcansky Svaty Martin on October 30, where they first approved the idea of an independent state in union with the Czechs the previous May. The influential priest and Slovak leader, Andrej Hlinka, was present again and the delegates approved a declaration that severed their relationship with Hungary, created a Slovak National Council, and demanded a union of Czechs and Slovaks in a new state.[19]

From Paris—where Beneš was permitted to join the Allies in negotiating the armistice with Austria-Hungary—Beneš took a moment on November 2 to write a letter to his wife, Hana, who had been imprisoned on account of her husband's activities. "I had heard how much you suffered," he said, "how bad it was, I had felt that it would be so. When I return, you will tell me everything, explain everything; you can now clearly understand that it was not all in vain."[20] A few days later, his heart was pounding and his head spinning as he found himself in the backseat of a flag-bedecked vehicle, gliding from Paris to Versailles on his way to an Allied meeting. "I could scarcely believe," Beneš later confessed, "in the reality of what was happening."[21]

The Great War's end on November 11, 1918, and the founding of Czecho-Slovakia removed every justification the legionnaires had ever heard for their fighting in Russia. Told by the Allies that they were fighting the Central Powers from Russia and told by the exile independence leaders that they were fighting on behalf of the Allies in order to earn a new nation of their own, the legionnaires now asked why they were fighting at all, with the war concluded, Austria-Hungary defeated, and Czecho-Slovakia proclaimed. Yet they still had to dodge the machine gun and artillery fire of a growing Red Army, which had halted the legionnaires by August 1918. Answers never came to the questions posed by the legionnaires, as the Allies dithered amongst themselves.

The Collapse of Austria-Hungary

BY AUTUMN 1918, the Central Powers were surrounded, the war would not end, their armies were defeated, the youthful Emperor Karl had run out of options, his former subjects were starving, and Germany, Vienna's sole ally, could not save her. The Habsburg authorities initially appealed to their subjects to maintain existing government structures, but they were ignored. After all, the emperor's Federalization Manifesto, though rejected in Washington, had confirmed that the emperor himself was willing to jettison the old regime and its historic realm. Feeling betrayed by their emperor, the Austrians quickly declared a Republic of German-Austria on October 30, 1918. But the Allied powers forbade a union with Germany. Budapest announced that the emperor's manifesto was a violation of the Compromise of 1867, essentially nullifying their union, and a Hungarian republic was declared in November 1918. Yugoslavia was founded on December 1, 1918, when the Kingdom of Serbs, Croats, and Slovenes was proclaimed under a Serb dynasty.

With a population smaller than the contemporary number of people living in the northeast corner of the United States, Austria-Hungary saw more than 2 million of its civilian and military population die as a result of the war. Throughout the war, Austria-Hungary placed about 8.5 million men in uniform, more than one-third of its male population. A total of 1.2 million died, half of them in action and the rest of wounds, illness,

Post-World War One Nations, Central & Eastern Europe

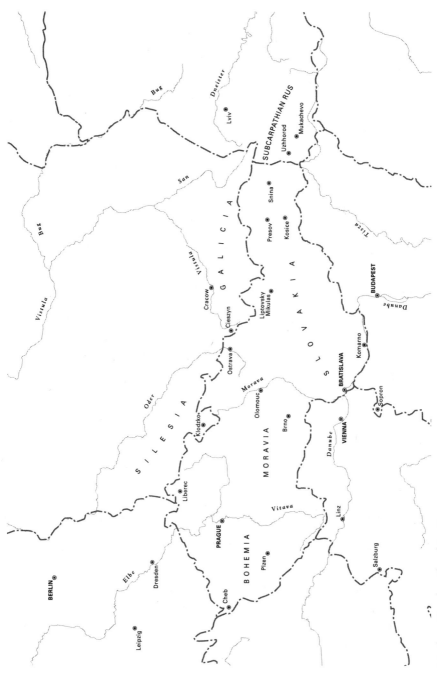

Modern Czecho-Slovakia, Pre-1993

or starvation. This does not include the 478,000 who died as prisoners of war, more than 20 percent of the 2,104,146 Austro-Hungarian soldiers taken prisoner in Russia.[22] If one includes a midrange of the estimates of the number of Habsburg civilians killed by the war (three hundred thousand to seven hundred thousand, or five hundred thousand), more than 2.1 million died altogether.[23]

THE CURRENCY OF dynasties and aristocracies had declined in a more democratic age, as did the unquestioned power of the Catholic Church in a more ecumenical and secular age. The army remained the last multinational institution of a regime whose legitimacy rested on its multinational character. The army's principal weakness, however, was that it was linked to a family dynasty whose rule was now ended. The professional Habsburg officer corps was largely dead and buried. Despite the weaknesses of the regime it represented and defended, the Austro-Hungarian army is thought to have performed reasonably well. "The fact remains," says historian Gunther E. Rothenberg, "that to the degree that the nationality problem could not be resolved in the Habsburg monarchy, or for that matter in Central Europe, it also could not be resolved within the army."[24] Moreover, as historian Josef Kalvoda points out, more Czechs died fighting for Austria-Hungary than joined the legion.[25]

On October 31 the emperor issued an order releasing the officer corps from their oaths to the dynasty, permitting them to join the armies of the new national governments, thereby destroying the Austro-Hungarian Army. Indeed, the army survived the dynasty, and its empire, by a few days. Its standard was last flown by an isolated unit in central Albania. Unaware that the war had ended and Austria-Hungary was no more, General Karl von Pflanzer-Baltin accepted the imperial salute as his men commenced their last march on November 21, 1918.

That November, however, there were simply not enough loyal soldiers to guard the Schönbrunn Palace in Vienna, where Emperor Karl remained with his family. Two platoons of youthful cadets volunteered to patrol the estate. News arrived on November 10 of German Kaiser Wilhelm's flight to Holland, and Karl's aides warned that his personal safety was imperiled unless he abdicated.[26] Karl refused, but early on the morning of November 11, he signed a proclamation, whose key point conceded something less than abdication: "The people, through its representatives, has taken over the government. I renounce all participation in the affairs of the state."[27] That evening, the family left for a remote castle.[28]

IN CZECHO-SLOVAKIA, PERHAPS because the exiles, émigrés, and prisoners of war had worked so long and fought so hard, the days of decision and ultimate victory could almost have gone unnoticed, even by some present. Step-by-step, various institutions, manned mostly by German authorities, handed over power to the Czechs. There were minor confrontations; when military commanders in Vienna ordered soldiers in Prague—mostly Romanian, Hungarian, or Austrian—to resist, telegraph and telephone lines between the two cities were cut off, allowing Czechs time to convince the garrisons in Prague to acquiesce. "This was the most dangerous moment in the revolution at home," Masaryk said.[29] Soon enough, however, the foreign soldiers in Prague departed to join their ethnic brethren in new nations, and Sokol volunteers were given arms and posted as guards at military establishments and ammunition stores. The Czechs in Prague urgently asked that Masaryk arrive as soon as possible; in the interim, Masaryk gave Kramar the authority to sign emergency measures in his absence.[30]

Overall, however, what people recalled was the anticlimactic way in which power changed hands. "In Prague, the Imperial Governor rang the secret number of the Czech National Committee, which he had known all along," reports historian A. J. P. Taylor. "They came round to the Castle. The Governor handed over his seals and keys. Then he left. The civil servants remained at their desks. Ten minutes of conversation had created Czecho-Slovakia as an independent country."[31] No serious violence accompanied the collapse of a monarchy hundreds of years old, a major European power with an administrative machinery that was among the most complex on earth, according to historian Joseph Redlich. "The official stamps were altered; the usual portrait of the head of the state on the office wall was removed, but the officials remained the same, and the countless laws and decrees through which they functioned remained in force with practically no alteration."[32] Recalling the origins of the revolt that brought down the Habsburgs, historian Taylor wrote, "In this strange way, the deathblow to an empire centuries old was struck far away on the railway platform at Chelyabinsk."[33]

In September 1915 Winston Churchill had swung in favor of the nationalities of Austria-Hungary, telling a reporter, "We want this war to settle the map of Europe on national lines and according to the true wishes of the people who dwell in the disputed areas. . . . We want a natural and harmonious settlement which liberates races and restores the integrity of nations."[34] The rise of Adolf Hitler, World War II, and the Soviet occupation of Eastern Europe changed his mind by the late 1940s. "There is not one of the peoples or provinces that constituted the Empire of the Habsburgs," he wrote in his history of World War II, which was published in 1948, "to whom gaining their independence has not brought the tortures which ancient poets and theologians had reserved for the damned."[35]

"It must be said, and said again," says historian Arthur J. May, "that nowhere in continental Europe, except in Switzerland, were the peculiar interests of the national minorities given more protection and consideration, unsatisfactory though they were, than in the Austrian half of the Dual Monarchy."[36] George F. Kennan notes, "The Austro-Hungarian Empire still looks better as a solution to the tangled problems of that part of the world than anything that has succeeded it."[37] Remarked one biographer of Emperor Franz Joseph, "The tragedy of Austria-Hungary was that it resembled a social-economic pedagogical institute for the nationalities, whose students burnt the building after having successfully passed the exams."[38]

Already deemed antiquated in its final years, Austria-Hungary was forgotten quickly after its demise, except in a few memoirs or works of nostalgic fiction, such as Joseph Roth's *The Radetzky March* and *The Emperor's Tomb*, Robert Musil's *The Man without Qualities*, and Stefan Zweig's *The World of Yesterday*, all of them misty memorials to an ethereal place and time. "Probably no other country in the history of

Europe underwent the transformation from a great power into a fantasy so quickly and spectacularly," wrote one author.[39] The realm now vanished, her peoples remained obscure. Says historian Adam Kozuchowski, "by the time it fell, this country was still exotic to the majority of European readers, not to mention Americans. Works in English or French about the monarchy were few, the peculiarities of its internal politics were mysterious even for the Germans, and the ethnographic map of the monarchy was full of names that remained unknown to its citizens inhabiting the other corner of the country."[40]

From the ruins of Austria-Hungary, in large part, arose the newly independent states of Czecho-Slovakia and Yugoslavia, Poland was again united and free, and Romania and Italy were enlarged. Austria and Hungary were reduced to separate, truncated versions of themselves. Hungary, which unlike "Austria" had defined boundaries, lost about two-thirds of its territory to Czecho-Slovakia, Romania, and Yugoslavia. Austria was left with a total population of fewer than 7 million people, fewer than in Czecho-Slovakia. Prague was awarded Bohemia, Moravia, and part of Silesia from the Austrian half of the realm, and the territories of Slovakia and Carpathian Rus—where resided the Ruthenians, often characterized as Ukrainian—from Hungary.[41] The war and its aftermath also awarded independence to Estonia, Finland, Latvia, and Lithuania.

On November 14, 1918, the Revolutionary National Assembly in Prague met for the first time. Prime minister–designate Kramář proclaimed the Habsburgs dethroned and the assembly declared Masaryk president and endorsed the proposed cabinet. From the United States, Masaryk sent messages to legionnaires everywhere, telling those in France and Italy they would return home, he said, and "commanded those in Russia and Siberia to stand by the Allies."[42] That same day, Slovak-American activist Josef Husek approached Albert P. Mamatey, president of the Slovak League, and showed him something. He had taken the original, penciled draft of the "Pittsburgh Agreement" and had it printed in an elaborate calligraphic design, clearly to make the accord seem more official, and perhaps binding. He fervently urged Mamatey to approach Masaryk and ask him to sign it again. Masaryk did not hesitate, which nurtured among the Slovaks an even greater assurance that they would enjoy autonomy.[43] The Slovak Americans also collected $200,000 for the new nation and forwarded it to Prague.[44]

"I do not know whether I am happy, and I could not describe my feelings," Masaryk said in his last public speech in the United States before returning to Prague, to lawyers in New York on November 16, 1918. "I have the feeling of responsibility. . . . The aim of this war is that these nations which have been oppressed by Prussia, Austria-Hungary, Turkey, and by old Russia—all of these nations must be liberated. You have a peculiar zone of nations going from Finland down to Greece—eighteen in all—and all of these eighteen nations must be reconstructed, liberated, and the foundation of future peace must be laid there. That is the great task."[45] When Masaryk emerged from the Vanderbilt Hotel in New York City on November 20 to board the *Carmania*, which would carry him across the Atlantic, he ran into a detachment of American sailors, his first military honor guard, "compelling me again and again to realize that I had ceased to be a private individual." Aboard ship a few days later, he realized, "Dear God, we'd actually done it!"[46]

In Russia, however, "filled with indignation and bitter disappointment," Sergeant Gustav Becvar said, "the legionnaires lost the last of their enthusiasm for the anti-Bolshevik cause."[47] On the heels of conquering Siberia, the Czechs and Slovaks had exhausted themselves in nonstop combat against a growing Red Army along the Volga River, waiting in vain for assistance from the Allies. Their dwindling forces increasingly lacked weapons, ammunition, winter clothing, medicine, sanitation facilities, and decent food. Large numbers of legionnaires began to throw down their rifles and refuse to fight—despite pleas from their officers. In late October, one such officer, Colonel Josef J. Švec, who had served from 1914 with the first volunteers in the Russian *družina* and who led the legionnaires that captured Kazan in 1918, retired to his train in shame and frustration—and shot himself dead.[48]

Angered by the coup that had installed Admiral Kolchak as "Supreme Ruler and Commander in Chief of all Russian Land and Sea Forces" on November 18, 1918, most of the men were increasingly bitter about what they felt was a betrayal by the Allies. They remained trapped in Siberia as Czechs and Slovaks at home celebrated a new country of their own, Czecho-Slovakia. Instead of joining the celebrations, they were expected to prop up a new Russian dictator. More to the point, the end of the war finally removed the threat of execution should they be returned to Austria-Hungary, a fear that had long kept the men together and fighting. The desire for national independence was always their aspiration, but the offer to fight for the Allies was merely transactional, a means to an end—and the transaction's terms had now changed. The legionnaires evacuated the Volga front entirely by the end of December, when Ufa fell to the Red Army. Štefánik was dispatched to Siberia to assess the problem and to try to improve the legionnaires' morale.

He arrived at Vladivostok with General Maurice Janin, commander of the legionnaires, on November 17. Janin remained behind while Štefánik traveled ahead to visit the legionnaires at the front. Reaching Yekaterinburg in early December, he encountered soldiers who were demoralized but respectful to him. Many refused to fight or move to the front. Battling war injuries from which he never fully recovered, Štefánik was thin and sickly; Syrový read Štefánik's welcoming remarks for him. Despite his weakness, on December 11, he ventured further west toward the front between Yekaterinburg and Kungur.[49] Štefánik met with legionnaires in small groups, speaking with them for hours at a time. "All that time," legionnaire František Kočí said, "Stefanik talked to them like a brother, like a soldier, like a minister and politician; he talked to them for four hours, ignoring his fatigue, often fainting from exhaustion. He was pleading, begging, demanding, and appealing to the feelings of the soldiers so much that some apparently began to cry."[50]

"Stefanik was revered by the troops," said Becvar. What he was required to tell the frontline soldiers northwest of Yekaterinburg, however, felt like another hammer blow. "You must hold out here in Siberia until the end, until the victory is won," said Štefánik, visibly struggling. "And this you must do relying only upon your own strength, for I can tell you authoritatively that no help from the Allies will come to this front. It is useless our discussing the rights and wrongs of the case. The fact of importance is that help will not come. Now you know just how things stand, and also the extent of the task that lies ahead."[51] This was a message that would not improve the men's morale and Štefánik was under no illusion he had succeeded by the time he left for Czecho-Slovakia to take up his post as minister of war. In his wake, two battalions of legionnaires refused to go to the front near Yekaterinburg in January 1919, according to Becvar, leading yet another officer, a sergeant, to shoot himself.[52]

While the legionnaires had already begun voting with their feet, Janin and Štefánik issued orders in January 1919 to make it official that the legionnaires were withdrawn from the anti-Bolshevik front. By the end of that month, they agreed to a new mission of guarding the Trans-Siberian Railway from the western cities of Yekaterinburg and Chelyabinsk to Irkutsk in the east, ostensibly to protect supplies, communications, and transport but also, it should be noted, to protect themselves. They began to exercise greater control of the trains from this point forward, prepared to place their own safety and transportation needs first.

No sooner had legionnaires begun to leave the front for garrison duty than they finally witnessed the arrival in Omsk in December 1918 of the Allied presence they had been waiting for. At the Omsk train station, the legionnaires were welcomed with fluttering Allied flags and a banner that said, "Welcome, brave Czecho-Slovak brethren!" Amidst crowds of officers, a Siberian army general greeted them with a flowery speech and bands played various national anthems. Marching into town, the men were toasted at a lavish luncheon, and in the afternoon a grand parade was held for the lone Allied soldier, French general Janin, who arrived just in time to supervise their guard duties. That night in their trains, the legionnaires indulged their bitterness and cynicism. "So the Allied help has come at last," one legionnaire cried out, "by lending us a fat general without troops."[53]

The Allies Dither, Churchill Fumes

ON JANUARY 14, 1919, Winston S. Churchill was awarded responsibility for the British military at precisely the moment when London's military options were blunted. Having served Prime Minister David Lloyd-George as minister for munitions since July 1917, Churchill was promoted to secretary of state for war and air two months after the armistice ended the war and four days before the Paris Peace Conference opened.[54] Everything intentional about Allied policy toward Russia was now irrelevant. "The Allies had only entered Russia with reluctance and as an operation of war; but the war was over," Churchill said. "They had made exertions to deny to the German armies the vast supplies of Russia; but these armies existed no more. They had set out to rescue the Czechs; but the Czechs had already saved themselves. Therefore every argument which had led to intervention had disappeared."

On the other hand, very little about Allied policy regarding Russia was, in fact, intentional, so very little changed. Confusion reigned not only among the Allies but within governments, as well, and this confusion was more acute in London than in other Allied capitals, since Great Britain stood out as the one ally pushing hardest to do more in Russia. The push originated almost solely from Churchill, who was moved in part by the debt owed to the anti-Bolsheviks that the Allies had encouraged, arguing that it would be dishonorable to abandon them to the reprisals that surely awaited them. Yet Churchill also began to perceive, unlike anyone else, the threat the Soviet regime would pose to world peace.

"Only the British intervened actively on the side of the anti-Bolshevik forces," concludes historian Richard Pipes, "and they did so in a half-hearted manner, largely at the initiative of one man, Winston Churchill."[55] "Of all the British leaders," says historian Ilya Somin, "only Winston Churchill, the state Secretary for War, was unequivocally convinced of the wisdom and viability of overthrowing the Bolsheviks by force."[56] While isolated among Allied leaders for his posture regarding

Russia, Churchill's views were shared by others outside of government. In June 1919, for example, the *New York Times* asked, "We have fought to make the world safe for democracy. Does that mean it shall be safe for democracy everywhere but in Russia?"[57]

On February 27, 1919, Churchill wrote to Lloyd-George that "the Allied powers in Paris have not decided whether they wish to make war upon the Bolsheviks or to make peace with them. They are pausing midway between these two courses with an equal dislike of either."[58] This uncertainty not only persisted, but was also perceived by others. Britain's deputy chief of the naval staff, Admiral James A. Fergusson, asked at a July 4, 1919, cabinet meeting, "Were we, or were we not, at war with the Bolsheviks?" To which the prime minister replied, "Actually, we are at war with the Bolsheviks, but we have decided not to *make* war. In other words, we do not intend to put great armies into Russia to fight the Bolshevik forces."[59]

Churchill continued to seek reliable lines of support for the anti-Bolshevik forces in Russia. Proving that his genius was not without its occasional failing, Churchill suggested as late as June 10, 1919, that the Czecho-Slovak legionnaires be redeployed into combat positions at the front, as a prelude to fighting their way north to Archangel, the same plan that, in part, prompted their revolt in 1918. "It is possible that they might welcome the prospect of cutting their way through to Archangel," Churchill wrote to General Knox, "and their eventual repatriation by this route, as this would be shorter and quicker than via Vladivostok."[60] Suggestions such as this one reflected a continued lack of relevant information reaching London, since such plans had been tried and failed already, to say nothing of the ignorance concerning the views of the Czecho-Slovaks. It also reflected a predisposition to treat the legionnaires as little more than pawns on a chessboard.

By December 1919 London and Paris agreed to end all further support for all of the White armies, and Churchill again dissented, again with an element of prophecy: "It is a delusion to suppose that all this year we have been fighting the battles of the anti-Bolshevik Russians," Churchill noted on December 15, 1919. "On the contrary, they have been fighting ours; and this truth will become painfully apparent from the moment that they are exterminated and the Bolshevik armies are supreme over the whole vast territories of the Russian Empire."[61]

Indeed, Churchill issued many prophetic warnings about Russia and Germany. One of his memos, dated February 17, read: "In five years, or even less, it will be apparent that the whole fruits of our victories have been lost at the Peace Conference, that the League of Nations is an impotent mockery, that Germany is stronger than ever, and that British interests in India are perilously affected. After all our victories we shall have quitted the field in humiliation and defeat." While this memo was not forwarded to his colleagues, in reply to an angry note from Lloyd-George, Churchill, in a February 21 letter that was, in fact, delivered, said, "Germany and Russia will have miseries and ambitions in common and their mighty national interests will be struggling for expression and restoration. When we have abandoned Russia, she will be restored by Germany and Japan, and these three powers together will constitute a menace for Britain, France and the United States very similar to that which existed before the present war."[62] In a speech in Parliament on July 29, he said, "I can never clear my mind from a sense of anxiety regarding the danger of a hostile Russia and a revengeful German. We should make a fatal mistake if we assume that the great victory which has been won can now be safely left to take care of itself, that we should not interest ourselves in the affairs of Russia, and that we should leave the Russian people to stew in their own juice."[63] "What will be said of the victors of 1918 if," Churchill asked, "while such fateful issues are taking shape, they remain destitute of any policy, openly admitting that they have no policy; unable to state whether they are at peace or war with the Bolshevik government, watching enterprise and enterprise carried almost to the point of success by weak and feeble Russian forces with which they were associated, yet never giving the aid which would have rendered these efforts effective."[64]

This entire episode gave birth to one of Churchill's most oft-quoted lines about Russia. "If I had been properly supported in 1919," he said in remarks to the National Press Club in Washington, DC, on June 28, 1954, at the height of the Cold War, "I think we might have strangled Bolshevism in its cradle, but everybody turned up their hands and said, 'How shocking.'"[65]

The Long Retreat

BY APRIL 1919 the Red Army began to advance, and it took Chelyabinsk and Yekaterinburg by August. White soldiers began to mutiny even far behind Admiral Kolchak's capitol at Omsk, whose residents became terror-stricken.[66] As the Whites retreated, chaos once again surrounded the legionnaires. They became increasingly unruly, prompting American and other officials to begin urging quick action to evacuate the men. In Paris, meanwhile, Allied leaders continued into the fall to debate and discuss the situation in Russia, which they did not fully grasp.

On September 3, Czecho-Slovak foreign minister Beneš made an urgent plea to the Allies to evacuate the legionnaires, indicating the issue was becoming a dangerous domestic political issue for the embryonic government in Prague.[67] The White House finally announced on September 22, 1919, a loan of $12 million to the Czecho-Slovak Republic to cover the costs of evacuating the legionnaires, and directed the US Shipping Board to allocate a sufficient number of ships. London and Washington ultimately agreed to share the costs of evacuating an estimated 55,000 Czechs and Slovaks, as well as thousands of other refugees, from Vladivostok.[68]

By October, with temperatures plunging to 10–15 degrees below zero Fahrenheit, the Whites began to evacuate Omsk; their long, horrendous retreat toward Irkutsk began, facing 1,500 miles of icy, snowbound tracks. On October 19 it was announced that the legionnaires would officially begin their evacuation toward Vladivostok the next day.[69] Kolchak and his aides began evacuating the city on November 11, 1919, in seven passenger and freight trains—one of which held the $210 million in Russian gold that remained—which sparked chaos throughout the city.[70]

Ordered to evacuate before Kolchak's regime fled Omsk, the legionnaires occupied trains in front of Kolchak, which prompted the admiral to blame his difficulties on the legionnaires, who were themselves struggling to obtain locomotives and fuel and discourage potential attacks.

Irkutsk was overtly hostile to Kolchak from the start. By November 25, the legionnaires in Irkutsk issued an announcement that, Harris said, publicly attacked Kolchak, reiterated their desire to leave Siberia, and hinted they would negotiate their exit with the Bolsheviks.[71] The threats tossed between Kolchak and the legionnaires began to escalate dangerously, with Kolchak threatening to have the tunnels around Lake Baikal blown up to stop the legion. Once again, the Czechs and Slovaks were surrounded, under threat, with their escape route imperiled. With no desire to fight their way across Siberia yet again, the legionnaires began negotiating with the anti-Kolchak opposition that had taken power in Irkutsk.

Kolchak's train reached Nizhneudinsk, about three hundred miles from Irkutsk, by December 27, where it was delayed again. In Irkutsk, legionnaires took up positions at the railway station, but Red Army troops were advancing from both the north and south, coming to within at least eighteen miles, according to US ambassador to Japan Roland S. Morris, who reported "no organized body of troops is now opposing its further advance."[72] The Allies remained unaware of the situation. Instead, Janin was directed by the Allied representatives at Irkutsk on January 1, 1920, to assume responsibility for Kolchak and "to ensure, as far as it is humanly possible to do so, the personal safety of Admiral Kolchak."

On January 5 orders reached the Czecho-Slovak Sixth Regiment at Nizhneudinsk, where Kolchak's trains idled; they were to escort Kolchak to Irkutsk, but only in a single coach and only if he agreed to surrender the Russian gold. He agreed to the terms in part because there were no other reliable troops; yet his anger toward the legionnaires did not soften.[73] Two cars for Kolchak and his government's prime minister, Viktor N. Pepelyayev, were attached to a legion train, and the convoy moved forward, greeted at most stations with angry demonstrations. At one station, rail workers refused to produce a locomotive the legionnaires needed unless they allowed twelve armed Russian guards to occupy Kolchak's coach; the legionnaires relented.

Irkutsk fell to a group of Socialist Revolutionaries and Mensheviks that called itself the Political Center by January 5, 1920. Significantly, General Janin, the commander of the legionnaires, had left Irkutsk. By now, even the Supreme Ruler of Russia gave up. On January 6, Kolchak sent a message to Janin saying he had resigned. Syrovy and Janin began discussing their options by telegraph as Kolchak approached Irkutsk. On January 14 his train pulled into Irkutsk station, now packed with armed Reds angrily demanding Kolchak's surrender.

At 6:00 p.m. on January 15, two Czech officers boarded Kolchak's coach, were ushered into his private quarters, and informed the admiral that General Janin ordered them to remove the legionnaires from his train and hand him over to the Political Center. The two officers shared with Kolchak that they did not approve of these orders, but that they had no choice. "So the Allies are betraying me?" Kolchak asked bitterly. He appeared otherwise very calm.

Kolchak and Pepelyayev were taken to a local prison, where the non-Bolshevik socialists in charge at Irkutsk began an extensive interrogation of the admiral. Outside the prison walls, control of the city passed to a Bolshevik Soviet on January 21.[74] Yet the remains of Kolchak's White Army approached. By February 2, his army had taken the last Trans-Siberian station short of Irkutsk. The city's Bolshevik soviet decided on the night of February 4-5 to execute Kolchak and Pepelyayev, subject to the Red Army's approval, which was given the evening of the 6. The legionnaires at Irkutsk had been exchanging fire with advancing Red Army units, but fire ceased on February 7, when they signed a truce. The legionnaires promised not to interfere with the detention of Kolchak and his entourage, and to leave the Russian gold under a combined guard of legionnaires and Red Army soldiers until the last legionnaire departed Irkutsk.[75] At dawn, Kolchak and Pepelyayev were led outside into the cold and executed by a firing squad.

Aftermath

THE DECISION BY the Czecho-Slovaks to turn Kolchak over to his enemies has long remained controversial. The legionnaires were culpable only in the eyes of those who remained unaware of their origins and aspirations and who saw them as mere tools of the Allies. Even as tools, the legionnaires started asking in the fall of 1918 why they were fighting and dying in Siberia for a failed cause promoted by the Allies, but one for which Allied soldiers would not fight. While US major general Graves did not know much about Russia before he served there, he spent a lot of time around the legionnaires. This made him one of the few Allied officials who were not surprised by the bitterness the soldiers began to feel the longer they fought in Russia. "These Czechs not only experienced great hardships during the winter of 1918 and 1919, but many of them lost their lives fighting the Bolsheviks in an effort to secure and keep control of the Trans-Siberian Railway, at the request of the Allies. Put yourself in the place of the Czech soldiers, and ask yourself if, under the circumstances, you would have any resentment?"[76]

Saving Kolchak would have added one more name to the ranks of the White Russian exiles at the cost of sacrificing the lives of more legionnaires, betraying both their hearts and historic aims, which had already been achieved thousands of miles away. As Václav Girsa, of the Russian branch of the National Council, had written in an open letter to the Allies on September 29, 1918, from Vladivostok, "There is limit to human endurance."

In early 1919 there were still at least sixteen thousand legionnaires approaching Irkutsk from the west.[77] Looking east, the men still anticipated combat with White forces east of Lake Baikal, which entirely controlled the city of Chita, a transit point for both the Trans-Siberian westward to Khabarovsk and the Chinese Eastern Railway southward to Harbin. Six trains were leaving Irkutsk for Vladivostok daily, but only two trains could get through each day.[78] Indeed, by February 18 the legionnaires were forced to abandon additional stalled trains still west of Irkutsk and proceed in wintry Siberian weather, "on foot and under fire," through the very hostile region around Irkutsk and Lake Baikal, conceded State Department counselor Frank L. Polk.[79]

Yet their difficulties did not prevent Polk from threatening to abandon the legionnaires if they did not hurry. He wrote Masaryk on February 17 to urge that his men "be moved to Pacific ports of embarkation at such times and in such numbers as will keep both our shipping assigned to this work, and the British shipping so assigned, fully engaged. However, if in actual practice this is not possible, it follows that American shipping cannot be held indefinitely at Pacific ports waiting to receive troops, and therefore, in this contingency it would have to be withdrawn and our obligations in the premises, financial or otherwise, considered as fulfilled." Polk also took this opportunity to tell Masaryk that Prague would also have to bear some of the costs of shipping the Polish, Yugoslav, and Romanian soldiers home.[80] All of which merely confirms that America's policy toward the legionnaires at times reached such chilling levels of indifference to their lives that it seemed almost as hostile, if not as homicidal, as Moscow's.

Despite all of this, generals and historians in the Allied West argued that the Czecho-Slovaks could—and should—take up arms yet again.[81] While General Graves scrupulously followed his orders not to intervene in Russia's internal affairs, the legionnaires were expected to remove from Russian soil the wanted leader of a failed insurgency. Yet again, the legionnaires were expected to risk their lives while Allied troops—having experienced much less combat and many fewer casualties than the legionnaires—were scampering up the gangplanks at Vladivostok. As early as October 20, 1919, US railroad expert John F. Stevens demanded that he and his men "be relieved quickly." In words about his men that could easily have been said of the legionnaires, he went on, "They all declare with truth they enlisted for the war and have served a year after [the close of the war] away from families and at pecuniary loss, that their efforts are useless under existing arrangement."[82] By the time Kolchak was executed in February 1920, US soldiers were already boarding ships.[83] As late as April 9, 1920—eight days after the last US troops steamed out of the harbor—there were still about six thousand legionnaires struggling to get to Vladivostok. Not until May 25 did all of them reach the city.[84]

Even then, in their final days and months in Russia, the good reputation of the Czechs and Slovaks did not desert them. As late as October 1919, Lieutenant Colonel Benjamin Johnson, who was decorated for his service with the US Russian Railway Service Corps, held the legionnaires in high regard, which is all the more credible when one learns that Johnson was an ardent defender of the Bolsheviks. Having spent months with the Czecho-Slovaks, he greatly admired their bearing and behavior, calling them "brown, hardened, trench-fighters, undoubtedly the greatest fighting men in the world. Some soldiers, these boys. Their young, boyish officers, so serious, so courteous, it has been a pleasure to know them." In October 1919 Johnson wrote to a friend, "My admiration for them exceeds my power of language . . . while they do not in the slightest degree strut or put on airs, they are the most self-confident bunch of men I have ever seen."[85]

CONCLUSION

AFTER CROSSING THE Atlantic on the *Carmania*, Tomáš G. Masaryk arrived in London by train on November 29, 1918. There he was greeted by a small crowd, a smattering of officials who were asking each other what Masaryk looked like, and his two most important British supporters, the journalists H. Wickham Steed and R. W. Seton-Watson. As the train pulled into the station to a royal salute from the Grenadier Guards, Seton-Watson said, "I could not help recalling that other arrival at a London terminus three-and-a-half years earlier, when no one else knew what train he was coming by, and when we between us dragged his heavy trunk along the platform, because there were no porters to be found."[1]

Masaryk met with and thanked many who had helped his cause, among them Steed and Seton-Watson, Foreign Secretary Arthur J. Balfour, and Secretary of State for War and Air Winston S. Churchill. Reaching Paris on December 7, he made the rounds there, too, thanking Aristide Briand, Prime Minister Georges Clemenceau, Foreign Minister Stéphen Pichon, and President Raymond Poincaré. He inspected the legionnaires, visited the wounded, and saw Edvard Beneš for the first time since Masaryk had left for Russia in May 1917. Beneš said, "he made no secret to me of the anxiety which he felt."[2] Masaryk next traveled to Italy, where King Victor Emmanuel greeted his train in Padua. On December 17, he left Italy with the legionnaires who had served in that country and arrived at a Czecho-Slovak frontier on December 20, where he was greeted by members of his family and various political figures. Spending the night at Budweis (České Budějovice, Czech Republic), the new president and his aides entered Prague the next day to tumultuous, cheering crowds, a motorcade, marching soldiers, fluttering flags, banners, and flowers.[3] "The nation welcomed him with enthusiasm and emotion, with unbounded gratitude and hope," Beneš said. "He was referred to as the people's liberator, and rightly so."[4]

Masaryk was reminded of the personal price he had paid—the son, Herbert, who died during his long absence; the daughter, Alice, who had been imprisoned; and even the wife he had known and loved, Charlotte. Suffering from depression, or something like a nervous breakdown, in addition to debilitating heart disease, she had been hospitalized in a sanitarium in May 1918, where Masaryk visited her on his first day back. Charlotte lingered for more than four years, living at the sanitarium, the presidential palace in Prague, and at their summer home in Lány, west of Prague. At the sanitarium, the president created a study in a room adjoining his wife's in order to spend more time with her as he worked. Charlotte died on May 13, 1923, and was buried in a plot at their home at Lány.[5]

Both Masaryk and Beneš, after Beneš's return from Paris, took up residence in Prague Castle, and among the new republic's parliamentary factions, their "Castle" group likewise stood above all the others.

Triumph and Tragedy

WHILE A CURSORY reading of history would imply that the Allies created the new countries of Europe, in fact the new states were created by leaders like Masaryk, who was clearly not only the indispensable leader for the Czechs and Slovaks, but also a model and inspiration for other nationalist leaders. Historian Victor S. Mamatey says, "the new nations of East Central Europe were not created by the Paris Peace Conference; they created themselves by their own efforts."[6] Masaryk knew from the very start that independence was possible and, more important, how to achieve it. Beneš said, "It was Masaryk's greatest merit that at the very outbreak of the war he was able to form a correct judgment of affairs, and to arrange his whole activity accordingly."[7]

Moreover, despite the unhappiness of Prague's ethnic minorities, particularly the nearly two million Slovaks and more than three million Germans among the new state's 13.3 million citizens, Masaryk and his allies established the only strong democracy in Central or Eastern Europe, despite the passions unleashed across the continent for socialism and fascism. National dictatorships took root in lands once wholly or partly ruled by the Habsburgs: Hungary, Yugoslavia, Poland, and even Austria itself, notes historian Edward Crankshaw.[8] Historian Norman Stone observes that Czecho-Slovakia honored individual minority rights, if not group rights, better "than anywhere else in that part of the world." It was the only democracy east of the Rhine by 1933.[9]

Yet it was not a perfect nation. While most Slovaks were happy to be liberated from Hungary and proud that fellow Slovaks helped to create the new nation, they expected the autonomy they had been promised, but it never came. Hans Kohn, the young officer from Prague who led reluctant Czechs into war and spent time as a POW, later became a scholar of nationalism. "As often happens among nationalists," Kohn says, "the Czech nationalist leaders showed little love for, or understanding of, the aspirations of the Slovak nationalists. Though the Czechs eagerly asserted their folk-originality against the Germans, they could not see any reason for the Slovaks to claim the same rights against the Czechs."[10] The only wholly Slovak member of the trinity of exiles who founded Czecho-Slovakia, Milan R. Štefánik, might have been able to convince Masaryk and Beneš of the need for Slovak autonomy. Given the population imbalance of the new republic, this seems unlikely, yet Stefanik was never given the opportunity.

Within days of declaring Czecho-Slovakia's independence, Beneš began negotiating with Paris for a formal military alliance with Masaryk's blessing, despite the fact that the new minister of war, Štefánik, was with the legionnaires in Russia. Štefánik was not consulted or informed of the establishment of the Provisional Government in Prague, and when the first Czecho-Slovak cabinet was installed on November 14, 1918, a prominent Czech, Václav Klofáč, was named minister of national defense, a position with more power and responsibility. Again without

Štefánik present, a military convention was signed between Prague and Paris on February 14, 1919. Štefánik's relationship with Beneš deteriorated, Masaryk dithered, and Štefánik started home. Štefánik secured a biplane in Rome, fired up the engine and, with two Italians on board, pointed it toward home. On May 4, 1919, as it approached Pressberg (Bratislava, Slovakia), the biplane suddenly lost altitude and crashed, and all three aboard were killed.[11] Štefánik was not yet forty years old. His elaborate funeral was one of the first major public ceremonies of the new nation.

In time, across Slovakia, Slovak history and values were ignored. Czech history and values were imposed by a government in Prague determined to bring enlightenment to the Slovaks. From heroes to holidays, from postage stamps to poets, Czech symbols took precedence. Education and civic life were secularized for a people who had had only their Catholicism to sustain them under Hungarian oppression. Many Czech teachers in Slovakia did not speak Slovak. Slovak history was absent from approved textbooks.[12] Resentment took hold from the start, mostly among Catholic Slovaks, who constituted a majority. American Slovaks deluged Prague with demands to implement the Pittsburgh Agreement, and the dispute raged through wars hot and cold until 1993, when the Czech Republic and Slovak Republic went their separate ways.

Masaryk and Woodrow Wilson kept up a regular correspondence. The new president of Czecho-Slovakia sent a New Year's telegram to Wilson on January 2, 1919: "In the first New Year in which after a long time of the darkness of war, light of freedom and peace is beginning to glimmer over Europe and world, I beg to greet you, Mr. President, on my own and our people's behalf from the free capital of the free Czecho-Slovak Republic."[13] On November 22, 1923, diplomats from the Czecho-Slovak embassy presented Wilson with two albums of photos of the many streets, squares, parks, bridges, and other public sites that were named for the American president.[14]

Masaryk was president of the new nation for seventeen years. And at the end of that time, his only wish was that Czecho-Slovakia be given enough time to develop, mature, and strengthen itself. "Often, even daily,

I say to myself, 'Thirty more years of peaceful, rational, efficient progress, and the country will be secure.'"[15] The new nation got only twenty good years. Nazi Germany demanded and received the German-speaking regions of the new country in 1938, and the following year Hitler's troops marched in and took the remainder. The communists took power in 1948 in the wake of the Red Army's "liberation" of Czecho-Slovakia three years earlier, and Moscow reasserted control with tanks to suppress the Prague Spring in 1968.

Thankfully, Masaryk never lived to see these events occur. He left office on December 14, 1935, at age eighty-five and in declining health. Beneš, who had been foreign minister for seventeen years, was elected the second president of Czecho-Slovakia by a strong majority six days later.[16] Masaryk died on September 14, 1937, and was buried next to Charlotte at Lány. His funeral, one historian says, was "the interwar period's final public national outpouring."[17]

Among his many legacies was a liberal-pacifist conviction that armed defense is sometimes necessary—he openly embraced this position, which is rarely articulated today in Europe. "I am a convinced pacifist, but I love the army," he said. "Even if there were no more war, there would still be a need for two basic military virtues in every man worthy of the name: discipline and courage. I may want peace, but that doesn't mean I will meet aggression unarmed; on the contrary. What I want is a practical peace, not a utopian one, and that means I'll dedicate the combined power of my brain and my love of country and humanity to keep the peace, but also, if attacked, to fight a war."[18] In a pointed warning to small nations everywhere, he said, "The problem of small nations is that we must do more than others and do it better. And if anyone sets upon us with force, we must hold our ground. Holding your ground is everything."[19]

Legacies of the Legionnaires

THE CHIEF LEGACY of the legionnaires remains the two nations that today exist—the Czech Republic and the Slovak Republic—in large part because of the courage and initiative of the legionnaires and the sacrifices they made in Russia. "There was, in the unfolding of events as between the Allies and Russia in the summer of 1918, no single factor that played a more significant role than the unique armed force known subsequently as the Czecho-Slovak Legion," concludes historian George F. Kennan.[20] While they fought in Russia, they made an indelible impression on the Allies, gaining for the exiles valuable political leverage. "My plan had been to get the army to France in 1918 and to bring it into action there in 1919," said Masaryk. "It never reached France, but we had an army and it made itself felt. That was the main thing."[21] Beneš also credited the legionnaires for giving him and Masaryk leverage. "In my opinion," he said, "it is often forgotten that our Siberian army was our strongest political factor at the end of the war and during the Peace Conference. I made use of its retention in Siberia to win our peace terms."[22]

THEIR EPIC MARCH across Siberia and the awe that their victories inspired were another legacy of the Czecho-Slovak Legion. President Wilson himself extolled their exploits when he reviewed a contingent of legionnaires who passed through the United States on their way home from Siberia to Europe. Wilson invited the men to the White House on July 18, 1919, where Bohemian-born US congressman Adolph J. Sabath also addressed the 1,050 troops in their native Czech.[23] Speaking from the White House portico alongside Ambassador Charles Pergler and Edith Bolling Galt Wilson, the president's wife, the president said:

> At the moment when adversity came to the armies with which you were fighting, and when darkness and discouragement cast a shadow upon your cause, you declined to be daunted by circumstances and retained your gallant hope. Your steadfastness in purpose, your unshaken belief in high ideals, your valor of mind, of body, and of heart have evoked the admiration of the world. In the midst of a disorganized people and subject to influences which worked for ruin, you consistently maintained order within your ranks, and by your example helped those

with whom you came in contact to re-establish their lives. I cannot say too much in praise of the demeanor of your brave army in these trying circumstances. . . . There is perhaps nowhere recorded a more brilliant record than the withdrawal of your forces in opposition to the armies of Germany and Austria, through a population at first hostile, or the march of your armies for thousands of miles across the great stretches of Siberia, all the while keeping in mind the necessity for order and organization.[24]

The legionnaires' service to democracy was another of their legacies. It might not have been a coincidence that Czecho-Slovakia enjoyed rare stability as a democracy in Europe and that its soldiers also enjoyed rare popularity. The legionnaires returned to Prague as patriots who had proved their loyalty to the new regime and who had gained valuable combat experience as well. Without these experiences, the army of the new republic would have consisted of Czechs and Slovaks who had simply exchanged Austro-Hungarian uniforms for different uniforms. Also, they might not have shed the unpopularity of Habsburg troops among the Czechs and Slovaks, or have embraced the new regime, without the life-or-death experiences in Russia that helped give birth to that regime. The legionnaires formed a key component of the Czecho-Slovak army. Those who continued to serve in Prague's new military, as well as the veterans who had served in Russia, France, and Italy, remained a powerful lobby that was influential in politics and, unsurprisingly, loyal to President Masaryk.

Departures

THE AMERICAN EXPEDITIONARY Force withdrew from Khabarovsk and the Trans-Baikal region to the west at the end of 1919, and on January 12, 1920, President Wilson announced that the US soldiers were coming home. The first ship sailed on January 17, 1920; the last ship carrying US troops steamed out of Vladivostok harbor on April Fool's Day 1920, with US general William S. Graves aboard, while a Japanese military band on the docks played "Hard Times Come Again No More." The American Expeditionary Force in Siberia (not including the troops sent to Russia's northern ports) suffered 170 deaths (135 from disease or accidents), 52 wounded, and 50 deserters.[25]

The US Army arranged for five troop transport ships to begin taking the legionnaires from Vladivostok.[26] Washington also loaned $12 million to the new Czecho-Slovak government, which allowed Beneš and his associates to lease additional ships. The first two American transports, the *America* and the *President Grant*, were scheduled to arrive February 10, 1920, but they were delayed until June.[27] Meanwhile, the legionnaires witnessed riotous unrest in Vladivostok and suffered the bitter cold of winter and the typhoons of summer.[28] One of their leaders, Václav Girsa, initially negotiated for legionnaires to occupy empty berths in Allied ships leaving the port. The disabled, wounded, and ill were given priority, as were older soldiers, soldiers with wives or children, and older or indigent Czech and Slovak émigrés. One hundred and thirty-nine of these passengers were the first to leave aboard the *Roma*, an Italian ship that departed on January 15, 1920. Yet arranging for ships and financing remained a difficult undertaking and it was not until the arrival of German passenger ships seized by the Allies that larger numbers of legionnaires could embark. The last ship transporting legionaires, the *Heffron*, departed from Vladivostok on September 2, 1920, though thousands of additional Austro-Hungarian POWs did not depart Vladivostok until 1922.

"On two crutches, I slowly reached the gang plank," recalled legionnaire Václav Medřický, one of the many legionnaires who experienced joy and relief, but also anxiety about what to expect. "The joints swollen by rheumatism in my legs hurt me terribly, but the thoughts of home strengthened me. What would meeting my family after five years be like?" Aboard a ship casting off from the docks, legionnaire Felčar Matějka said, "It would be hard to say what it meant when all the hands were waving, when all of the caps flew above our heads. It was an expression of joy over the definitive end of the lasting uncertainties of life. Today, nobody will attack me, ambush me, shoot me from behind, today for the first time I will sleep well again, although I am on the water. . . . When the littoral mountains are disappearing and only a grey band can be seen on the horizon, at last our eyes are getting moist and for the first time we are sorry, for something."[29] Another legionnaire, Jindřich Husák, said, "Each of us stared at the Russian landscape which we were leaving forever. Sad thoughts overwhelmed us. We felt sorry and grateful, happy and sad." They also worried. "A strange foreboding fell upon us," Husák said. "What would it look like at home? Shall we see all of those we left behind? We had spent so many years away as drifters. And what shall we do with our broken limbs and frayed nerves?"[30] Another, following the burial at sea of a legionnaire who died aboard ship of appendicitis, said, "I am sad and remember my home. I see in my mind that small village, a room illuminated by light, and in it a woman reading her man's letter—about his coming return. How glad she must be and how longingly she and her children are waiting his return! And yet, his body is floating in the wide sea and the jelly fish are attaching themselves like glue to his forehead, which was kissed for the last time by his wife some six years ago."[31]

A Czech official, Rudolf Raše, reported that the number of men, women, and children evacuated from Russia was 67,730. This included 56,459 legionnaires (53,455 noncommissioned officers and soldiers and 3,004 officers and military officials); 6,714 Czech and Slovak civilians, including emigres and former POWs who had not joined the legion; 2,433 wives and children, including a contingent of Russian brides of legionnaires and former POWs; and 1,935 foreigners whom the Czecho-Slovak National Council had agreed to transport on behalf of London and Washington.[32] The Americans and British, as promised, bore most of the burden of transporting the legionnaires, with twelve American ships transporting 53 percent of the total, and nine British vessels carrying 25 percent, with some ships making multiple trips. Most of the trips traveled south via the Indian Ocean to the Suez Canal and the ports of Trieste—the former Austro-Hungarian port on the Mediterranean, then a possession of Italy—Naples, or Marseilles, while others crossed the Pacific Ocean, with some stopping in the Hawaiian Islands, before docking at Vancouver, Canada, San Francisco, or San Diego. Cross-country train trips took them to the East Coast, where they embarked on ships for the transatlantic leg of their journeys, many to Hamburg, Germany, others to the Mediterranean ports. Still others traveled through the Panama Canal and crossed the Atlantic to the Mediterranean ports or Hamburg. From the start of major combat on the Eastern Front in August 1914 through late 1920, when the last legionnaires arrived home, the longest-serving of these soldiers were gone more than six years.

Most estimates say that a little over four thousand Czecho-Slovak legionnaires died in Russia—Masaryk estimated that forty-five hundred died in all of Russia, France, and Italy—and many of the dead in Russia are buried in towns and cities along the Trans-Siberian Railway in unmarked graves. Concentrations of grave sites are said to exist in Yekaterinburg, Krasnoyarsk, and Vladivostok, the port city that hosts the only real cemetery for almost two hundred of the dead.[33] A memorial honoring 126 legionnaires who died in the Chelyabinsk region was unveiled in October 2011 in Chelyabinsk, their names engraved in granite. This memorial replaces one constructed in 1919 but later destroyed by Soviet authorities after they retook the city. Chelyabinsk was the third such monument erected by the Czech Ministry of Defense, the two others being in Yekaterinburg and Nizhny Tagil.[34] In September 2014 a commemorative plaque was installed in Saint Sophia Square, Kiev, marking the establishment of the *družina*. Graves holding five legionnaires have been preserved in a nearby cemetery, though it is estimated that ninety-nine legionnaires died in the vicinity of Kiev.[35] In Vladivostok, across the Golden Horn Bay, up on the hillside where sits the city's Naval Cemetery, there is another memorial to the legionnaires, a towering 1918 monument with a sculptured falcon atop, the emblem of the Sokol, that marks the spot where 163 legionnaires are buried.

A Last Innocent Age

A DIFFERENT SET of assumptions governed ideas about political freedom, social justice, and democracy during the era of the Great War—this was the last innocent age of nationalism, which promised all of the above. Nationalism was not yet sullied by the xenophobic and hostile strains that emerged in Germany, Italy, and Japan in the 1930s; in the former Yugoslavia under Slobodan Milošević in the 1990s; or in Russia under Vladimir Putin more recently. Of course, many observers might easily forgive the Czechs and Slovaks for wanting what other nations in Europe—both Italy in 1861 and Germany in 1871 were unified under the principle of nationalism—had sought and attained.

The subjugation of the Czechs and Slovaks by an Austro-Hungarian German dynasty made their case more acute, of course, and wherever people felt subjected to foreign or illegitimate rule, nationalism in the early twentieth century seemed to represent an unqualified force for good. The Czechs and Slovaks, in particular, identified the quest for a nation of their own with the attainments of democracy and liberalism, since as second-class subjects they opposed the authority of the Habsburg monarchy, the influence of the Roman Catholic Church, and the social privileges and property interests of the nobility. Americans, too, can appreciate opposition to a monarchy, a state religion, and a hereditary aristocracy.

Ironically, Hans Kohn, the Bohemian who traveled with the Czecho-Slovak Legion and became perhaps the leading scholar on the subject of nationalism, told a colleague at the Foreign Policy Research Institute in Philadelphia as far back as 1966, that he was having trouble raising funds for his various studies of the subject. "They all tell me that nationalism is dead," Kohn said.[36] This at a time when national aspirations were bursting forth across Africa and Asia. Isaiah Berlin also noted how often, and erroneously, nationalism had been declared dead, principally because such declarations issue from elite opinion makers in the industrialized democracies. In an interview conducted in the late 1980s, he was asked, "But what makes you think that nationalism is still alive in European thought today?" He answered: "Oh, but it is one of the most powerful movements in the world today. Among the many things that the prophets in the nineteenth century foresaw, the growth of nationalism is not mentioned. They believed that nationalism was declining." He added, however, that "acute nationalism is just a reaction to humiliation, and top nations don't experience that. Nationalism is a reaction to wounds."[37] Within a year of the publication of these remarks, more than a dozen new nations would demand their independence from Moscow and a handful would demand independence from Belgrade; two years later the Slovak Republic would demand independence from Prague.

In his *History of the Idea of Progress*, Robert Nisbet says that intelligent persons once believed "the political state was more than a structure of law and polity; it was an exalted form of moral perfection or of a special kind of freedom, spiritual grace, or idealistic purity that was held to be man's supreme loyalty in the world, his consecrated duty of service, and his highest mode of true freedom."[38] A historian of Austria-Hungary, Robin Okey, observes, "a heightened national feeling was common to all reformist tendencies. For contemporaries the links were manifold. Did not civil equality logically presuppose national equality? Was not the nation the highest form of free association?"[39]

Masaryk shared these sentiments. Mere days before he sailed from the United States, he said that freedom relied on nationalism as much as democracy. "The principle of nationality is not a kind of modern European chauvinism. No. Nationality means something quite different. It is the endeavor of every nation—I say of every individual man—to unite with all mankind. We don't strive only for the uniting of smaller nations, but at the same time we are working for true internationalism. We do not like to have a Chinese Wall around these liberated nations, but we say—and this is our first national platform—the nation is the natural order of mankind."[40] The men who served with him in Russia agreed. One, Rudolf Raše, returning to his Bohemian village, was reminded of what it meant to belong to a place and its people, both living and dead. "And one feels and recognizes that the word 'homeland' is not an empty concept, but that there lies behind it the reality of that complicated combination of heredity, climate, memories, and the work of generations that creates a physical and intellectual singularity that is called a nation and that is tied to a certain piece of land. It is not sentimentality; it is not a false feeling."[41]

Determined to free themselves from an ancient monarchy, the legion-naires burst onto the world stage at the end of one era—and the dawn of another. These youngest sons of Europe's last medieval empire, among the last revolutionaries of the ancien régime, found themselves described in some quarters as the first counterrevolutionaries of a new era. Their experience found itself at odds with an emerging set of new political con-cepts and categories, which is one more reason why their story has been overlooked for so long.

NOTES

FOREWORD

1. John Anthony O'Brien, ed., *A Treasury of Great Thoughts, from Ancient to Modern Times* (New York: Frederick Fell, 1973), 155.

2. Winston Churchill, *The Unknown War: The Eastern Front*, vol. 5, *The World in Crisis* (New York: Charles Scribner's Sons, 1931).

3. Boris Pasternak, *Doctor Zhivago*, trans. Max Hayward and Manya Harari (New York: Pantheon Books, 1958), 454.

4. Herbert Butterfield, *The Whig Interpretation of History* (New York: W. W. Norton, 1965), 23.

5. Alois R. Nykl, "Czechoslovakia or Czecho-Slovakia?" *Slavonic and East European Review* 3, no. 4 (December 1944): 99–110.

INTRODUCTION

1. After the beginning of the war, the tsarist regime changed the name of the capital of Russia from Saint Petersburg to Petrograd to remove any taint of German influence, much as the German ruling family of Great Britain changed its Teutonic-sounding name to Windsor. Throughout this work, I refer to the former Russian capital as Saint Petersburg, the name that has since been restored, but I refer to the revolutionary Soviet of Workers' and Soldiers' Deputies as the Petrograd Soviet.

2. *Papers Relating to the Foreign Relations of the United States, 1918*, supp. 1, *The World War* (Washington, DC: US Government Printing Office, 1933), 1:174.

3. Arthur S. Link et al., eds., *The Papers of Woodrow Wilson*, vol. 47, *March 13–May 12, 1918* (Princeton, NJ: Princeton University Press, 1984), 215.

4. Gerard J. De Groot, *Douglas Haig, 1861–1928* (London: Unwin Hyman, 1988), 377–78.

5. Martin Gilbert, *The First World War: A Complete History* (New York: Henry Holt, 1994), 430.

6. Ironically, while the tsarist regime was hounded by accusations of German influence, the Bolsheviks received actual material support from Berlin and Vienna as a means of undermining the tsarist and provisional governments allied with France and Great Britain. See, for example, Z. A. B. Zeman, ed., *Germany and the Revolution in Russia*,

1915–1918: Documents from the Archives of the German Foreign Ministry (London: Oxford University Press, 1958); and Richard Pipes, *The Russian Revolution* (New York: Random House, 1990), 376–82 and 410–12.

7. Information in this section is from David Stevenson, *With Our Backs to the Wall: Victory and Defeat in 1918* (Cambridge, MA: Harvard University Press, 2011), 42–108, unless otherwise indicated.

8. Winston Churchill, *The World Crisis,* vol. 4, *1916–1918*, part 2 (New York: Charles Scribner's Sons, 1927), 412.

9. Martin Gilbert, *The First World War: A Complete History* (New York: Henry Holt, 1994), 407–8.

10. Thomas J. Fleming, *The Illusion of Victory: America in World War I* (New York: Basic Books, 2003), 86. While I include the United States in my use of the terms "Western Allies" and "Allies," the Wilson administration, keeping some distance from the aims of its partners, insisted the United States was merely an "Associated Power."

11. "The War with Germany: A Statistical Summary," by Col. Leonard P. Ayres, chief of the Statistics Branch of the General Staff, War Department (Washington, DC: US Government Printing Office, 1919).

12. Gilbert, *The First World War*, 444.

13. Karel Capek, *Talks with T. G. Masaryk*, trans. Dora Round, ed. Michael Heim (North Haven, CT: Catbird Press, 1995), 137.

14. T. G. Masaryk, *The Making of a State: Memories and Observations, 1914–1918* (London: George Allen & Unwin, 1927), 135, 162.

15. Ibid., 188.

16. Cyril Toman, "The Chelyabinsk Incident and What Followed," trans. Ivo Reznicek, from *Cestami odboje: Jak žily a kudy táhly čs. legie* [The Road to Resistance: How the Czech Legion Lived and Fought], ed. Adolf Zeman, vol. 4 [The Epic Journey] (Prague: Pokroku, 1928), 16–19.

17. Gustav Becvar, *The Lost Legion: A Czechoslovakian Epic* (London: Stanley Paul, 1939), 87–90.

CHAPTER 1

1. Joseph Roth, *The Radetzky March*, trans. Joachim Neugroschel (Woodstock, NY: The Overlook Press, 2002), 136.

2. Eduard Beneš, *My War Memoirs*, trans. Paul Selver (Boston and New York: Houghton Mifflin, 1928), 75

3. T. G. Masaryk, *The Making of a State: Memories and Observations, 1914–1918* (London: George Allen & Unwin, 1927), 25. Masaryk's home was then at 239 Thunova, currently listed as 13 ulice Mickiewiczova.

4. Joseph Redlich, *Austrian War Government* (New Haven, CT: Yale University Press, 1929), 84.

5. Maureen Healy, *Vienna and the Fall of the Habsburg Empire: Total War and Everyday Life in World War I* (Cambridge: Cambridge University Press, 2004), p. 9.

6. A Masaryk ally claimed that as many as twenty thousand Czech civilians were imprisoned during the war, with about five thousand hanged or shot; Vladimir Nosek, *Independent Bohemia: An Account of the Czecho-Slovak Struggle for Liberty* (New York: E. P. Dutton, 1918), 48. A critic of Masaryk said that as few as four Czech civilians were executed during 1914 and 1915 and that as few as one thousand Czechs were imprisoned for political offenses; Josef Kalvoda, *The Genesis of Czechoslovakia* (Boulder, CO: East European Monographs, 1986), 78–83 and 533–34n27.

7. T. Mills Kelly, "Traitors Everywhere! Political Trials in the Late Habsburg Monarchy," *Nationalities Papers* 27, no. 2 (June 1999): 175–89. Masaryk defended Šviha in court and in public, which tarnished his reputation and strained his relationship with Kramář, which was repaired only after Masaryk was in exile in 1915; Kalvoda, *The Genesis of Czechoslovakia*, 33 and 518n70.

8. Karel Čapek, *President Masaryk Tells His Story*, trans. Dora Round (London: George Allen & Unwin, 1934), 232–33.

9. Henry Wickham Steed, *Through Thirty Years, 1892–1922: A Personal Narrative* (New York: Doubleday, Page, 1924), 42–46. Unless otherwise noted, Steed's comments are from this source.

10. Arthur J. May, "R. W. Seton-Watson and British Anti-Hapsburg Sentiment," *American Slavic and East European Review* 20, no. 1 (February 1961): 40–54.

11. Henry Wickham Steed, *Through Thirty Years, 1892–1922: A Personal Narrative*, vol. 2 (New York: Doubleday, Page, 1924), 42.

12. J. Javurek, "My Happy October 28, 1914," trans. Ivo Reznicek, from *Cestami odboje: Jak žily a kudy táhly čs. legie* [The Road to Resistance: How the Czech Legion Lived and Fought], ed. Adolf Zeman, vol. 1 [From Austrian Bondage to Freedom] (Prague: Pokroku, 1926), 332–33.

13. Paul Selver, *Masaryk: A Biography* (London: Michael Joseph, 1940), 27. Unless otherwise noted, all biographical references come from this source, still the standard life of Masaryk in English.

14. Karel Čapek, *Talks with T. G. Masaryk*, trans. Michael Henry Heim (North Haven, CT: Catbird Press, 1995), 32.

15. See Barbara K. Reinfeld, "Charlotte Garrigue Masaryk, 1850–1923," in *Czechoslovak and Central European Journal* (Summer/Winter, 1989): 90–103, for many of the details about Charlotte and her life with Tomáš.

16. Emanuel Viktor Voska and Will Irwin, *Spy and Counterspy* (New York: Doubleday, Doran, 1940), 15, where Voska's meeting with Lord Kitchener is recounted. Kitchener was lost at sea in June 1916 when the British cruiser *Hampshire*, which was taking him to lead a mission in Russia, struck a mine.

17. R. W. Seton-Watson, *Masaryk in England* (New York: Macmillan, 1943), 55.

18. Masaryk, *The Making of a State*, 27.

19. Another possible explanation for his ability to leave the country was that he capitalized on his defense of the Czech police informer, Karel Šviha, by persuading Šviha's police contacts to let him go abroad. See Kalvoda, *The Genesis of Czechoslovakia*, 44 and 520–21n24.

20. In *Masaryk in England*, Seton-Watson says that he met Masaryk in 1910, but his sons say it was in 1907; Hugh and Christopher Seton-Watson, *The Making of a New Europe: R. W. Seton-Watson and the Last Years of Austria-Hungary* (Seattle: University of Washington Press, 1981), 55n11.

21. Memorandum reprinted in R. W. Seton-Watson, *Masaryk in England,* 40–47.

22. Hugh and Christopher Seton-Watson, *The Making of a New Europe,* 111.

23. The country was sufficiently ethereal that, officially, it had no permanent, legal name, since its owners, the Habsburgs, never saw the need to give it one. Austria-Hungary was its most common name after 1867. Other names included "the dual monarchy," the "Habsburg Monarchy," the "Austrian Empire," or simply, "Austria."

24. See Adam Kozuchowski, *The Afterlife of Austria-Hungary: The Image of the Habsburg Monarchy in Interwar Europe* (Pittsburgh, PA: University of Pittsburgh Press, 2013), 177.

25. Edward Gibbon, *History of the Decline and Fall of the Roman Empire* (New York: J. & J. Harper, 1831), 1:1.

26. Allan Janik and Stephen Toulmin, *Wittgenstein's Vienna* (New York: Simon and Schuster, 1973), 41.

27. H. Gordon Skilling, *T. G. Masaryk: Against the Current, 1882–1914* (University Park: Pennsylvania State University Press, 1994), 168.

28. Technically, he remained King Rudolf, never having received imperial coronation in Rome.

29. Marriage, inheritances, succession, and alliances at times extended Habsburg family rule to Italy, the Spanish Netherlands (present-day Belgium), Spain and its overseas dominions, as well as to Naples, Sicily, and Sardinia.

30. Gunther E. Rothenberg, *The Army of Francis Joseph* (West Lafayette, IN: Purdue University Press, 1976), ix.

31. Edmond Taylor, *The Fall of the Dynasties: The Collapse of the Old Order, 1905–1922* (New York: Dorset Press, 1963), 72.

32. Rita Krueger, *Czech, German, and Noble: Status and National Identity in Habsburg Bohemia* (Oxford: Oxford University Press, 2009), 24.

33. Robert A. Kann, *The Multinational Empire: Nationalism and National Reform in the Habsburg Monarchy, 1848–1918*, vol. 2, *Empire Reform* (New York: Columbia University Press, 1950), 305, 313.

34. For the role of the Bohemian nobility, see Krueger, *Czech, German, and Noble*.

35. It also spawned denominations known in the United States as the Moravian Church or Bohemian Brethren.

36. Arthur J. May, *The Hapsburg Monarchy, 1867–1914* (Cambridge, MA: Harvard University Press, 1951), 7.

37. Geoffrey Parker, *The Thirty Years' War* (London: Routledge & Kegan Paul, 1987), 49.

38. R. W. Seton-Watson, *A History of the Czechs and Slovaks* (London: Hutchinson, 1943), 116–17.

39. H. A. L. Fisher, *A History of Europe* (Boston: Houghton Mifflin, 1939), 629.

40. Robert A. Kann, *A History of the Habsburg Empire, 1526–1918* (Berkeley: University of California Press, 1974), 51.

41. Norman J. G. Pounds, *An Historical Geography of Europe, 1800–1914* (Cambridge: Cambridge University Press, 1985), 177.

42. Kann, *A History of the Habsburg Empire, 1526–1918*, 464.

43. Elizabeth Wiskemann, *Czechs and Germans: A Study of the Struggle in the Historic Provinces of Bohemia and Moravia* (London: Oxford University Press, 1938), 39–40.

44. C. A. Macartney, *The Habsburg Empire: 1790–1918* (New York: Macmillan, 1969), 767.

45. Wiskemann, *Czechs and Germans*, 59–60.

46. Robert A. Kann, *The Multinational Empire*, vol. 1, *Empire and Nationalities* (New York: Columbia University Press, 1950), 199.

47. Mark Twain, "Stirring Times in Austria," *Harper's New Monthly Magazine* 96 (March 1898): 530–40.

48. R. W. Seton-Watson, *A History of the Czechs and Slovaks*, 233.

49. C. A. Macartney, *The Habsburg Empire: 1790-1918* (New York: Macmillan, 1969), 755–56.

50. Indeed, one former student, having committed suicide in Berlin in 1884, named Masaryk his sole heir. The inheritance, 60,000 florins (guldens), made it possible in part

for Masaryk to publish a journal, the *Athenaeum*. See Kalvoda, *The Genesis of Czechoslovakia*, 19–20.

51. Macartney, *The Habsburg Empire, 1790–1918*, 733–34.

52. Hilsner was pardoned by Emperor Karl in the spring of 1918.

53. Steed, *Through Thirty Years, 1892–1922*, 309.

54. Skilling, *T. G. Masaryk*, 141.

55. R. W. Seton-Watson, *Masaryk in England*, 17–18.

56. Skilling, *T. G. Masaryk*, xiii.

57. "Thomas Masaryk—Maker of Czechoslovakia," *Times Literary Supplement*, March 3, 1950, 130.

58. Masaryk, *The Making of a State*, 26. Unless otherwise noted, material on Masaryk in the rest of this chapter is from this source.

59. Victor S. Mamatey, *The United States and East Central Europe, 1914–1918: A Study in Wilsonian Diplomacy and Propaganda* (Princeton, NJ: Princeton University Press, 1957), 20.

60. R. W. Seton-Watson, *Masaryk in England*, 37–38. In a speech at Charles University a few months before he died in 1994, Sir Karl Popper, the philosopher, recalled a young visitor to his family's Vienna home in the winter of 1915–16, when Popper was thirteen years old. The visitor was a family friend, Karl Schmidt, a young lawyer serving as an Austrian officer, whose job it was to investigate treasonous behavior and prepare prosecutions for a military tribunal. One of his active cases focused on Masaryk, a fugitive whom the young officer candidly confessed that he admired, despite the fact that Masaryk, whose exact whereabouts were then unknown, would have been executed if he were ever to be apprehended; Karl Popper, "Prague Lecture," May 25, 1994; online posting, Prague University website, http://old.lf3.cuni.cz/aff/p2_e.html.

61. Beneš, *My War Memoirs*, 35.

62. The English-language edition, published in 1919, was titled *The Spirit of Russia*.

63. Beneš, *My War Memoirs*, 34.

64. Arthur S. Link, *Wilson the Diplomatist: A Look at His Major Foreign Policies* (Baltimore, MD: Johns Hopkins University Press, 1957), 5.

65. Arthur S. Link, *Wilson: The Struggle for Neutrality, 1914–1915* (Princeton, NJ: Princeton University Press, 1960), 1.

66. Robert H. Zieger, *America's Great War: World War I and the American Experience* (Lanham, MD: Rowman & Littlefield, 2000), 21.

67. Link, *Wilson*, 53.

68. Woodrow Wilson, *The State: Elements of Historical and Practical Politics* (Boston: D. C. Heath, 1894), 338.

CHAPTER 2

1. Voltaire, *Philosophical Dictionary*, annotated by Abner Kneeland, vol. 1 (Boston: J. Q. Adams, 1836), 239.

2. Gustav Becvar, *The Lost Legion: A Czechoslovakian Epic* (London: Stanley Paul, 1939), 18–20.

3. Josef Krepela, "See You Again in Russia," trans. Ivo Reznicek, from *Cestami odboje: Jak žily a kudy táhly čs. legie* [The Road to Resistance: How the Czech Legion Lived and Fought], ed. Adolf Zeman, vol. 1 [From Austrian Bondage to Freedom] (Prague: Pokroku, 1926), 253–58.

4. Alon Rachamimov, *POWs and the Great War: Captivity on the Eastern Front* (Oxford: Berg, 2002), 43.

5. Josef Divis, "How We Dug Trenches at Minsk," trans. Ivo Reznicek, from *Cestami odboje* [The Road to Resistance], ed. Adolf Zeman, vol. 2 [In Captivity] (Prague: Pokroku, 1927), 166–70.

6. Boris Wuchterle, "The Capture of the Twenty-Eighth Regiment," trans. Ivo Reznicek, from *Cestami odboje* [The Road to Resistance], ed. Adolf Zeman, vol. 3 [Beginnings of Resistance] (Prague: Pokroku, 1927), 32–37.

7. Z. A. B. Zeman, *The Break-Up of the Habsburg Empire, 1914–1918: A Study in National and Social Revolution* (London: Oxford University Press, 1961), 55.

8. Ibid., 57. Zeman cites official Austrian reports on 55–56.

9. Adolf Zeman, "The Czech Company at the Front," trans. Ivo Reznicek, from *Cestami odboje* [The Road to Resistance], 3:29–32.

10. Oberst Maximilian Ehnl, *Österreich-Ungarns Letzter Krieg 1914-1918*, supplement to vol. 9 (Vienna: Kriegsjahr, 1917); lists units of the peacetime army in the summer of 1914, with the national composition of their noncommissioned officers and rank-and-file soldiers.

11. Peter Gay, *Freud: A Life for Our Time* (New York: W. W. Norton, 1988), 346.

12. Robert Seton-Watson, *A History of the Czechs and Slovaks* (London: Hutchinson, 1943), 285.

13. Johann Bauer, *Kafka and Prague*, trans. P. S. Falla (New York: Praeger, 1971), 14.

14. Hans Kohn, *Living in a World Revolution: My Encounters with History* (New York: Pocket Books, 1964), 81–87.

15. J. Javurek, "My Happy October 28, 1914," trans. Ivo Reznicek, from *Cestami odboje* [The Road to Resistance], [From Austrian Bondage to Freedom] (Prague: Pokroku, 1926), 1:332.

16. A. J. P. Taylor, *The Habsburg Monarchy, 1809–1918*, (London: Hamish Hamilton, 1948), 232.

17. Richard Georg Plaschka, "The Army and Internal Conflict in the Austro-Hungarian Empire, 1918," in *War and Society in East Central Europe*, vol. 19, *East Central European Society in World War I*, ed. Béla K. Király and Nandor F. Dreisziger (Boulder, CO: Social Science Monographs, 1985), 339.

18. Zeman, *The Break-Up of the Habsburg Empire, 1914–1918*, 51–54.

19. Béla K. Király, "Elements of Limited and Total Warfare," in *The Habsburg Empire in World War I: Essays on the Intellectual, Military, Political and Economic Aspects of the Habsburg War Effort*, ed. Robert A. Kann, Béla K. Király, and Paula S. Fichtner (Boulder, CO: East European Quarterly Press, 1977), 139.

20. Kohn, *Living in a World Revolution*, 85.

21. Eric Lohr, *Nationalizing the Russian Empire: The Campaign against Enemy Aliens during World War I* (Cambridge, MA: Harvard University Press, 2003), 5.

22. For information on enemy aliens in Russia, see Lohr, *Nationalizing the Russian Empire*; for information on the number of Slovaks in Russia, see Josef Orszagh, "The Slovaks at the Cradle of the Druzina," trans. Ivo Reznicek, from *Cestami odboje* [The Road to Resistance], ed. Adolf Zeman, 3:11–12.

23. Lohr, *Nationalizing the Russian Empire*.

24. Victor M. Fic, *Revolutionary War for Independence and the Russian Question* (New Delhi: Abhinav Publications, 1977), 2–5.

25. Arthur J. May, *The Passing of the Hapsburg Monarchy, 1914–1918* (Philadelphia: University of Pennsylvania Press, 1966), 1:258.

26. John F. N. Bradley, *The Czechoslovak Legion in Russia, 1914–1920* (Boulder, CO: East European Monographs, 1991), 13.

27. The older *Čechoslovan* ceased publication in late 1914 or early 1915, though it appeared again from 1916 to 1918. See Vojtech N. Duben, "Czech and Slovak Press Outside Czechoslovakia," in *The Czechoslovak Contribution to World Culture*, ed. Miloslav Rechcigl Jr. (The Hague: Mouton, 1964), 528–45.

28. For information on the early Česká Družina, see Josef Kalvoda, *The Genesis of Czechoslovakia* (Boulder, CO: East European Monographs, 1986), 60-67; Josef Kalvoda, "The Origins of the Czechoslovak Army, 1914–18," in *War and Society in East Central Europe*, vol. 19, *East Central European Society in World War I*, eds. Bela K. Kiraly and Nandor F. Dreisziger (Boulder, CO: Social Science Monographs, 1985), 419–22; and Fic, *Revolutionary War for Independence*, 1–51.

29. Bernard Pares, *My Russian Memoirs* (New York: AMS Press, 1969), 350–51.

30. Rachamimov, *POWs and the Great War*, 74.

31. Fic, *Revolutionary War for Independence*, 7.

32. Josef Kalvoda, "Czech and Slovak Prisoners of War in Russia during the War and Revolution," in *Essays on World War I: Origins and Prisoners of War*, ed. Samuel R. Williamson Jr. and Peter Pastor (New York: Brooklyn College Press, 1983), 223.

33. Adolf Zeman, "The Czech Company," trans. Ivo Reznicek, from *Cestami odboje* [The Road to Resistance], 3:5–11.

34. See Elsa Brändström, *Among Prisoners of War in Russia and Siberia* (London: Hutchinson, 1929); and Rachamimov, *POWs and the Great War*. Unless otherwise noted, statistics are from these two sources. Most analysts accept a midrange estimate of 2 million to 2.4 million for the total number of prisoners in Russia.

35. See two works by Josef Kalvoda, "The Origins of the Czechoslovak Army, 1914–18," in *War and Society in East Central Europe*, 19:419–22; and Kalvoda, "Czech and Slovak Prisoners of War in Russia during the War and Revolution," in *Essays on World War I*, 215–38. See also Zeman, *The Break-up of the Habsburg Empire, 1914–1918*, 131.

36. Josef Kyncl, "Marching Into Russia," trans. Ivo Reznicek, from *Cestami odboje* [The Road to Resistance], 2:129–34.

37. Brändström, *Among Prisoners of War in Russia and Siberia*, 49–50.

38. Novosibirsk was then known as Novonikolayevsk, but I use Novosibirsk throughout this work.

39. Brändström, *Among Prisoners of War in Russia and Siberia*, 206.

40. Rachamimov, *POWs and the Great War*, 213.

41. Karel Capek, *President Masaryk Tells His Story*, trans. DoraRound (London: George Allen & Unwin, 1934), 231.

42. In his war memoir, Masaryk called this a "second report," citing Seton-Hall's memorandum from Rotterdam in October 1914, forgetting that Steed first got a message to Sazonov in September 1914, through the Russian Embassy in London, about the desire and plans of Czech troops to defect to the Russian lines along the Eastern Front.

43. Eduard Beneš, *My War Memoirs* (Boston: Houghton Mifflin, 1928), 38.

44. Paul Selver, *Masaryk: A Biography* (London: Michael Joseph, 1940), 251. Unless otherwise noted, the information about Masaryk that follows is from this source.

45. Beneš, *My War Memoirs*, 41.

46. Ibid., 39.

47. See "Introduction" in Thomas Capek and Anna Vostrovsky Capek, *Bohemian (Čech) Bibliography* (New York: Fleming H. Revell, 1918).

48. Karel Čapek, *Talks with T. G. Masaryk*, trans. Michael Henry Heim (North Haven, CT: Catbird Press, 1995), 152.

CHAPTER 3

1. Arthur William Edgar O'Shaughnessy, *A Hundred Years of English Poetry*, ed. Edward B. Powley (Cambridge: Cambridge University Press, 1931), 107.

2. Lord Acton, "Nationality," in *Essays in the Liberal Interpretation of History*, ed. William H. McNeill (Chicago: University of Chicago Press, 1967), 146.

3. T. G. Masaryk, *The Making of a State: Memories and Observations, 1914–1918* (London: George Allen & Unwin, 1927), 40–41.

4. Josef Kalvoda, "The Origins of the Czechoslovak Army, 1914–18," in *War and Society in East Central Europe*, vol. 19, *East Central European Society in World War I*, ed. Béla K. Király and Nandor F. Dreisziger (Boulder, CO: Social Science Monographs, 1985), 419. At least another seven hundred Czechs found their way into the French army by 1915, according to Eduard Beneš, *My War Memoirs* (Boston: Houghton Mifflin, 1928), 91.

5. Emanuel Victor Voska and Will Irwin, *Spy and Counterspy* (New York: Doubleday, Doran, 1940), x–xi.

6. Ibid., 32–36.

7. Zbyněk Zeman and Antonin Klimek, *The Life of Edvard Beneš, 1884–1948* (Oxford: Clarendon Press, 1997). Unless otherwise indicated, information on Beneš comes from this source.

8. Masaryk, *The Making of a State*, 44–45; and Zeman and Klimek, *The Life of Edvard Beneš, 1884–1948*, 21.

9. O. D. Koreff, *Milan Rastislav Stefanik: A Short Biography* (Cleveland, OH: Slovak League of America, 1924); Thomas D. Marzik, "Milan Rastislav Stefanik and the Creation of Czecho-Slovakia," in *The Birth of Czechoslovakia*, ed. Sharon L. Wolchik and Ivan Dubovicky (Prague: Set Out, 1999), 29–36; Adolf Zeman, "In the Steps of General Stefanik," trans. Ivo Reznicek, in *Cestami odboje: Jak žily a kudy táhly čs. legie* [The Road to Resistance: How the Czech Legion Lived and Fought], ed. Adolf Zeman, vol. 1 [From Austrian Bondage to Freedom] (Prague: Pokroku, 1926), 19–34; and Masaryk, *The Making of a State*, 107–109. Unless otherwise indicated, information on Štefánik comes from these four sources.

10. Beneš, *My War Memoirs*, 84.

11. Ibid., 85.

12. Masaryk, *The Making of a State*, 107.

13. R. W. Seton-Watson, *Masaryk in England* (New York: Macmillan, 1943), 72.

14. Beneš, *My War Memoirs*, 39.

15. Masaryk, *The Making of a State*, 45 and 71; Zeman and Klimek, *The Life of Edvard Beneš, 1884–1948*, 18.

16. Cynthia Paces, *Prague Panoramas: National Memory and Sacred Space in the Twentieth Century* (Pittsburgh, PA: University of Pittsburgh Press, 2009), 24.

17. Paul Selver, *Masaryk: A Biography* (London: Michael Joseph, 1940), 195.

18. Masaryk, *The Making of a State*, 34; and Beneš, *My War Memoirs*, 50–51.

19. Josef Kalvoda, *The Genesis of Czechoslovakia* (Boulder, CO: East European Monographs, 1986), 46, 51, 91 n47, 536; and Masaryk, *The Making of a State*, 94.

20. Norman E. Saul, *The Life and Times of Charles R. Crane, 1858–1939* (Lanham, MD: Lexington Books, 2013), 50. Unless otherwise noted, all information about Crane and his family is from this source.

21. Patricia Watson, *Crane: 150 Years Together* (Stamford, CT: Crane, 2005). Chicago elected a Czech immigrant, Anton J. Cermak, as mayor in 1931. Standing with President-elect Franklin D. Roosevelt in Miami on February 15, 1933, Cermak was shot by an assassin aiming for Roosevelt; he died shortly thereafter.

22. Masaryk, *The Making of a State*, 28. According to Joseph Kalvoda, the amount was two hundred pounds sterling, see Kalvoda, *The Genesis of Czechoslovakia*, 44.

23. Thomas Čapek, *The Čechs (Bohemians) in America: A Study of their National, Cultural, Political, Social, Economic, and Religious Life* (New York: AMS Press, 1969), 268–69. Paris and London began supporting Masaryk's army in Russia after it established itself as a potential Allied army for the Western Front.

24. Masaryk, *The Making of a State*, 243.

25. Charles Pergler, *America in the Struggle for Czechoslovak Independence* (Philadelphia: Dorrance, 1926), 28.

26. Thomas Čapek and Anna Vostrovsky Čapek, *Bohemian (Čech) Bibliography* (New York: Fleming H. Revell, 1918), 53.

27. H. A. L. Fisher, *A History of Europe* (Boston: Houghton Mifflin, 1939), 1187.

28. Beneš, *My War Memoirs*, 502–503n15 and 23.

29. Voska and Irwin, *Spy and Counterspy*, 45.

30. Henry Wickham Steed, *Through Thirty Years, 1892–1922: A Personal Narrative* (New York: Doubleday, Page, 1924), 100.

31. Masaryk, *The Making of a State*, 79–80.

32. Zeman and Klimek, *The Life of Edvard Beneš, 1884–1948*, 23.

33. Masaryk, *The Making of a State*, 63.

34. Beneš, *My War Memoirs*, 58–59.

35. Seton-Watson, *Masaryk in England*, 60.

36. Masaryk's first work to be translated into English, it was published as *The Spirit of Russia* in 1919.

37. R. W. Seton-Watson, "The Origins of the School of Slavonic Studies," *Slavonic and East European Review* 17, no. 50 (January 1939): 360–71.

38. Beneš, *My War Memoirs*, 65–68; and Kalvoda, *The Genesis of Czechoslovakia*, 78.

39. For details on political oppression inside Austria-Hungary, see "Persecution of the Czechs, 1914-1917," in Cestmir Jesina, ed, *The Birth of Czechoslovakia* (Washington, DC: Czechoslovak National Council of America, 1968), 10–15; Vladimir Nosek, *Independent Bohemia: An Account of the Czecho-Slovak Struggle for Liberty* (New York: E. P. Dutton & Co., 1918), 19–25; and Kalvoda, *The Genesis of Czechoslovakia*, 71–83.

40. Gunther E. Rothenberg, *The Army of Francis Joseph* (West Lafayette, IN: Purdue University Press, 1976), 192.

41. C. A. Macartney, *The Habsburg Empire, 1790–1918* (New York: Macmillan, 1969), 818.

42. This same room would host the first meeting of the General Assembly of the new League of Nations, including the new nation of Czecho-Slovakia, when Geneva became the official headquarters of the League in 1920.

43. Selver, *Masaryk*, 255.

44. Masaryk, *The Making of a State*, 71–72.

45. Paces, *Prague Panoramas*, 74–82.

46. Years later, Vojta's granddaughter, Emilie Beneš, would marry Zbigniew Brzezinski, who served as national security adviser to President Carter.

47. Beneš, *My War Memoirs*, 33, 70–71.

48. Kalvoda, *The Genesis of Czechoslovakia*, 78.

49. In early 1916, Sychrava was expelled by the Swiss; he and the periodical moved across the border to France.

50. Seton-Watson, "The Origins of the School of Slavonic Studies," 369.

51. Kalvoda, *The Genesis of Czechoslovakia*, 53–55.

52. References to Beneš's activities in Paris in this section from Beneš, *My War Memoirs*, 76–78 and 111.

53. Unless otherwise noted, information in this section is from Victory S. Mamatey, "The United States and Czechoslovak Independence," in *Czechoslovakia: Crossroads and Crises, 1918-88*, ed. Norman Stone and Eduard Strouhal (New York: St. Martin's Press, 1989), 62–79; and Pergler, *America in the Struggle for Czechoslovak Independence*.

54. Woodrow Wilson, *The State: Elements of Historical and Practical Politics* (Boston: D. C. Heath, 1894), 338.

55. Selver, *Masaryk*, 166–72 and 210.

56. Seton-Watson, *Masaryk in England*, 125.

57. Mamatey, "The United States and Czechoslovak Independence," 66; and Kalvoda, *The Genesis of Czechoslovakia*, 69–70, 79, 83.

58. Jesina, ed., *The Birth of Czechoslovakia*, 1–4.

59. Beneš, *My War Memoirs*, 82.

60. Kalvoda, *The Genesis of Czechoslovakia*, 79.

61. Beneš, *My War Memoirs*, 73–74.

62. Ibid., 28

63. Selver, *Masaryk*, 258–59.

64. Kalvoda, *The Genesis of Czechoslovakia*, 79–81.

65. Betty M. Unterberger, "The Arrest of Alice Masaryk," *Slavic Review* 33, no. 1 (March 1974): 91–106.

66. Masaryk, *The Making of a State*, 92.

67. Ibid., 107. Indeed, Stefanik's health would suffer until his unexpected death shortly after the war.

68. Beneš, *My War Memoirs*, 84–86.

69. Based on notes made by Beneš, in ibid., 502n16.

70. Jesina, ed., *The Birth of Czechoslovakia*, 5–7.

71. M. Mark Stolarik, *The Role of American Slovaks in the Creation of Czecho-Slovakia, 1914–1918* (Cleveland, OH: Slovak Institute, 1968), 30.

72. Masaryk, *The Making of a State*, 122.

73. Ibid., 74–75, 86.

74. In their memoirs, both Foreign Minister Sazonov and Russian general Aleksei A. Brusilov blamed delays in recruitment on fears that among some of the captured or defecting Czech or Slovak soldiers would be double agents and agents provocateurs with hostile motives. See Sazonov, *Fateful Years, 1909–1916* (London: Jonathan Cape, 1928), 275; and Brusilov (spelled Brussilov in the book), *A Soldier's Note-Book, 1914–1918* (London: Macmillan, 1930), 192.

75. Gustav Becvar, *The Lost Legion: A Czechoslovakian Epic* (London: Stanley Paul, 1939), 32.

76. Paul Jankowski, *Verdun: The Longest Battle of the Great War* (Oxford: Oxford University Press, 2013), 116–23, 257–61; and Peter Hart, *The Somme: The Darkest Hour on the Western Front* (New York: Pegasus Books, 2008), 528.

77. Timothy C. Dowling, "The Brusilov Offensive," in *Essays on World War I*, ed. Peter Pastor and Graydon A. Tunstall (Boulder, CO: Social Science Monographs, 2012), 95.

78. Josef Mikolaj, "My Journey into Russian Captivity," trans. Ivo Reznicek, in *Cestami odboje* [The Road to Resistance] 1:243–46.

79. Graydon A. Tunstall, "Austria-Hungary and the Brusilov Offensive of 1916," *The Historian* 70, no. 1 (Spring 2008): 30–53.

80. Brusilov, *A Soldier's Note-Book, 1914–1918*, 191–92.

81. Tunstall, "Austria-Hungary and the Brusilov Offensive of 1916," 49; and Dowling, "The Brusilov Offensive," 104–105.

82. Gunther E. Rothenberg, "The Habsburg Army in the First World War, 1914–1918," in *War and Society in East Central Europe*, 19:295.

83. Gunther E. Rothenberg, *The Army of Francis Joseph* (West Lafayette, IN: Purdue University Press, 1976), 199.

84. Arthur J. May, *The Passing of the Hapsburg Monarchy, 1914–1918* (Philadelphia: University of Pennsylvania Press, 1966), 1:315.

85. Nicholas N. Golovine, *The Russian Army in the World War* (New Haven, CT: Yale University Press, 1931), 98.

86. Norman Stone, *World War One* (New York: Basic Books, 2009), 172.

87. Orlando Figes, *A People's Tragedy: The Russian Revolution, 1891–1924* (London: Jonathan Cape, 1996), 283.

88. Macartney, *The Habsburg Empire, 1790–1918*, 818.

89. Arthur J. May, *The Hapsburg Monarchy, 1867–1914* (Cambridge, MA: Harvard University Press, 1951), 38.

90. Ibid., 147.

91. Beneš, *My War Memoirs*, 144.

92. Nosek, *Independent Bohemia*, 52.

93. Richard Pipes, *The Russian Revolution* (New York: Random House, 1990), 244–45.

94. Golovine, *The Russian Army in the World War*, 98.

95. Pipes, *The Russian Revolution*, 202.

96. Unless otherwise indicated, information in this section is from Victor M. Fic, *Revolutionary War for Independence and the Russian Question* (New Delhi: Abhinav Publications, 1977), 22–51; and Kalvoda, *The Genesis of Czechoslovakia*, 85–107.

97. Kalvoda, *The Genesis of Czechoslovakia*, 137.

98. Ibid., 142.

99. Masaryk, *The Making of a State*, 87.

100. Kalvoda, *The Genesis of Czechoslovakia*, 147–48.

101. Ibid., 150–51.

102. "The Oath of the Czechoslovak Legion in Russia," in Jesina, ed., *The Birth of Czechoslovakia*, 17–18.

103. Betty Miller Unterberger, *The United States, Revolutionary Russia, and the Rise of Czechoslovakia* (Chapel Hill: University of North Carolina Press, 1989), 33–35; and Beneš, *My War Memoirs*, 154–58.

104. Masaryk, *The Making of a State*, 129–31.

105. Kalvoda, *The Genesis of Czechoslovakia*, 163.

106. "Wilson treated him like a glorified clerk," observes Justus D. Doenecke, *Nothing Less Than War: A New History of America's Entry into World War I* (Lexington: University Press of Kentucky, 2011), 9.

107. Unless otherwise noted, what follows is from Orlando Figes, *A People's Tragedy: The Russian Revolution, 1891–1924* (London: Jonathan Cape, 1996), 253–303; and Pipes, *The Russian Revolution*, 221–71.

108. Thomas Riha, *A Russian European: Paul Milyukov in Russian Politics* (Notre Dame, IN: University of Notre Dame Press, 1969), 268–69.

CHAPTER 4

1. Vladimir Nabokov, *Nikolai Gogol* (New York: New Directions Books, 1961), 31.

2. Unless otherwise noted, Orlando Figes, *A People's Tragedy: The Russian Revolution, 1891–1924* (London: Jonathan Cape, 1996), 307–53; and Richard Pipes, *The Russian Revolution* (New York: Random House, 1990), 272–337.

3. Victor M. Fic, *Revolutionary War for Independence and the Russian Question* (New Delhi: Abhinav Publications, 1977), 58.

4. Josef Kalvoda, *The Genesis of Czechoslovakia* (Boulder, CO: East European Monographs, 1986), 154–55.

5. Emil Lengyel, *Siberia* (New York: Random House, 1943), 202–9.

6. Arthur S. Link, *Wilson: Campaigns for Progressivism and Peace, 1916–1917* (Princeton, NJ: Princeton University Press, 1965), 393–95.

7. Betty Miller Unterberger, *The United States, Revolutionary Russia, and the Rise of Czechoslovakia* (Chapel Hill: University of North Carolina Press, 1989), 44–45; the account here of Wilson's decision for war is based, unless otherwise noted, on Arthur S. Link et al., eds., *The Papers of Woodrow Wilson*, 69 vols. (Princeton, NJ: Princeton University Press, 1983), vol. 41, *January 24–April 6, 1917*, 408–530; and Link, *Wilson: Campaigns for Progressivism and Peace, 1916–1917*, 396–97.

8. One source says that it may have been sooner, saying that Wilson "told the French Ambassador on about March 19" that he would recognize Russia "in order to encourage the effort of this great democracy"; Link, *Wilson: Campaigns for Progressivism and Peace, 1916–1917*, 396.

9. Robert Lansing, *War Memoirs of Robert Lansing* (Westport, CT: Greenwood Press, 1970), 235.

10. Ibid.

11. Ray Stannard Baker, *Woodrow Wilson: Life and Letters*, vol. 6, *Facing War, 1915–1917* (Garden City, NY: Doubleday, Doran, 1937), 501.

12. Arthur S. Link, *Woodrow Wilson: Revolution, War and Peace* (Wheeling, IL: Harlan Davidson, Inc., 1979), 2.

13. Thomas J. Knock, *To End All Wars: Woodrow Wilson and the Quest for a New World Order* (Princeton, NJ: Princeton University Press, 1992), 120–21.

14. Baker, *Woodrow Wilson*, 6:493.

15. Link, *The Papers of Woodrow Wilson*, vol. 41, *January 24–April 6, 1917*, 519–27.

16. George F. Kennan, *Soviet-American Relations, 1917–1920*, vol. 1, *Russia Leaves the War* (Princeton, NJ: Princeton University Press, 1956), 15. That no credit was accorded Lansing did not surprise House. Of Wilson, House wrote on March 28, "I do not think he does Lansing justice. Any man holding that place naturally comes in conflict with the president, particularly if he does not hold similar views, which is the case in this instance."

Their minds are not sympathetic." On April 2, he wrote, "I have noticed recently that [Wilson] holds a tighter rein over his Cabinet and that he is impatient of any initiative on their part. I think it is quite possible that he forgets from what source he receives ideas and suggestions." Link et al., eds., *The Papers of Woodrow Wilson*, vol. 41, *January 24–April 6, 1917*, 496–98, 528–30.

17. Barbara W. Tuchman, *The Zimmerman Telegram* (New York: Viking Press, 1958), 73.

18. Emanuel Victor Voska and Will Irwin, *Spy and Counterspy* (New York: Doubleday, Doran, 1940), viii.

19. Arthur S. Link, *Wilson: The Struggle for Neutrality, 1914–1915* (Princeton, NJ: Princeton University Press, 1960), 554–60 and 645–50.

20. R. W. Seton-Watson, *Masaryk in England* (New York: Macmillan, 1943), 96–100.

21. Betty M. Unterberger, "The Arrest of Alice Masaryk," *Slavic Review* 33, no. 1 (March 1974):92.

22. Lansing, *War Memoirs of Robert Lansing*, 239.

23. Link, *Wilson: Campaigns for Progressivism and Peace, 1916–1917*, 423–26.

24. Lansing, *War Memoirs of Robert Lansing*, 245–46.

25. John Keegan, *The First World War* (New York: Alfred A. Knopf, 1999), 372.

26. Lansing, *War Memoirs of Robert Lansing*, 260.

27. Robert Paul Browder and Alexander F. Kerensky, eds. *The Russian Provisional Government, 1917: Documents* (Stanford, CA: Stanford University Press, 1961), 1:157–58.

28. Ibid., 1044–46.

29. Ibid., 2:1098–1100.

30. Ibid., 2:1100–1101.

31. Pipes, *The Russian Revolution*, 337.

32. In this section, dates are Old Style (OS).

33. Unless otherwise indicated, information about Charles R. Crane and his family is from Norman E. Saul, *The Life and Times of Charles R. Crane, 1858–1939* (Lanham, MD: Lexington Books, 2013).

34. Lincoln Steffens, *The Autobiography of Lincoln Steffens* (New York: Harcourt, Brace, 1931), 743–46; and Pipes, *The Russian Revolution*, 298–99.

35. Crane's lone pessimism was shared by Lansing, who reported, "The Root Mission, excepting Charles R. Crane, have arrived and I had a long interview with them yesterday, preceded by one [meeting] in the morning with Mr. Root alone. I am astounded at their optimism. I cannot see upon what it is founded"; Lansing, *War Memoirs of Robert Lansing*, 337.

36. T. G. Masaryk, *The Making of a State: Memories and Observations, 1914–1918* (London: George Allen & Unwin, 1927), 133.

37. Paul Selver, *Masaryk: A Biography* (London: Michael Joseph, 1940), 146. Unless otherwise noted, biographical references come from this source, still the standard life of Masaryk in English.

38. A hostile Marxist-oriented review of Masaryk's book subsequently appeared in a German periodical called *Der Kampf*, written by none other than Trotsky, who in a few years would lead the Red Army against Masaryk's ad hoc Czecho-Slovak Legion.

39. Masaryk, *The Making of a State*, 134.

40. Eduard Beneš, *My War Memoirs* (Boston: Houghton Mifflin, 1928), 176.

41. Browder and Kerensky, eds. *The Russian Provisional Government, 1917*, 2:1044–45.

42. Masaryk, *The Making of a State*, 135.

43. Josef Kalvoda, "Czech and Slovak Prisoners of War in Russia during the War and Revolution," in *Essays on World War I: Origins and Prisoners of War*, ed. Samuel R. Williamson Jr. and Peter Pastor (New York: Brooklyn College Press, 1983), 223.

44. Masaryk, *The Making of a State*, 162.

45. Kalvoda, *The Genesis of Czechoslovakia*, 423.

46. Allan K. Wildman, *The End of the Russian Imperial Army* vol. 1, *The Old Army and the Soldiers' Revolt (March–April 1917)* (Princeton, NJ: Princeton University Press, 1980), 95; and Nicholas N. Golovine, *The Russian Army in the World War* (New Haven, CT: Yale University Press, 1931), 93.

47. Golovine, *The Russian Army in the World War*, 254–57.

48. Lt. Gen. Nicholas N. Golovine, *The Russian Army in the World War* (New Haven, CT: Yale University Press, 1931), 268.

49. Ibid., 272–73.

50. As the *družina* grew into an ever larger unit of the Russian army, it adopted different names and configurations. It became the Czecho-Slovak Rifle Regiment by 1916, was christened the Czecho-Slovak Rifle Brigade shortly thereafter, and by the fall of 1917 it consisted of the First and Second Czecho-Slovak Rifle Divisions. With its quasi-independent status under French command, it was called the Czecho-Slovak Corps. By 1919 it was renamed the Czecho-Slovak Army in Russia. To avoid confusion, I use a simpler nomenclature: *družina*, corps, or legion.

51. Josef Kohak, "In the Trenches of Zborov," trans. Ivo Reznicek, *Cestami odboje: Jak žily a kudy táhly čs. legie* [The Road to Resistance: How the Czech Legion Lived and Fought], ed. Adolf Zeman, vol. 3 [Beginnings of Resistance] (Prague: Pokroku, 1927), 77–79. For the ethnic composition of the infantry units, see supplement to vol. 9 of the official Austro-Hungarian history of the war, *Österreich-Ungarns Letzter Krieg 1914–1918* (Vienna: Kriegsjahr, 1917), by Oberst Maximilian Ehnl.

52. Ludek Navara, "The Incredible Story of Legionnaire Alois Vocasek," *Americke Listy*, September 25, 2003, p. D.

53. Masaryk, *The Making of a State*, 74.

54. Vaclav Koucký, "How Our Boys Took Us Prisoner at Zborov," trans. Ivo Reznicek, from *Cestami odboje* [The Road to Resistance], ed. Adolf Zeman, vol. 1, [From Austrian Bondage to Freedom] (Prague: Pokroku, 1926), 346–49.

55. "The Odyssey of the Czecho-Slovaks," in Charles F. Horne, ed. *Source Records of the Great War*, vol. 7 (New York: National Alumni, 1923).

56. Fic, *Revolutionary War for Independence*, 67–70, 157.

57. Kalvoda, *The Genesis of Czechoslovakia*, 172.

58. Masaryk, *The Making of a State*, pp. 157–58. Indeed, after the war, July 2 became a national holiday that commemorated the Battle of Zborov in Czecho-Slovakia. The new state's unknown soldier was selected from the Zborov battlefield.

59. George J. Kovtun, *Masaryk and America: Testimony of a Relationship* (Washington, DC: Library of Congress, 1988), 19.

60. Gunther E. Rothenberg, *The Army of Francis Joseph* (West Lafayette, IN: Purdue University Press, 1976), 202–03. On July 15, 1918, Hötzendorf was dismissed from the army to divert growing anger at the government.

61. Link, *Wilson: Campaigns for Progressivism and Peace, 1916–1917*, 314–15.

62. Arthur J. May, *The Passing of the Hapsburg Monarchy, 1914–1918* (Philadelphia: University of Pennsylvania Press, 1966), 1:495.

63. Ibid., 2:498.

64. Benes, *My War Memoirs*, 229–31.

65. M. Mark Stolarik, *The Role of American Slovaks in the Creation of Czecho-Slovakia, 1914–1918* (Cleveland, OH: Slovak Institute, 1968), 33.

66. May, *The Passing of the Hapsburg Monarchy, 1914–1918*, 1:309–35.

67. Beneš, *My War Memoirs*, 258.

68. Z. A. B. Zeman, *The Break-Up of the Habsburg Empire, 1914–1918: A Study in National and Social Revolution* (London: Oxford University Press, 1961), 123.

69. May, *The Passing of the Hapsburg Monarchy, 1914–1918*, 2:643.

70. Kalvoda, *The Genesis of Czechoslovakia*, 164–67.

71. Joseph Redlich, *Austrian War Government* (New Haven, CT: Yale University Press, 1929), 158.

72. C. A. Macartney, *The Habsburg Empire: 1790–1918* (New York: Macmillan, 1969), 823.

73. Victor S. Mamatey, "The Union of Czech Political Parties in the Reichsrat, 1916–1918," in *The Habsburg Empire in World War I: Essays on the Intellectual, Military, Political and Economic Aspects of the Habsburg War Effort*, ed. Robert A. Kann, Béla K. Király, and Paula S. Fichtner (Boulder, CO: East European Quarterly Press, 1977), 8–22.

74. Lansing, *War Memoirs of Robert Lansing*, 256–57.

75. Wildman, *The End of the Russian Imperial Army*, 1:95–96n41; and Golovine, *The Russian Army in the World War*, 98.

76. Golovine, *The Russian Army in the World War*, 101.

77. Figes, *A People's Tragedy*, 408–9.

78. Golovine, *The Russian Army in the World War*, 274.

79. Figes, *A People's Tragedy*, 451.

80. Keegan, *The First World War*, 366.

81. Kalvoda, *The Genesis of Czechoslovakia*, 178–79.

82. Masaryk, *The Making of a State*, 162.

83. Kalvoda, *The Genesis of Czechoslovakia*, 204, 227; and Vojtech N. Duben, "Czech and Slovak Press Outside Czechoslovakia," in *The Czechoslovak Contribution to World Culture*, ed. Miloslav Rechcigl Jr. (The Hague: Mouton, 1964), 540–41.

84. Kalvoda, "Czech and Slovak Prisoners of War in Russia during the War and Revolution," 224–25. At least some of these recruits emerged from a significantly smaller population of Czech and Slovak POWs than the original 210,000 to 250,000 prisoners in Russia that all sources agree upon, since by June 30, 1918, some 500,000 Austro-Hungarian POWs had been repatriated to Austria-Hungary. Contemporaneous US and British sources estimated the legion's strength in early 1918 at either 51,309 or 42,000, respectively. In March 1918 a legion officer, Captain Vladimir S. Hurban, reported to Masaryk that it numbered 50,000. Vladimir S. Hurban, "The Czech Exodus: A Siberian Epic: How 50,000 Determined Men Fought their Way from Moscow to Vladivostok," *Current History* 9, no. 3 (December 1918): 507–511. For the US report of December 10, 1918, that estimated the size of the legion at 51,309, see Josef Kalvoda, "The Origins of the Czechoslovak Army, 1914–18," in *War and Society in East Central Europe*, vol. 19, *East Central European Society in World War I*, ed. Béla K. Király and Nandor F. Dreisziger (Boulder, CO: Social Science Monographs, 1985), 424. The British War Office on April 1, 1918, corrected a Foreign Office estimate of the previous day that the legion numbered 70,000; the War Office said it numbered only 42,000 when it was stationed in Kiev in March 1918. In a memo Masaryk wrote to Lansing from Tokyo on April 10, 1918, based on

Hurban's report, he said the legion had 50,000 men. On May 10, the US military attaché in Russia reported, "The number of these troops is being daily increased by voluntary enlistments from among 40,000 *other* Czecho-Slovak prisoners of war in Russia." By July 2, Lansing reported it had grown to 55,000, with 15,000 at Vladivostok and 40,000 west of Irkutsk. On July 17, US consul John K. Caldwell reported 54,000 legionnaires, with another 5,000 to 20,000 Czech and Slovak POWs as potential recruits. *Papers Relating to the Foreign Relations of the United States, 1918, Russia* (Washington, DC: US Government Printing Office, 1932), 2:158, 241, 290. If a total of 15,000 POWs joined after the revolt in May 1918, which is quite possible, the legion would have numbered 65,000. Fic, *Revolutionary War for Independence*, 72, says that there were 46,714 early in 1918, who were joined by 15,000 that summer, bringing total strength to 61,714.

85. Masaryk, *The Making of a State*, 166–67.

86. Ibid., 163.

87. Václav Valenta, "The Origins of the Czechoslovak Artillery in Russia," trans. Ivo Reznicek, from *Cestami odboje* [The Road to Resistance] 3:145–51.

88. Based on the largest accepted estimate of 210,000 to 250,000 Czech and Slovak POWS, it would require 25 to 30 percent to reach the widely accepted estimate for the largest size of the legion, 60,000 to 65,000 men.

89. Unless otherwise noted, information in this section is from Figes, *A People's Tragedy*, 459–551; and Pipes, *The Russian Revolution*, 439–505. For this section, dates are Old Style, in accord with Soviet histories of the "October" revolution.

90. William Henry Chamberlin, *The Russian Revolution, 1917–1918: From the Overthrow of the Czar to the Assumption of Power by the Bolsheviks* (New York: Grosset & Dunlap, 1965), 1:294.

91. Figes, *A People's Tragedy*, 484.

92. Masaryk, *The Making of a State*, 169–70.

93. Wildman, *The End of the Russian Imperial Army*, vol. 2, *The Road to Soviet Power and Peace*, xv.

94. John W. Wheeler-Bennett, *Brest-Litovsk: The Forgotten Peace, March 1918* (New York: W. W. Norton, 1971), appendix I, 375.

CHAPTER 5

1. Astolphe, Marquis de Custine, *Empire of the Czar: A Journey Through Eternal Russia* (New York: Doubleday, 1989), 239.

2. George F. Kennan, *Soviet-American Relations, 1917–1920*, vol. 1, *Russia Leaves the War* (Princeton, NJ: Princeton University Press, 1956), 284–85; and vol. 2, *The Decision to Intervene* (Princeton, NJ: Princeton University Press, 1958), 17.

3. Ibid., 1:293–94.

4. Ibid., 1:309–13.

5. Ibid., 1:316–17.

6. Ibid., 1:322.

7. Ibid., 1:472.

8. *Papers Relating to the Foreign Relations of the United States, 1918, Russia* (Washington, DC: US Government Printing Office, 1932), 2:470–72.

9. Norman Stone, *World War One* (New York: Basic Books, 2009), 159–61.

10. Unless otherwise indicated, information in this section is from David Stevenson, *With Our Backs to the Wall: Victory and Defeat in 1918* (Cambridge, MA: Harvard University Press, 2011), 42–108.

11. Stone, *World War One*, 164.

12. Gerard J. De Groot, *Douglas Haig, 1861–1928* (London: Unwin Hyman, 1988), 376–77.

13. John Keegan, *The First World War* (New York: Alfred A. Knopf, 1999), 408.

14. David F. Trask, *The United States in the Supreme War Council: American War Aims and Inter-Allied Strategy, 1917–1918* (Middletown, CT: Wesleyan University Press, 1961), 12–13.

15. Martin Gilbert, *The First World War: A Complete History* (New York: Henry Holt, 1994), 420–21.

16. Robert Blake, ed., *The Private Papers of Douglas Haig, 1914–1919* (London: Eyre & Spottiswoode, 1952), 307.

17. T. G. Masaryk, *The Making of a State: Memories and Observations, 1914–1918* (London: George Allen & Unwin, 1927), 178.

18. Josef Kalvoda, *The Genesis of Czechoslovakia* (Boulder, CO: East European Monographs, 1986), 242–47.

19. Elsa Brändström, *Among Prisoners of War in Russia and Siberia* (London: Hutchinson, 1929), 236.

20. Kalvoda, *The Genesis of Czechoslovakia*, 213–17, 233.

21. Masaryk, *The Making of a State*, 263.

22. Eduard Beneš, *My War Memoirs* (Boston: Houghton Mifflin, 1928), 189–97, 262–68, 277.

23. The Soviet regime adopted the Gregorian calendar effective on February 1, 1918, which immediately became February 14, hence the loss of thirteen days in some histories. From that date Russia's calendar matched the calendar in the West.

24. Kalvoda, *The Genesis of Czechoslovakia*, 241–43.

25. Max Hoffman, *War Diaries and Other Papers*, trans. Eric Sutton (London: Martin Secker, 1929), 2:218–19.

26. "He Fought to Be Free: A Czech's Story," *Berwyn Life*, July 8, 1970, 1.

27. Kalvoda, *The Genesis of Czechoslovakia*, 245.

28. J. Čermak, "The Battle of Bakhmach," trans. Ivo Reznicek, from *Cestami odboje: Jak žily a kudy táhly čs. legie* [The Road to Resistance: How the Czech Legion Lived and Fought], ed. Adolf Zeman, vol. 3 [Beginnings of Resistance] (Prague: Pokroku, 1927), 218–21.

29. James Bunyan and H. H. Fisher, eds., *The Bolshevik Revolution, 1917–1918: Documents and Materials* (Stanford, CA: Stanford University Press, 1934), 432–51.

30. John W. Wheeler-Bennett, *Brest-Litovsk: The Forgotten Peace, March 1918* (New York: W. W. Norton, 1938), 269–75.

31. "The Minister in Bern to the Foreign Ministry," telegrams no. 568 and 603, March 31 and April 4, 1917, in Z. A. B. Zeman, ed., *Germany and the Revolution in Russia, 1915–1918* (London: Oxford University Press, 1958), 29–36.

32. Wheeler-Bennett, *Brest-Litovsk*, 407.

33. Alon Rachamimov, *POWs and the Great War: Captivity on the Eastern Front* (Oxford: Berg, 2002), 192; Brändström, *Among Prisoners of War in Russia and Siberia*, 244; and Gerald H. Davis, "The Life of Prisoners of War in Russia, 1914–1921," in *Essays on World War I: Origins and Prisoners of War*, ed. Samuel R. Williamson Jr. and Peter Pastor (New York: Social Science Monographs, 1983), 182–83.

34. Richard Pipes, *The Russian Revolution* (New York: Random House, 1990), 591.

35. Robert Lansing, *War Memoirs of Robert Lansing* (Westport, CT: Greenwood Press, 1970), 340.

36. Wheeler-Bennett, *Brest-Litovsk*, 143, 284–85.

37. Wheeler-Bennett, *Brest-Litovsk*, p. 332n3; and Kennan, *Soviet-American Relations, 1917–1920*, 2:45–46.

38. Kennan, *Soviet-American Relations*, 2:56.

39. William Manchester, *The Last Lion: Winston Spencer Churchill*, vol. 1, *Visions of Glory, 1874–1932* (Boston: Little, Brown, 1983), 617.

40. Gilbert, *The First World War*, 412.

41. Charles Seymour, ed., *The Intimate Papers of Colonel House*, vol. 3, *Into the World War* (Boston: Houghton Mifflin Company, 1928), 420.

42. Masaryk, *The Making of a State*, 188–89; and James Bunyan, ed., *Intervention, Civil War, and Communism in Russia, April–December, 1918: Documents and Materials* (Baltimore, MD: Johns Hopkins Press, 1936), 77.

43. Karel Čapek, *President Masaryk Tells His Story*, trans. Dora Round (London: George Allen & Unwin, 1934), 275.

44. Unless otherwise noted, the following account is based on Victor M. Fic, *Revolutionary War for Independence and the Russian Question* (New Delhi: Abhinav Publications, 1977), 213–15; and Gustav Becvar, *The Lost Legion: A Czechoslovakian Epic* (London: Stanley Paul, 1939), 63–70.

45. Čermak, "The Battle of Bakhmach," 3:218–21.

46. Vladimir S. Hurban, "The Czech Exodus: A Siberian Epic: How 50,000 Determined Men Fought Their Way from Moscow to Vladivostok," *Current History* 9, no. 3 (December 1918): 507.

47. Becvar, *The Lost Legion*, 64.

48. Bunyan, *Intervention, Civil War, and Communism in Russia*, 76.

49. Čermak, "The Battle of Bakhmach," 3:218–21.

50. Becvar, *The Lost Legion*, 70.

51. Josef Kyncl, "From Bahkmach to the Disembarking," trans. Ivo Reznicek, from *Cestami odboje* [The Road to Resistance], 3:230–38.

52. Rachamimov, *POWs and the Great War*, 192–193.

53. Harmon Tupper, *To the Great Ocean: Siberia and the Trans-Siberian Railway* (Boston: Little, Brown, 1965), 372. Unless otherwise noted, information in this section is from Tupper.

54. W. Bruce Lincoln, *The Conquest of a Continent: Siberia and the Russians* (New York: Random House, 1994), 41–43.

55. J. N. Westwood, *A History of Russian Railroads* (London: George Allen and Unwin, 1964), 184.

56. William Henry Chamberlin, *The Russian Revolution, 1917–1918: From the Overthrow of the Czar to the Assumption of Power by the Bolsheviks* (New York: Grosset & Dunlap, 1965), 1:418.

57. Horst Haselsteiner, "The Habsburg Empire in World War I: Mobilization of Food Supplies," in *War and Society in East Central Europe*, vol. 19, *East Central European Society in World War I*, ed. Béla K. Király and Nandor F. Dreisziger (Boulder, CO: Social Science Monographs, 1985), 87–90.

58. Wheeler-Bennett, *Brest-Litovsk*, 317–18.

59. Arthur J. May, *The Passing of the Hapsburg Monarchy, 1914–1918* (Philadelphia: University of Pennsylvania Press, 1966), 2:662–69.

60. Gunther E. Rothenberg, "The Army of Austria-Hungary, 1868–1918: A Case Study of a Multi-Ethnic Force," in *New Dimensions in Military History*, ed. Russell F. Weigley (San Rafael, CA: Presidio Press, 1975), 296.

61. May, *The Passing of the Hapsburg Monarchy, 1914–1918*, 2:720.

62. Arthur S. Link, *Wilson: Campaigns for Progressivism and Peace, 1916–1917* (Princeton, NJ: Princeton University Press, 1965), 25.

63. Ibid., 265–68.

64. May, *The Passing of the Hapsburg Monarchy, 1914–1918*, 2:572.

65. Lansing, *War Memoirs of Robert Lansing*, 261.

66. The telegram of December 13, 1917, is reprinted in Cestmir Jesina, ed., *The Birth of Czechoslovakia* (Washington, DC: Czechoslovak National Council of America, 1968), 18–19; also Kalvoda, *The Genesis of Czechoslovakia*, 257–58.

67. The declaration is reprinted in Jesina, *The Birth of Czechoslovakia*, 21–23.

68. Stanislav J. Kirschbaum, *A History of Slovakia: The Struggle for Survival* (New York: St. Martin's Press, 1995), 150.

69. M. Mark Stolarik, *The Role of American Slovaks in the Creation of Czecho-Slovakia, 1914–1918* (Cleveland, OH: Slovak Institute, 1968), 42–43.

70. *Papers Relating to the Foreign Relations of the United States, 1918*, supp. 1, *The World War* (Washington, DC: US Government Printing Office, 1933), 1:189–95.

71. Victor S. Mamatey, *The United States and East Central Europe, 1914–1918: A Study in Wilsonian Diplomacy and Propaganda* (Princeton, NJ: Princeton University Press, 1957), 234–35, 248.

72. Z. A. B. Zeman, *The Break-Up of the Habsburg Empire, 1914–1918: A Study in National and Social Revolution* (London: Oxford University Press, 1961), 160–62.

73. May, *The Passing of the Hapsburg Monarchy, 1914–1918*, 2:726.

74. Gunther E. Rothenberg, *The Army of Francis Joseph* (West Lafayette, IN: Purdue University Press, 1976), 204.

75. Lansing, *War Memoirs of Robert Lansing*, 261.

76. Arthur S. Link et al., eds., *The Papers of Woodrow Wilson*, 69 vols. (Princeton, NJ: Princeton University Press, 1983), vol. 48, *May 13–July 17, 1918*, 203–6.

77. See for example, "Bolsheviki Tell of a Vast Plot," *New York Times*, June 3, 1918, 3.

78. Link et al., eds., *The Papers of Woodrow Wilson*, 48:435–37; and Lansing, *War Memoirs of Robert Lansing*, 267–71.

79. Mamatey, *The United States and East Central Europe, 1914–1918*, 107.

80. Zeman, *The Break-Up of the Habsburg Empire, 1914–1918*, 184–87.

81. Hugh and Christopher Seton-Watson, *The Making of a New Europe: R. W. Seton-Watson and the Last Years of Austria-Hungary* (Seattle: University of Washington Press, 1981), 259–61, 276–87; May, *The Passing of the Hapsburg Monarchy, 1914–1918*, 2:607–8; and Mamatey, *The United States and East Central Europe, 1914–1918*, 242–43.

82. Beneš, *My War Memoirs*, 326.

83. Ray Stannard Baker, *Woodrow Wilson: Life and Letters*, vol. 8, *Armistice, March 1–November 11, 1918* (Garden City, NY: Doubleday, Doran, 1939), 177; Kalvoda, *The Genesis of Czechoslovakia*, 260–64; and Mamatey, *The United States and East Central Europe, 1914–1918*, 257–61.

84. Beneš, *My War Memoirs*, 372–75.

85. Ibid., 376–78.

86. Chamberlin, *The Russian Revolution, 1917–1918*, 1:368.

87. Bunyan and Fisher, eds., *The Bolshevik Revolution, 1917–1918*, 411–14, 427.

88. Chamberlin, *The Russian Revolution, 1917–1918*, 1:379.

89. Bunyan and Fisher, eds., *The Bolshevik Revolution, 1917–1918*, 425–26.

90. Ibid., 420.

91. Bunyan and Fisher, eds., *The Bolshevik Revolution, 1917–1918*, 420.

92. Emanuel Victor Voska and Will Irwin, *Spy and Counterspy* (New York: Double-day, Doran, 1940), 252–57.

93. The April 10 memorandum is reprinted in Link et al., eds., *The Papers of Woodrow Wilson*, vol. 47, *March 13–May 12, 1918*, 548–52.

94. Masaryk, *The Making of a State*, 195.

95. *Papers Relating to the Foreign Relations of the United States, 1918, Russia* (Washington, DC: US Government Printing Office, 1932), 2:132–33.

96. Kalvoda, *The Genesis of Czechoslovakia*, 287–93.

97. Becvar, *The Lost Legion*, 72–75.

CHAPTER 6

1. Victor Shea and William Whitla, eds., *Victorian Literature: An Anthology* (Oxford: John Wiley & Sons, 2015), 552–53.

2. Steven Stavropoulos, *The Beginning of All Wisdom: Timeless Advice from the Ancient Greeks* (New York: Marlowe & Company, 2003), 171

3. Josef Kalvoda, *The Genesis of Czechoslovakia* (Boulder, CO: East European Monographs, 1986), 174–76.

4. Arthur J. May, *The Passing of the Hapsburg Monarchy, 1914–1918* (Philadelphia: University of Pennsylvania Press, 1966), 1:358.

5. Rudolf L. Tokes, *Bela Kun and the Hungarian Soviet Republic: The Origins and Role of the Communist Party of Hungary in the Revolutions of 1918–1919* (New York: Frederick A. Praeger, 1967), 60–61.

6. Ivan Volgyes, "Hungarian Prisoners of War in Russia, 1916–1919," *Cahiers du Monde Russe et Soviétique*, no. 14 (1973): 64–65.

7. Arnold Krammer, "Soviet Propaganda among German and Austro-Hungarian Prisoners of War in Russia, 1917–1921," in *Essays on World War I: Origins and Prisoners of War*, ed. Samuel R. Williamson Jr. and Peter Pastor (New York: Brooklyn College Press, 1983), 244.

8. Ibid., 242–47.

9. Tokes, *Bela Kun and the Hungarian Soviet Republic*, 60.

10. Volgyes, "Hungarian Prisoners of War in Russia, 1916–1919," 65–66.

11. Elsa Brändström, *Among Prisoners of War in Russia and Siberia* (London: Hutchinson, 1929), 239–40.

12. J. F. N. Bradley, "The Czechoslovak Revolt against the Bolsheviks," *Soviet Studies* 15, no. 2 (October 1963): 132.

13. Edwin Erich Dwinger, *The Army behind Barbed Wire: A Siberian Diary*, trans. Ian F. D. Morrow (London: George Allen & Unwin, 1930), 261.

14. Volgyes, "Hungarian Prisoners of War in Russia, 1916–1919," 77–78.

15. Ibid., 67; Tokes, *Bela Kun and the Hungarian Soviet Republic*, 70; and Peter Pastor, "Hungarian Prisoners of War in Siberia," in *Essays on World War I*, ed. Peter Pastor and Graydon A. Tunstall (New York: Columbia University Press, 2012), 125.

16. Krammer, "Soviet Propaganda among German and Austro-Hungarian Prisoners of War in Russia, 1917–1921," 247.

17. John Bradley, *Allied Intervention in Russia* (London: Weidenfeld and Nicolson, 1968), 62.

18. John Erickson, "Red Internationalists on the March: The Military Dimension, 1918–1922," in *Russia and the Wider World in Historical Perspective*, ed. Cathryn Brennan and Murray Frame (New York: St. Martin's Press, 2000), 130.

19. T. G. Masaryk, *The Making of a State: Memories and Observations, 1914–1918* (London: George Allen & Unwin, 1927), 171.

20. Kalvoda, *The Genesis of Czechoslovakia*, 233, 241, 243–45; and Josef Kalvoda, "Czech and Slovak Prisoners of War in Russia during the War and Revolution," in *Essays on World War I: Origins and Prisoners of War*, ed. Samuel R. Williamson Jr. and Peter Pastor (New York: Brooklyn College Press, 1983), 225–27.

21. *Papers Relating to the Foreign Relations of the United States, 1918, Russia* (Washington, DC: US Government Printing Office, 1932), 2:248–60.

22. Kalvoda, "Czech and Slovak Prisoners of War in Russia during the War and Revolution," 230.

23. Josef Kyncl, "From Bahkmach to the Disembarking," trans. Ivo Reznicek, from *Cestami odboje: Jak žily a kudy táhly čs. legie* [The Road to Resistance: How the Czech Legion Lived and Fought], ed. Adolf Zeman, vol. 3 [Beginnings of Resistance] (Prague: Pokroku, 1927), 230–38.

24. Cecil Parrott, *The Bad Bohemian: The Life of Jaroslav Hašek, Creator of the Good Soldier Švejk* (London: Bodley Head, 1978), 30–191. Unless otherwise noted, all information about Hašek comes from this source.

25. Unless otherwise indicated, what follows is from Victor M. Fic, *Revolutionary War for Independence and the Russian Question: Czechoslovak Army in Russia, 1914–1918* (New Delhi: Abhinav Publications, 1977), 78–155.

26. Josef Kohak, "Stories of the Second Regiment after Zborov," trans. Ivo Reznicek, from *Cestami odboje* [The Road to Resistance], 3:155–60.

27. Fic, *Revolutionary War for Independence and the Russian Question*, 107–8.

28. Kalvoda, *The Genesis of Czechoslovakia*, 244.

29. Fic, *Revolutionary War for Independence and the Russian Question*, 149.

30. Vladimir S. Hurban, "The Czech Exodus: A Siberian Epic," *Current History* 9, no. 3 (December 1918): 509–510.

31. "Document No. 5," in Victor M. Fic, *The Bolsheviks and the Czechoslovak Legion* (New Delhi: Abhinav Publications, 1978), 386–89.

32. Brändström, *Among Prisoners of War in Russia and Siberia*, 247; and James Bunyan, ed., *Intervention, Civil War, and Communism in Russia, April–December 1918: Documents and Materials* (Baltimore, MD: Johns Hopkins Press, 1936), 281.

33. *Papers Relating to the Foreign Relations of the United States, 1918. Russia*, 2:309–314.

34. Richard Pipes, ed., *The Unknown Lenin: From the Secret Archive* (New Haven, CT: Yale University Press, 1996), 42–46.

35. Richard Pipes, *The Russian Revolution* (New York: Random House, 1990), 626.

36. Kalvoda, *The Genesis of Czechoslovakia*, 274–75.

37. David F. Trask, *The United States in the Supreme War Council: American War Aims and Inter-Allied Strategy, 1917–1918* (Middletown, CT: Wesleyan University Press, 1961), 102–115. Information about the deliberations of the Supreme War Council is from this source, unless otherwise indicated.

38. R. W. Seton-Watson, *Masaryk in England* (New York: Macmillan, 1943), 107.

39. Eduard Beneš, *My War Memoirs* (Boston: Houghton Mifflin, 1928), 357–58.

40. Bunyan, ed., *Intervention, Civil War, and Communism in Russia, April–December 1918*, 74–75.

41. Beneš, *My War Memoirs*, 365. In this English translation, the word "notified" is found in place of "communicated," which I believe was the intended meaning.

42. John Foster Fraser, *The Real Siberia: Together with an Account of a Dash through Manchuria* (London: Cassell and Company, 1902), 24.

43. *Guide to the Great Siberian Railway*, ed. A. I. Dimitriev-Mamonov and A. F. Zd-ziarski, trans. L. Kukol-Yasnopolsky (Saint Petersburg: Russian Ministry of Ways of Communication, 1900), 112.

44. Karl Baedeker, *Baedeker's Russia 1914* (London: George Allen & Unwin, 1914), 370.

45. Donald W. Treadgold, *The Great Siberian Migration: Government and Peasant in Resettlement from Emancipation to the First World War* (Princeton, NJ: Princeton University Press, 1957), 33, 96, 237.

46. Fic, *Revolutionary War for Independence and the Russian Question*, 243n66; Hurban, "The Czech Exodus," 508; and Kalvoda, *The Genesis of Czechoslovakia*, 310–11.

47. Bunyan, ed., *Intervention, Civil War, and Communism in Russia, April–December, 1918*, 80. Perhaps coincidentally, General Antonov-Ovseyenko was appointed Soviet ambassador to Czecho-Slovakia in the 1920s.

48. Kennan, *Soviet-American Relations, 1917–1920*, 2:140.

49. Bunyan, ed., *Intervention, Civil War, and Communism in Russia, April–December, 1918*, 80. Departing Moscow to investigate the claims made by the Omsk soviet, Klecanda died somewhat suddenly, from pneumonia, in Omsk on April 28, 1918.

50. Z. A. B. Zeman, *The Break-Up of the Habsburg Empire, 1914–1918: A Study in National and Social Revolution* (London: Oxford University Press, 1961), 207.

51. Bunyan, ed., *Intervention, Civil War, and Communism in Russia, April–December, 1918*, 81–82.

52. Josef Kyncl, "From Bahkmach to the Disembarking," trans. Ivo Reznicek, from *Cestami odboje* [The Road to Resistance], 3:230–38.

53. Jan Cinert, "Retreat from Kiev," in ibid., trans. Ivo Reznicek, in from *Cestami odboje* [The Road to Resistance], 3:205–8.

54. Gustav Becvar, *The Lost Legion: A Czechoslovakian Epic* (London: Stanley Paul, 1939), 79–82.

55. Bunyan, ed., *Intervention, Civil War, and Communism in Russia, April–December, 1918*, 82–85.

56. Ibid., 85; and Kalvoda, *The Genesis of Czechoslovakia*, 319–27.

57. "Distribution of Czechoslovak Trains on the Trans-Siberian Railway, May 27, 1918," annotated map in Victor M. Fic, *The Bolsheviks and the Czechoslovak Legion* (New Delhi: Abhinav Publications, 1978).

58. Edward T. Heald, *Witness to Revolution: Letters from Russia, 1916–1919*, ed. James B. Gibney (Kent, OH: Kent State University Press, 1972), 174.

59. Rev. Kenneth Dexter Miller Papers, IHRC1553, Box 1, Folder 10, Immigration History Research Center Archives, University of Minnesota.

60. Becvar, *The Lost Legion*, 88–89.

61. Indeed, the Czecho-Slovaks would quickly organize an entire telegraph company to control communications.

62. Pipes, *The Russian Revolution*, 515.

63. Leon Trotsky, *My Life: An Attempt at an Autobiography* (New York: Charles Scribner's Sons, 1930), 395.

64. Kalvoda, *The Genesis of Czechoslovakia*, 328.

65. Heald, *Witness to Revolution*, 269.

66. "Report of Sadlucky on the Chelyabinsk Incident," in Fic, *The Bolsheviks and the Czechoslovak Legion*, 393–95.

67. Ibid., 393–95.

68. John Keegan, *The First World War* (New York: Alfred A. Knopf, 1999), 389.

69. Bunyan, ed., *Intervention, Civil War, and Communism in Russia, April–December, 1918*, 86–92.

70. Kalvoda, *The Genesis of Czechoslovakia*, 330–33.

71. František Richter, "A Snapshot from Chelyabinsk," trans. Ivo Reznicek, from *Cestami odboje* [The Road to Resistance], ed. Adolf Zeman, vol. 4 [The Epic Journey] (Prague: Pokroku, 1928), 19–22.

72. Bunyan, ed., *Intervention, Civil War, and Communism in Russia, April–December, 1918*, 89–90.

73. Kennan, *Soviet-American Relations, 1917–1920*, 2:151, 155.

74. J. F. N. Bradley, "The Czechoslovak Revolt against the Bolsheviks," *Soviet Studies* 15, no. 2 (October 1963): 136.

75. Bunyan, ed., *Intervention, Civil War, and Communism in Russia, April–December, 1918*, 86–91.

76. Elena Varneck and H. H. Fisher, eds., *The Testimony of Kolchak and Other Siberian Materials*, trans. Elena Varneck (Stanford, CA: Stanford University Press, 1935), 240–41n165, n166, and n167.

77. Bunyan, ed., *Intervention, Civil War, and Communism in Russia, April–December, 1918*, 324–25.

78. This town was known as Novonikolayevsk at the time, but I use Novosibirsk throughout.

79. This town was known as Nikolsk-Ussuriysk at the time, but I use Ussuriysk throughout.

80. This town was known as Simbirsk at the time, but I use Ulyanovsk throughout.

81. This town was known as Verkhneudinsk at the time, but I use Ulan-Ude throughout.

82. Hurban, "The Czech Exodus," 509.

83. *Papers Relating to the Foreign Relations of the United States, 1918, Russia*, 2:184–87.

84. Hurban, "The Czech Exodus," 509.

85. *Papers Relating to the Foreign Relations of the United States, 1918, Russia*, 2:184–87.

86. Kalvoda, *The Genesis of Czechoslovakia*, 328.

87. Kennan, *Soviet-American Relations, 1917–1920*, 2:283–86, 290.

88. Bunyan, ed., *Intervention, Civil War, and Communism in Russia, April–December, 1918*, 96–98; Kalvoda, *The Genesis of Czechoslovakia*, 328.

89. Becvar, *The Lost Legion*, 100–114. The reference to forty rifles for four hundred men confirms Hurban's independent claim that every unit of one hundred legionnaires was limited to ten rifles. This account of the battle outside of Omsk relies mostly on Becvar's memoir.

90. *Papers Relating to the Foreign Relations of the United States, 1918, Russia*, 2:248–60.

91. Becvar, *The Lost Legion*, 115.

92. Bunyan, ed., *Intervention, Civil War, and Communism in Russia, April–December, 1918*, 92.

93. Josef Hosek, "The Bolshevik Captivity and Our Escape from It," trans. Ivo Reznicek, from *Cestami odboje* [The Road to Resistance], 4:65–73.

94. Samara was a major stop along the southern rail line leading to Siberia and Chelyabinsk. The city of Perm, which would also be contested by the legionnaires, was a key stop along the northern route through Yekaterinburg, which also connected to Chelyabinsk. The two lines joined at Omsk and continued as a single line to Chita.

95. Orlando Figes, *A People's Tragedy: The Russian Revolution, 1891–1924* (London: Jonathan Cape, 1996), 578.

96. Bunyan, ed., *Intervention, Civil War, and Communism in Russia, April–December, 1918*, 281.

97. Zbynék Zeman and Antonin Klimek, *The Life of Edvard Beneš, 1884–1948* (Oxford: Clarendon Press, 1997), 30–31.

98. R. H. Bruce Lockhart, *Memoirs of a British Agent* (London: Putnam, 1932), 284–85.

99. Kalvoda, *The Genesis of Czechoslovakia*, 336.

100. *Papers Relating to the Foreign Relations of the United States, 1918, Russia*, 2:248–60.

101. Kalvoda, *The Genesis of Czechoslovakia*, 336, 344–45.

102. Fic, *Revolutionary War for Independence and the Russian Question*, 204.

103. *Papers Relating to the Foreign Relations of the United States, 1918. Russia*, 2:309–314.

104. W. Somerset Maugham, *A Writer's Notebook* (New York: Penguin Books, 1984), 138.

105. Masaryk, *The Making of a State*, 256.

106. Winston S. Churchill, *The World Crisis*, vol. 4, *The Aftermath* (New York: Charles Scribner's Sons, 1929), 87.

107. Letter to US Rep. James Ambrose Gallivan, August 22, 1918, in *The Letters of Theodore Roosevelt*, ed. Elting E. Morison (Cambridge, MA: Harvard University Press, 1954), 1363–66. Roosevelt's Nobel Peace Prize included a cash prize of $36,735, which was held in trust until 1917, when it was returned to him, with interest. In August of that year, the amount, now $45,483, was distributed by the former president to various charities related to the war.

108. Normal E. Saul, *The Life and Times of Charles R. Crane, 1858–1939* (Lanham, MD: Lexington Books, 2013), 150.

109. Masaryk, *The Making of a State*, 181.

110. Seton-Watson, *Masaryk in England*, 101–102.

111. Beneš, *My War Memoirs*, 359.

112. *Papers Relating to the Foreign Relations of the United States, 1918, Russia*, 2:184.

CHAPTER 7

1. William S. Graves, *America's Siberian Adventure, 1918–1920* (New York: Peter Smith, 1941), 354.

2. Josef Kalvoda, *The Genesis of Czechoslovakia* (Boulder, CO: East European Monographs, 1986), 347–48.

3. Gustav Becvar, *The Lost Legion: A Czechoslovakian Epic* (London: Stanley Paul, 1939), 116.

4. Ibid., 116–24.

5. Ibid., 124–28. The legionnaires adopted several bears or bear cubs, at least two of which returned with them to Prague.

6. *Papers Relating to the Foreign Relations of the United States, 1918, Russia* (Washington, DC: US Government Printing Office, 1932), 2:230–31, 275, 290–92.

7. Ibid., 2:226.

8. Ibid., 2:265, 290–92.

9. John J. Stephan, *The Russian Far East: A History* (Stanford, CA: Stanford University Press, 1994), 129, 132.

10. *Papers Relating to the Foreign Relations of the United States, 1918, Russia*, 2:235, 261–62.

11. James Bunyan, ed., *Intervention, Civil War, and Communism in Russia, April–December, 1918: Documents and Materials* (Baltimore, MD: Johns Hopkins Press, 1936), 314–18; and *Papers Relating to the Foreign Relations of the United States, 1918, Russia*, 2:275.

12. Eduard Beneš, *My War Memoirs* (Boston: Houghton Mifflin, 1928), 394.

13. *New York Times*, August 15, 1918, 4.

14. *Papers Relating to the Foreign Relations of the United States, 1918. Russia*, 2:261, 264, 319.

15. The line was clear via the Chinese Eastern Railway linking Vladivostok to Chita, and westward as far as the Urals; the line running north from Vladivostok to Khabarovsk and westward to Chita was cleared a few days later.

16. Richard Pipes, *The Russian Revolution* (New York: Random House, 1990), 832–33. Pipes argues the camps, while precipitated by Soviet concern about the Czechs, were systemic aspects of Bolshevik rule. See *Russian Revolution*, 789–843. While the camps would have no doubt been established without the legion's revolt, the two are indelibly linked.

17. Arno J. Mayer, *The Furies: Violence and Terror in the French and Russian Revolutions* (Princeton, NJ: Princeton University Press, 2000), 282.

18. "Answers to Questions Put by the Representative of the Czechoslovak Corps, Vaclav Neubert," May 31, 1918, in *How the Revolution Armed: The Military Writings and Speeches of Leon Trotsky*, vol. 1, *The Year 1918*, trans. Brian Pearce (London: New Park Publications, 1979), 280.

19. "Order of June 4, 1918," in *How the Revolution Armed*, 1:282.

20. Richard Pipes, "Trotsky the Jew," a review of *Leon Trotsky: A Revolutionary's Life*, by Joshua Rubenstein, *Tablet*, October 17, 2011.

21. Robert Service, *Stalin: A Biography* (Cambridge, MA: Harvard University Press, 2005), 158.

22. Anne Applebaum, *Gulag: A History* (New York: Doubleday, 2003), 8–9.

23. R. W. Seton-Watson, *Masaryk in England* (New York: Macmillan, 1943), 24–25.

24. Karel Capek, *President Masaryk Tells His Story* (London: George Allen & Unwin, 1934), 231.

25. T. G. Masaryk, *The Making of a State: Memories and Observations, 1914–1918* (London: George Allen & Unwin, 1927), 206.

26. Unless otherwise noted, information about Masaryk in this section is from Paul Selver, *Masaryk: A Biography* (London: Michael Joseph, 1940).

27. Masaryk, *The Making of a State*, 255.

28. Ibid., 206.

29. Charles Pergler, *America in the Struggle for Czechoslovak Independence* (Philadelphia: Dorrance, 1926), 47–48; and George J. Kovtun, *Masaryk and America: Testimony of a Relationship* (Washington, DC: Library of Congress, 1988), 31–32.

30. Karel Čapek, *Talks with T. G. Masaryk*, trans. Michael Henry Heim (North Haven, CT: Catbird Press, 1995), 174.

31. Kalvoda, *The Genesis of Czechoslovakia*, 287, 293.

32. Kovtun, *Masaryk and America*, 37–38.

33. Ibid., 48.

34. Ibid., 22.

35. *Papers Relating to the Foreign Relations of the United States, 1918*, Supp. 1, 1:808.

36. M. Mark Stolarik, *The Role of American Slovaks in the Creation of Czecho-Slovakia, 1914–1918* (Cleveland, OH: Slovak Institute, 1968), 48.

37. "Czecho-Slovak Agreement," in *The Birth of Czechoslovakia*, ed. Cestmir Jesina (Washington, DC: Czechoslovak National Council of America, 1968), 35.

38. Pergler, *America in the Struggle for Czechoslovak Independence*, 25, 40, 61.

39. Beneš, *My War Memoirs*, 395.

40. Richard Henry Ullman, *Angelo-Soviet Relations, 1917–1921* (Princeton, NJ: Princeton University Press, 1961), 2:192.

41. George F. Kennan, *Soviet-American Relations, 1917–1920*, vol. 2, *The Decision to Intervene* (Princeton, NJ: Princeton University Press, 1958), 345–46.

42. *Papers Relating to the Foreign Relations of the United States, 1918, Russia*, 2:179–80.

43. *Papers Relating to the Foreign Relations of the United States, 1918, Russia* (Washington, DC: U.S. Government Printing Office, 1931), 1:519–21.

44. Kennan, *Soviet-American Relations, 1917–1920*, 2:303.

45. *Papers Relating to the Foreign Relations of the United States, 1918, Russia*, 2:181, 189, 206–7.

46. Kalvoda, *The Genesis of Czechoslovakia*, 347–49, 356.

47. *Papers Relating to the Foreign Relations of the United States, 1918, Russia*, 2:224–26.

48. David F. Trask, *The United States in the Supreme War Council: American War Aims and Inter-Allied Strategy, 1917–1918* (Middletown, CT: Wesleyan University Press, 1961), 116–17. Information about the deliberations of the Supreme War Council are from this source, 116–22, unless otherwise indicated.

49. Kennan, *Soviet-American Relations, 1917–1920*, 2:310, 366.

50. Ibid., 2:384.

51. Ibid., 2:311.

52. Beneš, *My War Memoirs*, 506n52.

53. Kennan, *Soviet-American Relations, 1917–1920*, 2:386.

54. *Papers Relating to the Foreign Relations of the United States, 1918, Russia*, 2:472, 486.

55. Ibid., 2:188.

56. Ibid., 2:195.

57. Ibid., 2:259.

58. Z. A. B. Zeman, ed., *Germany and the Revolution in Russia, 1915–1918* (London: Oxford University Press, 1958), 130, 133, 137; and Pipes, *The Russian Revolution*, 616–18.

59. Pipes, *The Russian Revolution*, 631–35.

60. Richard Pipes, ed., *The Unknown Lenin: From the Secret Archive* (New Haven, CT: Yale University Press, 1996), 12, 50–53.

61. John Keegan, *The First World War* (New York: Alfred A. Knopf, 1999), 391.

62. George F. Kennan, *Soviet-American Relations, 1917–1920*, vol. 1, *Russia Leaves the War* (Princeton, NJ: Princeton University Press, 1956), 282.

63. Ibid., 1:455.

64. John O. Crane and Sylvia Crane, *Czechoslovakia: Anvil of the Cold War* (New York: Praeger, 1982), xviii.

65. Kalvoda, *The Genesis of Czechoslovakia*, 289–90.

66. Long's memorandum is reprinted in Kovtun, *Masaryk and America*, 32–33.

67. See, for example, "Bolsheviki Tell of a Vast Plot," *New York Times*, June 3, 1918, 3.

68. Arthur S. Link et al., eds., *The Papers of Woodrow Wilson*, 69 vols. (Princeton, NJ: Princeton University Press, 1985), vol. 48, *May 13–July 17, 1918*, 273, 283.

69. Charles Seymour, ed., *The Intimate Papers of Colonel House*, vol. 3, *Into the World War* (Boston: Houghton Mifflin, 1928), 408.

70. John W. Long and C. Howard Hopkins, "T. G. Masaryk and the Strategy of Czechoslovak Independence: An Interview in Russia on 27 June 1917," in *Slavonic and East European Review* 56, no. 1 (January 1978): 88–96, 96n47.

71. Kovtun, *Masaryk and America*, 57–58.

72. Kennan, *Soviet-American Relations, 1917–1920*, 1:282.

73. *New York Times*, June 20, 1918, 5.

74. Victor S. Mamatey, *The United States and East Central Europe, 1914–1918: A Study in Wilsonian Diplomacy and Propaganda* (Princeton, NJ: Princeton University Press, 1957), 285–86.

75. Herbert Adolphus Miller, "What Woodrow Wilson and America Meant to Czechoslovakia," in *Czechoslovakia: Twenty Years of Independence*, ed. Robert J. Kerner (Berkeley: University of California Press, 1940), 71–75.

76. *Papers Relating to the Foreign Relations of the United States, The Lansing Papers, 1914–1920* (Washington, DC: US Government Printing Office, 1940), 2:361–362.

77. Kennan, *Soviet-American Relations, 1917–1920*, 2:388.

78. Kalvoda, *The Genesis of Czechoslovakia*, 295–96.

79. Seymour, ed., *The Intimate Papers of Colonel House*, 3:410.

80. *Papers Relating to the Foreign Relations of the United States, The Lansing Papers, 1914–1920*, 2:364.

81. Kennan, *Soviet-American Relations, 1917–1920*, 2:391.

82. Ibid.

83. Bunyan, ed., *Intervention, Civil War, and Communism in Russia, April–December, 1918*, 106–8; and Trask, *The United States in the Supreme War Council*, 122.

84. Z. A. B. Zeman, *The Break-Up of the Habsburg Empire, 1914–1918: A Study in National and Social Revolution* (London: Oxford University Press, 1961), 214.

85. Trask, *The United States in the Supreme War Council*, 116–17.

86. Seymour, ed., *The Intimate Papers of Colonel House*, 3:418, and 418n1.

87. Kennan, *Soviet-American Relations, 1917–1920*, 2:292–93.

88. *The Times* (London), August 12, 1918, 6, in Cestmir Jesina, ed., *The Birth of Czechoslovakia* (Washington, DC: Czechoslovak National Council of America, 1968), 63–64.

89. "The Socialist Fatherland in Danger," speech, July 29, 1918, in Leon Trotsky, *How the Revolution Armed: The Military Writings and Speeches of Leon Trotsky*, vol. 1: *The Year 1918*, trans. Brian Pearce (London: New Park Publications, 1979), 286.

90. Kennan, *Soviet-American Relations, 1917–1920*, 2:395.

91. Peyton C. March, *The Nation at War* (Garden City, NY: Doubleday, Doran, 1932), 124–26. Lansing subsequently explained to the Japanese ambassador that the US troop presence would actually amount to 8,763 men and 251 officers, though only 7,398 were combat troops. *Papers Relating to the Foreign Relations of the United States, 1918, Russia*, 2:346.

92. Ray Stannard Baker, *Woodrow Wilson: Life and Letters*, vol. 8, *Armistice, March 1–November 11, 1918* (Garden City, NY: Doubleday, Doran, 1939), 266.

93. *Papers Relating to the Foreign Relations of the United States, 1918, Russia*, 2:287–90.

94. Kennan, *Soviet-American Relations, 1917–1920*, 2:482–85.

95. Trask, *The United States in the Supreme War Council*, 124–27.

96. Kennan, *Soviet-American Relations, 1917–1920*, 2:411–13.

97. Bunyan, ed., *Intervention, Civil War, and Communism in Russia, April–December, 1918*, 102–3; and Kennan, *Soviet-American Relations, 1917–1920*, 2:370–71.

98. "The State Secretary to the Minister in Moscow," telegram no. 246, June 1, 1918, and "The First Quartermaster General to the State Secretary," June 9, 1918, in Zeman, *Germany and the Revolution in Russia, 1915–1918*, 129, 134–36.

99. Kennan, *Soviet-American Relations, 1917–1920*, 2:371–72.

100. Bunyan, ed., *Intervention, Civil War, and Communism in Russia, April–December, 1918*, 132–35; and Kennan, *Soviet-American Relations, 1917–1920*, 2:374–76.

101. The Angara Dam was built several miles west of Irkutsk in 1950, flooding the Trans-Siberian tracks along the Angara between Irkutsk and Lake Baikal. As a result, a new double-track line was extended southward from Irkutsk to Slyudyanka at the southern tip of the lake, where it reconnects with the main line. The Trans-Siberian now bypasses the tunnels and Lake Baikal almost entirely, though a single track along the lake is used for tourists.

102. *Papers Relating to the Foreign Relations of the United States, 1918, Russia*, 2:309–14.

103. Becvar, *The Lost Legion*, 133–34.

104. At the time, Babushkin was known as Mysovsk, but I use Babushkin throughout.

105. Becvar, *The Lost Legion*, 136–42.

106. Ibid., 142–46.

107. Ibid., 150.

CHAPTER 8

1. Rudyard Kipling, *The Collected Poems of Rudyard Kipling*, introduction and notes by R. T. Jones (Hertfordshire, UK: Wordsworth Editions Limited, 1994), 204.

2. Unless otherwise noted, information in this section on the Romanovs is from Helen Rappaport, *The Last Days of the Romanovs: Tragedy at Ekaterinburg* (New York: St. Martin's Griffin, 2008).

3. Ibid., 141. Masaryk took umbrage afterward at the suggestion of a chain of causation between the advance of the legionnaires and the decision to execute the tsar, as if that causation somehow made the Czecho-Slovaks responsible for the murders. That responsibility has always rested with Lenin and his associates. T. G. Masaryk, *The Making of a State: Memories and Observations, 1914–1918* (London: George Allen & Unwin, 1927), 258–59.

4. George Leggett, *The Cheka: Lenin's Political Police* (Oxford: Clarendon Press, 1981), 66. Rappaport says there were nine assassins, all but one of them Russian, but Pipes agrees with Leggett that five or six were Hungarian, citing the authoritative report by Nicholas A. Sokolov, chairman of the commission that investigated the killings. Richard Pipes, *The Russian Revolution* (New York: Random House, 1990), 773, 771. Robert K. Massie reaches the same conclusion in *Nicholas and Alexandra* (New York: Atheneum, 1967), 513–14.

5. Formerly Simbirsk, Ulyanovsk was renamed in honor of Vladimir Lenin after his death in 1924.

6. James Bunyan, ed., *Intervention, Civil War, and Communism in Russia, April–December, 1918: Documents and Materials* (Baltimore, MD: Johns Hopkins Press, 1936), 277–300.

7. Ibid., 104–5.

8. Eduard Beneš, *My War Memoirs* (Boston: Houghton Mifflin, 1928), 393.

9. *Papers Relating to the Foreign Relations of the United States, 1918, Russia* (Washington, DC: US Government Printing Office, 1932), 2:248–60.

10. George F. Kennan, *Soviet-American Relations, 1917–1920*, vol. 2, *The Decision to Intervene* (Princeton, NJ: Princeton University Press, 1958), 294–95.

11. Ibid. *The Decision to Intervene*, devotes an entire chapter to this misunderstanding, 2:296–321.

12. *Papers Relating to the Foreign Relations of the United States, 1918, Russia*, 2:211–12.

13. Josef Kalvoda, *The Genesis of Czechoslovakia* (Boulder, CO: East European Monographs, 1986), 353–54.

14. J. F. N. Bradley, "The Czechoslovak Revolt against the Bolsheviks," *Soviet Studies* 15, no. 2 (October 1963): 144.

15. *Papers Relating to the Foreign Relations of the United States, 1918, Russia*, 2:226. It was this request for 100,000 troops that found its way into the Supreme War Council's formal plan for an Allied intervention a few days later.

16. Bunyan, ed., *Intervention, Civil War, and Communism in Russia, April–December, 1918*, 106.

17. Kennan, *Soviet-American Relations, 1917–1920*, 2:317.

18. Bunyan, ed., *Intervention, Civil War, and Communism in Russia, April–December, 1918*, 109; and Victor S. Mamatey, *The United States and East Central Europe, 1914–1918: A Study in Wilsonian Diplomacy and Propaganda* (Princeton, NJ: Princeton University Press, 1957), 293.

19. *Papers Relating to the Foreign Relations of the United States, 1918, Russia*, 2:505–512.

20. Kennan, *Soviet-American Relations, 1917–1920*, 2:378–79, 422–27.

21. *Papers Relating to the Foreign Relations of the United States, 1918, Russia*, 2:513–16, 520.

22. R. H. Bruce Lockhart, *Memoirs of a British Agent* (London: Putnam, 1932), 311.

23. Peyton C. March, *The Nation at War* (Garden City, NY: Doubleday, Doran, 1932), 131.

24. *Papers Relating to the Foreign Relations of the United States, 1918, Russia*, 2:319–20.

25. Zbyněk Zeman and Antonin Klimek, *The Life of Edvard Beneš, 1884–1948* (Oxford: Clarendon Press, 1997), 30–31.

26. Unless otherwise noted, the following is from William Clarke, *The Lost Fortune of the Tsars*, revised and updated (London: Weidenfeld & Nicolson, 1996), 229–39; and J. D. Smele, "White Gold: The Imperial Russian Gold Reserve in the Anti-Bolshevik East, 1918–? (An Unconcluded Chapter in the History of the Russian Civil War)," in *Europe-Asia Studies* 46, no. 8 (1994): 1317–47.

27. Pipes, *The Russian Revolution*, 234.

28. Orlando Figes, *A People's Tragedy: The Russian Revolution, 1891–1924* (London: Jonathan Cape, 1996), 580–81.

29. Bunyan, ed., *Intervention, Civil War, and Communism in Russia, April–December, 1918*, 289–90, 295.

30. Gustav Becvar, *The Lost Legion: A Czechoslovakian Epic* (London: Stanley Paul, 1939), 175.

31. Beneš, *My War Memoirs*, 359.

32. *Papers Relating to the Foreign Relations of the United States, 1918, Russia*, 2:174.

33. Kennan, *Soviet-American Relations, 1917–1920*, 2:391.

34. *Papers Relating to the Foreign Relations of the United States, 1918, Russia*, 2:199–200.

35. Becvar, *The Lost Legion*, 191.

36. *Papers Relating to the Foreign Relations of the United States, 1918, Russia*, 2:236–41.

37. Ibid., 2:241–45.

38. Ibid., 2:264.

39. Ibid., 2:342.

40. Ibid., 2:360–61.

41. Bradley, "The Czechoslovak Revolt against the Bolsheviks," 141.

42. Bunyan, ed., *Intervention, Civil War, and Communism in Russia, April–December, 1918*, 336–38.

43. William S. Graves, *America's Siberian Adventure, 1918–1920* (New York: Peter Smith, 1941), 1–4.

44. Newton D. Baker, "Foreword," in Graves, *America's Siberian Adventure, 1918–1920*, x.

45. Ray Stannard Baker, *Woodrow Wilson: Life and Letters*, vol. 8, *Armistice, March 1–November 11, 1918* (Garden City, NY: Doubleday, Doran, 1939), 316–17.

46. Graves, *America's Siberian Adventure, 1918–1920*, 57–59.

47. Stanislav Zak, "To Vladivostok and Back to Yekaterinburg with General Gajda," trans. Ivo Reznicek, *Cestami odboje: Jak žily a kudy táhly čs. legie* [The Road to Resistance: How the Czech Legion Lived and Fought], ed. Adolf Zeman, vol. 4 [Anabasis] (Prague: Pokroku, 1928), 211–15.

48. Graves, *America's Siberian Adventure, 1918–1920*, 60–61.

49. Arthur S. Link et al., eds., *The Papers of Woodrow Wilson*, 69 vols. (Princeton, NJ: Princeton University Press, 1986), vol. 49, *July 18–September 13, 1918*, 185, 203.

50. Ibid., vol. 47, *March 13–May 12, 1918*, 131–32.

51. Kennan, *Soviet-American Relations, 1917–1920*, vol. 1, *Russia Leaves the War* (Princeton, NJ: Princeton University Press, 1956), 283; and 2:71–75.

52. See "The Unsung Internationalists," chapter six.

53. "Deputy Erzberger to the State Secretary," December 7, 1917 (enclosure dated December 5), in Z. A. B. Zeman, ed., *Germany and the Revolution in Russia, 1915–1918* (London: Oxford University Press, 1958), 98–99.

54. Vladimir S. Hurban, "The Czech Exodus: A Siberian Epic: How 50,000 Determined Men Fought their Way from Moscow to Vladivostok," *Current History* 9, no. 3 (December 1918): 508.

55. Kennan, *Soviet-American Relations, 1917–1920*, 2:248–60.

56. Bunyan, ed., *Intervention, Civil War, and Communism in Russia, April–December, 1918*, 94.

57. *Papers Relating to the Foreign Relations of the United States, 1918, Russia*, 2:230–31.

58. David F. Trask, *The United States in the Supreme War Council: American War Aims and Inter-Allied Strategy, 1917–1918* (Middletown, CT: Wesleyan University Press, 1961), 113.

59. Bunyan, ed., *Intervention, Civil War, and Communism in Russia, April–December, 1918*, 111.

60. Becvar, *The Lost Legion*, 157–58.

61. *Papers Relating to the Foreign Relations of the United States, The Lansing Papers, 1914–1920* (Washington, DC: US Government Printing Office, 1940), 2:374.

62. *Papers Relating to the Foreign Relations of the United States, 1918, Russia*, 2:360–61.

63. Baker, *Woodrow Wilson: Life and Letters*, vol. 8, *Armistice, March 1–November 11, 1918*, 384.

64. Graves, *America's Siberian Adventure, 1918–1920*, 68.

65. *Papers Relating to the Foreign Relations of the United States, 1918, Russia*, 2:543–44.

66. Ibid., 2:544–46, 551, 555.

67. US troop presence in Archangel and Murmansk grew to 4,907 soldiers, all of whom were withdrawn by July 1919. Combat deaths were 109, while 35 died from wounds, and 100 died of disease or from accidents; the wounded numbered 305. March, *The Nation at War*, 150–51.

68. *Papers Relating to the Foreign Relations of the United States, 1918, Russia*, 2:351.

69. Ibid., 2:323–24.

70. *Papers Relating to the Foreign Relations of the United States, The Lansing Papers, 1914–1920*, 2:379–81.

71. Leon Trotsky, *My Life: An Attempt at an Autobiography* (New York: Charles Scribner's Sons, 1930), 395–97.

72. Unless otherwise indicated, information about the Red Army is from John Erickson, "The Origins of the Red Army," in *Revolutionary Russia*, ed. Richard Pipes (Cambridge, MA: Harvard University Press, 1968); and Orlando Figes, "The Red Army and Mass Mobilization during the Russian Civil War, 1918–1920," *Past & Present*, no. 129 (November 1990): 168–211.

73. Orlando Figes, *A People's Tragedy: The Russian Revolution, 1891–1924* (London: Jonathan Cape, 1996), 591.

74. Trotsky, *My Life*, 411–19.

75. Ibid., 401–2.

76. Ibid., 402–7.

77. "About the Victory," in *How the Revolution Armed: The Military Writings and Speeches of Leon Trotsky*, vol. 1, *The Year 1918*, trans. Brian Pearce (London: New Park, 1979), 347.

78. Pipes, *The Russian Revolution*, 629.

79. *Papers Relating to the Foreign Relations of the United States, 1918, Russia*, 2:369–70.

80. Trotsky, *My Life*, 407.

81. Kennan, *Soviet-American Relations, 1917–1920*, 2:416.

82. *Papers Relating to the Foreign Relations of the United States, 1918, Russia*, 2:364.

83. Ibid., 2:375.

84. Ibid., 2:374–75.

85. Ibid., 2:379.

86. *New York Times*, September 18, 1918, 8.

87. *Papers Relating to the Foreign Relations of the United States, 1918, Russia*, 2:383–84.

88. Ibid., 2:381–82.

89. Memorandum by Breckinridge Long, September 17, 1918, reprinted in George J. Kovtun, *Masaryk and America: Testimony of a Relationship* (Washington, DC: Library of Congress, 1988), 40–41.

90. Articles reprinted in Cestmir Jesina, ed., *The Birth of Czechoslovakia* (Washington, DC: Czechoslovak National Council of America, 1968), 79–81.

91. *Papers Relating to the Foreign Relations of the United States, 1918, Russia*, 2:387–90.

92. *Papers Relating to the Foreign Relations of the United States, The Lansing Papers, 1914–1920*, 2:386–87.

93. Ibid., 2:386–91.

94. *Papers Relating to the Foreign Relations of the United States, 1918, Russia*, 2:392–94.

95. Ibid., 2:404.

96. John Bradley, *Allied Intervention in Russia* (London: Weidenfeld and Nicolson, 1968), 108–10.

97. *Papers Relating to the Foreign Relations of the United States, 1918, Russia*, 2:402–3.

98. Elena Varneck and H. H. Fisher, eds., *The Testimony of Kolchak and Other Siberian Materials*, trans. Elena Varneck (Stanford, CA: Stanford University Press, 1935), 98–105, 144–45.

99. Varneck and Fisher, eds., *The Testimony of Kolchak and Other Siberian Materials*, 146–47.

100. Ibid., 248n190.

101. Beneš, *My War Memoirs*, 375–79.

102. Ibid., 411.

103. *Papers Relating to the Foreign Relations of the United States, 1918,* supp. 1, *The World War* (Washington, DC: US Government Printing Office, 1933), 1:808.

104. Ibid., 1:816.

105. Beneš, *My War Memoirs*, 387.

106. *Papers Relating to the Foreign Relations of the United States, 1918,* supp. 1, *The World War*, 1:816–17.

107. Jesina, ed., *The Birth of Czechoslovakia*, 54–55.

108. *Papers Relating to the Foreign Relations of the United States, 1918,* supp. 1, *The World War*, 1:818.

109. While the document does not appear in *Papers Relating to the Foreign Relations of the United States,* Charles Pergler, Masaryk's closest aide in the United States, said it was much like a document he quotes in *America in the Struggle for Czechoslovak Independence* (Philadelphia: Dorrance, 1926), 50–55.

110. *Papers Relating to the Foreign Relations of the United States, 1918,* supp. 1, *The World War*, 1:824–25.

111. Link et al., eds., *The Papers of Woodrow Wilson*, 49:485–86, 511–12.

112. Pergler, *America in the Struggle for Czechoslovak Independence*, 55–56.

113. Beneš, *My War Memoirs*, 421–23.

114. Unless otherwise indicated, information about the Mid-European Union is from Arthur J. May, "H. A. Miller and the Mid-European Union of 1918," *American Slavic and East European Review* 16, no. 4 (December 1957): 473–88; and Herbert Adolphus Miller, "What Woodrow Wilson and America Meant to Czechoslovakia," in *Czechoslovakia: Twenty Years of Independence*, ed. Robert J. Kerner (Berkeley: University of California Press, 1940), 71–87.

115. Masaryk, *The Making of a State*, 224.

116. Baker, *Woodrow Wilson*, vol. 8, *Armistice, March 1–November 11, 1918*, 395, 417.

117. Graves, *America's Siberian Adventure, 1918–1920*, 144.

118. Link et al., eds., *The Papers of Woodrow Wilson*, 53:227–29.

119. *Papers Relating to the Foreign Relations of the United States, 1918, Russia*, 2:574.

CHAPTER 9

1. Reinhold Niebuhr, *Moral Man and Immoral Society: A Study in Ethics and Politics* (Louisville, KY: Westminster John Knox Press, 2013), 91.

2. *Papers Relating to the Foreign Relations of the United States, 1918,* supp. 1, *The World War* (Washington, DC: US Government Printing Office, 1933), 1:846–47.

3. T. G. Masaryk, *The Making of a State: Memories and Observations, 1914–1918* (London: George Allen & Unwin, 1927), 268.

4. See George J. Kovtun, *The Czechoslovak Declaration of Independence: A History of the Document* (Washington, DC: Library of Congress, 1985). Unless otherwise noted, information about the constitution is from this source.

5. Miller is thought to have authored the first article on Bohemian nationalism published in the United States, "Nationalism in Bohemia and Poland," in *North American Review* 200, no. 709 (December 1914): 879–86.

6. Herbert Adolphus Miller, "What Woodrow Wilson and America Meant to Czechoslovakia," in *Czechoslovakia: Twenty Years of Independence*, ed. Robert J. Kerner (Berke-

ley: University of California Press, 1940), 83–84. The men who edited the constitution at the American Agricultural Association offices, 1125 Fourteenth Street NW, according to George J. Kovtun, "then dispersed, never to meet again for any other purpose." *The Czechoslovak Declaration of Independence*, 25.

7. Ray Stannard Baker, *Woodrow Wilson: Life and Letters*, vol. 8, *Armistice, March 1–November 11, 1918* (Garden City, NY: Doubleday, Doran, 1939), 496–99. While the names of Masaryk, Beneš, and Štefánik appeared at the bottom of the declaration with their new official titles, Štefánik was actually in Tokyo on his way to meet with the leaders of the Czecho-Slovak Legion in Russia and Beneš was shuttling between Paris and London.

8. Masaryk, *The Making of a State*, 270, 273.

9. *Papers Relating to the Foreign Relations of the United States, 1918*, supp. 1, *The World War*, 1:367–69.

10. Masaryk, *The Making of a State*, 268–69, 355.

11. R. W. Seton-Watson, *A History of the Czechs and Slovaks* (London: Hutchinson, 1943), 309.

12. *Papers Relating to the Foreign Relations of the United States, 1918*, supp. 1, *The World War*, 1:392–93.

13. Baker, *Woodrow Wilson: Life and Letters*, 8:496.

14. *The Times* (London), October 17, 1918, 5.

15. Masaryk, *The Making of a State*, 233, 237–38.

16. Miller, "What Woodrow Wilson and America Meant to Czechoslovakia," 87.

17. Zbyněk Zeman and Antonin Klimek, *The Life of Edvard Beneš, 1884–1948* (Oxford: Clarendon Press, 1997), 32–34; Z. A. B. Zeman, *The Break-Up of the Habsburg Empire, 1914–1918: A Study in National and Social Revolution* (London: Oxford University Press, 1961), 221; and *Papers Relating to the Foreign Relations of the United States, 1918*, supp. 1, *The World War*, 1:392–94.

18. Cestmir Jesina, ed., *The Birth of Czechoslovakia* (Washington, DC: Czechoslovak National Council of America, 1968), 105–6. As a result, October 28 was subsequently observed as Independence Day in the republic.

19. Stanislav J. Kirschbaum, *A History of Slovakia: The Struggle for Survival* (New York: St. Martin's Press, 1995), 145–47, 151–52.

20. Zeman and Klimek, *The Life of Edvard Beneš, 1884–1948*, 53. The authors say that he was in Geneva, but Beneš's memoirs say that he arrived in Paris on November 1.

21. Eduard Beneš, *My War Memoirs* (Boston: Houghton Mifflin, 1928), 460–62.

22. While I use the more widely accepted figures of 1.2 million combat-related deaths, and 2,104,146 Habsburg POWs, a separate figure for deaths among POWs is given by István Deák, *Beyond Nationalism: A Social and Political History of the Habsburg Officer Corps, 1848–1918* (New York: Oxford University Press, 1992), 192–93.

23. Leo Grebler and Wilhelm Winkler, *The Cost of the World War to Germany and Austria-Hungary* (New Haven, CT: Yale University Press, 1940), 146–47.

24. Gunther E. Rothenberg, "The Army of Austria-Hungary, 1868–1918: A Case Study of a Multi-Ethnic Force," in *New Dimensions in Military History*, ed. Russell F. Weigley (San Rafael, CA: Presidio Press, 1975), 254.

25. Josef Kalvoda, "Czech and Slovak Prisoners of War in Russia during the War and Revolution," in *Essays on World War I: Origins and Prisoners of War*, ed. Samuel R. Williamson Jr. and Peter Pastor (New York: Brooklyn College Press, 1983), 217.

26. Rothenberg, "The Army of Francis Joseph," 220.

27. Gordon Brook-Shepherd, *The Austrians: A Thousand-Year Odyssey* (New York: Carroll & Graf, 1996), 228–29. After at least one attempt to regain his throne, Emperor Karl died of tuberculosis on April 1, 1922, in enforced exile with his family on the Portuguese island of Madeira, north of the Canary Islands.

28. Martin Gilbert, *The First World War: A Complete History* (New York: Henry Holt, 1994), 505; Norman Stone, "Army and Society in the Habsburg Monarchy, 1900–1914," *Past & Present* 33 (April 1966): 95–111.

29. Masaryk, *The Making of a State*, 352.

30. Beneš, *My War Memoirs*, 458.

31. A. J. P. Taylor, *The First World War* (New York: G. P. Putnam's Sons, 1963), 244.

32. Joseph Redlich, *Austrian War Government* (New Haven, CT: Yale University Press, 1929), 167.

33. Taylor, *The First World War*, 226.

34. Arthur J. May, *The Passing of the Hapsburg Monarchy, 1914–1918* (Philadelphia: University of Pennsylvania Press, 1966), 1:251.

35. Winston Churchill, *The Second World War* (London: Cassell, 1948), 1:8.

36. Arthur J. May, *The Hapsburg Monarchy, 1867–1914* (Cambridge, MA: Harvard University Press, 1951), 477.

37. George F. Kennan, *The Decline of Bismarck's European Order: Franco-Russian Relations, 1875–1890* (Princeton, NJ: Princeton University Press, 1979), 423.

38. Eugene Bagger, *Franz Joseph: Eine Personlichkeits-Studie* (Vienna: Amalthea Verlag, 1927), 27.

39. Adam Kozuchowski, *The Afterlife of Austria-Hungary: The Image of the Habsburg Monarchy in Interwar Europe* (Pittsburgh, PA: University of Pittsburgh Press, 2013), 174–75.

40. Ibid., 27.

41. Often lumped in with Ukrainians, these rural people have also been known as Rusyns, Uhro-Rusyns, Carpatho-Russians, and Carpatho-Ukrainians. I use Ruthenian throughout this work. With few exceptions, they occupied the northeastern corner of the Hungarian kingdom, living as farmers, shepherds, or woodcutters in the Carpathian Mountains. Like the Czechs and Slovaks, their American brethren had a say in their union with Czecho-Slovakia, holding two meetings in 1918 to consider the issue in the Pennsylvania towns of Homestead and Scranton. Paul R. Magocsi, "The Ruthenian Decision to Unite with Czechoslovakia," *Slavic Review* 34, no. 2 (June 1975): 360–81.

42. Masaryk, *The Making of a State*, 285.

43. M. Mark Stolarik, *The Role of American Slovaks in the Creation of Czecho-Slovakia, 1914–1918* (Cleveland, OH: Slovak Institute, 1968), 49–50.

44. Masaryk, *The Making of a State*, 94.

45. George J. Kovtun, *Masaryk and America: Testimony of a Relationship* (Washington, DC: Library of Congress, 1988), 42.

46. Masaryk, *The Making of a State*, 286; and Karel Čapek, *Talks with T. G. Masaryk*, trans. Michael Henry Heim (North Haven, CT: Catbird Press, 1995), 178.

47. Gustav Becvar, *The Lost Legion: A Czechoslovakian Epic* (London: Stanley Paul, 1939), 195.

48. Ibid., 176.

49. Josef Broz, "After Kolchak's Coup," trans. Ivo Reznicek, *Cestami odboje: Jak žily a kudy táhly čs. legie* [The Road to Resistance: How the Czech Legion Lived and Fought], ed. Adolf Zeman, vol. 4 [Anabasis] (Prague: Pokroku, 1928), 361–63.

50. František Kočí, "General Stefanik's Visit with the Fifth Regiment in the Urals," trans. Ivo Reznicek, from *Cestami odboje* [The Road to Resistance], 4:364–68.

51. Becvar, *The Lost Legion*, 196.

52. Ibid., 202–3.

53. Ibid., 205–6.

54. Information for this section is from Winston S. Churchill, *The World Crisis,* vol. 4, *The Aftermath* (New York: Charles Scribner's Sons, 1929), 164–86, 240–88; and Martin Gilbert, ed., *Winston S. Churchill: The Stricken World, 1916–1922*, companion vol. 4, parts 1, 2, 3 (Boston: Houghton Mifflin Company, 1978), unless otherwise noted.

55. Richard Pipes, *The Russian Revolution* (New York: Random House, 1990), 607.

56. Ilya Somin, *Stillborn Crusade: The Tragic Failure of Western Intervention in the Russian Civil War, 1918–1920* (New Brunswick, NJ: Transaction Publishers, 1996), 18.

57. *New York Times,* June 30, 1919, 10.

58. Gilbert, ed., *Winston S. Churchill,* companion vol. 4, part 1, 555.

59. Ibid., part 2, 728.

60. Ibid., part 1, 680.

61. Ibid., part 2, 978.

62. Ibid., part 1, 550.

63. Ibid., part 2, 774n1.

64. Ibid., part 2, 964.

65. Richard Langworth, ed., *Churchill by Himself: The Definitive Collection of Quotations* (New York: Public Affairs, 2008), 381. Churchill also mentioned "strangling Bolshevism" in a March 1949 speech at MIT.

66. *Papers Relating to the Foreign Relations of the United States, 1919, Russia* (Washington, DC: U.S. Government Printing Office, 1937), 206–9.

67. Ibid., 296–97.

68. Ibid., 298–303, 318–21.

69. Ibid., 533.

70. Ibid., 224–25.

71. Ibid., 226–27.

72. *Papers Relating to the Foreign Relations of the United States, 1920* (Washington, DC: U.S. Government Printing Office, 1936), 3:485–87.

73. Peter Fleming, *The Fate of Admiral Kolchak* (New York: Harcourt, Brace & World, 1963), 187; and Gustav Becvar, *The Lost Legion: A Czechoslovakian Epic* (London: Stanley Paul, 1939), 235–36.

74. Elena Varneck and H. H. Fisher, eds., *The Testimony of Kolchak and Other Siberian Materials,* trans. Elena Vck (Stanford, CA: Stanford University Press, 1935), 7, 215–16.

75. *Papers Relating to the Foreign Relations of the United States, 1920*, 3:564–65.

76. William S. Graves, *America's Siberian Adventure, 1918–1920* (New York: Peter Smith, 1941), 73, 82.

77. *Papers Relating to the Foreign Relations of the United States, 1920*, 3:561.

78. Ibid., 3:499–500.

79. Ibid., 3:502–3.

80. Ibid., 3:563–64.

81. See, for instance, Peter Fleming, *The Fate of Admiral Kolchak* (New York: Harcourt, Brace & World, 1963), 224–29.

82. *Papers Relating to the Foreign Relations of the United States, 1919, Russia*, 534–35.

83. *Papers Relating to the Foreign Relations of the United States, 1920*, 3:502.

84. Ibid., 3:566, 569.

85. Frederick C. Giffin, "An American Railroad Man East of the Urals, 1918–1922," in *The Historian* 60, no. 4 (Summer 1998): 812–19.

CONCLUSION

1. R. W. Seton-Watson, *Masaryk in England* (New York: Macmillan, 1943), 114.

2. Eduard Beneš, *My War Memoirs* (Boston: Houghton Mifflin, 1928), 485.

3. T. G. Masaryk, *The Making of a State: Memories and Observations, 1914–1918* (London: George Allen & Unwin, 1927), 327–32. He arrived almost exactly four years after departing Prague.

4. Beneš, *My War Memoirs*, 486.

5. Barbara K. Reinfeld, "Charlotte Garrigue Masaryk, 1850–1923," in *Czechoslovak and Central European Journal* (Summer/Winter, 1989): 90–103.

6. Victor S. Mamatey, *The United States and East-Central Europe, 1914–1918: A Study in Wilsonian Diplomacy and Propaganda* (Princeton, NJ: Princeton University Press, 1957), 384.

7. Beneš, *My War Memoirs*, 498.

8. Edward Crankshaw, *The Habsburgs: Portrait of a Dynasty* (New York: Viking Press, 1971), 13.

9. Norman Stone, "Introductory Essay: Czechoslovakia," in *Czechoslovakia: Crossroads and Crises, 1918–88*, ed. Norman Stone and Edward Strouhal (New York: St. Martin's Press, 1989), 3.

10. Hans Kohn, "Romanticism and Realism Among Czechs and Slovaks," *The Review of Politics* 14, no. 1 (January 1952): 38.

11. Zbynek Zeman and Antonin Klimek, *The Life of Edvard Beneš, 1884–1948* (Oxford: Clarendon Press, 1997), 36–41; and Thomas D. Marzik, "Milan Rastislav Štefánik and the Creation of Czecho-Slovakia," in *The Birth of Czechoslovakia*, ed. Sharon L. Wolchik and Ivan Dubovicky (Prague: Set Out, 1999), 33–34. Today, the main international airport at Bratislava, the capital of the Slovak Republic, is named in honor of Štefánik.

12. Nadya Nedelsky, *Defining the Sovereign Community: National Identity, Individual Rights and Minority Membership in the Czech and Slovak Republics* (Philadelphia: University of Pennsylvania Press, 2009), 74–77.

13. George J. Kovtun, *Masaryk and America: Testimony of a Relationship* (Washington, DC: Library of Congress, 1988), 63–64.

14. Ibid., 65–66.

15. Karel Čapek, *Talks with T. G. Masaryk*, trans. Michael Henry Heim (North Haven, CT: Catbird Press, 1995), 185.

16. Victor S. Mamatey, "The Development of Czechoslovak Democracy, 1920–1938," in *A History of the Czechoslovak Republic, 1918–1948*, ed. Victor S. Mamatey and Radomir Luza (Princeton, NJ: Princeton University Press, 1973), 152–56.

17. Cynthia Paces, *Prague Panoramas: National Memory and Sacred Space in the Twentieth Century* (Pittsburgh, PA: University of Pittsburgh Press, 2009), 159.

18. Čapek, *Talks with T. G. Masaryk*, 187.

19. Ibid., 60.

20. George F. Kennan, *Soviet-American Relations, 1917–1920*, vol. 2, *The Decision to Intervene* (Princeton, NJ: Princeton University Press, 1958), 136.

21. Masaryk, *The Making of a State*, 261.

22. Beneš, *My War Memoirs*, 368.

23. Charles Pergler, *America in the Struggle for Czechoslovak Independence* (Philadelphia: Dorrance, 1926), 57.

24. *Papers Relating to the Foreign Relations of the United States, 1919, Russia* (Washington, DC: US Government Printing Office, 1937), 286–87.

25. Peyton C. March, *The Nation at War* (Garden City, NY: Doubleday, Doran, 1932), 130–32; John J. Stephan, *The Russian Far East: A History* (Stanford, CA: Stanford University Press, 1994), 139–40; and Frederick Harris, et al., eds., *Service with Fighting Men: An Account of the Work of the American Young Men's Christian Associations in the World War* (New York: Association Press, 1922), 456.

26. March, *The Nation at War,* 129.

27. *Papers Relating to the Foreign Relations of the United States, 1919, Russia,* 322.

28. Unless otherwise indicated, information about the evacuation of the legionnaires is from Rudolf Raše, "The Evacuation," trans. Ivo Reznicek, from *Cestami odboje* [The Road to Resistance], 5:94–104.

29. Felčar Matějka, "From the Last Journey across Siberia to the Great Ocean," trans. Ivo Reznicek, from *Cestami odboje* [The Road to Resistance], 5:107–32.

30. Jindřich Husák, "The First Ones are Returning Back Home," trans. Ivo Reznicek, from *Cestami odboje* [The Road to Resistance], 5:158–65.

31. Adolf Zeman, "A Burial in the Open Sea," trans. Ivo Reznicek, from *Cestami odboje* [The Road to Resistance], 5:276–79.

32. These numbers are perhaps indirectly corroborated by a report of the YMCA—Harris, et al., eds., *Service with Fighting Men*—which provides two different numbers for Czechs and Slovaks evacuated at Vladivostok: 53,026 (p. 325) and 67,217 (p. 456), without explanation. Yet the YMCA's first number is very close to the number of noncommissioned officers and soldiers (53,455) given by Rudolf Raše and the second figure is very close to Raše's given total number of all men, women, and children evacuees (67,730).

33. Michael Mainville, "Legion Graves in Disrepair," *Prague Post,* May 1, 2003.

34. Tom Jones, "New Memorial to Czechoslovak Legionaries Divides Russian City," *Czech Position,* October 20, 2011.

35. "Commemorative Plaque to Mark Czechoslovak Legions in Kyiv," *Prague Post,* August 12, 2014.

36. Interview with Kohn's former colleague, Alvin Rubinstein, PhD, October 8, 1999.

37. Isaiah Berlin and Rain Jahanbegloo, *Conversations with Isaiah Berlin* (New York: Charles Scribner's Sons, 1991), 101.

38. Robert Nisbet, *History of the Idea of Progress* (New York: Basic Books, 1980), 268.

39. Robin Okey, *The Habsburg Monarchy c. 1765–1918: From Enlightenment to Eclipse* (New York: St. Martin's Press, 2001), 106.

40. Kovtun, *Masaryk and America,* 41–44.

41. Rudolf Raše, "In Europe Again after All Those Years," trans. Ivo Reznicek, from *Cestami odboje: Jak žily a kudy táhly čs. legie* [The Road to Resistance: How the Czech Legion Lived and Fought], ed. Adolf Zeman, vol. 5 [Home] (Prague: Pokroku, 1929), 348–51.

BIBLIOGRAPHICAL ESSAY

Very few books on the exploits and significance of the Czecho-Slovak Legion have ever been published in English, and fewer of those remain in print.

Before this volume, the three most recent works in English include *The Czech Legion 1914–20*, by David Bullock, a forty-eight-page paperback published in 2009 by Osprey Publishing, a publisher well known for its very brief military histories. Two others are Joan McGuire Mohr, *The Czech and Slovak Legion in Siberia, 1917–1922* (Jefferson, NC: McFarland, 2012), and Brent Mueggenberg, *The Czecho-Slovak Struggle for Independence, 1914–1920* (Jefferson, NC: McFarland, 2014).

The largest and most detailed study of the Czecho-Slovak Legion in English is Victor M. Fic's four-volume diplomatic and military history of the Russian Civil War, poorly translated into English and poorly organized. Two of the volumes are out of print. The titles are *Revolutionary War for Independence and the Russian Question: Czechoslovak Army in Russia, 1914–1918* (New Delhi: Abhinav Publications, 1977); *The Bolsheviks and the Czechoslovak Legion: The Origin of Their Armed Conflict, March–May 1918* (New Delhi: Abhinav Publications, 1978); *The Collapse of the American Policy in Russia and Siberia, 1918: Wilson's Decision Not to Intervene, March–October 1918* (Boulder, CO: East European Monographs, 1995; distributed by Columbia University Press); and *The Rise of the Constitutional Alternative to Soviet Rule in 1918: Provisional Governments of Siberia and All-Russia: Their Quest for Allied Intervention* (Boulder, CO: East European Monographs, 1998; distributed by Columbia University Press).

An academic text is *The Czechoslovak Legion in Russia, 1914–1920*, by John F. N. Bradley, also published by East European Monographs and distributed by Columbia University Press. Still in print, this slender volume cites no sources and has no index.

A work that qualifies as an English text in print, *The Czech Legions in Siberia*, is an angry memoir by Konstantin W. Sakharow, a White Russian officer who had strongly negative opinions of the Czecho-Slovak Legion. Originally published as *Die Tschechischen Legionen in Sibirien* (Berlin-Charlottenburg: Heinrich Wilhelm Hendriock Verlag, 1930), it was brought out in a very limited English edition by Buda Publishing in 1992.

The only history published for a wide audience and still in print is a British history by Henry P. B. Baerlein, *The March of the Seventy Thousand* (London: Leonard Parsons, 1926). Reprinted in 1971 by Arno Press, it is difficult to locate. Baerlein was a prolific travel writer whose many books included *Baltic Paradise*, *Romanian Oasis*, and *Spain Yesterday and Tomorrow*. His work on the legion cites very few sources.

Of the eight out-of-print works devoted solely or largely to this subject, the only one written for a wide audience of interested readers is Edwin P. Hoyt, *The Army without a Country* (New York: Macmillan, 1967). Hoyt was another prolific author of popular works of nonfiction, such as *Marilyn: The Tragic Venus* and *Jumbos and Jackasses*. While Hoyt claimed to have used "rare contemporary sources," he identified few of them and offered no footnotes. There is also a very good firsthand account by Gustav Becvar, *The Lost Legion* (London: Stanley Paul, 1939), whose author was a member of the legion. The remaining out-of-print works include *Perish by the Sword: The Czechoslovakian Anabasis and Our Supporting Campaigns in North Russia and Siberia, 1918–1920* by military historian R. Ernest Dupuy (Harrisburg, PA: Military Service Publishing, 1939), which devotes as much attention to the US military intervention in Russia as to the activities of the legion.

The out-of-print literature also includes three very brief, celebratory summaries published by government agencies or patronage societies in the years immediately following the return of the legionnaires to Czecho-Slovakia: *Heroic Story of the Czecho-Slovak Legions*, by A. Beaumont (Prague: Czechoslovakian Foreigners' Office, 1919), an eighty-four-page account by a British war correspondent; Rudolph Medek, *The Czechoslovak Anabasis across Russia and Siberia* (London: Czech Society, 1929), a forty-five-page version by a member of the Czechoslovak National Council; and H. J. O'Higgins, *March of the Czechoslovaks across Siberia* (New York: Czechoslovak Art Club, 1918), a twenty-eight-page pamphlet.

While I draw on several hundred original documents and firsthand accounts (memoirs, diaries, letters, interviews, and official documents), many of them translated from Czech, German, Hungarian, or Russian, this bibliography includes only those works that offer substantive material related to the Czecho-Slovak Legion in Russia.

For a review of related literature, see Jonathan D. Smele, *The Russian Revolution and Civil War, 1917–1921: An Annotated Bibliography* (London: Continuum, 2003).

BIBLIOGRAPHY

Illuminating this story in the English-speaking world are more than one hundred personal accounts by the members of the Czecho-Slovak Legion, translated into English for the first time by Ivo Reznicek, PhD. Fully 460 personal accounts by 197 legionnaires were brought together in a five-volume work, *Cestami odboje: Jak žily a kudy táhly čs. legie* [The Road to Resistance: How the Czech Legion Lived and Fought], that was published in Prague between 1926 and 1929, but subsequently suppressed by the Nazi and Soviet regimes. Carefully selected from the 460 stories and translated into English are 107 firsthand accounts that are most relevant to this story. The five volumes of *The Road to Resistance* are:

Zeman, Adolf, ed. *Cestami odboje: Jak žily a kudy táhly čs. legie* [The Road to Resistance: How the Czech Legion Lived and Fought]. Vol. 1 [From Austrian Bondage to Freedom]. Prague: Pokroku, 1926.

———. *Cestami odboje: Jak žily a kudy táhly čs. legie* [The Road to Resistance: How the Czech Legion Lived and Fought]. Vol. 2 [In Captivity]. Prague: Pokroku, 1927.

———. *Cestami odboje: Jak žily a kudy táhly čs. legie* [The Road to Resistance: How the Czech Legion Lived and Fought]. Vol. 3 [Beginnings of Resistance]. Prague: Pokroku, 1927.

————. *Cestami odboje: Jak žily a kudy táhly čs. legie* [The Road to Resistance: How the Czech Legion Lived and Fought]. Vol. 4 [Anabasis]. Prague: Pokroku, 1928.

————. *Cestami odboje: Jak žily a kudy táhly čs. legie* [The Road to Resistance: How the Czech Legion Lived and Fought]. Vol. 5 [Home]. Prague: Progress Publishing, 1929.

ADDITIONAL ORIGINAL DOCUMENTS AND REFERENCES

"*Aide-memoire* of the Secretary of State to the Allied Ambassadors," July 17, 1918. Reprinted in George F. Kennan, *Soviet-American Relations, 1917–1920*, vol. 2, *The Decision to Intervene*. Princeton, NJ: Princeton University Press, 1958) pp. 482–85.

Baker, Ray Stannard. *Woodrow Wilson: Life and Letters*. Garden City, NY: Doubleday, Doran, 1927–39. Vol. 6, *Facing War, 1915–1917*.

————. *Woodrow Wilson: Life and Letters*. Garden City, NY: Doubleday, Doran, 1927–39. Vol. 7, *War Leader, 1917–1918*.

————. *Woodrow Wilson: Life and Letters*. Garden City, NY: Doubleday, Doran, 1927–39. Vol. 8, *Armistice, March 1–November 11, 1918*.

Bowder, R. P., and A. F. Kerensky, eds. *The Russian Provisional Government, 1917: Documents*. 2 vols. Stanford, CA: Stanford University Press, 1961.

Bunyan, James, ed. *Intervention, Civil War, and Communism in Russia, April–December, 1918: Documents and Materials*. Baltimore: Johns Hopkins Press, 1936.

————, and H. H. Fisher, eds. *The Bolshevik Revolution, 1917–1918: Documents and Materials*. Stanford, CA: Stanford University Press, 1934.

Butt, V. P., A. B. Murphy, N. A. Myshov, and G. R. Swain, eds. *The Russian Civil War: Documents from the Soviet Archives*. New York: St. Martin's Press, 1996.

Czechoslovak Philatelic Society of Great Britain. *The Field Post of the Czechoslovak and Allied Forces in Russia, 1918–1920*. Kent: Czechoslovak Philatelic Society of Great Britain, 1991.

Findlay, John, and Dorothy Findlay. "Letters from Vladivostok, 1918–1923." *The Slavonic and East European Review* 45, no. 105 (July 1967): 497–530.

Golder, Frank Alford, ed. *Documents of Russian History, 1914–1917*. Translated by Emanuel Aronsberg. Gloucester, MA: Peter Smith, 1964.

Heald, Edward T. *Witness to Revolution: Letters from Russia, 1916–1919*. Edited by James B. Gidney. Kent, OH: Kent State University Press, 1972.

Jesina, Cestmir, ed. *The Birth of Czechoslovakia*. Washington, DC: Czechoslovak National Council of America, 1968. Includes 102 original documents.

Koenker, Diane P., and Ronald D. Bachman, eds. *Revelations from the Russian Archives: Documents in English Translation*. Washington, DC: Library of Congress, 1997.

Link, Arthur S., et al., eds. *The Papers of Woodrow Wilson*. 69 vols. Princeton, NJ: Princeton University Press, 1966–94.

Palmer, Svetlana, and Sarah Wallis, eds. *Intimate Voices from the First World War*. New York: HarperCollins, 2003.

Seymour, Charles, ed. *The Intimate Papers of Colonel House*. 4 vols. Boston: Houghton Mifflin, 1926–28.

Sworakowski, Witold S. "A Churchill Letter in Support of the Anti-Bolshevik Forces in Russia in 1919." *Russian Review* 28, no. 1 (January, 1969): 77–82.

US Department of State. *Papers Relating to the Foreign Relations of the United States, 1918, Russia*. 3 vols. Washington, DC: US Government Printing Office, 1931–33.

————. *Papers Relating to the Foreign Relations of the United States, 1918,* Supplement 1, *The World War*. 2 vols. Washington, DC: US Government Printing Office, 1933.

————. *Papers Relating to the Foreign Relations of the United States, 1919, Russia.* Washington, DC: US Government Printing Office, 1937.

————. *Papers Relating to the Foreign Relations of the United States, 1920.* 3 vols. Washington, DC: US Government Printing Office, 1935–36.

————. *Papers Relating to the Foreign Relations of the United States: The Lansing Papers, 1914–1920.* 2 vols. Washington, DC: US Government Printing Office, 1939–40.

Varneck, Elena, and H. H. Fisher, eds. *The Testimony of Kolchak and Other Siberian Materials.* Translated by Elena Varneck. Stanford, CA: Stanford University Press, 1935.

Wieczynski, Joseph L., ed. *The Modern Encyclopedia of Russian and Soviet History.* 59 vols. Gulf Breeze, FL: Academic International Press, 1976–96.

MEMOIRS AND FIRST-PERSON ACCOUNTS

Ackerman, Carl W. *Trailing the Bolsheviki: Twelve Thousand Miles with the Allies in Siberia.* New York: Charles Scribner's Sons, 1919.

Beaumont, A. *Heroic Story of the Czecho-Slovak Legions.* Prague: Czechoslovakian Foreigners' Office, 1919.

Becvar, Gustav. *The Lost Legion: A Czechoslovakian Epic.* London: Stanley Paul, 1939.

Beneš, Eduard. *My War Memoirs.* Translated by Paul Selver. New York: Houghton Mifflin, 1928.

Brändström, Elsa. *Among Prisoners of War in Russia and Siberia.* London: Hutchinson, 1929.

Buxhoeveden, Baroness Sophie. *Left Behind: Fourteen Months in Siberia, December 1917–February 1919.* London: Longmans, 1929.

Čapek, Karel. *President Masaryk Tells His Story.* London: George Allen & Unwin, 1934.

Churchill, Winston S. *The World Crisis.* Vol. 4: *The Aftermath.* New York: Charles Scribner's Sons, 1929.

————. *The World Crisis.* Vol. 5: *The Eastern Front.* New York: Charles Scribner's Sons, 1931.

Colton, Ethan T., Sr. "With the Y.M.C.A. in Revolutionary Russia." *Russian Review* 14, no. 2 (April, 1955): 128–39.

Dotsenko, Paul S. *The Struggle for a Democracy in Siberia, 1917–1920: Eyewitness Account of a Contemporary.* Stanford, CA: Hoover Institution Press, 1983.

Duncan, William V. "A Siberian Notebook [The Czechoslovak Campaign against the Bolsheviks]," *The Yale Review* 9, no. 1 (October 1919): 154–84.

Dyboski, Roman. *Seven Years in Russia and Siberia, 1914–1921.* Translated, edited, and annotated by Marion Moore Coleman. Cheshire, CT: Cherry Hill Books, 1971. Original Polish edition: Warsaw: Nakład Gebethnera i Wolffa, 1922.

Guins, George C. "The Siberian Intervention, 1918–1919." *Russian Review* 28, no. 4 (October 1969): 428–40.

Graves, William S. *America's Siberian Adventure, 1918–1920.* New York: Jonathan Cape & Harrison Smith, 1931.

Kohn, Hans. *Living in a World Revolution: My Encounters with History.* New York: Pocket Books, 1965.

Lansing, Robert. *War Memoirs of Robert Lansing.* Westport, CT: Greenwood Press, 1970.

Lewis, Brackett. *Eyewitness Story of the Occupation of Samara, Russia, by the Czechoslovak Legion in June 1918.* Washington, DC: Czechoslovak Society of Arts and Sciences in America, 1977.

Lichtenstein, Gaston, ed. *Repatriation of Prisoners of War from Siberia: A Documentary Narrative.* Richmond, VA: William Byrd Press, 1924.

Lloyd George, David. *War Memoirs of David Lloyd George.* Vol. 6, *1918.* Boston: Little, Brown, 1937.

Lockhart, R. H. Bruce. *Memoirs of a British Agent.* London and New York: G. P. Putnam's Sons, 1932.

Long, John W., and C. Howard Hopkins. "T. G. Masaryk and the Strategy of Czechoslovak Independence: An Interview in Russia on 27 June 1917." *Slavonic and East European Review* 56, no. 1 (January 1978): 88–96.

Machar, Josef S. *The Jail: Experiences of 1916.* Translated by Paul Selver. Oxford: Basil Blackwell, 1921.

Masaryk, Alice G. "From an Austrian Prison." *Atlantic Monthly* 126, no. 227 (November 1920): 577–87.

———. "The Prison House." *Atlantic Monthly* 126, no. 228 (December 1920): 770–79.

Masaryk, Tomáš G. *The Making of a State: Memories and Observations, 1914–1918.* New York: F. A. Stokes, 1927.

Medek, Rudolf. *The Czechoslovak Anabasis across Russia and Siberia.* London: Czech Society, 1929.

Nosek, Vladimir. *Independent Bohemia: An Account of the Czecho-Slovak Struggle for Liberty.* New York: E. P. Dutton, 1918.

O'Higgins, H. J. *March of the Czechoslovaks across Siberia.* New York: Czechoslovak Art Club, 1918.

Pergler, Charles. *America in the Struggle for Czechoslovak Independence.* Philadelphia: Dorrance, 1926.

Petroff, Serge P. *Remembering a Forgotten War: Civil War in Eastern European Russia and Siberia, 1918–1920.* Boulder, CO: East European Monographs, 2000.

Sakharow, Konstantin W. *The Czech Legions in Siberia.* Akron, OH: Buda Publishing Co., 1992.

Seton-Watson, R. W. *Masaryk in England.* Cambridge: Cambridge University Press, 1943.

Smirnov, M. I. "Admiral Kolchak." *The Slavonic and East European Review* 11, no. 32 (January 1933): 373–87.

Steed, Henry Wickham. *Through Thirty Years, 1892–1922: A Personal Narrative.* New York: Doubleday, Page, 1924.

Trotsky, Leon. *The History of the Russian Revolution.* Translated by Max Eastman. 3 vols. Ann Arbor, MI: University of Michigan Press, 1932.

———. *How the Revolution Armed: The Military Writings and Speeches of Leon Trotsky.* 5 vols. London: New Park Publications, 1979–81.

———. *My Life: An Attempt at an Autobiography.* New York: Charles Scribner's Sons, 1930.

Voska, Emanuel Victor, and Will Irwin. *Spy and Counterspy.* New York: Doubleday, Doran, 1940.

Ward, John. *With the "Die-Hards" in Siberia.* New York: George H. Doran, 1920.

Williams, Maynard Owen. "The Fighting Czecho-Slovaks." In *World's War Events: Recorded by Statesmen, Commanders, Historians, and by Men Who Fought or Saw the Great Campaigns,* edited by Francis J. Reynolds and Allen L. Churchill. Vol. 3. New York: P. F. Collier & Son, 1919.

Young Men's Christian Association. Frederick Harris, et al., eds. *Service with Fighting Men: An Account of the Work of the American Young Men's Christian Associations in the World War.* New York: Association Press, 1922.

SECONDARY SOURCES

Baerlein, Henry P. B. *The March of the Seventy Thousand.* London: Leonard Parsons, 1926.

Balawyder, A. "The Czechoslovak Legion Crosses Canada, 1920." *East European Quarterly* 6, no. 2 (June 1972): 177–91.

Bisher, Jamie. *White Terror: Cossack Warlords of the Trans-Siberian.* New York: Routledge, 2005.

Boterbloem, Kees. "Hasek, Svejk, and the Czechoslovak Legion." In *Essays on World War I*, edited by Peter Pastor and Graydon A. Tunstall. Boulder, CO: Social Science Monographs, 2012. Distributed by Columbia University Press.

Bradley, John F. N. *Allied Intervention in Russia.* London: Weidenfeld and Nicolson, 1968.

———. "The Allies and Russia in the Light of French Archives (7 November 1917–15 March 1918)." *Soviet Studies* 16, issue 2 (October 1964): 166–85.

———. *Civil War in Russia, 1917–1920.* New York: St. Martin's Press, 1975.

———. *The Czechoslovak Legion in Russia, 1914–1920.* Boulder, CO: East European Monographs, 1991. Distributed by Columbia University Press.

———. "The Czechoslovak Revolt against the Bolsheviks." *Soviet Studies* 15, issue 2 (October 1963): 124–51.

Bullock, David. *Armored Units of the Russian Civil War: Red Army.* Oxford: Osprey Publishing, 2006.

———. *The Czech Legion 1914–20.* Oxford: Osprey Publishing, 2009.

———, and A. Deryabin. *Armored Units of the Russian Civil War: White and Allied.* Oxford: Osprey Publishing, 2003.

Carley, Michael Jabara. *Revolution and Intervention: The French Government and the Russian Civil War, 1917–1919.* Kingston and Montreal: McGill-Queen's University Press, 1983.

Chamberlin, William Henry. *The Russian Revolution, 1917–1921.* 2 vols. New York: Macmillan, 1965.

Chen, Edgar, and Emily Van Buskirk. "The Czech Legion's Long Journey Home." *MHQ: The Quarterly Journal of Military History* 13, no. 2 (Winter 2001): 42–53.

Connaughton, Richard M. *The Republic of Ushakovka: Admiral Kolchak and the Allied Intervention in Siberia, 1918–1920.* New York: Routledge, 1990.

Davis, Donald E., and Eugene P Trani. "The American YMCA and the Russian Revolution." *Slavic Review* 33, no. 3 (September, 1974): 469–91.

Davis, Gerald H. "The Life of Prisoners of War in Russia, 1914–1921." In *Essays on World War I: Origins and Prisoners of War*, edited by Samuel R. Williamson Jr. and Peter Pastor. New York: Social Science Monographs, 1983.

Deák, István. "The Habsburg Army in the First and Last Days of World War I: A Comparative Analysis." In *War and Society in East Central Europe*, vol. 19, edited by Bela K. Kiraly and Nandor F. Dreisziger. New York: Social Science Monographs, 1985.

Decsy, János. "The Habsburg Army on the Threshold of Total War." In *War and Society in East Central Europe*, vol. 19, edited by Béla K. Király and Nandor F. Dreisziger. New York: Social Science Monographs, 1985.

Dunscomb, Paul E. *Japan's Siberian Intervention, 1918–1922*. Lanham, MD: Lexington Books, 2011.

Dupuy, R. Ernest. *Perish by the Sword: The Czechoslovakian Anabasis and Our Supporting Campaigns in North Russia and Siberia, 1918–1920*. Harrisburg, PA: Military Service Publishing Co., 1939.

Ferrell, Robert H. *Woodrow Wilson and World War I, 1917–1921*. New York: Harper & Row, 1985.

Fic, Victor M. *The Bolsheviks and the Czechoslovak Legion: The Origin of Their Armed Conflict, March–May 1918*. New Delhi: Abhinav Publications, 1978.

———. *The Collapse of the American Policy in Russia and Siberia, 1918: Wilson's Decision Not to Intervene (March–October 1918)*. Boulder, CO: East European Monographs, 1995. Distributed by Columbia University Press.

———. *Revolutionary War for Independence and the Russian Question: Czechoslovak Army in Russia, 1914–1918*. New Delhi: Abhinav Publications, 1977.

———. *The Rise of the Constitutional Alternative to Soviet Rule in 1918: Provisional Governments of Siberia and All-Russia: Their Quest for Allied Intervention*. Boulder, CO: East European Monographs, 1998. Distributed by Columbia University Press.

Figes, Orlando. *A People's Tragedy: A History of the Russian Revolution*. New York: Viking, 1997.

———. "The Red Army and Mass Mobilization during the Russian Civil War, 1918–1920." *Past & Present*, no. 129 (November 1990): 168–211.

Fleming, Peter. *The Fate of Admiral Kolchak*. New York: Harcourt, Brace & World, 1963.

Foglesong, David S. *America's Secret War against Bolshevism: U.S. Intervention in the Russian Civil War, 1917–1920*. Chapel Hill: University of North Carolina Press, 1995.

Footman, David. *Civil War in Russia*. New York: Frederick A. Praeger, 1961.

Gilbert, Martin. *Winston S. Churchill*. Vol. 4, *The Stricken World, 1916–1922*. Boston: Houghton Mifflin, 1975.

———. *Winston S. Churchill*. Companion vol. 4: Parts 1, 2, 3. Boston: Houghton Mifflin, 1978.

Glos, Blanka Ševčík, and George E Glos. *Czechoslovak Troops in Russia and Siberia during the First World War*. New York: Vantage Press, 2000.

Goldhurst, Richard. *The Midnight War: The American Intervention in Russia, 1918–1920*. New York: McGraw-Hill, 1978.

Grubbs, Carolyn B. "American Railroaders in Siberia, 1917–1920." *Railroad History*, no. 150 (Spring 1984): 107–14.

Hanak, Harry. "France, Britain, Italy and the Independence of Czechoslovakia in 1918." In *Czechoslovakia: Crossroads and Crises, 1918–1988*, edited by Norman Stone and Eduard Strouhal. New York: St. Martin's Press, 1989.

Hoyt, Edwin P. *The Army without a Country*. New York: Macmillan, 1967.

Jahelka, Joseph. "The Role of the Chicago Czechs in the Struggle for Czechoslovak Independence." *Journal of the Illinois State Historical Society* 31, no. 4 (December 1938): 381–410.

Jeffreys-Jones, Rhodri. "W. Somerset Maugham: Anglo-American Agent in Revolutionary Russia." *American Quarterly* 28, no. 1 (Spring 1976): 90–106.

Kalvoda, Josef. "Czech and Slovak Prisoners of War in Russia during the War and Revolution." In *Essays on World War I: Origins and Prisoners of War*, edited by Samuel R. Williamson Jr. and Peter Pastor. New York: Social Science Monographs, 1983.

———. *The Genesis of Czechoslovakia*. Boulder, CO: East European Monographs, 1986. Distributed by Columbia University Press.

———. "Masaryk in America in 1918." *Jahrbücher für Geschichte Osteuropas* 27 (1979): 85–99.

———. "The Origins of the Czechoslovak Army, 1914–1918." In *War and Society in East Central Europe*, vol. 19, edited by Béla K. Király and Nandor F. Dreisziger. New York: Social Science Monographs, 1985.

———. "The Origins of Czechoslovakia (Russia—The Home Front)." In *Czechoslovakia: Crossroads and Crises, 1918–1988*, edited by Norman Stone and Eduard Strouhal. New York: St. Martin's Press, 1989.

Kawakami, K. K. "The Far Eastern Republic of Siberia." *Current History* 16, no. 1 (April 1922): 123–27.

Kennan, George F. *Russia and the West under Lenin and Stalin*. Boston: Little, Brown, 1961.

———. *Soviet-American Relations, 1917–1920*. Vol. 1, *Russia Leaves the War*. Princeton, NJ: Princeton University Press, 1956.

———. *Soviet-American Relations, 1917–1920*. Vol. 2, *The Decision to Intervene*. Princeton, NJ: Princeton University Press, 1958.

Khvostov, Mikhail. *The Russian Civil War: The Red Army*. Oxford: Osprey, 2002.

———. *The Russian Civil War: White Armies*. Oxford: Osprey, 2004.

Kinvig, Clifford. *Churchill's Crusade: The British Invasion of Russia, 1918–1920*. London: Hambledon Press, 2006.

Kohn, Hans. "Romanticism and Realism among the Czechs and Slovaks." *Review of Politics* 14, no. 1 (January 1952): 25–46.

Koreff, O. D. *Milan Rastislav Stefanik: A Short Biography*. Cleveland, OH: Slovak League of America, 1924.

Kovtun, George J. *The Czechoslovak Declaration of Independence: A History of the Document*. Washington, DC: Library of Congress, 1985.

———. *Masaryk and America: Testimony of a Relationship*. Washington, DC: Library of Congress, 1988. Krammer, Arnold. "Soviet Propaganda among German and Austro-Hungarian Prisoners of War in Russia, 1917–1921." In *War and Society in East Central Europe*, vol. 5, edited by Béla K. Király. New York: Social Science Monographs, 1983.

Levin, N. Gordon, Jr. *Woodrow Wilson and World Politics: America's Response to War and Revolution*. London: Oxford University Press, 1968.

Lincoln, W. Bruce. *Passage through Armageddon: The Russians in War and Revolution*. New York: Simon and Schuster, 1986.

———. *Red Victory: A History of the Russian Civil War*. New York: Simon and Schuster, 1989.

Link, Arthur S. *The Struggle for Neutrality, 1914–1915*. Princeton, NJ: Princeton University Press, 1960.

———. *Wilson: Campaigns for Progressivism and Peace, 1916–1917*. Princeton, NJ: Princeton University Press, 1965.

———. *Wilson: Confusion and Crises*. Princeton, NJ: Princeton University Press, 1964.

———. *Woodrow Wilson: Revolution, War, and Peace*. Princeton: Princeton University Press; Arlington Heights, IL: Harlan Davidson Press, 1979.

Luckett, Richard. *The White Generals: An Account of the White Movement and the Russian Civil War*. New York: Viking Press, 1971.

Luvaas, Jay. "A Unique Army: The Common Experience." In *The Habsburg Empire in World War I*, edited by Robert A. Kann, Béla K. Király, and Paula S. Fichtner. Boulder, CO: East European Quarterly, 1977.

MacMillan, Margaret. *Paris 1919: Six Months That Changed the World*. New York: Random House, 2001.

Magocsi, Paul R. "The Ruthenian Decision to Unite with Czechoslovakia." *Slavic Review* 34, issue 2 (June 1975): 360–81.

Mamatey, Victor S. "The Czech Wartime Dilemma: The Habsburgs or the Entente?" In *War and Society in East Central Europe,* vol. 19, edited by Béla K. Király and Nandor F. Dreisziger. New York: Social Science Monographs, 1985.

———. "The Union of Czech Political Parties in the Reichsrat, 1916–1918." In *The Habsburg Empire in World War I,* edited by Robert A. Kann, Béla K. Király, and Paula S. Fichtner. Boulder, CO: East European Quarterly, 1977.

———. "The United States and Czechoslovak Independence." In *Czechoslovakia: Crossroads and Crises, 1918–1988,* edited by Norman Stone and Eduard Strouhal. New York: St. Martin's Press, 1989.

———. *The United States and East Central Europe, 1914–1918: A Study in Wilsonian Diplomacy and Propaganda*. Princeton, NJ: Princeton University Press, 1957.

———, and Radomír Luža. *A History of the Czechoslovak Republic, 1918–1948*. Princeton, NJ: Princeton University Press, 1973.

Manning, Clarence A. *The Siberian Fiasco*. New York: Library Publishers, 1952.

Mawdsley, Evan. *The Russian Civil War*. Boston: Allen and Unwin, 1987.

May, Arthur J. "R. W. Seton-Watson and British Anti-Hapsburg Sentiment." *American Slavic and East European Review* 20, issue 1 (February 1961): 40–54.

Melton, Carol Willcox. *Between War and Peace: Woodrow Wilson and the American Expeditionary Force in Siberia, 1918–1921*. Macon, GA: Mercer University Press, 2001.

Miller, Herbert Adolphus. "What Woodrow Wilson and America Meant to Czechoslovakia." In *Czechoslovakia: Twenty Years of Independence*. Berkeley, CA: University of California Press, 1940.

Moffat, Ian C. D. "Forgotten Battlefields: Canadians in Siberia 1918–1919." *Canadian Military Journal* 8, no. 3 (Autumn 2007): 73–83.

Mohr, Joan McGuire. *The Czech and Slovak Legion in Siberia, 1917–1922*. Jefferson, NC: McFarland, 2012.

———. "No Longer Forgotten: The Czecho-Slovak Legion in Siberia." *Slovo: A Publication of the National Czech and Slovak Museum and Library* 1, no. 2 (Winter 2000): 4–9.

Morley, James William. *The Japanese Thrust into Siberia, 1918*. New York: Columbia University Press, 1954.

Mueggenberg, Brent. *The Czecho-Slovak Struggle for Independence, 1914–1920*. Jefferson, NC: McFarland, 2014.

Nykl, Alois. "Czechoslovakia or Czecho-Slovakia?" *Slavonic and East European Review* 3, no. 4 (December 1944): 99–110.

Occleshaw, Michael. *Dances in Deep Shadows: The Clandestine War in Russia, 1917–1920*. New York: Carroll & Graf, 2006

O'Grady, Joseph P. *The Immigrants' Influence on Wilson's Peace Policies*. Lexington: University Press of Kentucky, 1967.

Parry, Albert. "Charles R. Crane, Friend of Russia." *Russian Review* 6, no. 2 (Spring 1947): 20–36.

Pereira, Norman G. O. *White Siberia: The Politics of the Civil War*. Montreal: McGill-Queen's University Press, 1996.

Pipes, Richard. *Russia under the Bolshevik Regime*. New York: Alfred A. Knopf, 1993.

———. *The Russian Revolution*. New York: Random House, 1990.

Rachamimov, Alon. *POWs and the Great War: Captivity on the Eastern Front*. Oxford: Berg, 2002.

Radkey, Oliver H. *The Unknown Civil War in Soviet Russia: A Study of the Green Movement in the Tambov Region, 1920–1921*. Stanford, CA: Hoover Institution Press, 1976.

Rees, H. Louis. *The Czechs during World War I: The Path to Independence*. Boulder, CO: East European Monographs, 1992.

Reinfeld, Barbara K. "Charlotte Garrigue Masaryk, 1850–1923." *Czechoslovak and Central European Journal* (Summer/Winter 1989): 90–103.

Rothenberg, Gunther E. *The Army of Francis Joseph*. West Lafayette, IN: Purdue University Press, 1976.

———. "The Habsburg Army in the First World War: 1914–1918." In *War and Society in East Central Europe*, vol. 19, edited by Bela K. Kiraly and Nandor F. Dreisziger. New York: Social Science Monographs, 1985.

Saul, Norman E. *War and Revolution: The United States and Russia, 1914–1921*. Lawrence: University Press of Kansas, 2001.

Selver, Paul. *Masaryk: A Biography*. London: Michael Joseph, 1940.

Seton-Watson, Hugh, and Christopher Seton-Watson. *The Making of a New Europe: R. W. Seton-Watson and the Last Years of Austria-Hungary*. Seattle: University of Washington Press, 1981.

Seton-Watson, R. W. *A History of the Czechs and Slovaks*. London: Hutchinson, 1943.

Skilling, H. Gordon. *T. G. Masaryk: Against the Current, 1882–1914*. University Park: Pennsylvania State University Press, 1994.

Smele, Jonathan D. *Civil War in Siberia: The Anti-Bolshevik Government of Admiral Kolchak, 1918–1920*. Cambridge: Cambridge University Press, 1996.

———. "White Gold: The Russian Imperial Gold Reserve in the Anti-Bolshevik East, 1918—? (An Unconcluded Chapter in the History of the Russian Civil War)." *Europe-Asia Studies* 46, no. 8 (1994): 1317–47.

Smith, Canfield F. *Vladivostok under Red and White Rule: Revolution and Counterrevolution in the Russian Far East, 1920–1922*. Seattle: University of Washington Press, 1975.

Snow, Russell E. *The Bolsheviks in Siberia, 1917–1918*. London: Associated University Presses, 1977.

Somin, Ilya. *Stillborn Crusade: The Tragic Failure of Western Intervention in the Russian Civil War, 1918–1920*. New Brunswick, NJ: Transaction Publishers, 1996.

Speed, Richard B., III. *Prisoners, Diplomats, and the Great War: A Study in the Diplomacy of Captivity*. New York: Greenwood Press, 1990.

Stewart, George. *The White Armies of Russia: A Chronicle of Counter-Revolution and Allied Intervention*. New York: Macmillan, 1933.

Stolarik, M. Mark. *The Role of American Slovaks in the Creation of Czecho-Slovakia*. Cleveland, OH: Slovak Institute, 1968.

Swain, Geoff. *The Origins of the Russian Civil War*. London: Longman, 1995.

Swain, G. R. "Maugham, Masaryk and the Mensheviks." *Revolutionary Russia* 7, no. 1 (June 1994): 78–97.

Trani, Eugene P. "Woodrow Wilson and the Decision to Intervene in Russia: A Reconsideration." *Journal of Modern History* 48, no. 3 (September 1976): 440–61.

Tunstall, Graydon. "The Collapse of the Austro-Hungarian Army in 1918." In *Essays on World War I*, edited by Peter Pastor and Graydon A. Tunstall. Boulder, CO: Social Science Monographs, 2012. Distributed by Columbia University Press.

———. "Traitors or Scapegoats? The Desertion of Czech Soldiers in World War I." In *Essays on World War I*, edited by Peter Pastor and Graydon Tunstall. New York: Columbia University Press, 2011.

Ullman, Richard. *Britain and the Russian Civil War, November 1918–February 1920*. Princeton, NJ: Princeton University Press, 1968.

———. *Intervention and the War: Anglo-Soviet Relations, 1917–1921*. Princeton, NJ: Princeton University Press, 1961.

Unterberger, Betty Miller. *America's Siberian Expedition, 1918–1920: A Study of National Policy*. Durham, NC: Duke University Press, 1956.

———. "The Arrest of Alice Masaryk." *Slavic Review* 33, issue 1 (March 1974): 91–106.

———. *The United States, Revolutionary Russia, and the Rise of Czechoslovakia*. College Station: Texas A&M University Press, 2000.

———. "Woodrow Wilson and the Russian Revolution." In *Woodrow Wilson and a Revolutionary World, 1913–1921*, edited by Arthur S. Link, 49–104. Chapel Hill: University of North Carolina Press, 1982.

Völgyes, Iván. "Hungarian Prisoners of War in Russia, 1916–1919." *Cahiers du Monde Russe et Sovietique* 14 (1973): 54–85.

Wallace, William V. "Masaryk and Benes and the Creation of Czechoslovakia: A Study in Mentalities." In *T. G. Masaryk (1850–1937)*, edited by Harry Hanak. London: Macmillan, 1989, vol. 3, *Statesman and Cultural Force*.

Wheeler-Bennett, John W. *Brest-Litovsk: The Forgotten Peace, March 1918*. New York: W. W. Norton, 1938.

White, John Albert. *The Siberian Intervention*. Princeton, NJ: Princeton University Press, 1950.

Wightman, Gordon. "T. G. Masaryk and the Czechoslovak Legion in Russia." In *T. G. Masaryk (1850–1937)*, edited by Harry Hanak. (London: Macmillan, 1989), vol. 3, *Statesman and Cultural Force*.

Williams, Rowan A. "The Odyssey of the Czechs." *East European Quarterly* 9, no. 1 (Spring 1975): 15–38.

Zeman, Zbyněk A. B. *The Break-Up of the Habsburg Empire, 1914–1918: A Study in National and Social Revolution*. London: Oxford University Press, 1961.

———. *The Masaryks: The Making of Czechoslovakia*. New York: I. B. Taurus, 1990.

———, and Antonin Klimek. *The Life of Edvard Benes, 1884–1948: Czechoslovakia in Peace and War*. Oxford: Clarendon Press, 1997.

INDEX

Index

© 2015 Karen Carey Photography, LLC

Kevin J. McNamara followed the path taken by the Czecho-Slovak Legion shortly after the fall of the Soviet Union, traveling almost two thousand miles along the Trans-Siberian Railway. He was subsequently awarded research grants by the Earhart and Tawani Foundations to acquire and translate from Czech to English firsthand accounts by the men who had served in the legion, which were published in Prague in the 1920s but were suppressed following the Nazi and Soviet conquests of Czecho-Slovakia.

A former journalist for Calkins Media Inc. and aide to the late US congressman R. Lawrence Coughlin, McNamara is an associate scholar of the Foreign Policy Research Institute in Philadelphia, PA, and a former contributing editor to its quarterly journal, *Orbis: A Journal of World Affairs*. He earned a BA in journalism and an MA in international politics from Temple University, where he was a student of the noted military historian Russell F. Weigley. He lives in Glenside, PA.

PublicAffairs is a publishing house founded in 1997. It is a tribute to the standards, values, and flair of three persons who have served as mentors to countless reporters, writers, editors, and book people of all kinds, including me.

I. F. STONE, proprietor of *I. F. Stone's Weekly*, combined a commitment to the First Amendment with entrepreneurial zeal and reporting skill and became one of the great independent journalists in American history. At the age of eighty, Izzy published *The Trial of Socrates*, which was a national bestseller. He wrote the book after he taught himself ancient Greek.

BENJAMIN C. BRADLEE was for nearly thirty years the charismatic editorial leader of *The Washington Post*. It was Ben who gave the *Post* the range and courage to pursue such historic issues as Watergate. He supported his reporters with a tenacity that made them fearless and it is no accident that so many became authors of influential, best-selling books.

ROBERT L. BERNSTEIN, the chief executive of Random House for more than a quarter century, guided one of the nation's premier publishing houses. Bob was personally responsible for many books of political dissent and argument that challenged tyranny around the globe. He is also the founder and longtime chair of Human Rights Watch, one of the most respected human rights organizations in the world.

.   .   .

For fifty years, the banner of Public Affairs Press was carried by its owner Morris B. Schnapper, who published Gandhi, Nasser, Toynbee, Truman, and about 1,500 other authors. In 1983, Schnapper was described by *The Washington Post* as "a redoubtable gadfly." His legacy will endure in the books to come.

Peter Osnos, *Founder and Editor-at-Large*